Peace Operations

Additional Praise for *Peace Operations*

"*Peace Operations* is an important addition to the peace operations literature. It is based on a comprehensive review of regional efforts in peace operations, and it develops an innovative analysis of national and regional motivations for participating in peace operations. This book makes major contributions to our understanding of these critical issues. It will be an authoritative source for scholars and students, as well as policymakers and practitioners."

> —**Chantal de Jonge Oudraat**, associate vice president, Jennings Randolph Program for International Peace, United States Institute of Peace

"The world of peacekeeping is volatile, uncertain, and often just downright perplexing. This collection of excellently informed and refreshingly clear essays provides a sure-footed guide to this important but complex dimension of international security."

> —**Richard Gowan**, associate director for policy, Center on International Cooperation, New York University and former coordinator, *Annual Review of Global Peace Operations*

"The contributions in this book offer problem solving perspectives on national and regional trends in peace operations that seem to be expanding in scope. In a period when peace operations are taken to mean whatever an observer wants them to mean, and when such operations are regarded as a panacea for managing crises, this book should prove valuable in contributing to knowledge about how the world order is disciplined."

> —**Michael Pugh**, professor of peace and conflict studies, Department of Peace Studies, University of Bradford

Peace Operations

Trends, Progress, and Prospects

Donald C. F. Daniel

Patricia Taft &

Sharon Wiharta, *Editors*

A joint project of the
Center for Peace and Security Studies of
the School of Foreign Service,
Georgetown University;
the Fund for Peace;
and
the Stockholm International Peace
Research Institute

Georgetown University Press
Washington, D.C.

Georgetown University Press, Washington, D.C.
www.press.georgetown.edu

LIBRARY OF CONGRESS CATALOGING-IN-PUBLICATION DATA
Peace operations : trends, progress, and prospects /
Donald C. F. Daniel, Patricia Taft, and Sharon Wiharta, editors.
　　p.　　cm.
"A joint project of the Center for Peace and Security Studies of
the School of Foreign Service, Georgetown University; the Fund for
Peace; and, the Stockholm International Peace Research Institute."
Includes bibliographical references and index.
ISBN-13: 978-1-58901-209-7 (alk. paper)
1. Security, International. 2. Peacekeeping forces. 3. Conflict
management—International cooperation. 4. Peace-building—
International cooperation. I. Daniel, Donald C. (Donald Charles),
1944– II. Taft, Patricia. III. Wiharta, Sharon. IV. Georgetown
University. Center for Peace and Security Studies. V. Fund for
Peace. VI. Stockholm International Peace Research Institute.
JZ5588.P43 2008
341.5′84—dc22 2007048035

∞ This book is printed on acid-free paper meeting the requirements
of the American National Standard for Permanence in Paper for
Printed Library Materials.

15 14 13 12 11 10 09 08 　 9 8 7 6 5 4 3 2
First printing
Printed in the United States of America

Contents

PART II
Micro View: Within Regions and Nations

Tables and Figures

Acknowledgments

The editors wish to thank Georgetown University's Center for Peace and Security Studies (CPASS) for sponsoring this project, and in particular Daniel Byman for his enthusiasm and support, and Ellen McHugh for her administrative support. We would like to thank the United States Institute of Peace (USIP) and the National Defense University (NDU) for their generous support of this endeavor. We are grateful to the editors at Georgetown University Press for their guidance and patience. Throughout the project, we benefited from the wisdom and guidance of Colonel James Murtha (USMC), who was crucial in helping us shape the chapters on core and specialized military capacities. Thanks to Jason Ladnier for his contributions to this volume and support throughout the project. We are also grateful to Bo Huldt, Annika Hilding-Norberg, and Michael Pugh for their valuable comments on earlier drafts of the book. Finally, we would like to extend warm thanks to Katrin Heuel, Benjamin Margo, Edwin Yuen, Mark A. Loucas, Ian Born, Colin Costello, and Caspar Trimmer, who contributed much to the research, writing, and editing of this book.

Acronyms

ACDS	African Chiefs of Defense Staff
ACOTA	Africa Contingency Operations Training Assistance
ACRF	African Crisis Response Force
ACRI	African Crisis Response Initiative
ACSRS	African Center for Strategic Research and Studies
ACTORD	activation order
ACTREQ	activation requirement
ACTWARN	activation warning
AMIB	African Union Mission in Burundi
AMIS	African Union Mission in Sudan
AMISOM	African Union Mission in Somalia
AMM	Aceh Monitoring Mission
AMPH ST	amphibious support
AMU	Arab Maghreb Union
ANAD	Accord de Non Aggression et D'Assistance en Matiere de Defense
APC	armored personnel carrier
APEC	Asia-Pacific Economic Cooperation
APPM	Armed Political Parties and Movements
ARF	ASEAN Regional Forum
ARPCT	Alliance for the Restoration of Peace and Counter-Terrorism
ASC	ASEAN Security Community
ASEAN	Association of Southeast Asian Nations
ASF	African Standby Force
AU	African Union
BDF	Botswana Defense Force
BPST	British Peace Support Team
CAA	Conference of American Armies
CAECOPAZ	Centro Argentino de Entrenamiento Conjunto para Operaciones de Paz
CAR	Central African Republic
CARICOM	Caribbean Community
CDC	Community of Democratic Choice
CDRF	Collective Rapid Deployment Force
CECOPAC	Centro de Entrenamiento Conjunto de Operaciones de Paz de Chile
CEMAC	Economic and Monetary Community of Central African States
CENCAMEX	Centro de Capacitación para Misiones en el Exterior
CEN-SAD	Community of Saharan and Sahelian States
CFAC	Conferencia de Fuerzas Armadas de CentroAmerica
CFSP	Common Foreign and Security Policy
CG	Coast Guard
CHOD	Chief of Defense
CIMIC	civil military coordination
CIS	Commonwealth of Independent States
CIVPOL	civilian police

CNDD-FDD   Conseil national pour la defense de la democratie-Forces pour la defense
              de la democratie
CoESPU   Centre of Excellence for Stability Police Units
COIN ACFT   counterinsurgency aircraft
COMESA   Common Market for Eastern and Southern Africa
CONOPS   concept of operations
COPAX   Peace and Security Council in Central Africa
CPP   Cambodian People's Party
CPP   Conflict Prevention Pool
CPX   command post exercise
CRC   crowd and riot control
CSTO   Collective Security Treaty Organization
CV   aircraft carrier
DC   designated troop contributing country
DDR   disarmament, demobilization, and reintegration
DFID   Department for International Development
DITF   Darfur Integrated Task Force
DPKO   Department of Peacekeeping Operations (UN)
DRC   Democratic Republic of Congo
EAC   East African Community
EACC   Euro-Atlantic Cooperation Council
EASBRIG   East African Standby Brigade
ECCAS   Economic Community of Central African States
ECOMOG   ECOWAS Cease-fire Monitoring Group
ECOMICI   ECOWAS Mission in Côte d'Ivoire
ECOMIL   ECOWAS Mission in Liberia
ECOWAS   Economic Community of West African States
ECSC   European Coal and Steel Community
EDF   European Development Fund
EEC   European Economic Community
EGF   European Gendarmerie Force
EPG   Eminent Persons Group (ASEAN)
ESDP   European Security and Defense Policy
ESS   European Security Strategy
ETF   Engineer Task Force
EU   European Union
EUCS   EU Cell at SHAPE
EUMC   EU Military Committee
EUMS   EU Military Staff
EURATOM   European Atomic Energy Community
FCO   Foreign and Commonwealth Office
FNL   Forces nationales de liberation
FTX   field training exercises
FYROM   Former Yugoslavian Republic Of Macedonia
G70   70 nominal and noncontributors
G87   87 designated contributors
G157   157 potential contributors
GAM   Free Aceh Movement

GDP	Gross Domestic Product
GNI	Gross National Income
GPOI	Global Peace Operations Initiative
GUAM	Georgia, Ukraine, Azerbaijan, and Moldova
HELO	helicopter
HIS	higher or major impact state
HQ	headquarters
IAPF	Inter-American Peace Force
ICISS	International Commission on Intervention and State Sovereignty
ICRC	International Committee of the Red Cross
ICTY	International Criminal Tribunal for the Former Yugoslavia
ICU	Union of Islamic Courts
IFOR	Implementation Force
IGAD	Intergovernmental Authority on Development
IGASOM	IGAD Peace Support Mission to Somalia
IGO	intergovernmental organization
IMB	International Maritime Bureau
IMF	International Monetary Fund
INTERFET	International Force for East Timor
IPA	International Peace Academy
ISAF	International Security Assistance Force
ISDSC	Inter-State Defense and Security Committee (SADC)
IVF	infantry fighting vehicle
JAM	Joint Assessment Mission (AU)
JTF	Joint Task Force
KAIPTC	Kofi Annan International Peacekeeping Training Centre
KFOR	Kosovo Force (NATO)
KPS	Kosovo Police Service
LIS	lower or limited impact state
LURD	Liberians United for Reconciliation and Democracy
MALSINDO	Malaysia, Indonesia, and Singapore
MFA	Ministry of Foreign Affairs
MFO	Multinational Force and Observers
MFO-Haiti	Multinational Force Haiti
MIF	Multinational Interim Force
MILREP	military representative
MINURSO	UN Mission for the Referendum in Western Sahara
MINUSTAH	UN Stabilization Mission in Haiti
MNF	multinational force
MNF-I	Multinational Force Iraq
MoD	Ministry of Defense
MODEL	Movement for Democracy in Liberia
MOMEP	Military Observer Mission Ecuador-Peru
MONUC	UN Organization Mission in the Democratic Republic of Congo
MOU	memorandum of understanding
MP	maritime patrol
MRU	Mano River Union
NAC	North Atlantic Council

NATO	North Atlantic Treaty Organization
NCO	noncommissioned officer
NGO	nongovernmental organization
NIS	new independent states
NLA	National Liberation Army
NLW	nonlethal weapon(s)
NMC	NATO Military Committee
NNC	nominal and noncontributor
NP	national police
NPFL	National Patriotic Front for the Liberation of Liberia
NRC	notable rising contributor
NRF	NATO Response Force
NSO	NATO Standardization Organization
NWC	National War College Nigeria
OAS	Organization of American States
OAU	Organization of African Unity
OFR	Operation Focus Relief
OECS	Organization of Eastern Caribbean States
ONUB	UN Operations in Burundi
ONUMOZ	UN Operation in Mozambique
OSCE	Organization for Security and Co-operation in Europe
P3	USA, UK, and France
PAE	Pacific Architects and Engineers
PACOM	Pacific Command
PC	patrol craft
PKO	peacekeeping operations
PoCo	Political Committee
PPC	Pearson Peacekeeping Centre
PSC	Peace and Security Council (AU)
PSC	Political and Security Committee (EU)
PSO	Peace Support Operations
PSOD	Peace Support Operations Division (AU)
PSTC	Peace Support Training Centre
R&D	research and development
REC	Regional Economic Communities
ReCAAP	Regional Cooperation Agreement on Combating Piracy and Armed Robbery against Ships in Asia
RECAMP	Renforcement des capacités Africaines de maintien de la paix
RECON	reconnaissance
RDF	rapid deployment force (CIS)
RO	regional organization
RPTC	Regional Peacekeeping Training Centre (SADC)
RSS	Regional Security System
SACEUR	Supreme Allied Commander Europe
SADC	Southern African Development Community
SAPSD	South African Protection and Support Detachment
SAR	search and rescue
SCO	Shanghai Cooperation Organization

SDF	Self Defense Force
SEEBRIG	South-East Europe Brigade
SFOR	Stabilization Force (NATO)
SG/HR	High Representative for CFSP
SHAPE	Supreme Headquarters Allied Powers Europe
SHIRBRIG	Standing High Readiness Brigade
SIPRI	Stockholm International Peace Research Institute
SLOCS	sea lane of communication
SOP	standard operating procedures
SOR	statement of military requirements
SRCC	Special Representative of the Chairman of the AU Commission
SRSG	Special Representative to the Secretary-General
SPU	special police unit
TCC	troop-contributing country
TPT	transport aircraft
UAV	unmanned aerial vehicle
UN	United Nations
UNAMET	UN Mission in East Timor
UNAMSIL	UN Assistance Mission in Sierra Leone
UNAVEM	UN Angola Verification Missions
UNDOF	United Nations Disengagement Observer Force
UNDP	United Nations Development Programme
UNEF	UN Emergency Force
UNFICYP	UN Peacekeeping Force in Cyprus
UNIFIL	UN Interim Force in Lebanon
UNITAF	Unified Task Force
UNMEE	UN Mission in Ethiopia and Eritrea
UNMIH	UN Mission in Haiti
UNMIK	UN Mission in Kosovo
UNMIL	UN Mission in Liberia
UNMIS	UN Mission in Sudan
UNMISET	UN Mission of Support in East Timor
UNMOGIP	UN Military Observer Group in India and Pakistan
UNOCI	UN Mission in Côte d'Ivoire
UNOSOM	UN Operation in Somalia
UNPROFOR	UN Protection Force
UNSCR	UN Security Council Resolution
UNTAC	UN Transitional Authority in Cambodia
UNTAET	UN Transitional Authority in East Timor
UNTSO	UN Truce Supervision Organization
USSOUTHCOM	U.S. Southern Command
UXO	unexploded ordinance
TEU	Treaty on European Union
TGoB	Transitional Government of Burundi
WBG	World Bank Group
WDI	World Development Indicators
WEU	Western European Union

Introduction

DONALD C. F. DANIEL AND SHARON WIHARTA

Peace operations have undergone several evolutions in the last decade and a half, both in terms of the type of operations launched and in the way they are perceived. In recent years, the demand for peace operations has grown significantly, leading to a steady rise in the number conducted annually since 2002. Along with this rise is an explosive growth in the number of troops required for them and in the number of countries participating in them. In 2006, about 60 percent of the world's countries contributed nearly 150,000 troops to peace operations. The number of operations with mission strengths of over 5,000 personnel in 2006 was twice the number of missions of this size in 2000.[1] The large-scale deployments are, among other things, a reflection of heightened international political appreciation of the value of peace operations and a reaffirmation by many states of the United Nations (UN) Security Council's commitment to "a responsibility to protect populations from genocide, war crimes, ethnic cleansing and crimes against humanity."[2]

The current trend toward expanded peace operations is rooted in the experiences of the 1990s.[3] Developments in that period have been extensively documented and analyzed in published literature, much of which has underscored the more problematic nature of operations.[4] Numerous studies have diagnosed the problems and suggested changes in practice for institutions and nations authorizing and carrying out missions. Their focus has been predominantly on operations mandated by and executed through the UN, even though regional organizations—with the UN's encouragement—and ad hoc coalitions have come to account for half of the operations on a yearly basis.

Particularly since 2000, published attention has been increasingly directed to how these non–UN entities have supplemented or supplanted "UN coverage."[5] Much of this more recent literature concentrates particularly on European (including NATO) and African developments, since these regions have been the most active in addressing their respective institutional and national needs. Still rare are studies that systematically look at other regions.[6] Rarer yet are those that compare troop contributors and noncontributors within and across regions to determine either what they have in common or how they differ across a range of characteristics and capabilities.[7]

This volume goes beyond the published literature by concentrating on trends in and prospects for regional and national capacities to undertake peace operations. It does not ignore the UN—probably the most oft-mentioned organization in the volume—but considers it against the backdrop of what regional institutions and ad hoc coalitions are doing to carry out their own missions. It breaks relatively new ground with some of the questions it raises, some of the information and conclusions it offers, and in the evidence and methodologies employed in some of the chapters. While the book updates trends and developments identified in earlier works, it also addresses long-standing shortfalls in the literature.

The book is divided into two sections. Part I focuses on global trends and prospects *across* regions and nations; part II addresses trends and prospects *within* regions and nations. The conclusion draws together various findings and assesses the prospects for peace operations in light of both positive and negative trends.

Part I answers relatively basic questions that have not yet been addressed comprehensively due to a lack of detailed time-series data about national contributions to missions, especially those conducted by non–UN entities. Tabulating UN statistics poses the lesser challenge, since the data can be found on the UN's website and in paper records at the New York headquarters. While sorting through paper files is tedious, the records at least are accessible at one location and relatively complete. Such is not the case with data for operations undertaken by regional institutions and coalitions of the willing. Collecting these statistics is a time-consuming, labor-intensive slow march across thousands of sources from institutional internet sites (most of which remain hit or miss in what they provide) to scholarly analyses and news articles. The level of effort needed to generate a comprehensive and cross-checked database is enormous.[8]

A unique feature of this volume is that it brings together the results of major data-gathering projects undertaken at Georgetown University's Center for Peace and Security Studies (CPASS), the Stockholm International Peace Research Institute (SIPRI), and the Folke Bernadotte Academy (FBA). While aggregated SIPRI data have been available through its yearbooks for nearly fifteen years, it was only two years ago that the institute began to provide disaggregated yearly national data. It was at about the same time that both the CPASS and the FBA projects had accumulated and vetted enough data to allow for initial use in published research. Each effort is conducted independently with its own operational definitions, criteria, and counting rules.[9] The respective databases should be viewed as complementary rather than competitive.

A second relatively unique feature of this volume is that it attends not only to regions that have an established institutional track record in peace operations but also to regions that do not. Much has been written about Europe and Africa because there is much to say about what their institutions have done and are doing; the chapters devoted to them in this volume do a superb job of updating their developments. Far less has yet been published about other regions precisely because their institutions have done less. However, this volume examines them to answer two fundamental questions rarely addressed elsewhere: If little or nothing has been done institutionally in a region, why not? And what should be expected?

The five chapters in part I address a variety of fundamental questions about trends in and prospects for peace operations worldwide, the breakdown between two basic mission types (interstate and intrastate), the number of troops deployed overall, the number deployed by basic mission type, the regional distribution of operations, the characteristics of troop contributors, the factors that affect troop availability, the division of labor between UN and non–UN entities, and finally some generic capabilities that have become or are becoming more important for success in complex peacekeeping and hazardous operations.

Part I appropriately begins with a chapter by FBA professor Birger Heldt that challenges widely held views about the relation between UN and non–UN entities. Its focus on that relation, and its lengthy time perspective, 1948 through 2005, provides a solid foundation for better informed reading of the volume's later chapters. In chapter 2, Georgetown professor Donald C. F. Daniel and research assistants Katrin Heuel and Benjamin Margo employ data from 2001 through 2005 for a broader and more in-depth look at an issue introduced by Heldt: the characteristics of nations that contribute troops to missions. In chapter 3, Daniel adds data through 2006 to help explain why such small percentages of national ground forces deploy to peace operations. Chapter 4 builds on the expertise and peace operations experience of a retired Marine colonel, Gary Anderson, to spotlight a concern rarely addressed outside of specialized military publications: the types of combat and associated support capabilities that must be made available to deployed forces if hazardous missions are to remain on the peace operations to-do list. Chapter 5, written by FFP's Patricia Taft, parallels Anderson's article. It builds on Taft's wide-ranging travels as a policy-oriented analyst to spotlight trends and prospects in the niche capabilities needed to conduct complex "nation-building" operations.

Part II deals with trends and prospects *within* regions and nations. Specifically, this section looks at how regional mechanisms and institutions respond to the circumstances that call for peacekeeping both within and outside of their own region. A particular strength of the book is that the chapter authors for part II either are natives or have long-standing experience working in or on the region. Each chapter provides an overview of the institutional capacity to conduct peace operations and seeks to assess its degree of maturity and sophistication. Among the factors addressed are the level of institutional capacity, the existence of a common peacekeeping doctrine, the availability of peacekeeping training centers, and the extent of intraregional military cooperation, training, and exercises. Consistent with the ongoing debate on these issues, particular attention is given to the relationship between individual regional organizations and the UN and to the relative advantages and disadvantages of burden-sharing between them.

The chapters also explore regional political dynamics as well as cultural and ideational characteristics, such as regional views on the use of force or the proper role of the UN vis-à-vis peace operations. Specific attention is given to factors that drive countries to contribute troops to peace operations, or that constrain them from making such contributions. These may include concerns about regional or subregional stability, global power distributions, regional and subregional competition or cooperation, past experiences with peace-keeping, ideational frameworks, national interests concerns, and preferences for working through the UN, regional institutions, or ad hoc coalitions.

In chapter 6, Mark Malan examines ongoing work to build institutional mechanisms in Africa to make political decisions about operations, along with the serious challenges to building capabilities needed to train peacekeep-ers, plan missions, and sustain deployments. He delves into the relationship between the continentwide African Union and the region's relatively well-developed subregional organizations—a unique feature of the African conti-nent. He considers the significant roles that external actors play in supporting national and institutional capacity-building.

Bastian Giegerich addresses European-based institutions in chapter 7. The chapter looks at the ongoing development of the European Union (EU) and the North Atlantic Treaty Organization (NATO), and at their unique capabili-ties to operate out of area. While Anderson, in chapter 4, argues that Euro-pean nations can contribute more to "hazardous" operations, Giegerich offers reasons for the restrictions they impose.

In chapter 8, on peacekeeping operations in the new independent states (NIS), Alexander Nikitin and Mark Loucas explore the roles that Russia played both individually and through the Commonwealth of Independent States (CIS). The chapter also examines the potential role of other emerging regional bodies, such as the intraregional Collective Security Treaty Organiza-tion (CSTO), the Shanghai Cooperation Organization (SCO), and the GUAM (Georgia, Ukraine, Azerbaijan, and Moldova) group.

In chapter 9, John Fishel recounts the history of peace operations in Latin America and examines the apparent revival of the willingness of countries such as Argentina, Brazil, and Chile to play major roles. At the institutional or collective level, Fishel points particularly to the potential that exists in the Central American, Andes, and Caribbean subregions.

The slow normative shift toward peace operations in Southeast and North-east Asia and the emergence of actors such as China and Japan are critically examined by Mely Caballero-Anthony in chapter 10. She suggests that the motivating factor driving these changes may be more a matter of *realpolitik* than internalization of any "responsibility to protect" norm.

In his chapter on South Asia, Dipankar Banerjee focuses on the long-standing experience of Bangladesh, India, Nepal, and Pakistan in peace op-erations as well as the more recent efforts of Sri Lanka. He contrasts the large role that South Asian states have traditionally played in UN peace operations around the globe with their inability to develop institutions to serve their own regional needs or collectivize their efforts.

Paul Pillar's chapter on the Greater Middle East explains the decline in the role of regional organizations (such as the Arab League) in peace operations and why, notable exceptions aside, most countries there (including those with large militaries) are not major contributors to peacekeeping efforts. He looks at these trends in the context of the domestic and regional political problems that dominate the agendas and decisions of the governments in the area.

Finally, the volume's editors did not attempt to impose a uniform definition of peace operations on the authors, nor did they even impose the requirement that all authors use the same term. Strapping an international group of independent thinkers down to such Procrustean beds would have been pointless. In several chapters the authors explicitly define the term they use; in others the definition can be derived from the context. The mushrooming of terms in the 1990s to replace "peacekeeping" reflects the mushrooming of activities that "peacekeepers" were asked to undertake. One reason for a general lack of uniformity in the broader literature on this subject is disagreement over whether all such activities properly fall under the rubric of whatever it is that succeeded peacekeeping as traditionally understood. A major feature of the NIS chapter in this volume speaks directly to this last point. At the end, each reader may have to settle for the position taken by U.S. Supreme Court Justice Potter Stewart in the obscenity case *Jacobellis v. Ohio* (1964). Admitting an inability to offer a generally agreed upon operational definition of hard core pornography, the Justice nevertheless declared, "I know when I see it." He then moved on to render his judgment.

Part I
Macro View
Across Regions and Nations

Chapter 1

Trends from 1948 to 2005: How to View the Relation between the United Nations and Non-UN Entities

Birger Heldt

This book looks at regional and national trends in peace operations, and at prospects for carrying them out. It also assesses how recent developments in attitudes and capabilities might shape the future. This chapter places these issues in a larger global context by looking at the overall panoply of operations—UN-led as well as non-UN-led—from 1948 to 2005.

In light of the prevalence of modern peacekeeping operations, it might be said that the UN invented peacekeeping. However, the general phenomenon did not originate with the UN, as instances of peacekeeping can be traced back at least to the mid-nineteenth century.[1] Indeed, the UN Charter encourages peace initiatives by intergovernmental organizations (IGOs) or coalitions of states, and a series of Charter articles stipulate that non-UN-led initiatives should be the first option.[2] Since the mid-1990s the UN has also worked to increase the contribution of regional arrangements to peacekeeping operations, conflict prevention, and other security enhancing measures and to coordinate such contributions with UN efforts.[3]

Regional IGOs, subregional IGOs, regional ad hoc coalitions of states, and even individual states have in recent years taken on larger peacekeeping roles within and sometimes outside their regions. However, this development and the related perception of dominance by non-UN actors has raised concerns that, if true, could have large policy implications. One concern is that reliance on non-UN actors may undermine the UN's global role.[4] Another concern is that an increased responsibility for peacekeeping of non-UN actors may decrease the access of developing countries to the well-trained and well-equipped peacekeepers from troop-contributing countries (TCCs) in the developed world that are supplied through UN operations.[5] More to the point, regions (such as Africa) with considerable demand for peacekeeping are said to have the least indigenous capacity to meet that demand. They cannot afford a lesser UN peacekeeping capacity, as they are believed to be incapable of meeting the peacekeeping demand by themselves. In contrast, developed countries would stand to lose little from consistently taking sole care of their own peacekeeping needs, since wealthy regions generally do not experience any major demand for peacekeeping.

The implicit assumptions behind these concerns are that the occurrence of one set of operations (non-UN) negatively conditions the occurrence of another set of operations (UN), and that participation in one set negatively conditions participation in the other. In essence, non-UN operations are believed to crowd out and take precedence over UN operations. At play here is an assumption of a competitive relationship.[6]

The first claim concerning the occurrence of non-UN versus UN operations is empirical and not inherently false. At the same time, it may be claimed to be unrealistic. Given the large costs and manpower needs of modern and ambitious peacekeeping operations, it appears unlikely that many regions (apart from perhaps Europe) would be able and willing to handle the costs by themselves instead of preferring the UN (and thus the international community) to do so. The second claim, concerning participation, while reasonable at first glance, may be logically flawed: a low demand for peacekeeping within wealthy regions could actually mean that their peacekeeping resources can be put at the disposal of the UN for use in other regions. Instead, it is poor countries that should become tied up in their own regions, and thus should be less able to contribute to UN operations.

Ultimately, both claims are subject to empirical verification, and the empirical record presented in this chapter throws concerns about the UN's future role and call on troop resources into relief. The first part of this chapter provides a bird's-eye view of the institutional or macro trends at the global level to assess whether non-UN dominance and related concerns are supported by historical data. It describes which entities carried out peacekeeping, how often, and with what amount of personnel. In particular, it highlights the division of labor between the UN, on the one hand, and regional IGOs and national coalitions of the willing, on the other. The chapter's second part offers another bird's-eye view—this time at the national or micro level. It complements the first part by describing the dynamics of participation across national wealth. In assessing whether the dire predictions about non-UN versus UN operations have any currency, the second part asks whether certain types of states have become more or less prominent TCCs, whether that pool has diversified over time, and whether the TCCs to UN operations differ from the contributions to non-UN operations.

Institutional Trends, 1948–2005

Throughout history there has generally been an even division of labor between the UN and non-UN actors in areas of conflict prevention and conflict management.[7] From 1948 to 2005 non-UN actors initiated sixty-eight operations and the UN sixty.[8] Of the non-UN operations, twenty-eight were either recognized (welcomed, endorsed, commended, or approved) or authorized by UN Security Council resolutions.[9]

As illustrated by figure 1.1, the numbers for UN-led and non-UN-led operations follow a similar pattern over time. Until the end of the cold war, around 1990, there are no dramatic shifts in absolute numbers, which are low. The growth of UN operations began in 1988, whereas the increase in operations carried out by other actors began in 1992. There were also more UN operations at most points in time. The lines suggest a positive relationship between UN and non-UN operations; moreover, they suggest that the UN may have a leading, or exemplar, role in that it carried out the first operations, initiated the large increase in peacekeeping operations in the latter part of the period, and had more operations ongoing at almost every point in time. Since the mid-1990s the UN has also taken on a leading role by inducing non-UN actors to take on a larger role, and this may constitute an important part of the explanation for the recent growth in non-UN operations.

While non-UN operations have grown in numbers, there is limited evidence of an emerging dominance. The number of non-UN led operations was higher during some brief periods, particularly the mid-1950s, late 1960s, early 1970s, 1999, and 2003–4. Regardless of the explanations for these cycles, the fact remains that the UN handled more and more cases at the same time that non-UN actors were carrying out more operations than ever before. The increasing number of non-UN operations hides the persistent, and at times increased, inability of these actors to meet the demand for peacekeeping on their own. There is therefore no historical support for the conjecture that non-UN peacekeeping may serve to undermine the UN's role as peacekeeper.

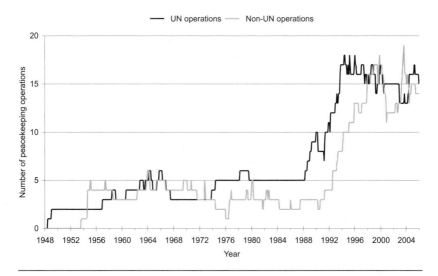

Figure 1.1. Trends in Peacekeeping Operations, 1948–2005

Had the conjecture been accurate, then we should have been able to discern comparatively less UN peacekeeping—or at least the beginning of a trend in that direction—in the 1960s. Moreover, if there is a simple and consistent negative long-term impact of non-UN operations on the number of UN operations, then such repeated cycles of a numerical dominance of non-UN operations should not have occurred. Instead, non-UN operations should have crowded out UN operations once and for all decades ago when the first instance of non-UN dominance occurred. There is also a positive—not negative—short-term relationship between the number of UN and non-UN operations.[10] Non-UN operations have thus not crowded out UN operations, but rather the two have thrived together. In addition, non-UN operations have not challenged the UN; rather, they have complemented UN operations and have often sought the UN's material support as well as Security Council endorsements.[11]

An analysis of data disaggregated into operations deployed in intra- and interstate conflicts from 1948 to 2005 adds detail to the above conclusion while also exposing some qualifications. First, the UN deployed seventeen operations in interstate conflicts, while non-UN actors deployed eighteen operations, of which none were recognized or authorized by UN Security Council resolutions. Second, figure 1.2 shows an upward trend in the number of UN operations, while a different trend applies to non-UN operations. Peacekeeping in interstate conflicts was dominated by non-UN initiatives between 1953 and 1973, but since then there has been a move toward greater reliance on the UN in such conflicts, while the number of non-UN operations has been fairly constant. In December 2005 the UN carried out six operations in interstate conflicts, while there were two non-UN operations.[12] In addition, there is only a very weak relationship—and a negative one at that—between the two types of operations.[13] This indicates that the UN does not inspire a trend in, or serve as an exemplar for, peacekeeping in interstate conflicts. Nor do the UN's operations result in fewer non-UN operations. Rather, the two peacekeeping patterns are virtually independent of each other. This indicates that non-UN operations cannot serve to undermine or diminish the UN's role in interstate conflicts in the short or long term. Moreover, should any such detrimental link exist, then it is not straightforward but confined to some particular cases or contexts, and thus with only very minor policy implications. It also means that whatever factors motivate or allow the UN to intervene are not the same as those that motivate non-UN actors to intervene. Had the factors been identical, then the two actors' patterns of peacekeeping would have been strongly related. Consequently, we cannot understand why non-UN actors deploy peacekeepers in interstate cases by using the same models that we use for analyzing why the UN deploys peacekeepers.

The pattern for intrastate conflicts is different. The UN deployed forty-four intrastate operations between 1948 and 2005, while non-UN actors deployed fifty-one, of which twenty-eight were recognized or authorized by UN Security Council resolutions. Figure 1.3 shows that UN operations occurred in two blocks of time. The first block, from 1960 to 1974, involved only a few

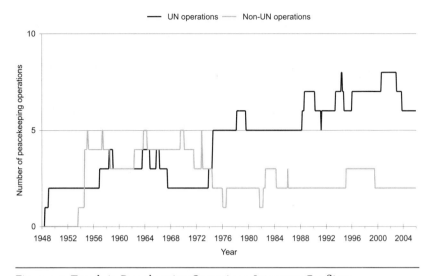

Figure 1.2. Trends in Peacekeeping Operations, Interstate Conflicts, 1948–2005

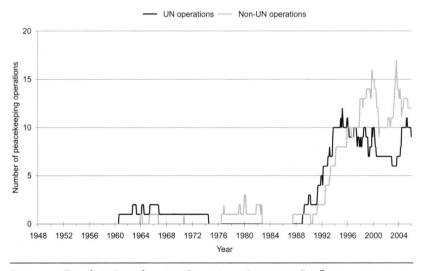

Figure 1.3. Trends in Peacekeeping Operations, Intrastate Conflicts, 1948–2005

operations. The second, from 1989 to 2005, consisted of a larger number (between six and twelve operations in any one month). The only intrastate operations between the mid-1970s and early 1980s were led by non-UN entities, but they were few in number both then and throughout the period up to the 1990s. During the 1990s, non-UN operations followed the same pattern of steady increases as did UN missions; in fact, the number of non-UN intrastate operations surpassed UN operations after 1998. Indeed, during 1996–2005 non-UN operations outnumbered UN operations by 50 percent. This gap in favor of non-UN operations arose just as the UN initiated the aforementioned process of encouraging regional peacekeeping efforts, suggesting that the UN's efforts were influential. By 2005 the gap had narrowed.

The verdict is still out on whether the UN's role as peacekeeper in intrastate conflicts has been undermined by recent developments, or whether we are observing another temporary cycle. To assess this we will need additional years of observations. However, the situation in 2005 suggests that we are approaching the end of yet another cycle. Yet as also noted above, there is no historical support for the conjecture that non-UN peacekeeping undermines the UN's role as peacekeeper. Had the conjecture been accurate, then we should have been able to discern comparatively less UN peacekeeping—or at least the beginning of a trend in that direction—in earlier decades. The observable cycles thus indicate the absence of a simple and consistent negative impact. We can also note that the historical patterns of UN and non-UN operations in intrastate conflicts are positively—not negatively—associated.[14] The two types of operations thus thrive together, and overall appear to share burdens and (particularly during recent years) coordinate rather than compete.

Moving the analysis to the regional level offers additional insights. Table 1.1 shows the regional distribution of operations from 1948 to 2005. It shows that the UN deployed nine operations in the Middle East, nine in Asia, twenty-three in Africa, eleven in Europe, and nine in the Americas. As for non-UN operations, twenty-four were deployed in Africa, sixteen in Asia, fourteen in Europe, eight in the Middle East, and seven in the Americas.

Non-UN operations characterize some regions, but in different ways. The most conspicuous pattern is that in the Americas the UN has been entrusted to address intrastate conflicts, while non-UN actors have addressed interstate conflicts. In the Middle East the UN has dealt only with interstate conflicts, while non-UN actors have addressed both intrastate and interstate conflicts. In Africa the two types of actors have been almost equally active. In Europe and Asia, non-UN actors have been considerably more active across the board with one minor exception: the UN was employed twice in European interstate operations, whereas non-UN actors were not deployed at all.

The radically different intervention patterns in the Americas and the Middle East raise the question of how these patterns may be explained. A closer look at the Middle East suggests that all the intrastate operations basically concerned the same conflict and area. Three of the operations were deployed in Lebanon, and the fourth in Jordan. The conflicts were also interconnected. In this case the Arab League handled two of the missions in Lebanon; a couple

Table 1.1. Number of Peacekeeping Operations, by Actor and Conflict, 1948–2005

Region	UN-led operations		Non–UN-led operations	
	Interstate	*Intrastate*	*Interstate*	*Intrastate*
Africa	3	20	3	21
Asia	3	6	6	10
Americas	0	9	5	2
Europe	2	9	0	14
Middle East	9	0	4	4

Note: Appendix is used as source. UNFICYP is counted twice, as it was an intrastate peace-keeping operation until 1974, after which it became an interstate operation. MNF I is also counted twice, as it too was an intrastate and an interstate peacekeeping operation.

of central Arab states handled the mission in Jordan; and a western ad hoc coalition intervened in the Lebanon.[15] Similarly, of the UN's nine interstate operations in the Middle East, five were related to the Arab–Israeli conflict, while two were related to Iraq.

A similar pattern applies to interstate operations in the Americas. Four out of five interstate operations took place in Central America, and three of the conflicts involved Honduras. Moreover, El Salvador and Nicaragua were each involved in two of the conflicts, whereas two of the conflicts were between the same parties. The Organization of American States (OAS) handled all cases in Central America.[16] Again, this pattern of interconnectedness is similar to the one in the Middle East, and it may offer an explanation for the intervention pattern: having initiated peacekeeping, the same type of actor (UN or non-UN actors) tends to end up handling all subsequent peace operations in interconnected conflicts. Europe shows a similar clustering pattern, in that eight of the UN's operations concern conflicts within the Balkans. Instances of clustering of operations and peacekeepers can be found in other regions as well. For instance, of the UN's nine operations in the Americas, five took place in Haiti.

History appears to matter in such instances, as peacekeeping appears to be characterized by "stickiness" or inertia.[17] This pattern suggests that initial decisions essentially determined which organization will be involved in the long run in interconnected conflicts (or conflict complexes). If this interpretation is accurate, dire predictions of non-UN dominance, and of a weakened global role for the UN, may come true if non-UN actors consistently carry out the first attempt to keep the peace in such settings. However, since decisions about peacekeeping are made on a case-by-case basis in concert with the UN, and since such conflict complexes are unusual, it appears uncertain that such a scenario would actually materialize.

It is important to note that actors from outside regions carried out thirteen of the non-UN operations between 1948 and 2005. Such out-of-area operations were common in Asia and fairly evenly distributed in the Middle East and Africa, but they were rare in the Americas.[18] Hence, two thirds of the non-UN operations in Asia, and half of the operations in the Middle East, were not carried out by the region's member states. Out-of-area operations appear meanwhile to be mainly a thing of the past, since during the past twenty years only four such operations were launched. The important insight is that 20 percent of the non-UN operations were not confined to the regions of the TCCs. Non-UN peacekeeping is thus not synonymous with geographically narrow interests, as has often been implicitly assumed, but rather it has had a global reach that mirrors the UN's operations.

A region that deserves more attention is Asia. It is unique in its pattern of nonintervention by regional actors, and of interventions by ad hoc coalitions of the willing rather than regional IGOs. Almost half of the non-UN operations, and all of the operations in interstate conflicts, were out of area. The intrastate operations carried out by countries from within the region were small in size and consisted almost solely of those deployed in Papua New Guinea, and the Solomon Islands; moreover, these operations were mostly composed of a few small TCCs. Only one of the large East Asian countries, Malaysia, participated in a small operation (the International Monitoring Team), while a few major states (Malaysia, the Philippines, Republic of Korea, and Thailand) took part in the International Force for East Timor (INTERFET) operation.

Asia, saddled with tragic historic legacies that hamper interstate cooperation, lacks regional structures and institutionalized preparedness for peacekeeping-like conflict management.[19] In addition, some of the Asian conflicts are located in pivotal member states. There are also unresolved interstate issues that reinforce mutual distrust: the Taiwan dispute has flared up over the years; there is still formally a state of war on the Korean peninsula; the border conflict between India and Pakistan has caused several wars and repeated skirmishes; and there are sea border disputes in North East Asia that could well escalate because of undersea resources. In short, historic legacies and festering interstate disputes create barriers for intraregional operations and open the way for out-of-area operations. This sets Asia apart from other regions of the world. This is not to claim that there are no unsettled interstate disputes in the Middle East, only that there are not as many acute or manifest conflicts as in Asia.

Number of Peacekeepers

Figure 1.4 presents the monthly number of UN peacekeepers and constitutes an alternative measure of peacekeeping activity that could generate different conclusions. From 1948 to 1956 very few peacekeepers—and only military observers—were deployed. This changed after the 1956 Suez crisis, which led to the deployment of the first United Nations Emergency Force (UNEF I). It is commonly regarded as the first "real" peacekeeping operation, since it was composed of troops rather than only military observers, and since it was of considerable size. The number of UN peacekeepers increased sharply in 1960 with the Congo (Leopoldville) operation that lasted until 1964, after which time they decreased. Another sharp increase took place from 1991 to 1998, as the UN's peacekeepers reached a high point of almost 78,000 personnel

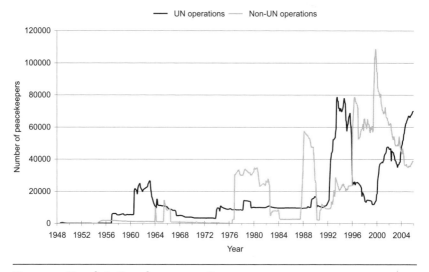

Figure 1.4. Trends in Peacekeepers, 1948–2005

in July 1993. This increase was mainly caused by the operations in Cambodia, the former Yugoslavia, and Somalia. A final phase began in 1999, so that by December 2005 the number of UN peacekeeping forces had reached 70,000. The last fifteen years, characterized by dramatic changes in terms of deployed UN personnel, end with another surge in peacekeeping forces.

The first—and still ongoing—non-UN operation was deployed between the two Koreas in 1953; it consists of a small monitoring mission. Peaks, involving some 10,000–15,000 peacekeepers in the mid-1960s, are accounted for by the British operation in Cyprus before the deployment of the follow-up UN mission, and by the operation in the Dominican Republic. Another peak of more than thirty thousand peacekeepers during the late 1970s and early 1980s relates to the Arab League's intervention in Lebanon. The peak in the late 1980s of nearly sixty thousand peacekeepers reflects the Indian peacekeeping operation in Sri Lanka, and the numbers for the second half of the 1990s are mostly due to NATO operations in the Balkans. After a high of almost 110,000 peacekeepers in 1999, the number dropped to 39,000 by December 2005.

In terms of fielded personnel the UN dominated until the mid-1970s, with no consistent pattern thereafter: non-UN operations dominated from the late 1970s to the early 1980s, and during the late 1980s; the UN dominated during the mid-1980s and the first half of the 1990s; thereafter, non-UN actors dominated again for the rest of the decade. By December 2005, the number of UN peacekeepers exceeded non-UN ones by 80 percent. Important to remember is that on a number of occasions, intrastate operations shifted from one actor to another. For instance, many of the TCCs in the UN Protection Force (UN-PROFOR) for Bosnia were incorporated into the NATO-led successor Implementation Force (IFOR). In some other cases, notably in Africa, non-UN missions converted into UN missions while keeping most of the previous personnel. To some extent such shifts or conversions explain the sharp change in 1996 (when the number of peacekeepers in non-UN operations sharply increased and UN peacekeepers sharply decreased) and changes during the past three to four years when the number of UN peacekeepers increased at the same time as non-UN peacekeepers decreased.

It is therefore not possible to discern a gradual change toward greater or lesser reliance on the UN; instead, one can discern a cyclical pattern. There is, again, no evidence of a long-term detrimental effect of non-UN operations on UN operations. Figure 1.4 suggests also that there is a short-term—and positive rather than negative—association between the resources that the UN and non-UN actors have utilized for peacekeeping.[20] Apparently, the resources that one actor is able to recruit do not negatively influence the resources available to the other actor.

Given the UN's effort to coordinate its own and non-UN actors' peacekeeping operations, this pattern is not surprising. It suggests also that the UN's efforts have been successful. Differentiating the operations into interstate and intrastate operations yields conclusions identical with those of figures 1.2 and 1.3. That is, the UN has for some thirty years been the primary supplier of peacekeepers to interstate conflicts, although the relationship is actually positive instead of weakly negative as in figure 1.2. For intrastate conflicts, the pattern is somewhat weaker than in figure 1.4.

As noted earlier, there are concerns that an increase in non-UN operations would hurt access to ready peacekeepers for the regions in need. If true, non-UN dominance should have led the UN to become less involved in the region with the greatest need: Africa. However, the data tell another story: for the 1989–2005 period Africa received a large part of the UN's peacekeeping resources, particularly for the period 2000–5. For instance, in December 2005 Africa received 76 percent of the UN's peacekeeping personnel.[21] The past decade has been one marked by a UN focus on—not neglect of—Africa. Whereas the quality of troops is not taken into account in this analysis, this is nevertheless an additional piece of information that puts to rest fears that the UN's pool of peacekeeping resources would decrease due to non-UN operations, and that regions in the greatest need for peacekeeping would be left to their own devices. It also indicates that the UN picks it cases and sends peacekeepers to regions where the need is greatest, and that the increased contribution by regional actors to peacekeeping may have enabled the UN to more actively pursue conflict management in Africa.[22] Hence a rationale behind the UN's efforts to promote non-UN missions: to allow the UN to carry out peacekeeping in regions of need. The UN's strategy has in this sense been successful.

Number of Troop-Contributing Countries

As there seems to be no overall competition between UN and non-UN operations—and no general negative consequences of non-UN operations for the occurrence of UN operations and the number of deployed UN peace-keepers—one may assume that concerns about competition for TCCs are un-grounded as well: if the first is not the case, then the second should not be the case either. The analysis below sets set such logic aside in favor of empirical inquiry into whether participation in non-UN operations undermines partici-pation in UN operations.

Figure 1.5 shows that the number of TCCs to UN operations has been al-most constantly growing since the UN started to focus on intrastate conflicts in the early 1990s. This number is also positively associated with the number of fielded peacekeepers (see figure 1.4).[23] Non-UN missions display a similar pattern: there is an upward trend, though more irregular, and it is positively associated with the number of non-UN peacekeepers.[24] There is nothing in this graph indicating that TCCs are turning away from the UN toward non-UN missions, as the number of TCCs to UN operations exceeds the number of TCCs to non-UN operations by a wide margin. There is also a strong posi-tive—not negative—global relationship from 1970 to 2005 between the two curves.[25] While suggestive, a global relationship does not definitively reveal whether *individual* countries become more or less inclined to participate in UN operations due to participation in non-UN operations. However, a statis-tical analysis at the country level shows a positive—not negative—relation-ship: for any given year participation in non-UN missions is positively—not negatively—associated with participation in UN missions.[26] Instead of com-petition and crowding out, the statistics show that the interaction is to a large extent characterized by sharing the very same TCCs.

This growth in TCCs may indicate that a norm has been established and is spreading: as the number of TCCs increases, it may create pressure on other

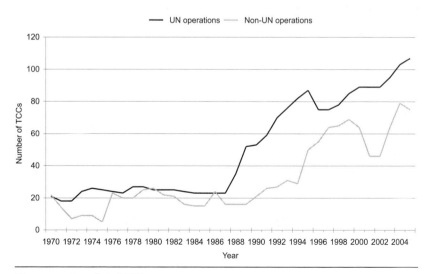

Figure 1.5. Trends in TCCs, 1970–2005

countries to enlist. In addition, the higher number of TCCs lessens the burden
on any individual country. And the less the burden on individual countries, the
more likely it is that additional countries will enlist. Moreover, once a country
has been a TCC, it may have passed an important hurdle that makes it easier for
the UN and non-UN actors to enlist in future missions. In all, these interpretations suggest that we are observing a self-reinforcing process of growth that
may originally have taken off due to the UN's efforts to make regional actors
assume more responsibility (cf. endnote 3), and whose positive self-reinforcing
nature spills over between UN and non-UN peacekeeping operations.

National Trends, 1970–2005

As mentioned earlier, since non-UN dominance in the sphere of peacekeeping has not become predominant, one may on logical grounds consider the
second concern about global competition for TCCs as unrealistic. The empirical evidence also provides support for this insight. However, at the same time
we may ask whether the characteristics of TCCs have changed. If wealthy
countries, with their superior peacekeeping resources, are likely to no longer
be placed at the UN's disposal due to involvement in non-UN operations, then
an important change has occurred. However, and as earlier noted, the logic
behind these fears implies that it is poor countries that should become tied up
in their own regions, and thus that they—not wealthy countries—should be
less likely to contribute to UN operations. This section assesses the accuracy
of these scenarios.

Figure 1.6 shows the average TCC GDP per capita in comparison to the
world GDP per capita, adjusted for inflation. A score of 1 at the Y-axis indicates that the average TCC GDP per capita is on par with the average world
GDP per capita. Thus, the figure shows that wealthier countries were prominent in UN operations from 1970 through the late 1980s, after which the
less wealthy countries have increasingly kept the peace for the UN. There
has also been a slow downwards movement in terms of TCC wealth since the
late 1990s. As additional TCCs are now mainly recruited from less and less
developed countries, a downward trend is an unavoidable consequence of the
expansion of the UN TCC roster. Nonetheless, the average TCC by 2005 had
a GDP per capita some 40 percent higher than the world average. Whereas
TCCs have become less wealthy, they are still on average semideveloped.

The relatively prominent participation of wealthy countries in UN operations through the late 1980s appears easy to explain. One possible explanation is that UN operations were mostly a matter of interstate peacekeeping
until 1989. Because the operations were few (cf. figure 1.1) and mostly small
in size (cf. figure 1.4), the UN did not need to look beyond developed countries in order to find TCCs. A second possible reason is that the countries that
came out of colonization during the 1950s and 1960s were poor, preoccupied
with domestic consolidation, and had in general no armed forces suitable for

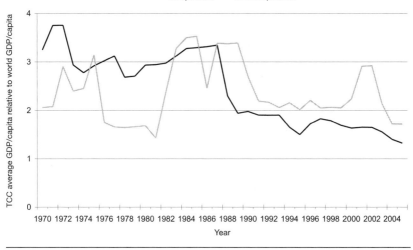

Figure 1.6. Trends in TCC Relative Wealth, 1970–2005

peacekeeping. Still another possible reason is the focus on interstate cases: their low risks did not cause a strong inducement to spread the burden.

This pattern changed when the emphasis shifted to intrastate peacekeeping in the final years of the 1980s. The drop in average TCC wealth coincides with the peacekeeping operations in Namibia and Angola. There were apparently not enough developed countries willing to assume the higher costs and increased risks of such intrastate missions. Hence, the UN cast a wider net, and thus developing countries needed to come on board. However, and as mentioned earlier, whereas the number of peacekeepers has fluctuated widely during the past fifteen years, no similarly wide variation can be discerned in average TCC wealth. This suggests that, from the perspective of wealth, the UN's TCCs by now constitute a fairly consistent but increasingly broad pool of nations.

Non-UN operations have evolved in a slightly different way, and they have fluctuated more widely. It is also difficult to discern any long- or medium-term trend. The pattern is rather inconsistent, and by 2005 the average TCC wealth for both types of operations was basically identical. In general, since 1983 TCCs in non-UN operations have been slightly wealthier than those in UN operations, with wider differences in the late 1980s and in the late 1990s through the first years of the present decade. Such patterns are consistent with concerns that non-UN operations are drawing especially wealthy TCCs away from UN operations. However, the difference during the years 1988–91 is also related to trends in peacekeeping as illustrated in previous figures, that is, that the UN started to expand its peacekeeping activities in 1988, and the non-UN actors did likewise a few years later; this provides a more natural explanation for the gap during these few years. Moreover, the patterns throughout the 1990s and since 2004 do not confirm any trend toward wealthy countries increasingly and consistently confining themselves to non-UN missions while avoiding UN missions: the TCC wealth trend for UN operations is flat from 1998 to 2004, whereas the pattern for non-UN operations is unstable. Apparently, there is no simple connection or crowding-out effect.

Instead, it may be conjectured that the pattern of TCC wealth reflects the location of particular conflicts. The UN, in contrast, recruits at a global level, thereby providing for a more stable pattern of wealth among TCCs, as the pool of potential TCCs is not dependent on the location of the conflict where peace is to be kept. In reality, the picture of intervention by non-UN actors is complicated. The reason has to do with the more than a dozen out-of-area operations that were carried out by mainly developed countries. Without these operations, the wealth pattern of TCCs to non-UN operations would have tilted in the direction of lower average wealth. In other words, what keeps TCC wealth up for non-UN operations is a pattern of developed states keeping the peace in poor—rather than their own—regions. As such, they are serving as substitutes for the UN in conflict-stricken regions.

Regardless of those forces that are pushing countries to contribute, the overall insight is that across the period from 1970 to 2005, the economic characteristics of TCCs do not consistently and substantially differ across UN-led and non–UN-led operations. There is no evidence that UN-led and non–UN-led operations are increasingly confined to poor and rich TCCs respectively, or any aggregate indications that, in general, either poor or wealthy countries have participated in non-UN operations at the expense of participation in UN operations. There is also no evidence of a negative—but rather of a weak positive—relationship between the lines for the entire period as well as the subperiod from 1995 to 2005.[27] This indicates that UN and non-UN operations do not in general compete for the same type of TCCs. To the extent that the wealth of TCCs to non-UN operations conditions the wealth of TCCs to UN missions, it does so in a positive manner.

This aggregate analysis raises the question of whether the intervention pattern for individual *rich* countries has changed, as has sometimes been feared would be the outcome of the increase in non-UN operations. To assess this, a regression analysis was run focusing on countries whose GDP per capita was at least three times the world's per capita GDP. According to this analysis, a positive relationship between participation in non-UN operations and participation in UN operations is at hand for the period from 1970 to 2004. When rerunning the analysis for the subperiod 1995–2004, the relationship is even stronger.[28] For wealthy countries, participation in non-UN operations does not negatively affect participation in UN operations; rather, it positively affects that participation. A second question is whether the intervention patterns for developing countries have changed. Thus, the analysis was rerun for all countries with a GDP per capita less than the world average. For the entire period 1970–2004, as well as for the subperiod 1995–2004, the relationship between participation in UN and non-UN operations was positive

for developing countries. Once again, and perhaps more surprisingly, participation of developing countries in non-UN operations positively affects their
participation in UN operations.

The analysis so far has only considered participation in peacekeeping operations, not the size of those contributions. If poor countries are increasingly
supplying most of the peacekeepers to the UN at the same time that wealthy
countries are becoming more likely to contribute to non-UN operations, then
one can argue that wealthy countries have been backing away from the UN,
and that this may be due to an increased focus on non-UN operations. Unfortunately, there is no easily accessible monthly country-level data available for
personnel contributions to most non-UN operations. It is far easier to find
monthly data at the mission level. Country-specific figures can often be determined for some periods of some operations with the help of case studies
and official documents. However, because of the large data gaps, there generally arises an unclear degree of measurement error if there is an attempt to
impute or interpolate data to generate substitutes for missing monthly data
points. Availability of accurate monthly country-level data for UN operations
is secured through the monthly summaries of contributions to peacekeeping
operations available since 1991, and for periods before that through docu-
mentation in the UN archives in New York, and including mission reports of
the secretary-general. This data situation means that it is not possible to use
statistical tools to accurately assess whether a causal relationship exists between the personnel contributions of individual countries to UN and non-UN
operations. However, the UN data do make possible a descriptive analysis of
whether the wealth of states has conditioned contributions to UN operations.
Whereas such an analysis does not address the possible crowding-out effect of
non-UN operations, it will at least tell us whether there has been a change in
the wealth of TCCs.

Figure 1.7 speaks to this issue by showing the cumulative share of personnel contributions to UN operations as conditioned by the wealth of countries
for three time periods: 1991–95, 1996–2000, and 2001–5. It is evident that a
change has taken place. During 1991–95, countries that were below the world
average GDP per capita (that is, countries to the left of 1 at the x-axis, as 1 indicates the world average) contributed around 50 percent of all the peacekeepers. During 1996–2000, the figure increased to almost 65 percent, and during
2001–5 the figure was almost 90 percent. It was not the medium-wealthy
countries (i.e., countries that are 1 to 4 times as wealthy as the world average,
and thus located between 1 and 4 at the X-axis) that scaled back their contributions, but rather the ones that were 4 to 6 times as wealthy as the world average. The latter category contributed around 30 percent of the peacekeepers
during 1991–95; some 20 percent during 1996–2000; and around 10 percent
during 2001–5. The scaling back of contributions by the wealthiest countries
may not appear surprising considering their limited number and the sharp
increase in TCCs during the past fifteen years (see figure 1.5). Yet the data
show that the wealthiest countries have not maintained their contributions.
Because of the paucity of data, it is not possible to assess the extent to which

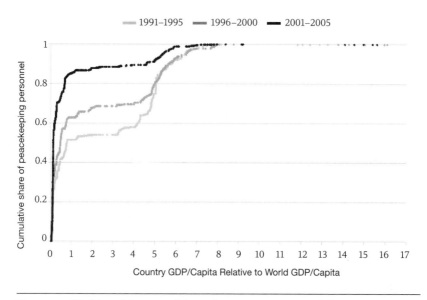

Figure 1.7. Wealth and Personnel Contributions to UN Peacekeeping, 1991–2005

this dynamic has been influenced by changes in contributions to non-UN operations. One may nevertheless note that in recent years, wealthy countries have been dominating non-UN operations.[29] This pattern is mainly caused by the large non-UN operations in the Balkans. When those conflicts become dormant, and assuming no new and large out-of-area operations for wealthy states, this pattern can be expected to change drastically.

Lurking behind figure 1.7 is the possibility that there may be some individual countries that account for this large growth in contributions by less wealthy countries, rather than a comprehensive scenario whereby the growth is pretty evenly distributed among such countries. Table 1.2 sheds some light on this issue by showing the top ten UN TCCs for the same three periods: 1991–95, 1996–2000, and 2001–5.

As indicated by this table, less wealthy countries have increasingly supplied the bulk of peacekeepers. There are also only developing and low-income countries among the top ten contributors for 2001–5; four developed countries were part of the top ten for 1996–2000, whereas the figure is three out of ten for 1991–95. Yet a closer look reveals that a few contributors consistently contribute, and at a significantly large magnitude. India, Pakistan, Bangladesh, Ghana, Jordan, and (to a less extent) Nepal were among the top ten throughout all three periods. This indicates that it is not really the case that poor countries have increasingly supplied the bulk of peacekeepers, but instead that some less wealthy *particular* countries have done so, and for an extended period. The conclusion is that the decreased contributions from wealthy countries have been replaced by contributions from a handful of less

Table 1.2. Top Ten Contributors to UN Peacekeeping Operations, 1991–2005 (%)

1991–1995	1996–2000	2001–2005
France, 9.9	India, 6.5	Pakistan, 12.0
Pakistan, 7.0	Bangladesh, 5.9	Bangladesh, 11.9
United Kingdom, 6.0	Poland, 4.9	India, 7.0
India, 4.6	Ghana, 4.7	Nigeria, 6.4
Canada, 4.5	Jordan, 4.0	Ghana, 5.1
Bangladesh, 4.0	Pakistan, 3.8	Jordan, 4.4
Nepal, 3.2	Austria, 3.7	Kenya, 3.6
Jordan, 3.1	Finland, 3.6	Nepal, 3.5
Ghana, 2.9	United States, 3.5	Uruguay, 3.2
Poland, 2.8	Ireland, 3.4	Ukraine, 2.4

Sources: Data for the period 2001–5 are from the UN Department of Peacekeeping Operations (DPKO) website. Data for 1991–2000 are from monthly summaries of contributions to peacekeeping operations supplied by the UN Department of Peacekeeping Operations in 2001. UN Department of Peacekeeping Operations (DPKO), *United Nations Peacekeeping*, www.un.org/Depts/dpko/dpko/index.asp.

wealthy countries rather than from less wealthy countries in general. UN peacekeeping today is thus to an important extent the business of a few large and less wealthy countries.

The Prospects for Peacekeeping

An inventory of global and national patterns of peacekeeping, coupled with some very simple calculations and visual inspection of data trends, does not offer support for concerns that non-UN operations may undermine the UN's future global role. The historical pattern is instead characterized by cycles, coexistence, and coordination rather than by competition.

As for concerns that participation in non-UN missions may decrease the UN's access to well-trained and well-equipped peacekeepers from the developed world, the picture is not clear. In terms of participation, there is no negative effect but rather a positive one. Hence, UN and non-UN missions appear indirectly to assist each other in creating a pool of potential TCCs. As such, the promotion of non-UN missions has served to strengthen the UN's capacity for peacekeeping, just as experience from UN missions may have conditioned many countries to enter into non-UN missions. In terms of the number of supplied peacekeepers to UN missions, the share of UN peacekeepers from the richest countries has decreased, but it is not clear how to interpret this change. It may be due to an increase in poor TCCs, or it may have been caused by the richest countries' contributions to the very large non-UN operations in the Balkans (which are in essence acting as proxies for the UN—and as follow-ups to previous UN missions—as well as being endorsed by the UN). For a rich country like Sweden, the latter has been the case. Yet even if the latter interpretation explains most of this pattern, it is somewhat difficult to regard it as a crowding-out effect, since these non-UN operations are proxying for the UN and following up on earlier UN missions. It is also important to remember that, whereas poor countries are increasingly supplying the UN with peacekeepers, behind this trend is the important fact that the suppliers are mainly a few large and less wealthy countries rather than this category of states as a whole.

What do the insights in this chapter mean for the future of peacekeeping? They may mean that the global supply of TCCs is more secure than ever, and that the foundation for future peacekeeping has been laid. Such a situation will arguably make it easier to establish operations than before, unless there arises some traumatic deadlock in the UN system. Nonetheless, there is still one point of concern: contributions to UN operations mainly come from a handful of large and poor countries. While one may argue that their dominance is natural and reasonable given their combined size, it is still the case that, should these countries change their policies, the UN will face a challenge to find replacements for their contributions. This means that the UN needs to consider how to diversify its pool of contributors so that it becomes less dependent on a few countries. This is one of the larger issues for the future of peacekeeping.

The increased number of TCCs means an increased demand for reform of UN peacekeeping. At the same time, it will become more difficult to reach a consensus on the nature of such reforms. It remains to be seen what the end result will be. Perhaps the easiest predictions are that reforms will come slowly at best and that peacekeeping will be carried out in the medium-term future pretty much as it has been in the past.

Chapter 2

Distinguishing among Military Contributors

DONALD C. F. DANIEL, KATRIN HEUEL,
AND BENJAMIN MARGO

Introduction

Is there a profile for most of the states that have recently contributed military personnel to peace operations? What kinds of governments do they have? How wealthy, developed, and internally stable are they? Are they technologically well-connected with the rest of the world? Do they have large, medium, or small ground forces? From what regions do they hail? Do the profiles of most major contributors differ from those of most minor contributors? Are profiles changing? What are the implications for the availability of troops for peace operations? Published literature has had relatively little to say that is either systematic or comprehensive about these issues.[1] This chapter attempts to help fill that gap, and it does so within this book's trends and prospects framework.

Drawing on troop-contribution data for 2001 through 2005, together with data about national traits or characteristics, four sets of trend questions are addressed:

- What are the profiles of the majority of designated troop-contributing countries (DCs), and are they markedly different from those for most nominal and noncontributors (NNCs)?
- Which states have had relatively major impacts on contributions, and which have had more limited impacts? Do the traits of the former differ from those of the latter?
- How have the characteristics of all contributors changed over the period, and who were the notable rising contributors (NRCs)—that is, those whose impacts seemed to become more significant over time? How do their characteristics compare to those of the other groups?
- Which characteristics seem the most salient with regard to how much and how often a state contributes?

Building on the above analyses, we address three near-term prospect issues:

- Based largely on their characteristics, which nominal and noncontributors have the most potential for becoming designated contributors over the next few years?
- Of the limited impact contributors, which have the most potential for becoming higher impact states?
- In light of all the above, what are the overall prospects for the makeup of the troop-contributor community over the next few years? Are significant changes in the offing and what could these changes mean for the availability of military personnel?

After defining basic analytic concepts, we describe our peace operations database and how it was put together. We move on to outline the national characteristics of interest and the data relied on to profile each state. We then present findings, first for trends and then for potential prospects. The answers to the last set of prospects questions will serve as our conclusions.

Basic Concepts, the Peace Operations Database, and Group Rankings

A *peace operation* is defined as a military intervention in an area of crisis or conflict by a force that is usually multinational in makeup and operating under a mandate issued by one or more international security organizations. The intent of the interveners must be to quell anticipated or ongoing violence generated by the indigenous parties and/or to help them move toward a sustainable peace. A peace operation can encompass traditional peacekeeping (the interposition of a neutral force to separate former belligerents who have consented to the force's presence), complex peacekeeping (the restoration of law and order, basic services, and governmental authority in a largely consensual environment), peace enforcement (the threat or use of coercion to induce the indigenous parties to implement an international mandate intended to restore or maintain stability), and postconflict stabilization (efforts to restore governmental and social services in an occupied country).[2]

The starting points for determining which operations to include in the database were the compilations of peace missions for 2001 through 2005 found in the Stockholm International Peace Research Institute's (SIPRI) *Yearbook on Armaments, Disarmaments, and International Security*. We found comprehensive information on national military contributions to be more readily available for those years than for earlier periods. This was true for press reports and in websites administered by organizations conducting peace operations (such as the UN for data after October 2000, the African Union, and the EU through its Europa portal) and by think tanks (such as SIPRI itself or the Institute for Security Studies in South Africa). A second reason for focusing on these particular years is our assumption that the 2001–05 period provides a better indication of a country's willingness and capability to undertake peace operations over the next few years than would earlier periods.

For the purposes of our analyses, a country is designated a *troop contributor* if it provided at least one hundred troops to any one mission. Although about 112 states provided military personnel to peace operations between 2001 and 2005, we estimated that only 87 contributed at least 100 troops to at least one mission in any given year. The other twenty-five *nominal contributors*—those that provided some personnel but fewer than one hundred troops to any operation—were excluded from the troop-contributor database. Doing so reduced skewing of contribution aggregates toward the low end, and it also makes it possible to focus on unit contributors per se. That is, countries can detail personnel to missions in two ways: they can assign them as separate individuals or as part of a unit such as a company or battalion. Small missions (e.g., those of no more than 100 to 200 or so military personnel) are generally easy to staff and may be made up entirely of individual detaillees. However, most missions are larger and necessitate unit detailing. We chose one hundred as a minimum because it is the generally accepted low end of a company-size unit; we assumed that any country's contribution of one hundred or more troops to an operation consisted of one or more formed units.[3]

The eighty-seven designated contributors (or the G87) are, of course, a subset of the larger international community, and out of the nearly two hundred existing sovereignties, we identified 157 as *potential contributors* (the G157). They were nations (excluding Iraq) whose ground forces (army and naval infantry) totaled at least 800 troops, the size of the smallest national force (Gambia's) belonging to a designated contributor.[4]

Alongside the eighty-seven designated contributors in the G157 are seventy *nominal and noncontributors* (the NNCs or the G70). It is they to whom one would turn when seeking new designated contributors. As noted earlier, particular attention will be paid to their prospects by comparing the profiles of G70 states to those in the G87.

We drew on a variety of sources to estimate national contributor totals; the sources included the SIPRI database, *Military Balance*, UN Department of Peacekeeping Operations (DPKO) monthly summaries, official government and organization websites, think tank and information-dissemination websites, and press accounts. Accessing data for UN operations is relatively simple because its DPKO site provides monthly national contribution totals from October 2000 on; we looked at the month when overall military contributions were the highest overall for the year and then went to each nation's contribution for that particular month. There is no similar source for non-UN operations; our estimates for them required triangulating the troop levels from scattered sources.

As noted earlier, we excluded those nations that provided less than 100 troops from the designated contributor data base in order to avoid skewing aggregates toward the low end. We also excluded U.S. participation in the stabilization operation in Iraq to avoid the opposite since U.S. Iraq deployments by themselves roughly equaled the yearly total for all other national deployments for 2003 through 2005. To avoid double-counting, we also attended to the rollover of missions as one mission directly succeeded another in the same location. The designation of the follow-on mission was usually due to major changes in the mandate or in the organizational leadership of the original mission.[5] E.g., on June 1, 2004, the UN through its ONUB mission took over peace operations responsibility for Burundi from the African Union and its AMIB mission. The 860 Ethiopian troops in the AU mission simply rolled over to UN authority (trading their green AU berets for blue UN ones). Thus Ethiopia's 2004 national contributor total was credited with 860 for *both* operations and not with 1,720, the total that would arise if one simply added Ethiopia's contributions across missions—the normal way of arriving at an annual total for a country—without concern for rollover.

In order to compare states within the G87, their yearly contributions were added together and divided by the number of years for which they contributed. The result was an overall 2001 to 2005 "years-giving average" for each country. The averages were ranked in descending order and divided into quartiles such that each country was given a score of 1 through 4, 4 being the largest.

While size of contribution is obviously a critical measure of a country's performance, we also attended to another critical measure: sustainability of contributions on a year-by-year basis. Countries that consistently contribute to peace operations can be viewed as the dependable core—or "go-to"—members of the international community.

By adding together a country's quartile ranking and its number of contributor years, we arrived at an overall composite score for each country. The best score, 9, belongs to consistent five-year contributors ranked at quartile level 4. The lowest score, 2, is for one-year contributors at quartile level 1.

The National Profiles Database

Seven traits are relied upon to form a profile for each state. One is *geographic location*, with the regions—Africa (sub-Saharan), the Americas, the CIS (Commonwealth of Independent States), East Asia and the Pacific, Europe, North Africa and the Mideast, and South Asia—corresponding to the U.S. State Department geographic bureau breakdown, except for our distinguishing the CIS states from Europe.

Each of the remaining six traits is divided into three "quality" levels. The first of these traits is *size of active ground forces*—ground forces being those elements of each nation's military that overwhelmingly account for the number of troops contributed. In our analysis large ground forces are those with 100,000 or more personnel; medium ground forces range from 25,000 to 99,999; and small forces are below 25,000. The next five traits—collectively termed a country's societal characteristics—are *governance, income, development level, internal stability,* and *international technological connectivity.*

Governance data are from Freedom House. Countries it rated as "free" in its combined index are referred to in this chapter as "democracies," "partly free" as "anocracies," and "not free" as "autocracies."[6] Nearly all income classifications are from the World Bank Group's (WBG) gross national income per capita data.[7] The WBG utilized four categories: high, upper middle, lower middle, and low; we collapsed the upper and lower middle categories into one middle-income group.[8] Level of development was based on the UN Development Program's human development index—encompassing life expectancy, educational attainment, and adjusted real income.[9] It too placed countries into one of three groups, which we labeled highly developed, lesser developed, and least developed. With a few exceptions, information on internal stability was derived from the Center for International Development and Conflict Management's Peace and Conflict Ledger at the University of Maryland, which classifies countries based on eight capacity indicators for building domestic peace and avoiding destabilizing political crises.[10] Adopting the Ledger's three-fold breakdown, we characterized states as stable, less stable, and least stable. International technological connectivity is a trait that we derived from aggregating a state's ranking in three areas: minutes per person of international voice traffic in and out of the country, number of internet users per one thousand people in the country, and the country's international internet bandwidth bits per person as found in the World Bank's Development Indicators and, where necessary, supplemented with data from the UN's Conference on Trade and Development.[11] A country's rankings in each connectivity area were added and served as the basis for an aggregate ranking. For instance, the aggregate leader is Switzerland. Its fourth-place rankings for voice traffic and bandwidth and its 14th place among internet users gave it a composite score of 22, the lowest and thus best of all the 157 states; in contrast, Myanmar's composite score of 464 placed it last. The states in the top third of the composite rankings were credited with high connectivity, those in the middle with medium connectivity, and the bottom third with low connectivity.

Appendix 2.1 identifies the 157 potential contributors and profiles each state in alphabetical order. It is number-coded for societal characteristics and ground forces, with 1 identifying the highest level states (i.e., democratic, high income, stable, etc.), 2 for states with mid-range values, and 3 for states with the lowest values. The numbers make it possible to come up with mean scores for groups, whereby the lower the number, the higher the quality of governance, income, development level, internal stability, and international technological connectivity for that group. The mean scores thus derived provide a ready basis for comparing groups.

The "majority profiles" attributed to a group refers to the characteristics that apply to most of the states in the group. For example, table 2.1, column 1, shows that most of the 157 potential contributors are democratic and anocratic (73 percent), medium to low in income (78 percent), stable (52 percent), highly to lesser developed (76 percent), and have medium to small ground forces (77 percent).

Trend Findings

This section lays out the core trends derived from the analysis. It divides the contributors into groups and compares the characteristics profiles of each group to one another and to that of the nominal and noncontributors. It also identifies notable rising contributors and specifies which characteristics seem most salient for predicting a state's propensity to become a high-impact donor.

Overall Aggregate Trends

Overall contributions (excluding the U.S. in Iraq) ranged from a low of 101,400 in 2002 to a high of 149,000 in 2004. The number of designated contributor countries ranged from the low fifties early in the period to the upper seventies at its end. The mean average contribution for all states over the five years was 1,551 personnel; the median was 767. The difference between the mean and median indicates the critical role played by the larger contributors—a point to which we will return.

Figure 2.1 is a matrix that lists all 87 DCs by their composite score for size of contribution by quartile (the y-axis) combined with the number of years they contributed (the-x axis). States with the best showing are top right; the lowest scorers are bottom left. What is striking about the figure is the correlation between consistent contributors and size of contribution. Of the forty-six five-year contributors, three-quarters (35) contributed at level 3 or 4; of the forty-one less-than-five-year contributors, four-fifths (33) are at level 1 or level 2.

The G87 Majority Profiles

As seen in column 2 of table 2.1, most of the 87 contributors are democratic, stable, highly or lesser developed, with high to medium connectivity. Most impressive are the majorities for democratic governance (55 percent) and stability (60 percent). While it is impossible to arrive at majority profiles for per capita income and ground force size, table 2.2 addresses what proportion of potential contributors by trait actually made contributions. The table shows how higher quality states tend more often to be contributors than do lower quality states. Specifically, two-thirds to three-quarters of all democratic, wealthy, stable, highly developed, well-connected states with large ground forces are contributors, compared with only one-quarter to one-half of autocratic, poor, least stable, least developed states with low connectivity and small ground forces. Anocratic, middle income, less stable, less developed states with medium connectivity and medium ground forces fell in the middle; in every category about 50 percent of them are designated contributors.

In absolute numbers, the European and African states are the most heavily in evidence, totaling 48 states or 55 percent of all contributors. (See table 2.1., bottom of column 2.) There were fourteen contributors from the Americas, eleven from the Asia/Pacific countries, and only eleven from the CIS, North African/Mideast, and South Asian states collectively. When one asks, however, which region is proportionally best relative to the number of potential contributors in a given region, the South Asian states by far come out on top. Of the six states located in South Asia, five, or 83 percent, are contributors. The only other region significantly overrepresented is Europe, at 77 percent.

Quartile– (number of troops contributed)					
4 (> 1973)			Ethiopia SCORE = 7		Bangladesh, Canada, France, Germany, Ghana, Greece, India, Italy, Morocco, Nepal, Netherlands, Nigeria, Pakistan, Poland, Russia, South Africa, Spain, Turkey, Ukraine, United Kingdom, United States SCORE = 9
3 (781–1973)		Brazil, Guinea, Namibia, Rwanda, United Arab Emirates SCORE = 5		Japan, Romania SCORE = 7	Australia, Austria, Belgium, Denmark, Finland, Hungary, Jordan, Kenya, S. Korea, Norway, Portugal, Senegal, Sweden, Uruguay SCORE = 8
2 (334–780)	Egypt SCORE = 3	Chile, Guinea-Bissau, Honduras, Sri Lanka SCORE = 4	Benin, Bulgaria, China (PR), El Salvador, New Zealand, Niger, Togo SCORE = 5	Philippines SCORE = 6	Argentina, Colombia, Czech Republic, Fiji, Ireland, Slovakia, Thailand, Tunisia, Zambia SCORE = 7
1 (100–333)	Albania, Guatemala, Malawi, Peru SCORE = 2	Azerbaijan, Dominican Republic, Lithuania, Mali, Nicaragua, Slovenia SCORE = 3	Chad, Congo (RO), Gabon, Gambia, Georgia, Indonesia, Latvia, Mongolia, Mozambique, Singapore SCORE = 4		Bolivia, Switzerland SCORE = 6
DC years–	1	2	3	4	5

Figure 2.1. Designated Contributor Matrix

Table 2.1. Percentages for Traits and Regions (%)

	G (157)[a]	DC (87)[b]	NNC (70)[c]	HIS (47)[d]	LIS (40)[e]	NRC (24)[f]
Governance						
Democracy	64 (41)	48 (55)	16 (23)	32 (68)	16 (40)	13 (54)
Anocracy	50 (32)	28 (32)	28 (31)	12 (26)	16 (40)	8 (33)
Autocracy	43 (27)	11 (13)	32 (46)	3 (6)	8 (20)	3 (13)
Income/capita						
High	34 (22)	25 (29)	9 (13)	20 (43)	5 (13)	3 (13)
Medium	71 (45)	38 (44)	33 (48)	17 (36)	21 (53)	13 (54)
Low	52 (33)	24 (28)	28 (40)	10 (21)	14 (35)	8 (33)
Stability						
Stable	81 (52)	52 (60)	28 (40)	30 (64)	22 (55)	12 (50)
Less stable	49 (31)	26 (30)	24 (34)	13 (28)	13 (33)	7 (29)
Least stable	27 (17)	9 (10)	18 (26)	4 (9)	5 (13)	5 (21)
Development						
Highly developed	48 (31)	34 (39)	14 (20)	26 (55)	8 (20)	6 (25)
Less developed	71 (45)	35 (40)	36 (51)	15 (32)	20 (50)	13 (54)
Least developed	38 (24)	18 (21)	20 (29)	6 (13)	12 (30)	5 (21)
Connectivity						
High	52 (33)	34 (39)	18 (26)	26 (55)	8 (20)	6 (25)
Medium	53 (34)	30 (34)	23 (33)	12 (26)	18 (45)	11 (46)
Low	52 (33)	23 (26)	29 (41)	9 (19)	14 (35)	7 (29)
Ground Forces						
Large	37 (24)	25 (29)	12 (17)	20 (43)	5 (13)	13 (54)
Medium	45 (29)	23 (26)	22 (31)	12 (26)	11 (28)	8 (33)
Small	75 (48)	39 (45)	36 (51)	15 (32)	24 (60)	3 (13)
Region						
Africa (S-S)	42 (27)	21 (24)	21 (30)	7 (15)	14 (35)	6 (26)
Americas	24 (15)	14 (16)	10 (14)	5 (11)	9 (26)	3 (13)
Asia/Pac	21 (13)	11 (13)	10 (14)	5 (11)	6 (15)	3 (13)
CIS	12 (8)	4 (5)	8 (11)	2 (4)	2 (5)	1 (4)
Europe	35 (22)	27 (31)	8 (11)	21 (45)	6 (15)	3 (13)
N. Africa/ Mideast	17 (11)	5 (6)	12 (17)	3 (6)	2 (5)	2 (9)
S. Asia	6 (4)	5 (6)	1 (1)	4 (9)	1 (3)	5 (21)

[a] G = Potential Contributors (157 countries)
[b] DC = Designated Contributors (87 countries)
[c] NNC = Nominal and Noncontributors (70 countries)
[d] HIS = Higher- or Major-Impact States (47 countries)
[e] LIS = Lower- or Limited-Impact States (40 countries)
[f] NRC = Notable Rising Contributors (24 countries)

Table 2.2. Proportion of Potential Contributors by Trait That Are Designated Troop-Contributing Countries

Characteristics	Number of Contributors	Number of Potential Contributors	Percentage (column 2/ column 3)
All	87	157	55
Governance			
Democratic	48	64	75
Anocratic	28	50	56
Autocratic	11	43	26
Income			
High	25	34	74
Middle	38	71	54
Low	24	52	46
Stability			
Stable	52	81	64
Less stable	26	49	53
Least stable	9	27	33
Development			
Highly developed	34	48	71
Less developed	35	71	49
Least developed	18	38	47
Connectivity			
High	34	52	65
Medium	30	53	57
Low	23	52	44
Ground Forces			
Large	25	37	68
Medium	23	45	51
Small	39	75	52
Region			
Africa	21	42	50
Americas	14	24	58
Asia-Pacific	11	21	52
CIS	4	12	33
Europe	27	35	77
North Africa/Middle East	5	17	29
South Asia	5	6	83

North Africa/Mideast and the CIS were significantly underrepresented with 29 and 33 percent of their regions, respectively, being troop contributors. Half to three-fifths of states in Africa, Asia/Pacific, and the Americas were donors.

Comparing the Contributors to the Nominal and Noncontributors
The majority profiles of the seventy NNCs both overlap and contrast markedly with those of the eighty-seven designated contributors (see table 2.1, columns 2 and 3) Whereas most contributors are democratic, stable, and highly developed with high to medium connectivity, most nominal and noncontributors are anocratic or autocratic, stable or less stable, and lesser developed with medium to low connectivity. Where the two groups differ least is in ground forces, with small forces being most prominent to both. In every trait, however, the G87 exhibits higher quality. The G87 states consistently have lower—that is, better—mean scores with the biggest differences being in governance (especially) and stability (see figure 2.2).

Regionally, sub-Saharan Africa (with twenty-one states) and North Africa/ Mideast (with twelve states) form the largest groups among the nominal and noncontributors, while South Asia (with one state) is the smallest. All other regions have eight to ten states.

Comparing Higher-Impact and Lower-Impact States
Contributors with scores of 7 through 9 in table 2.1 can justifiably be considered as higher- or major-impact states (HISs), and those with scores of 2 though 6 as lower- or limited-impact states (LISs). To be a major-impact donor, a contributor must have provided troops for at least three of the five years and done so at least at the level of the second quartile. There are forty-seven HISs, and nearly all exceed those minimal standards. Only nine are in the

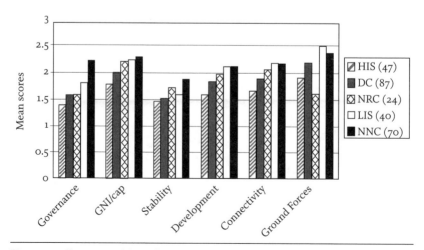

Figure 2.2 Comparing Mean Scores

second quartile, and only three did not contribute for the five consecutive years. The average contribution among the major donors was 2,600 troops. There are forty LISs, with the vast majority of them contributing three years or less and at quartile levels one or two. Their average contribution was 350 troops.

When comparing profiles, one sees that the higher-impact contributors have consistently better national qualities than the lower-impact ones (see table 2.1, columns 4 and 5). The HIS are democratic, wealthy or of middle income, highly developed, and well connected. Most of the LIS are democratic or anocratic, middle income, lesser or least developed, with medium or low connectivity. A healthy plurality of major contributors has large ground forces; a majority of nominal and noncontributors have small ground forces. The greatest overlap is in stability. Most states in both groups are stable, but the percentage for the HIS (64) is more impressive than that for the LIS (55).

Considering the differences in average contributions, it is not surprising that the greatest contrast in mean scores pertains to the size of ground forces. The mean scores also show that the lower-impact contributors collectively resemble the nominal and noncontributors more than they resemble their higher-impact counterparts (see figure 2.2).[12] Indeed, the nominal and noncontributors have a better ground forces score than do the LIS, and the income, development, and connectivity scores for both groups are practically the same. Reaffirming the significance of governance and stability for all contributors, however, is the fact that the lower-impact states do better for both traits than do the nominal and noncontributor states.

The regional picture largely reinforces the foregoing in that the Europeans have the highest numbers of states among both the eighty-seven contributors and the high-impact states (27 and 21 states, respectively), while the Africans have the largest among both the low-impact states and the nominal and noncontributors (14 and 21, respectively). All other regions have three to seven states among the HIS, and one to nine states among the LIS. Most impressive is that three-fifths of all potential European contributors and two-thirds of all potential South Asian contributors are among the HIS.

Changes over Time

What has been presented to this point constitutes a static picture for the period from 2001 through 2005. Table 2.3, however, presents a dynamic picture. It lists the changes in the characteristics of the contributors by year and by moving averages—the latter being good indicators of overall trends since they smooth peaks and valleys in time series data. The picture is one of gradually decreasing quality over time—modestly for governance and stability, more significantly for ground forces, and most significantly for income, development, and connectivity—as the overall number of contributors increased from the low fifties in 2001 and 2002 to the upper seventies by 2004 and 2005.

Highlighting those states that significantly raised their levels of contributions over time provides another dynamic look. Table 2.4 lists twenty-four

Table 2.3. Year-by-Year Mean Scores and Moving Averages

Group	Years-Giving Average	Ground Forces	Governance	Income	Stability	Development	Connectivity
2001(51)	2329	2.02	1.45	1.76	1.41	1.57	1.65
2002(52)	2311	1.98	1.44	1.73	1.40	1.54	1.60
2003(73)	1747	2.16	1.49	1.97	1.47	1.78	1.84
2004(79)	1667	2.14	1.52	1.99	1.49	1.80	1.86
2005(76)	1721	2.07	1.54	1.97	1.53	1.80	1.86
Moving Averages							
		2.00	1.45	1.75	1.41	1.55	1.62
		2.07	1.47	1.85	1.43	1.66	1.72
		2.15	1.51	1.98	1.48	1.79	1.85
		2.10	1.53	1.98	1.51	1.80	1.86
Biggest Difference		0.15	0.08	0.23	0.10	0.25	0.24

countries whose two-year moving averages increased by at least five hundred troops, that is, their final moving average was five hundred or more troops higher than their first. We chose five hundred because it is the low end of the average battalion size—the battalion being the basic building block for most peace operations forces. As noted above, moving averages smooth peaks and valleys. Such smoothing was especially useful here since many of the contributors had their best year in 2004, dropping in 2005. Moving averages do not "penalize" states that understandably lowered their contribution in the year after they reached their high.

Since only six of the twenty-four are low-impact states, the picture is more one of major contributors pulling away than one of limited contributors moving up. The least impressive showings are by the North Africa/Mideast and CIS groups (with two and one states, respectively, on the list). The American and East Asian/Pacific states are again in the middle (three each); so too are the Europeans (four states, three of which are from Eastern Europe).[13] The Africans have the highest absolute number (six) while the South Asians are again impressive since every contributor from the region (five states) made the list.

Comparing the quality of the NRCs to that of the broader community of contributors yields interesting similarities and contrasts. As seen in figure 2.2, column 5, the NRCs are less wealthy, developed, and well connected than the eighty-seven designated contributors as a group. They are also relatively less stable, though high stability is significant to both (50 percent and 60 percent, respectively) as is democratic governance (54 and 55 percent). Large ground forces provide the greatest contrast: 54 percent of the NRCs have them as opposed to 29 percent of the broader community. These results underscore the significance of quality governance, stability, and size of ground forces. They also suggest that the overall quality of the major contributors may gradually lessen if the twenty-four continue their rise as prominent contributors.

Table 2.4. Notable Rising Contributors

States	Type	States	Type
AFRICA		ASIA	
Ethiopia	HIS	China	LIS
Namibia	LIS	Japan	HIS
Nigeria	HIS	Korea, RO	HIS
Rwanda	LIS		
Senegal ·	HIS	AMERICAS	
South Africa	HIS	Argentina	HIS
		Brazil	LIS
SOUTH ASIA		Uruguay	HIS
Bangladesh	HIS		
India	HIS		
Nepal	HIS	NORTH AFRICA/MIDEAST	
Pakistan	HIS	Jordan	HIS
Sri Lanka	LIS	Morocco	HIS
		CIS	
EUROPE		Ukraine	HIS
Bulgaria	LIS		
Poland	HIS		
Romania	HIS		
United Kingdom	HIS		

The Most Salient Characteristics

While it seems that the higher the quality of a state, the greater its propensity to contribute, there are three (possibly four) traits that seem more significant than the others. The first two are governance and stability. When comparing designated contributors and the nominal and noncontributors, the greatest distinctions were in governance (particularly so) and stability. Indeed, only in governance and stability do the low impact states exhibit higher quality than the nominal and noncontributors. In each of the five years, furthermore, governance and stability were not only the highest quality traits but also the ones that saw the least downward movement in quality. In addition, both democratic governance and high stability are significant for notable rising contributors as well.

The third trait is the size of ground forces. There is clearly a relation between size of ground forces and size of contribution. States with large forces averaged contributions of 3,477 troops over the five years, those with medium averaged 1,007, and those with small averaged 637. In addition, size of ground forces seems particularly salient at both the upper and lower ends. That is, while only 37 of the 157 potential contributors possess large ground forces, 25 are contributors, 20 are high impact states, and 13 are among the 24 notable rising contributors. Conversely, there does seem to be a bottom line in force size below which it becomes highly improbable that a state will become a designated contributor. The lower-end threshold is a ground force of about 4,000 (of the 87 designated contributors, only four [4.6 percent] had smaller ground forces).

A fourth trait may be regional location. Specifically, can we speak of a regional ethos or sentiment for or against participation in peace operations? On a prima facie basis, there would seem to be a positive ethos among both the South Asian and the European states since both are so heavily overrepresented as a proportion of their regions not only as designated contributors (83 and 77 percent, respectively) but also as high-impact contributors (60 and 67 percent). Conversely, both the CIS and North Africa/Mideast would seem to have little regional enthusiasm as only 33 and 29 percent of their numbers are designated contributors. Although Africa is much in evidence in absolute numbers—there are twenty-one African states among the designated contributors and six among the notable rising contributors—the fact remains that only 50 percent of African states are designated contributors. This places them in the same set as the Americas (58 percent) and East Asia and the Pacific (52 percent). That is, their percentages make it difficult to attribute to them either a positive or negative regional ethos.

Findings about Potential Prospects

Our prospects analysis seeks to identify two overall groups of states: those nominal and noncontributors whose characteristics suggest they have the best potential to move into the ranks of low-impact states, and those low-impact contributors whose characteristics and record of contributions show them to have the best potential to move up to the higher-impact category.

Designated Contributor Prospects

Since there is considerable overlap in the profiles of the nominal and noncontributors and the low impact states, there should be many good prospects, but the numbers fall when one extends the analysis. While nineteen NNC states fit the LIS profile, nine were eliminated because their militaries did not reach the four thousand personnel bottom line identified above.[14] Notwithstanding its possession of large ground forces, Taiwan was eliminated as well (PRC political pressure would surely cause Taiwan to be blackballed by fellow states, and it has no hope of ever joining the United Nations).

The remaining nine are Bahrain, Botswana, Croatia, Cyprus, Kuwait, Macedonia, Mexico, Paraguay, and Venezuela. Mexico's and Venezuela's prospects are enhanced, so to speak, by their being the only states with large and medium-sized ground forces, respectively. Croatia, Cyprus, and Macedonia may have an advantage by being from Europe, a region whose members generally show a high inclination to participate in peace operations; Bahrain and Kuwait may be analogously disadvantaged since their region, the Mideast, is one with a low ethos.

High-Impact Prospects

When analyzing which low-impact states have the best potential to move up to the higher category, one can look not only at a state's characteristics but also at its record of performance from 2001 through 2005; that is, one can look at whether the trajectory of its contributions showed if it was in fact on the way up. Because the trajectory trend trumps all other factors, it provides the starting point.

Eleven states made the trajectories cut. Six were already identified as the low impact states among the notable rising contributors group, that is, as donors whose final moving averages were at least five hundred troops above their beginning averages. Of the six, Brazil, China, and Sri Lanka are advantaged by possessing large ground forces; Bulgaria and Rwanda have midsized forces, and Namibia has small forces. The remaining five are Benin, Chile, El Salvador, Niger, and Togo, and they can be viewed as modestly rising contributors. Each was a designated donor for at least two years and had a final moving average above the lower end of the second quartile (334 troops), the minimum quartile for all high-impact states. Chile has a medium-sized force; the other four have smaller forces.

Of the eleven, Chile is the only contributor among the entire LIS group that fully meets the HIS societal profile criteria. Notwithstanding the considerable characteristics gaps between the low- and higher- impact states, its achievement remains at least mildly surprising considering that the LIS are forty strong.[15] Four more minor contributors, however, did come close. El Salvador fell one level below the bar in development, and Brazil, Bulgaria, and Namibia (all NRCs) were one level below in connectivity as well as development.

Benin, China, Niger, Rwanda, Sri Lanka, and Togo do not at all match the societal characteristics profile of the majority of high-impact states. But if they continue on their trajectories, they will join that minority subset of high impact contributors (four South Asian states, six African states, and Russia) that do not closely resemble the majority profile.[16]

Should the present HIS group lose no members and should all eleven prospects move up to join it, there would be five more African states and three more Latin American ones among the HIS. East Asia-Pacific, Europe, and South Asia would increase their presence by one state each, and there would be no growth for the North Africa/Mideast area.

Pushing Trends into the Future: Some Possible Overall Prospects

In light of what has been presented earlier, significant change in the membership of the DC community is not soon in the offing. Only nine states among the nominal and noncontributors were identified as new designated contributor prospects, and two of them were from regions with a low ethos for contributing. In addition, seven of the nine have small ground forces, suggesting that their contributions might not add very much to troop totals even if they did participate. Indeed, any major increase in the number of new contributors will probably have to include several states from outside the majority contributor profile.

Any major increase in contributed troops, furthermore, would almost certainly come from existing donors. The combined number of notable and modestly rising contributors is not insignificant: twenty-nine in all. Several may well fall off or plateau, but twenty-nine is a good base from which to do so, particularly since it includes thirteen states with large forces, seven with medium-sized forces, and only seven with small forces.

The majority profiles for the overall contributor community and its high impact subset assuredly will continue to reflect the higher quality states. Admittedly, ongoing trends indicate that the community is becoming somewhat less elite except for ground force size. Furthermore, the notable rising contributors are already less privileged as a group than the majority of the high-impact states. With only one (Chile) of the eleven high-impact prospects fully meeting the HIS majority profile, the profile will surely experience lower quality societal scores should even a few of the prospective candidates for entry into the HIS actually move up. That is, the profile will move in the direction of states that are not as democratic, wealthy, developed, stable, or well-connected; it should also become more African and Latin American. All shifts, however, would almost certainly be very gradual, particularly for governance and stability. As shifts occur, one can hope that they will reflect greater participation by states with large ground forces since such forces provide the best means by which to make significant contributions.

Appendix 2.1

National Profiles Database[a]

State Name	Size of Ground Forces	Govern- ance	Wealth	Stability	Develop- ment	Connec- tivity	Region[b]
Afghanistan	2	3	3	3	3	3	SA
Albania	3	2	2	1	2	2	Eu
Algeria	1	3	2	3	2	2	NM
Angola	1	3	3	3	3	3	Af
Argentina	2	1	2	1	1	2	Am
Armenia	2	2	2	3	2	2	Eu
Australia	2	1	1	1	1	1	AP
Austria	2	1	1	1	1	1	Eu
Azerbaijan	2	3	2	3	2	3	CIS
Bahrain	3	2	1	1	1	1	NM
Bangladesh	1	2	3	2	2	3	SA
Belarus	2	3	2	1	2	2	CIS
Belgium	3	1	1	1	1	1	Eu
Belize	3	1	2	1	2	1	Am
Benin	3	1	3	1	3	3	Af
Bolivia	2	2	2	1	2	2	Am
Bosnia	3	2	2	2	2	2	Eu
Botswana	3	1	2	1	2	2	Af
Brazil	1	1	2	1	2	2	Am
Brunei	3	3	1	1	1	1	AP
Bulgaria	2	1	2	1	2	2	Eu
Burk Faso	3	2	3	3	3	3	Af
Burundi	2	2	3	3	3	3	Af
Cambodia	2	3	3	3	2	3	AP
Cameroon	3	3	3	2	2	3	Af
Canada	3	1	1	1	1	1	Am
Cape Verde	3	1	2	1	2	2	Af
Central Afr R	3	3	3	3	3	3	Af
Chad	2	3	3	2	3	3	Af
Chile	2	1	2	1	1	1	Am
China, PR	1	3	2	2	2	2	AP
Colombia	1	2	2	1	2	2	Am
Congo	3	2	3	3	3	3	Af
Congo, DR	2	3	3	3	3	3	Af
Côte d'Ivoire	3	3	3	3	3	3	Af
Croatia	3	1	2	1	1	1	Eu
Cuba	2	3	2	1	1	2	Am
Cyprus	3	1	1	1	1	1	Eu
Czech	2	1	2	1	1	1	Eu

National Profiles Database

State Name	Size of Ground Forces	Govern-ance	Wealth	Stability	Develop-ment	Connec-tivity	Region[b]
Denmark	3	1	1	1	1	1	Eu
Djibouti	3	2	2	2	3	3	Af
Dom Rep	3	1	2	1	2	2	Am
Ecuador	2	2	2	2	2	2	Am
Egypt	1	3	2	2	2	2	NM
El Salvador	3	1	2	1	2	1	Am
Equit Guin	3	3	2	2	2	3	Af
Eritrea	1	3	3	2	3	3	Af
Estonia	3	1	2	1	1	1	Eu
Ethiopia	1	2	3	3	3	3	Af
Fiji	3	2	2	2	2	2	AP
Finland	3	1	1	1	1	1	Eu
France	1	1	1	1	1	1	Eu
Gabon	3	2	2	2	2	2	Af
Gambia	3	2	3	2	3	3	Af
Georgia	3	2	2	2	2	2	CIS
Germany	1	1	1	1	1	1	Eu
Ghana	3	1	3	2	2	3	Af
Greece	1	1	1	1	1	1	Eu
Guatemala	2	2	2	2	2	2	Am
Guinea	3	3	3	3	3	3	Af
Guinea-Bis	3	2	3	3	3	3	Af
Guyana	3	1	2	1	2	1	Am
Honduras	3	2	2	1	2	2	Am
Hungary	3	1	2	1	1	1	Eu
India	1	1	3	2	2	3	SA
Indonesia	1	2	2	2	2	3	AP
Iran	1	3	2	3	2	2	NM
Ireland	3	1	1	1	1	1	Eu
Israel	1	1	1	2	1	1	NM
Italy	1	1	1	1	1	1	Eu
Jamaica	3	1	2	1	2	1	Am
Japan	1	1	1	1	1	1	AP
Jordan	2	2	2	2	2	2	NM
Kazakhstan	2	3	2	1	2	2	CIS
Kenya	3	2	3	2	3	3	Af
Korea, DPR	1	3	3	2	3	3	AP
Korea, RO	1	1	1	1	1	1	AP
Kuwait	3	2	1	1	1	1	NM
Kyrgyzstan	3	3	3	2	2	2	CIS
Laos	2	3	3	2	2	3	AP
Latvia	3	1	2	1	1	1	Eu

National Profiles Database

State Name	Size of Ground Forces	Govern- ance	Wealth	Stability	Develop- ment	Connec- tivity	Region[b]
Lebanon	2	3	2	3	2	2	NM
Lesotho	3	1	3	2	3	3	Af
Liberia	3	2	3	3	3	3	Af
Libya	2	3	2	2	2	2	NM
Lithuania	3	1	2	1	1	2	Eu
Luxembourg	3	1	1	1	1	1	Eu
Macedonia	3	2	2	1	2	2	Eu
Madagascar	3	2	3	2	3	3	Af
Malawi	3	2	3	1	3	3	Af
Malaysia	2	2	2	2	2	1	AP
Mali	3	1	3	1	3	3	Af
Malta	3	1	1	1	1	1	Eu
Mauritania	3	3	3	2	3	3	Af
Mexico	1	1	2	1	1	1	Am
Moldova	3	2	3	1	2	2	CIS
Mongolia	3	1	3	1	2	3	AP
Morocco	1	2	2	2	2	2	NM
Mozambique	3	2	3	2	3	3	Af
Myanmar	1	3	2	3	2	3	AP
Namibia	3	1	2	1	2	2	Af
Nepal	2	2	3	3	2	3	SA
Netherlands	2	1	1	1	1	1	Eu
New Zealand	3	1	1	1	1	1	AP
Nicaragua	3	2	3	1	2	2	Am
Niger	3	2	3	2	3	3	Af
Nigeria	2	2	3	3	3	3	Af
Norway	3	1	1	1	1	1	Eu
Oman	2	3	2	1	2	2	NM
Pakistan	1	3	3	3	3	3	SA
Papua NG	3	2	3	1	2	3	AP
Paraguay	3	2	2	1	2	2	Am
Peru	2	1	2	2	2	2	Am
Philippines	2	1	2	1	2	2	AP
Poland	1	1	2	1	1	1	Eu
Portugal	2	1	1	1	1	1	Eu
Qatar	3	3	1	1	1	1	NM
Romania	2	1	2	1	2	1	Eu
Russia	1	3	2	2	2	2	CIS
Rwanda	2	3	3	3	3	3	Af
Saudi Arabia	2	3	2	2	2	2	NM
Senegal	3	1	3	2	3	2	Af
Serbia(Yug)	2	1	2	2	2	2	Eu

National Profiles Database

State Name	Size of Ground Forces	Govern-ance	Wealth	Stability	Develop-ment	Connec-tivity	Region[b]
Sierra Leone	3	2	3	3	3	3	Af
Singapore	2	2	1	1	1	1	AP
Slovakia	3	1	2	1	1	1	Eu
Slovenia	3	1	1	1	1	1	Eu
South Africa	2	1	2	1	2	2	Af
Spain	1	1	1	1	1	1	Eu
Sri Lanka	1	2	2	2	2	2	SA
Sudan	1	3	3	3	2	3	Af
Suriname	3	1	2	1	2	1	Am
Sweden	3	1	1	1	1	1	Eu
Switzerland	3	1	1	1	1	1	Eu
Syria	1	3	2	2	2	2	NM
Taiwan	1	1	1	1	1	1	AP
Tajikistan	3	3	3	3	2	3	CIS
Tanzania	3	2	3	2	3	3	Af
Thailand	1	1	2	2	2	2	AP
Timor	3	2	3	2	3	3	AP
Togo	3	3	3	2	3	2	Af
Trin-Tob	3	2	2	1	1	1	Am
Tunisia	2	3	2	2	2	2	NM
Turkey	1	2	2	2	2	2	Eu
Turkmenistan	2	3	2	2	2	3	CIS
Uganda	2	2	3	3	3	3	Af
Ukraine	1	2	2	1	2	2	CIS
United Ar Em	2	3	1	1	1	1	NM
United King	1	1	1	1	1	1	Eu
United States	1	1	1	1	1	1	Am
Uruguay	3	1	2	1	1	1	Am
Uzbekistan	2	3	3	2	2	3	CIS
Venezuela	2	2	2	1	2	2	Am
Vietnam	1	3	3	2	2	2	AP
Yemen	2	2	3	2	3	3	NM
Zambia	3	2	3	2	3	3	Af
Zimbabwe	2	3	2	1	3	2	Af

[a] The numerical scoring allows a way to compare states based on the characteristics identified at the head of the first six columns. The lower the number, the larger a country's ground force and the higher the level of its governance (with democracy being the highest), wealth, internal stability, development, and international technological connectivity.

[b] Regional abbreviations: Af=Africa (sub-Sahara); Am=Americas; AP=Asia-Pacific; CIS=Commonwealth of Independent States; Eu=Europe; NM=North Africa and Mideast; SA=South Asia

Chapter 3

Why So Few Troops from among So Many?

Donald C. F. Daniel

Introduction

The period 2001 through 2006 saw an impressive increase of 36,000 designated troop contributions to peace operations, with the highest total (155,000) ever occurring in the final year.[1] Nonetheless, planners faced considerable difficulties finding appropriate military personnel to man and sustain missions.[2] While as many as thirty or more countries may provide troops to a single mission, it is not unusual that only one third or less of the contributors supply the weapons-carrying infantry battalions and brigades that constitute the central building blocks for most peace operations. The remaining national participants may offer vital support or niche capabilities (see chapter 5, this volume), but the nature of those capabilities (often organized around small battalions or companies, some of them multinational in makeup or fully manned by civilians) is such that their military contributions tend to be far smaller.

The difficulties in finding available troops can initially seem puzzling, however, when one considers that there are approximately 20 million active military personnel in 163 countries around the globe, and 14.3 million in ground forces (army and naval infantry) alone (i.e., the main type of forces found in peace operations).[3] For the purposes of argument, if we assume that all of the 155,000 troops contributed in 2006 were ground personnel, then from a macro perspective only about one percent of all global active ground forces—and less than two percent of combined designated contributor ground forces—participated in peace operations at any point in 2006. From a micro or individual national perspective, on average only about 3.4 to 5 percent (median and mean, respectively, with the former being the more representative) of a contributor's active ground forces were deployed.[4] As shown in table 3.1, these proportions are not greatly different from those seen in earlier years—a fact that suggests a continuing pattern. Why are these percentages consistently low? Why so few troops from among so many?

This chapter forwards propositions that provide perspectives and some answers, albeit partial and general ones. The first two propositions address the demand side of peace operations, that is, what they require and how the

Table 3.1. Comparing Ground Force Pools and Percentages Deployed in 2001, 2003, 2006

	2001	2003	2006
Total ground force pool for all states worldwide combined	14,368,830	14,338,255	14,313,103
Total ground force pool for all designated contributors combined	6,254,320	8,723,790	9,275,267
Total designated troop contributions	115,206	126,502	155,113
Total troop contribution as percent of worldwide pool of ground forces	0.8	0.8	1.1
Total troop contribution as percent of worldwide pool of designated contributor ground forces	1.8	1.5	1.7
Mean average percent of own forces deployed by contributors	5.6	5.0	5.1
Median average percent of own forces deployed by contributors	3.8	3.3	3.4

requirements have generally become more challenging since the early 1990s. Propositions three and four look to supply side, in other words, to military-technical issues affecting the ability of states to stand up and sustain missions. Proposition five addresses another supply side dimension: political considerations that cause a state to stay out of an operation or limit its level of involvement when it does participate. The final proposition offsets the pessimistic tone of the prior discussion by summarizing recent developments that may herald gradual but important improvements in the pool of potential contributors.

Demand Side Propositions

Proposition one: Peace operations differ significantly as to their level of difficulty, with some being among the most challenging of all military activities. When assembling a peace operations force, the authorities in mandating organizations and national capitals focus on several issues. The first concerns the types of tasks the deployed force will be called on to undertake (see table 3.2 for a detailed listing). If the mission is largely of the traditional peacekeeping variety, the force will be expected to interpose itself between formerly warring parties, help them draw down their forces, and undertake other confidence-building measures. If engaged mainly in complex peacekeeping or stabilization operations, the force may be called on to establish a safe and secure environment in the aftermath of an internal conflict and to restore governmental and basic social services. If the tasks involve peace enforcement or humanitarian intervention, the force will have to be ready to conduct both defensive and offensive combat operations. If the mission involves a combination of these tasks, then the force should be one that is versatile and able to

Table 3.2. Peace Operations Tasks

Basic Peacekeeping	Challenging: Stabilization Operations	Very Challenging: Enforcement Operations/ Humanitarian Interventions
Interpose buffer force between belligerents	Carry out some/all basic peacekeeping tasks	Carry out some or all of basic, complex/stabilization operational tasks
Monitor observance of cessation of hostilities	Assist in maintenance of secure and stable environment overall	Induce parties to adhere to agreements
Supervise withdrawal of opposing forces from buffer	Maintain visible presence and patrols	Guarantee security of populations at risk and of aid materials
Confirm repositioning of opposing forces	Protect government buildings, leaders	Ensure security/movement of mission/reconstruction teams
Supervise buffer zone to ensure no intrusions	Assist conduct of elections and security of polling sites	Facilitate/establish writ of transitional/elected authorities
Continuously liaise with military headquarters of both sides	Assist in/reestablish essential services, transport, ports, roads	Forcibly disarm belligerents and disruptive elements
Investigate incidents	Protect key sites (e.g., ports, power and water supply, markets)	Secure weapons cantonment[a] sites
Conduct challenge inspections	Ensure security and free movement of mission personnel	Conduct sanction, embargo, and exclusion zone operations
Conduct land, air, and/or water patrols	Provide security, free movement for civilians when possible	Control air space and adjoining waters
Man checkpoints/observation points/crossings	Deal with threats to mandate implementation	Mentor and support local police and armed forces
Provide security for monitors	Deter outbreaks of violence	Protect major events (from elections to large assemblies)
Maintain small mobile reserve for contingencies	Protect humanitarian services and access to services	Arrest war criminals
	Assist in provision of basic medical services	Maintain own robust quick reaction force
	Assist local/international police in event of riots, violence	
	Verify withdrawal/nonreturn of foreign forces/arms	
	Monitor borders/prevent infiltrations/smuggling	
	Supervised cantonment of weapons	
	Assist in/supervise DDR and repatriation	
	Assist in mine clearance/EOD and in awareness programs	
	Investigate allegations of atrocities	
	Keep population informed of developments	
	Make provisions for "911" needs (possibly from outside operation area)	

[a]Cantonment refers to separating soldiers from their weapons and storing the weapons securely.

coordinate the variety of military units assembled to perform the different tasks.

The second concern is that of the circumstances that will confront the peace operations force:

- What risks will the force face and, particularly, how much consent (or resistance) will it confront from the indigenous parties and local populations? Have the indigenous parties given their full consent to the mission? How solid is their consent? How much opposition can be expected from obstructionists such as extreme nationalists, génocidaires, war criminals, and organized crime groups?
- What is the size and topography of the operating areas in-country? Will the troops be widely dispersed across great distances? Will natural barriers (mountains, forests, deserts, bodies of water) hinder easy movement or provide cover for resistance elements?
- In what condition are the indigenous infrastructures for transport and basic services? Are roads and bridges usable? Will helicopters and track vehicles be needed? How will troops and the populations in the operating area get access to potable water and electricity?

While the above questions focus on the in-country circumstances that the force will face, planners also have three exogenous concerns:

- How much time is available before the mission must begin? Which contributors can meet, for instance, the UN deployment time guidelines of thirty days for simple peacekeeping operations and ninety days for more complex ones? Alternatively, which contributors can deploy within a week to contain fast-breaking humanitarian disasters?
- How far must the troop contingents travel to get to the country of operation, and how will they get there? Will they deploy within their own neighborhood or region, or will it be to another continent, possibly across a wide ocean? Who will transport them and their equipment?
- Do provisions have to be made for emergency backup or withdrawal under fire should the peace force suddenly find itself in harm's way? In other words, from where will quick-response "911" support come?

Table 3.3 is a simplified listing of factors for assessing the level of challenge posed by a given peace operation. The factors noted in any column can mix and match with those in another. Obviously a basic peacekeeping mission occurring with the full consent of the belligerents in a small area with excellent infrastructure would need far fewer troops, firepower, and breadth of organic support than an enforcement mission occurring over a large area where the ground transport and basic services infrastructures are heavily damaged.

Table 3.3. Simplified Listing of Factors for Assessing the Level of Difficulty of Generic Peace Operations

	Level of difficulty		
Conditioning factor	Easy	Challenging	Very challenging
Mandated tasks/type of operation	Mainly basic peacekeeping	Complex/stabilization operations	Enforcement/ humanitarian intervention
Consent or resistance from local parties	Full consent	Some resistance	Widespread resistance
Number of personnel judged necessary	Tens to low thousands	Up to low tens of thousands	Several tens of thousands
Geographic size of operations area	Small	Medium	Large
Ability to concentrate peace support forces	Considerable	Some	Widespread dispersion
Distance from donor nation to operation area	Near/in neighborhood	In region/ continent	Far/trans- continental
Time to deploy significant PO force	Several months	Several weeks/ few months	Days
Availability of "outside" emergency backup	Quick response force nearby	Some forces if prior warning	Reliance on own forces only
Transport and services infrastructure in operation area	Excellent/ extensive	Damaged/limited	Widespread, heavy damage
Terrain/climate in operation area	Flat/moderate	Varies/varies	Mountainous or desert/ extremes

In particular, the operations undertaken with little or no consent from some or all of the indigenous factions are among the most challenging of all military activities. Unlike in consent-based peacekeeping, the personnel in these operations may face a range of resistance that can be either centrally coordinated or sporadic—such as roadblocks manned by drunken, armed irregulars. Unlike their counterparts in conventional wars, the peace operations personnel in general cannot assume that their task is full-fledged combat aiming at victory. Rather, the same personnel that are expected to engage in muscular, even violent, peace operations are also expected to do so with the lightest touch possible and with minimal collateral damage as they seek to cement or encourage a peace process, as well as help rebuild a nation. To succeed, such missions usually require that the peace operations force establish a robust military presence that makes clear to the local parties that they should cooperate rather than resist.

Proposition two: Since the early 1990s, challenging and very challenging missions—those that stress the quantity and qualities of the deployed forces—have come to dominate the peace operations landscape.[5] The period from 1948 through 1988 is sometimes referred to as the first generation of peacekeeping because most missions during that era were of the traditional consent-based variety involving two state parties. During that period the largest (nearly twenty thousand troops) and most challenging mission was ONUC (the French acronym for the United Nations Mission to the Congo), an early 1960s peace enforcement operation that proved so taxing and politically charged that it took nearly three decades before comparable missions were again undertaken.

It was in the 1990s that a trend arose within the international community for conducting complex peacekeeping and enforcement missions in the midst of or in the aftermath of civil conflicts. By midpoint in the decade, about half of the twenty-six operations under way at the time were challenging or very challenging. Such missions, in turn, drove large increases in the numbers of personnel deployed. From roughly 24,000 personnel in missions in 1991, the number rose to about 140,000 in 1994 before dropping off to a low of 76,000 in 1998; troop levels thereafter subsequently began rising again. The makeup of many missions also changed as both more heavily armed units and more "nation-building" capable troops (such as engineers, military police, civil affairs, and health care specialists) deployed and worked alongside civilian nongovernmental aid and relief organizations. Table 3.4 gives examples of the overall size and military components found in six representative basic, challenging, and very challenging operations. It illustrates how the number of troops and their variety in both combat and support capabilities increase as the level of challenge rises.

Because of the trend toward challenging or dangerous missions in the 1990s, the decade saw a plethora of new concepts that tried to capture the new dynamics of peacekeeping missions. To many observers, "peacekeeping" no longer described what the "peacekeepers" were about, and terms such as "complex peacekeeping," "wider peacekeeping," "muscular peacekeeping," "peace enforcement," and "coercive inducement" were crafted to fill the conceptual gap.

Supply Side Propositions

Against the backdrop of the demand side propositions are supply side ones that address the complications that surround obtaining the necessary personnel to undertake peace operations. The first of these is proposition three: A minority of states—those that are superior in ground forces quantity and in armed forces quality—have disproportionate significance on the manning and sustaining of missions. Figure 3.1 illustrates the global distribution of ground forces by quantity of personnel. It shows how the distribution is quite uneven among contributors; with relatively few states having sizable ground elements and many possessing modestly sized forces. Specifically, of 163 states with active ground forces in 2006, only 38 contributed positively to the global mean of 88,000 personnel per nation; the remaining 125 were below the mean. Half of all states had no more than 21,000 personnel at their disposal.

Table 3.4. Illustrative Force Packages by Mission Type

Basic Peacekeeping Operation	Challenging: Stabilization Operation	Very Challenging: Enforcement of Humanitarian Intervention
UNDOF: 1,048 troops at December 2006	MINUSTAH: 6,561 troops at December 2006	SFOR: Approximately 18,000 troops at January 2002
2 infantry battalions	7 infantry battalions (~4550)	1 armed battle group
1 logistical battalion	2 infantry companies (~400)	5 mechanized infantry brigades
2 headquarter units	4 infantry platoons (~100)	5 mechanized infantry battalions
2 MP units	2 armed infantry companies (~400)	1 airborne brigade
2 signal platoons	1 armed infantry platoon (~25)	1 airborne infantry battalion
(83 military observers seconded from UNTSO)	2 engineering companies (~300)	1 infantry battalion
	1 engineering platoon (~25)	1 infantry company
UNMEE: 4200 troops as planned	Medical companies (~100)	1 infantry platoon
Military observers (220)	MPs (~100)	2 engineering battalions
3 infantry battalions (2400)	2 air groups	1 engineering company
Mobile reserve company (195)	Headquarters (~100)	1 transport company
1 construction engineering company (195)	Special forces/language	1 logistical platoon
3 field engineers/mine clearance (585)	Civilian affairs	100 support personnel
Headquarters company (165)		Civilian affairs
MP company (80)	UNTAC: Approximately 15,900 troops at mid-1993	Psychological operations
Guard/administrative company (190)	Military observers (485)	Special forces
Medical company (90)	10 infantry battalions (10,200)	Forensic specialists
Transport company (95)	3 engineering battalions/ 1 company (2,230)	Mortuary teams
	Headquarters company (204)	
	Air support group (326)	IFOR: Approximately 54,000 troops at March 1996
	1 signals battalion (582)	17 mechanized infantry battalions
	1 medical battalion, 1 company, 3 platoons (541)	2 mechanized artillery battalions
	MP company (160)	1 artillery battalion
	4.67 logistical companies (872)	3 airborne infantry battalions
	Naval unit (376)	1 airborne battalion
	Civilian affairs	1 armored company
		2 armored reconnaissance companies
		1 armored reconnaissance squad
		1 reconnaissance squad
		1 transport battalion
		3 transport companies
		5 engineering battalions
		1 engineering company
		1 signals regiment
		1 helicopter battalion
		1 helicopter company
		1 helicopter squad
		Civilian affairs
		Psychological operations
		Special forces
		Forensic specialists
		Mortuary teams

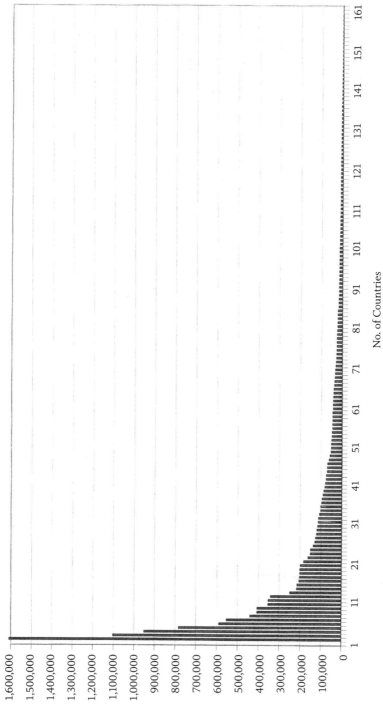

Figure 3.1. Quantitative Distribution of Active Ground Forces, 2006

As seen in chapter 2, the size of ground forces made a significant difference to the size and impact of national contributions from 2001 through 2005; the same trend applies to 2006. Of the 38 states above the quantitative mean, 24 were designated contributors with a mean average of 4,329 troops and a median of 2,307 troops. The mean and median contributions, respectively, for the remaining 55 designated contributors (all part of the 125 states below the global mean) were far smaller: 931 and 498. Not surprising in light of those numbers is the collective impact of the 24 designated contributors with large ground forces: though constituting less than one-third of total designated contributors worldwide, they accounted for two-thirds of all contributions. In short, without them it would have been impossible to man and sustain labor-intensive, challenging operations.

Unlike quantitative measures, simple measures of quality are elusive, but crude proxies are available. One such measure is a nation's national defense budget: the higher the budget, the higher the assumed quality. A shortfall of this measure, however, is that for some nations with very large militaries the size of the budget can remain more a function of a military's size than of its quality. To control for this circumstance, an alternate measure divides the budget by the number of active personnel in a country's military to arrive at spending per individual. This measure assumes that higher spending per individual is a function of greater personnel remunerations (often associated with a fully professional military), higher-end equipment, and better training. Figure 3.2 reflects the latter measure, and it reveals the same pattern as the quantitative distribution: only a few states (with only eight overlapping with the high-quantity group) possess high-quality militaries, while most of the others have militaries of very modest quality. Of the 157 states for which data were available, 37 were above the mean of $46,000 per force member; the remaining 120 were below.[6] Half of all the states spent $14,000 per member or less. There were 25 designated contributors among the top 37, and they had mean and median contributions of 3,111 and 1,190 troops respectively in 2006. Among the 120 states were the remaining 54 contributors, and they averaged a mean of 1,430 and a median of 600 troops. As a group, the 25 high contributors, constituting less than one-third of all contributors, accounted for 50 percent of all contributions. While their overall significance thus would not seem to rise to the same level as that for the 24 high-quantity states that provided two-thirds of all contributed troops, it was even more critical to the non-UN missions. The latter constituted 58 percent of all operations in 2006, and high quality forces accounted for 78 percent of the troops provided in those missions.[7] (In contrast, they provided only 18 percent of all forces in the ten UN missions.) In short, it would have been impossible to man and sustain non-UN missions (nearly all of which are challenging to very challenging) without the participation of nations possessing high quality militaries.

To summarize, while there may be 163 states worldwide that possess ground forces, only about 62 (less than 40 percent) possess the number or quality of forces critical to manning and sustaining labor-intensive, challenging, and very challenging missions.[8] In 2006 forty-two of these states were

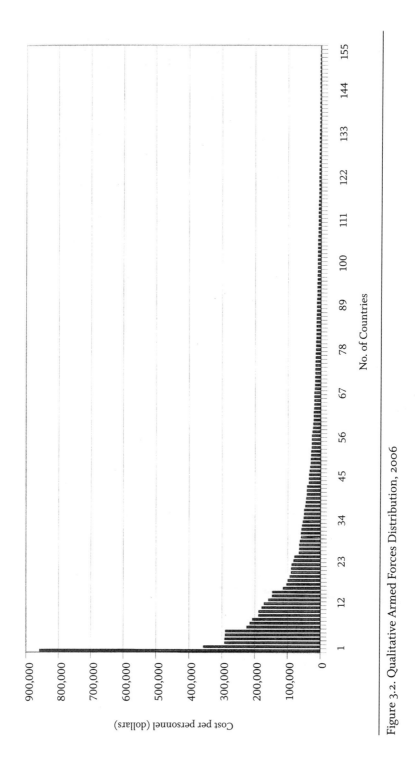

Figure 3.2. Qualitative Armed Forces Distribution, 2006

designated contributors, and twenty were not. Each of the latter had its own reasons for staying away; some of these reasons will be discussed below after proposition four is presented.

Proposition four: No matter how many troops are in a nation's ground forces, only a small percentage can normally be expected to deploy at any one time to a peace operation. At least three factors are at play here. One is that, as seen in some of the other chapters in this volume, many nations have laws restricting the ability of command authorities to order the deployment of forces outside the nation's boundaries, with severe restrictions particularly on the deployment of conscripts. It is not possible here to estimate how many nations have such legal restrictions, but in 2006 at least forty-nine drafted conscripts who, in many armies, made up the bulk of the active personnel.

A second factor is the makeup of a nation's forces, with the more advanced militaries usually having a wider variety of personnel. The availability of specific information makes the U.S. Army a ready example. In 2003 there were 480,000 personnel in its ranks, but only about a quarter (123,000) were "trigger-pullers" or combat-specialists, and only about 50 percent of them were in the mobile light and medium weight units most often relied upon to perform basic peacekeeping and security functions in peace operations.[9] Alongside them are the support troops (such as military police, construction elements, medical practitioners, and public affairs specialists) that are important for restoring and sustaining basic services and infrastructures in complex operations. Shortages in any of these forces can lead to "HD/LD," or high demand/low-density problems, where the low-density units (i.e., those in short supply) are overused so as to meet the demand. Shortages also lead to the creation of purpose-built battalions or brigades, which are put together by cannibalizing personnel and equipment from other units. The knock-on effect on these other units is sharply reduced readiness.[10]

A third factor is rotation cycles. Nations cannot be expected to deploy forces to peace operations when they themselves are at war or in a war-readiness state. Hence, peace operations deployments usually fall into peace-time cycles. The oft-cited rule of thumb is that peacetime units are in a one-in-three rhythm, that is, one deployed (usually for six months or one year), one preparing to deploy, and one in postdeployment rest and reconstitution. This cycle means that the percentage of a nation's forces deployed at one time may not be the most accurate indicator of the stress on its military; rather, it may be more accurate to multiply that percentage by at least three. Thus, if the average state in 2006 donated a median of 3.4 percent and a mean of 5.1 percent of its armed forces, then the impact on its forces, if one assumes a sustained commitment, is more on the order of 10.2 or 15.3 percent (median or mean) under this standard rule of thumb.

Complicating this picture is that the rule of three may understate the situation for many militaries. Because unit rotations are interspersed with personnel rotations, transit times to and from deployment areas, special training regimens, responses to unexpected contingencies, time-consuming adjustments to new equipment or procedures, and reconstitution after cannibalization, normal rotation cycles can be closer to one in four or five.[11] If a one-in-four rule is applied to militaries generally, then on average a contributor committed to sustained effort would have 13.6 or 20.4 percent (mean or median) of its ground forces tied up in a peace operations deployment cycles.

Proposition five: While these technical factors limit how many troops a nation might deploy, the ultimate determinants are political considerations. Such considerations fall into several categories. The first is a nation's international security concerns. Specifically, how confident is a government that deploying some of its forces abroad will not reduce its ability to protect its homeland or to meet its alliance commitments? For instance, of the twenty high quality or quantity states that did not deploy in 2006, North Korea, Eritrea, and several states in the Mideast (particularly Iran, Israel, Kuwait, Saudi Arabia, and Syria) were probably influenced by such considerations.

A second category consists of internal security concerns, particularly challenges to the integrity of the homeland, the nation's way of life, and the viability of its form of government or of its established leadership. Such concerns probably had significant impact on at least five of the twenty nonparticipants: Algeria, Iraq, Myanmar, North Korea, and Sudan.

A third category is that of national leadership insecurities. There are at least two dimensions to this category. One is that the more challenging the mission (particularly the greater the prospect of national casualties or exposure to diseases such as AIDS), the more a national leader (particularly when facing election or possessing only a thin parliamentary majority) might be unwilling to risk public opinion or legislative backlash. In 2006 Japan backed away from its earlier participation in the Iraq operation, and one reason may have been the unpopularity of its Iraq deployment with Japanese voters. A change of government, with Prime Minister Abe taking over from Koizumi, probably provided the opportunity for Japan to mark paid to its military role in Iraq. A second dimension is that some national leaders fear that, while abroad, their deployed troops may pick up "wrong" ideas about their own country and its political system, culture, religious practices, ideology, or leadership—ideas that the leaders do not want brought back to the homeland. This factor may explain the nonparticipation in peace operations of some high-quality and conservative Islamic states of the Mideast or high-quantity states such as Myanmar and North Korea.

A fourth category may be a desire to avoid "blackballing." For instance, the consistent criticism to which Israel (a high-quality state) is subjected in the United Nations would certainly dampen any domestic willingness to participate in UN and possibly other operations. Similarly, any attempt by Taiwan (another high-quality state ousted from the UN with the PRC's accession) to participate would probably face criticism from the PRC and those states that wish to curry favor with it.

Finally, national pride coupled with an inferiority complex may restrict the willingness of some states to deploy if they fear that their deployed troops will not compare favorably with troops of other nations when working together.

Countries whose troops may have high rates of HIV may also be reluctant to deploy them for fear that their troops will be shunned and the nation subjected to negative publicity.

Proposition six: Alongside the bearish factors proposed above are more bullish ones that could slowly increase the pool of available troops. The first is that peace operations, including dangerous ones, are now an accepted and prominent feature of the international political landscape. The 36,000 troop increase in designated contributions during this decade is impressive; so too are the facts that 2006's total is the highest yet, and that (as described in chapter 2) there were twenty-four notable rising contributors for the 2001 through 2005 period. Such trends are in marked contrast to the experience of the 1960s when, as noted earlier, ONUC had a considerable dampening effect on the willingness of states to undertake highly challenging operations. An ONUC-moment did occur in the mid-1990s in the aftermath of several unsuccessful operations, especially in Somalia and the Balkans, but that disillusionment was temporary. Peace operations are now consistently promoted as a mechanism for dealing with instabilities worldwide; as seen in the regional chapters of this volume, an oft-discussed agenda item (though results are slow to materialize) at the UN and in other international security fora is how better to prepare to conduct them. Such discussions, even in East Asia, often follow expressions of regret within a region that it did not respond well to some local disaster. Not surprisingly, a prominent contemporary element of foreign and military aid to African states and organizations is the enhancement of peacekeeping capacities.

A second factor, overlapping the first, is that participation in peace operations is one way that states can enhance their prestige. Some see participation as proving that they are players of global scope. This is true not only of established medium powers such as the UK and France, but also of rising powers such as China and India. States also participate in peacekeeping to show that they are responsible international citizens worthy of respect. This is the case for many members of the traditional peacekeeping "fire brigade," such as Canada and the Scandinavians. It is the case as well for most recently admitted members of the EU and NATO. Others, such as Brazil, Nigeria, and South Africa, may link participation to their desire to be seen as regional leaders and as candidates for a permanent seat in the Security Council. Still others, like Germany, Japan, and South Korea, may see such participation as part of their "coming out" as "normal" countries that possess regionally or globally significant economic or military clout.

A third factor is more prosaic but no less important: the steady increase in the number of peacekeeping training centers. Very few existed prior to the 1990s, but since 1993 Argentina, Australia, Bangladesh, Bosnia, Canada, Chile, Croatia, Ghana, India, Ireland, Norway, South Africa, Sweden, and the United States, among others, have either opened their own centers or hosted international ones.[12]

A fourth factor, overlapping with the third, is that at least three organizations, as well as many countries, are striving to improve the quality of their militaries with some of the armed forces becoming smaller but more agile and deployable. Three developments are worthy of note in this regard. One is an increase either in specifically targeted peace operations capabilities or in rapid deployment units and assets. Experiencing such changes are NATO (with its Response Force), the EU (with its battlegroups), the AU (with its regional battalions), as well as Argentina, Britain, Canada, Chile, China, Denmark, Finland, Germany, the Netherlands, Russia, and Sweden, among others.[13] A second development is that several countries are restructuring their militaries to increase professionalism and reduce reliance on conscripts. These countries include Belgium, Bulgaria, Chile, the Czech Republic, Italy, Poland, Romania, Russia, Slovenia, Slovakia, South Korea, and South Africa.[14] A third development is that important members of today's peacekeeping "fire brigade," such as Australia, Canada, Jordan, India, and Pakistan, are increasing the size of their militaries and/or their defense spending.[15] While many of these same countries may struggle with budget issues and popular pressures for increased social spending, the net effect of all three developments should be a slow increase in the overall quality of militaries available for global peace operations.[16]

Conclusions

This chapter sought to answer a simple question: why do so few troops engage in peace operations when there are so many present in national militaries? The answer is not simple, and this analysis does not claim to settle the matter. More than providing definitive answers, this chapter puts the problem into perspective. There are 163 national militaries collectively and 20 million personnel under arms, but not all are equal in the peace operations arena. Quantity and quality count for a great deal. Nations with high-quantity ground elements can more easily deploy high numbers than nations with smaller ones. Nations with high-quality forces can more easily take on operations where the challenges would be too daunting for less well-equipped and maintained forces. Everything, of course, is relative. As one African general put it, the nature of most peace operations in Africa is often such that African peacekeeping forces do not need the cutting edge equipment that the Americans feel they must have. African militaries in African settings usually can do well with last-generation weapons as long as they have enough of them—more a quantity than a quality issue—and have forces trained in using them.[17] They need, for example, mark-1, mod-able, trucks—not $100,000 humvees.

Only about sixty national militaries are of high quantity and/or quality, and each has its own national laws controlling deployments, professional-versus-conscript mix, occupational specialties, and rotation cycles. Consider the deployment of combat specialists who form the core of challenging missions by a country with a ground force that equals the world's mean of 88,000 personnel. If we accept (1) that all the personnel are professional with no legal or political restrictions on their deployments, (2) that one-third are "trigger-pullers," (3) that no more than half of the latter are appropriate for deploying for peace operations, and (4) that they deploy in a one-in-four cycle, then 3,650 or 4.2 percent might deploy at one time. Only eight high-quantity states contributed 3,650 or more personnel in 2006, and among the critical high quality states only eight contributed 4.2 or more percent of their ground forces.[18] Eliminating the overlaps among the high-quality and high-quantity states results in a total of twelve. Such a small number brings us back to the question: why so few? The answer goes back to the assumptions laid out earlier in this paragraph—that "all [the deployers] are professional with no legal or political restrictions." The political factor—addressed briefly in proposition five—is ultimately determinative. For in-depth analysis of this factor, I refer the reader to the regional chapters in this volume.

Chapter 4

Preparing for the Worst: Military Requirements for Hazardous Missions

GARY ANDERSON

Military personnel deployed to peace operations since the 1990s have been operating in increasingly hostile and dangerous environments, often where residual pockets of fighting occur, such as in Afghanistan and the Democratic Republic of the Congo. Despite this emerging trend, little sustained attention has been given to specific military-centered requirements for undertaking hazardous operations. This chapter addresses the need for practitioners and academics alike to consider current and future on-the-ground challenges of hazardous peace operations and the requisite military capabilities to address them, such as the imperative for strong leadership at mission start-up and the utilization of nonlethal weapons. Such issues are central to any volume that addresses trends and prospects in peace operations. This chapter highlights several capabilities that can enhance or, in some cases, be required for success in hazardous operations. The list is more illustrative than it is exhaustive and reflects the judgments of the author, a retired United States Marine officer who has served in United Nations peace operations and who has had the benefit of recent and direct observation of two hazardous operations: United Nations Interim Force in Lebanon (UNIFIL) and the International Security Assistance Force (ISAF).

The first section of the chapter describes the minimal requirement for mission leadership in predeployment and initial deployment phases. This requirement is different than the others that are highlighted in that it encompasses a variety of military capabilities and has an important political element. The other requirements, involving specific individual military capabilities, addressed in the next section, are much narrower in scope.

Capacity to Lead at Mission Start-up

In the decade after the debacles in Somalia, Rwanda, and Srebrenica, the world's ability to undertake effective peace operations remains uneven at best. Some of this is due to institutional friction within the UN and regional organizations that call for or undertake peace missions. However, in many cases the problems center on who participates in missions and what they can do to ensure the success of a mission. The problem is particularly acute when it comes to responding quickly to crises where the peace operations forces expect considerable resistance to their presence. Establishing such missions often revolves around the issue of "Who can lead?" The leaders are those nations that form the initial nucleus of the mission's military headquarters and that provide the core military units that the other military contingents fall in on.

In an ideal situation, the UN or the various regional mechanisms that undertake peace operations would have a combined, multinational headquarters and a robust and well-trained force standing by. The landmark Panel on United Nations Peace Operations Report of 2000 (also referred to as the *Brahimi Report*) made a number of recommendations on improving the UN's capacities to conduct peace operations. The report included specific recommendations about mission leadership; but perhaps due to sensitivity about not offending member states, the subject of choosing nations as leaders was not addressed. The report primarily dealt with the criterion for the selection of headquarters personnel when a mission is established.[1] Essentially, a mission leader must have the capacity to deploy rapidly, and immediately upon arrival in theatre must be able to effectively control and coordinate all peacekeeping forces. The number of countries that possess this ability is limited. Only the United States, a few NATO allies (such as France, Germany, and the United Kingdom), and non-NATO forces (such as Australia) have the capacity to do this.

The issue of the UN having a standby interim headquarters ready for rapid response was not addressed in the *Brahimi Report* apart from a recommendation that a pool of one hundred trained personnel be prepared to augment deployed contingents for peace operations. At the present time the only standby headquarters specifically created to serve UN needs, the Standing High Readiness Brigade (SHIRBRIG), is an international initiative, consisting of sixteen states that work together and combine resources so that an interim quick-response headquarters (but not an associated robust force) can be deployed quickly. It provided the initial headquarters in 2000 for the United Nations Mission to Eritrea-Ethiopia (UNMEE) and the nucleus of the force headquarters for the UN Mission in Sudan (UNMIS) in 2005. It also provided small numbers of advisory personnel for the UN Mission in Liberia (UNMIL) in 2003 and the UN Advance Mission in Sudan (UNAMIS) in 2004. While SHIRBRIG generally participates only in nonhazardous missions, the member states "are prepared to examine more robust operations on a case-by-case basis." However, any movement in this direction will probably be very slow and methodical.[2]

At the regional institutional level, only NATO is suited to provide both quick-response mission leadership and combat forces for hazardous operations. The EU has made important strides in developing its own capabilities, but it still has far to go (see chapter 7, this volume). The AU has aspirations, but a lack of institutional and national resources will hamper significant progress for years if not decades to come. Hence, NATO aside, when hazardous missions must be stood up today, the harsh reality is that the best choice is to find a major national contributor with military capacity in terms of forces, command, and control to temporarily take the lead as the United States did in Somalia in 1992–93. Australia played a similar role in Timor-Leste in 1999, as did South Africa for the AU mission in Burundi in 2002 and for the UN mission in the DRC.

Leonard Hawley is an individual with long-standing leadership experience in peace operations as a result of having held the peacekeeping "account" on the staff of the U.S. National Security Council and having been a deputy assistant secretary in both the Department of Defense and the State Department during the Clinton presidency. He has given considerable thought to the issue of mission leaders and the concept of lead nations, and he has laid out the following ideal characteristics for an effective leader:

1. Recognized disposition for nonintervention in the region;
2. Strong domestic public support for long, difficult, and costly commitments;
3. Strong diplomatic and military connections with supporting major powers;
4. Previous defense cooperation arrangements in the region;
5. Professional competence in the nation's defense forces;
6. Internal intelligence collection capacity—both political and security;
7. Strong financial management capacity for the coalition;
8. Sophisticated public information and media affairs capacity;
9. A well-founded international reputation.[3]

No country fits the Hawley model, and few would even come close. If one focused on military capabilities alone, the list of states with rapid and robust globally deployable forces is extremely short. It would include the United States, the United Kingdom, France, and possibly Russia (were the latter determined to undertake a distant mission, though it is better described as a regional leader). The regional list is longer and could include Australia, Brazil, Germany, India, Italy, Nigeria, Turkey, and South Africa, but all have considerable shortcomings, not the least of which involves strategic airlift capabilities and, for some, organic sustainability while deployed.

Some states that do not wish to lead a mission could serve as enablers to help others participate. For example, the United States enabled UNOSOM I in Somalia with strategic airlift of supplies before it felt compelled to intervene in Unified Taskforce, UNITAF (the UN sanctioned, but U.S.-led mission that was replaced by UNOSOM II). Likewise the United States contributed substantial strategic lift, intelligence, and command and control support to the Australian-led, UN-sanctioned operation—INTERFET—in East Timor. France and the United Kingdom have both provided temporary and specialized combat support to UN forces in various African operations, such as the UN Mission in Côte d'Ivoire (UNOCI) and the UN Assistance Mission in Sierra Leone (UNAMSIL). The UN itself is a major enabler by providing for the commercial transport of contingents not able to deploy forces on their own. The UN also maintains "start-up" kits at its logistic base in Brindisi, Italy, contracting for logistics services and reimbursing contributing countries approximately $1,000 per troop per month. The fact remains, however, that the UN is not itself a mechanism that can rapidly put all the pieces together to launch a hazardous mission.

Six Long-standing or Potentially Emerging Shortfalls

Efforts to address the following shortfalls would greatly increase capacity in these areas.

Helicopters

In hazardous missions, helicopters can be an important force multiplier in that they allow commanders to move troops quickly to where they are needed; yet the provision of helicopter support is too often a catch-as-catch-can affair. Few deploying contingents can bring helicopters with them to the country where the operation is taking place. As a result, either the mandating organization must provide the helicopters or the burden falls on a small subset of mission participants. Since the early to mid-1990s the UN has contracted for helicopter support, and it has been able to take advantage of surplus helicopter capabilities among the former Soviet states, especially Ukraine. In UNIFIL, the Italians have borne much of the responsibility for providing helicopters. The United Kingdom and the United States did the same for the NATO-led International Security Assistance Force (ISAF) in Afghanistan, but a shortage of helicopters remained an issue in August 2006.[4] Because U.S. and U.K. assets were already stretched thin, other NATO countries were asked to deploy more of their own.[5] The ISAF example illustrates the frequent shortage of helicopters even in operations where most of the participants are from advanced militaries.

Night Operations Capabilities

A continuing problem in hazardous missions is a lack of night operations capabilities, both to defend against local resistant parties that attack the peace operation force at night and, if appropriate, to take the offensive against them when they move and regroup under the cover of night. This has been a problem in a number of operations, particularly in Somalia and Lebanon. During UNIFIL operations in Lebanon in 1986–87, when Hezbollah and other groups in the loosely affiliated national resistance often operated at night, there were frequent complaints from Israel that UNIFIL forces were letting the Lebanese insurgents own the night. Israel conceded that UNIFIL was fairly diligent in manning its checkpoints and patrolling during the day, but claimed that the UNIFIL contingents did not do so at night. A UNIFIL investigation revealed that most contingents were not trained or equipped for night operations.[6]

Despite this, no significant improvement occurred at the time in UNIFIL or, it seems, in other UN operations. When the U.S.-led coalition entered Somalia in 1992 in support of UNOSOM I, the U.S. Marines who provided most of the troops regularly patrolled at night. In the UN operation that followed (UNOSOM II), the contingents were challenged by the Somali militia led by general Aideed. The Somalis did not generally fight much past ten at night, but they did make aggressive use of the early hours of darkness. The UNOSOM II staff noted that most contingents were not conducting night operations.[7] Again, an investigation revealed that the contingents were simply not trained or equipped for effective night operations.[8]

It remains unclear to the author whether the situation in UN operations has improved significantly, but it is worth noting that in the aftermath of the Israeli invasion of south Lebanon in 2006, UNIFIL was reinforced considerably. The Italians and the French have served as lead nations, and by all accounts UNIFIL forces today are reasonably able to operate at night. As far as UN operations are concerned, however, this operation is probably the exception rather than the norm by virtue of having two nations possessing advanced militaries in the lead—something not found in most UN missions.

Advanced Urban Operations Capabilities

Conducting any type of peace operation in an urban environment where spoilers or obstructionists have a free hand can be the most difficult of all military activities to undertake. Spoilers can easily hide and fire from apartment blocks, shops, schools, or places of worship. Any defensive response by peace forces can lead to significant collateral damage and contribute to turning the local population away from the peace mission. The shortcomings in urban capabilities that featured prominently in Bosnia, Kosovo, and Somalia are now the norm in many missions. Urban operations are particularly labor-intensive and require a very high degree of situational awareness provided by both human intelligence and technical systems (such as unmanned aerial reconnaissance); they also require excellent communications and coordination among the civilian and military peace personnel. A former U.S. Marine Corps commandant noted that in modern urban operations, any force has to be capable of fighting in three different "blocks." It has to be prepared to transition rapidly from humanitarian (or state-building) operations in one block, to complex peace enforcement (also called stability and support operations by some countries) in another, and to combat in a third.[9] Very few contributors have the capability to operate successfully in all three "blocks," much less to transition smoothly from one to another. Efforts along these lines are possibly most advanced in the United States, Australia, the United Kingdom, France, Belgium, the Netherlands, Canada, and Italy.

Advanced Nonlethal Weapons (NLW) Capabilities

The asymmetric tactic of using civilian crowds to mask gunmen or to fight from buildings, where combatants and noncombatants are intermingled, is the weapon of choice for many of the nonstate opponents that peace operations face today, particularly in failed or failing countries. The kinetic nonlethal weapons available today can be outranged by most small caliber lethal firearms as well as by slings and stones such as those used by Palestinian youths against the Israelis. The lack of effective nonlethal capabilities precipitated the fighting between the UN and Somalia militiamen in the summer of 1993 when a crowd attacked a Pakistani unit. The Pakistanis had to make a choice between using lethal force or rifle butts in response. They chose the latter. Too late, they discovered that the crowd, which included women and children, was masking armed gunmen. Twenty-four Pakistani peacekeepers were brutally murdered in the incident, which precipitated the hunt for General Aideed and the subsequent Battle of the Black Sea Market portrayed in the book and movie *Blackhawk Down*.

Similarly, in 2003 an incident in Fallujah, Iraq, probably went a long way toward turning the occupation of Iraq into an insurgency, rather than the intended peace operation, when U.S. soldiers fired into a crowd where some gunmen were moving among demonstrators. Twelve civilians were killed in an incident deeply resented by the residents; it is still cited as a primary reason for anti-American feelings.[10]

Directed energy weapons, which have ranges reaching to the line of sight, would have been of immense help in incidents such as the two cited above. However, adding those tools to the peace operations kit remains a contentious issue. The human rights community and civilian aid agencies, such as the International Committee of the Red Cross (ICRC), are opposed to the idea of using directed energy nonlethal weapons. They have two concerns. The first is that they could be used as weapons of torture; the second is that they could be used to suppress legitimate human rights demonstrations. Any weapon can be misused, but one that does not kill or maim should not be written off merely because it has the potential for misuse.

At the other end of the spectrum, national militaries are reluctant to buy expensive nonlethal systems, arguing that niche requirements do not outweigh the need for other military hardware. The positions of these two interest groups have largely slowed and, in some cases, stifled nonlethal-weapon development. The question of whether capable nonlethal weapons will become part of the peace operations tool kit remains in question at this writing.[11]

Air Protection and Air Defense: Emerging Shortfalls?

In Somalia in 1993 General Aideed's militia spread a rumor that it had Stinger missiles from Afghanistan. The rumor was evidently untrue but it did ground UN-contracted aircraft (soaring commercial insurance rates were a major reason) until the rumor could be debunked.[12] This was only the first instance of a problem that would grow substantially for peace operations forces, including ISAF in Afghanistan. Protecting their own aircraft may require that peace operations personnel be equipped with and trained to use appropriate sensors and countermeasures. This was not critical during early peace support operations, when anti-aircraft systems were expensive and hard for nonstate actors to obtain. Now they are proliferating. In Iraq, insurgents are getting more sophisticated in their anti-air tactics, and they share that information with other radicals.

As for air defense, UNIFIL today faces a relatively unique problem in the history of peacekeeping. Its job involves keeping Israel and Hezbollah apart in the aftermath of Hezbollah rocket attacks into Israel—and Israel's subsequent invasion of south Lebanon—in 2006. In the course of doing its job, UNIFIL has already had one confrontation with the Israeli Air Force.[13] In addition, Israel's nonstate opponent, Hezbollah, has an air capability in the form of Iranian supplied Ababil unmanned aerial vehicles (UAV) that can be used for both reconnaissance and attacks.[14] In peace operations prior to the Israeli-Hezbollah conflict in 2006, nonstate actors rarely posed an aerial threat.[15] This potential exposure to future air attacks should sensitize peace operations planners to consider whether they should add air defense systems to a mission's tool kit.

Counterinsurgency Resources and Coordination: Other Emerging Shortfalls?

It is probably too early to determine whether counterinsurgency resources and operational coordination are across-the-board deficiencies, but nonstate actors, who lack the capability to conduct stand-up fights against conventional military forces, have been active to a greater or lesser degree in past operations such as in Haiti, Somalia, Congo, and Afghanistan. Traditional counterinsurgency doctrines tend to be oriented toward turning back challenges to established governments, rather than challenges to the establishment of new governmental capacities. Very few nations have yet been able to develop a doctrine for the latter circumstances, or been able to develop the types of capabilities (including those for psychological operations) suited to counterinsurgency. The United States is working in both areas, yet its experiences in both Iraq and Afghanistan have not been especially praiseworthy. If there are peace operation shortfalls here, they will remain so for many years to come.

As for coordination, John Mackinlay, in a thoughtful analysis on peace operations in the post–September 11 era, sensibly argues, among other things, that success against insurgents requires "reducing the number of moving parts."[16] What he means is that there has to be particularly strong leadership for such a mission. One dimension of such leadership is imposing "very stringent rules" about resort to "opt-out procedures" by national contingents. Yet enacting such rules runs counter to the inclinations of nearly all states concerned about casualties to their forces. This was very much in evidence in Somalia in 1993, when several nations, most notably Italy and Pakistan,

generally limited the activities of their forces to those activities typical of traditional peacekeeping rather than of peace enforcement.[17] In Afghanistan, the
primary limitations have come from France and Germany, although smaller
contingents have also imposed limitations. This may be acceptable for some
niche contributors, but less so from major core contributors such as Germany
and France. Actions such as theirs put the burden of hazardous operations on
contingents that do not restrict the use of their forces. This shortcoming is
one that, while it may be lessened in some cases, will almost certainly never
go away.

Conclusion

Hazardous missions have become increasingly common in peace operations
for more than a decade, and they must be expected whenever a violent humanitarian crisis occurs. If the missions are to be successful, implementing
measures such as those suggested above (by no means an exhaustive list) will
become the norm. However, troop contributors cannot be expected to confront hazards if they are incapable of doing so. How many countries will be
willing to develop the requisite capabilities remains to be seen. In the end,
however, the most pernicious shortfall may be not what contingents are capable of doing but rather what they are allowed to do by their own national
governments.

Chapter 5

Preparing Nations for Peace: Specialized Requirements for Complex Missions

PATRICIA TAFT

As the conflicts of the past two decades have demonstrated, the days of traditional peacekeeping operations are over. Recent wars, most of which have been internal conflicts in weak and failing states, have become increasingly violent and complex and have required specialized resources and skill sets beyond those found in traditional, Chapter VI, United Nations (UN) peacekeeping missions of the past. In today's peacekeeping operations, efforts to quell violence and stabilize the environment, reintegrate combatants, deal with spoilers, and rebuild critical infrastructure often must occur simultaneously. In addition, as numerous prior studies have shown, a failure of the international community to address the "security vacuum" that often plagues postconflict environments has greatly hampered efforts to establish the rule of law and rebuild indigenous institutions. In both planning and executing a peacekeeping operation, the international community has repeatedly failed to adequately anticipate the full range of resources and specialized skills needed for the task, from the military intervention to the follow-on peacekeeping and reconstruction elements of the mission.

These specialized capacities have proven essential in numerous peacekeeping operations but to date are ad hoc and have not been formally catalogued so as to be of use in strategic planning at the international or regional level. In order to address the complex conflict and postconflict environments that the international community currently finds itself engaged in around the world, it is crucial to review what constitutes specialized capacities, where they have proven critical, which countries currently possess them, which countries plan to develop them, and what overall national attitudes condition their willingness to deploy them in an operation.

Recent operations, from Africa to the Balkans, have demonstrated that the experiences and specialized capacities that nations and regional organizations bring to peacekeeping operations have frequently proven critical to the success of the mission. Specialized capacities, also sometimes referred to as "niche" capacities, can include gendarmerie forces and formed police units, engineers, medical and chemical/biological units, special operations forces, search and rescue teams, and unexploded ordinance disposal (UXO)/ demining teams. Specialized capacities can also refer to particular airlift and logistical capabilities deemed crucial in the deployment and sustainability of peacekeeping troops to and within a theater of operations. This chapter is by no means meant to be an exhaustive review of all specialized capacities that nations have contributed—and that they can potentially contribute—to peacekeeping operations, but rather a critical regional review of those that have proven crucial in past operations with a view toward those that may be available in the future.

Gendarmerie Forces/Stability Police Units

The utility of stability police in peacekeeping operations has become increasingly apparent over the past ten years since their introduction in Bosnia in 1996. Stability police, or gendarmerie forces, are trained to execute a wide variety of tasks that fall between traditional war fighting and civilian policing. Stability police have proven to be a vital asset in modern peacekeeping operations to bolster the efforts of traditional military and regular police forces. The tasks that stability police are trained to perform include crowd control, intelligence gathering, surveillance, border patrol, countering terrorism, crime and insurgency, and arrest and interdiction. Stability police can be deployed as units and bring lethal force to bear in a peacekeeping mission. They can also perform the functions of civilian police and address the postconflict "public security gap" that exists in many peacekeeping operations.

The "public security gap," as defined by Oakely, Dziedzic, and others, refers to the critical time period in a mission when the need for the use of blunt military force to combat overt violence, including revenge killings and major civil unrest, has ended but the environment is still too unstable for the military to turn over public security details to regular civilian police.[1] In such missions, from Bosnia to Côte d'Ivoire to Haiti, national military forces have repeatedly found themselves maintaining public order, often taking on tasks that they are neither trained nor mandated to execute. In these environments, which have come to define modern-day peacekeeping operations, international civilian police are also often inadequate as both their training and mandates may prevent the use of lethal force or, in some cases, they may be unarmed. It is in these settings, which define the "public security gap," that "spoilers" and others interested in derailing the peace process may become entrenched, causing myriad corollary effects that eventually spell the overall doom of the mission.

Stability police, however, have proven critical in restoring law and order in peacekeeping missions and addressing the public security gap that exists between the time when military contingents pull back and that when international civilian police assume primary security responsibilities. Beyond their indigenous training as an "intermediate force capacity" between regular military forces and civilian police, stability police are able to deploy rapidly, sustain an autonomous logistical support capacity, and operate independently of, or in concert with, military forces in the initial and immediate follow-on stages of a peacekeeping operation. They are also less costly than international police provided by the UN and can be tasked to perform daily mission requirements, including more public security-related functions than soldiers, who are estimated to be able to perform only 50–60 percent of "outside the wire" duties while stability police are capable of performing up to 90 percent of such tasks.[2]

In Africa, most countries that are former colonies of France or Belgium still possess national gendarmerie forces. Senegal, however, has proven the most willing to deploy its gendarmerie forces in peacekeeping missions, particularly in the Democratic Republic of Congo and Haiti. In both missions, Senegalese gendarmes were able to operate in mixed units with other Francophone gendarmerie forces, largely due to a commonality in language but also to interoperability stemming from French bilateral training assistance programs that provide standardized equipment. Rwanda, a country that has emerged over the past several years as one of Africa's newest willing contributors to peacekeeping operations, also possesses a national gendarmerie force, as does Cameroon. Both of these countries have demonstrated a willingness to deploy both their military and police forces to peacekeeping operations on the continent and further afield. For them to deploy outside of the continent, they will need additional outside training and assistance.

Indeed, many countries on the continent face a consistent lack of resources in basic equipment, from bullets to proper uniforms. In addition, corrupt or authoritarian African leaders often utilize the special skills and training of these elite forces to form their own "praetorian guard" in order to quell public dissent and commit widespread human rights abuses. This is not a situation that has been seen only in Africa, as will be clear in the discussion of Latin America later in this chapter. One of the most glaring cases of a government employing the national gendarmerie to protect its own interests was in Côte d'Ivoire, where the relatively well-trained and equipped national gendarmerie was quickly co-opted by President Laurent Gbagbo and utilized throughout that country's civil war to commit some of the most brutal acts of repression and torture against government opponents.

In the Americas, Argentina is one of the region's oldest and most tested peacekeeping contributors, with experience in the first UN missions in the Middle East. Argentina has long considered peacekeeping part of its foreign policy agenda and has performed well (particularly the national gendarmerie) in the multitude of operations to which it has contributed. In the post-junta era, the use of the armed forces and the gendarmerie in peacekeeping operations was seen as a vital tool to improve the country's reputation, both domestically and internationally, after the full extent of human rights abuses committed under the military dictatorship were revealed. In addition, as one official in the Argentinean Ministry of Defense remarked, "In the beginning, it was a good way to get them out of the country so that people would forget their ties to the Peron era."[3]

Argentina's gendarmerie force has been deployed alongside its armed forces in peacekeeping operations for years. In addition, Argentina has a specialized training center for its gendarmerie peacekeepers, Centro de Capacitación para Misiones en el Exterior (CENCAMEX). In Bosnia and Kosovo, the gendarmerie has, at different times, functioned as a critical part of the Multinational Specialized Unit (now the Integrated Police Unit) and the Special Police Unit (SPU), similar structures utilizing the intermediate force capacities of gendarmerie or special police units; both are trained to serve under civilian or military control depending on the mission. In both settings, the Argentinean gendarmerie has provided critical capacities in riot control and counternarcotics, weapons, and human trafficking, as well as investigation and arrest.[4] While gendarmerie forces in Argentina are highly valued at home, their presence in peacekeeping operations that fall within the "chapter 6½" category, or those missions that fall between traditional, chapter 6, self-defense missions and those that mandate the outright use of force to protect civilians, should continue to be assessed in light of the challenges posed by complex operations that require an intermediate force capacity.[5]

Chile also has an intermediate force capacity, the *Carabineros*, which participate in peacekeeping training and have earned a reputation for both flexibility and neutrality in peacekeeping operations. Like other gendarmerie forces in the region, the *Carabineros* are modeled on the Italian *Carabinieri*. They provide force protection for Chilean armed forces deployed abroad and can operate independently in peacekeeping operations. Like Argentina's gendarmerie, Chile's *Carabineros* are considered a valuable asset at home but have been deployed to international peacekeeping missions in the past, most notably to the UN Stabilization Mission in Haiti (MISNUSTAH). In the MINUSTAH mission, the Chilean gendarmerie earned high marks for their willingness and professionalism in confronting some of Haiti's worst gang violence that threatened to once again destabilize the peacekeeping mission in late 2005.[6] Although the Chilean Ministry of Defense (MOD) does not envision its forces, either military or special police, playing a robust role in upcoming peacekeeping operations that occur out of area, their professionalism as demonstrated in Haiti may provide a valuable asset in those missions to which they are deployed alongside the Chilean armed forces in the future. As of late 2006, Chilean Embassy officials stated that, while Chile has no immediate plans to deploy its *Caribineros* independently of its armed forces, it would consider such deployments on a "case by case" basis.[7]

In Europe, a promising initiative aimed at institutionalizing a standing gendarmerie capacity was the creation of the European Gendarmerie Force (EGF), a joint effort by France, Italy, Spain, the Netherlands, and Portugal. The EGF is comprised of a core of eight hundred gendarmerie officers, trained under a common European Security and Defense Policy (ESPD) doctrine and able to be deployed in thirty days for intervention and postconflict peacekeeping missions. An additional 2,300 officers comprise a standby capacity. The first EGF commander was French, a post subsequently handed over to an Italian colonel in mid-2007. The EGF headquarters are based in Vincenza,

Italy, also home to the international gendarmerie training facility, the Centre of Excellence for Stability Police Units (CoESPU). The EGF completed its second Command Post Exercise (CPX) in April 2006 and was declared fully operational in July of the same year. In recognition of the unique capacities that special police forces bring to peace and stability environments, the EGF is available to deploy under the mandates of the Organization for Security and Cooperation in Europe (OSCE), the UN, or NATO. Participation in the EGF is open to all EU countries, with Poland indicating a desire to join in late 2006. While the EGF is primarily comprised of forces from Western European countries, it hopes that the future admission of Poland and other Eastern European countries will lead to a full expansion of its ranks so as to include all new EU members who currently possess special police capacities and are willing to deploy exclusively to peacekeeping operations.[8]

While Western European countries with gendarmerie forces have a long-standing reputation for professionalism and competence in peacekeeping operations, recent trends have indicated that traditional contributors, such as France and Italy, are sending fewer gendarmes abroad. Rather, these countries are focusing efforts on training gendarmerie forces for future deployments to peacekeeping operations. At the 2004 G-8 Summit in Sea Island, Georgia, Italy took the lead in creating the Center of Excellence for Stability Police Units (CoESPU). CoESPU is tasked with developing doctrine and common operational procedures for stability police in peacekeeping. In December 2005, twenty-nine senior officers completed the first high-level course, followed by ninety-eight company-level forces representing Jordan, Kenya, India, Morocco, Cameroon, and Senegal, who graduated in March 2006. CoESPU employs a "training the trainer" model that strives to develop an institutionalized capacity for training gendarmerie officers for peacekeeping operations worldwide.

Although Western European countries with gendarmeries have tended to focus their efforts on building the capacities of other nations' special police units for peacekeeping through training, Eastern European countries have also been expanding their role. Romania stands out as the only country in Southeastern Europe that, like Italy, France, and Spain, possesses a national gendarmerie force. The first deployment of the Romanian gendarmerie was in 1999 to Kosovo, where it now serves under the United Nations Mission in Kosovo (UNMIK) and is known as the Romanian Special Police Unit (SPU). The Romanian SPU consists of 115 gendarmes, of which 12 are officers and the rest are noncommissioned officers (NCOs). The SPUs, under UNMIK police command, are the first forces to be deployed to deal with riots or other violent demonstrations that require a more robust policing capacity than United Nations Civilian Police (CIVPOL) or the Kosovo Police Services (KPS) can provide. In Peja, the Romanian SPU took the lead in creating a stability police unit within the KPS to "leave behind an intermediate force capacity within the indigenous police structure," as one officer noted. As has been demonstrated by the brutal March 2004 riots that gripped the province and by the subsequent violence leading to the decision about Kosovo's independence, the potential for violence to escalate beyond the capabilities of civilian police remains a distinct possibility in the province. The creation of an indigenous stability police force is therefore crucial in ensuring that the province will be able to provide for its own security when the UN and NATO eventually leave.[9]

The Romanian SPU, like the Italian and French units, has extensive training in riot control, search and rescue, investigation, drugs and weapons interdiction, VIP escort, and dangerous arrests. In April 2002 the Romanian SPU provided critical backup support in putting down a demonstration in the divided northern city of Mitrovica, which turned violent as the crowd began to throw hand grenades at a Polish SPU. It has also successfully performed, alone and in conjunction with other SPUs, arrests of dangerous war criminals wanted by the International Criminal Tribunal for the Former Yugoslavia (ICTY) and successful interceptions of major drugs and weapons caches. The Romanian SPU is also adept at operating in the rugged mountainous terrain in the Balkans, crucial in stopping illegal cross-border trafficking. The Romanian gendarmerie is currently under the civilian command of UNMIK but, like the Italian *Carabinieri*, can also be placed under the military chain of command in a peacekeeping operation.[10] This flexibility is important in the deployment of stability police to peacekeeping operations as it removes a critical caveat that often hampers how gendarmerie forces can be employed abroad.[11]

Romania, as both a new EU and NATO member, sees an evolving role for its military and gendarmerie forces in both UN and non-UN missions. Following the deployment of the first Romanian SPU to Kosovo in 1999, the national gendarmerie training school in Bucharest instituted a wide range of courses tailored to meet the challenges of complex peacekeeping operations. These include training on drugs and weapons interception, arrest and rendition of high-value suspects, and anti-terrorism and counter-insurgency tactics. In addition, the Romanian gendarmerie, like those in Italy and France, sees itself playing an increasing role in establishing or rebuilding indigenous special police units as part of leaving behind this capacity in postconflict states. However, for the foreseeable future, Romania comprises one of the most willing contributors of special police units for peacekeeping operations in Europe.

Engineering, Medical, and Chemical/Biological Units

Increasingly in today's peacekeeping operations, reconstruction and the provision of civilian services must often occur in hostile or transitional environments. Key services include the provision of engineering units critical for rebuilding destroyed infrastructure as well as rapidly deployable medical teams and chemical and biological units. Over the past decade countries that are not willing or able to be significant contributors to peacekeeping operations or to provide strategic leadership have begun developing specialized capacities in these areas.

In Liberia, Chinese engineering companies have been critical in helping to rebuild destroyed civilian infrastructure, while a joint Hungarian-Romanian engineering company helped rebuild destroyed bridges in Bosnia in the wake of the civil war. South Korea has also developed a peacekeeping battalion, known as "Evergreen," which is specifically designed to provide engineering and medical support for peacekeeping operations. The Evergreen battalion has been deployed to Somalia and East Timor, and it is comprised of rapidly deployable engineering and medical personnel as well as approximately two hundred infantry troops and support elements. South Korea also deployed a medical unit in support of the UN mission in Western Sahara (MINURSO), and it views the provision of engineering and medical support units as a critical role for South Korean participation in peacekeeping operations.

Another country that has not been a long-standing contributor to peacekeeping or postconflict operations but that enjoys a solid reputation for military professionalism and the rapid provision of humanitarian assistance is Thailand. Particularly in East Timor as a troop-contributing nation and in Aceh as an Indonesian-invited monitoring force, Thailand has shown strength in the provision of specialized capacities that have been evaluated positively by both host nations and other countries.[12] Thailand's first peacekeeping mission under UN auspices was in Cambodia (UNTAC), where it provided two engineer battalions. Currently, Thailand has a light infantry and armored battalion as well as a medical unit readily available to deploy to an operation. In 2002, Thailand also made ready an engineering battalion for rapid deployment in support of Coalition efforts in Afghanistan. Thailand has also sent engineering and medical units to Iraq, and it envisions the provision of specialized engineering and humanitarian assistance units as crucial to its peacekeeping policy in the future, since it is unlikely to ever become a major troop contributor.[13]

Other countries in East and Southeast Asia are also embracing the role of being contributors of specialized capacities to peacekeeping operations rather than contributors of mass. With the exception of Indonesia and, potentially, the Philippines, the trend of providing specialized capacities rather than significant numbers of "boots on the ground" is likely to continue. However, as demonstrated in East Timor, the provision of specialized capacities can be critical for the success of the mission. In addition to Thailand and South Korea, Singapore also provided emergency medical units and other disaster relief services that deployed quickly.[14]

With the exception of Uruguay, countries in Latin America are likely to curtail their participation in peacekeeping operations to the provision of specialized capacities such as engineering and medical units, particularly in operations occurring outside of the hemisphere. Brazil, however, is becoming an experienced leader within the region in the provision of emergency medical services, a capacity that it also plans to expand to make ready for rapid deployment to peacekeeping operations. The Brazilian armed forces have broad experience in deploying mobile hospitals into the interior of the country with teams experienced in emergency triage, dental surgery, the containment of epidemics, and the provision of vaccinations and other basic medical services. While the Brazilian government currently does not envision contributing significant numbers of troops to peacekeeping in the coming years, the country does see a role for itself as a future provider of specialized requirements, like search and rescue teams and rapidly deployable medical units.

In Europe, many of the newer members of NATO and the European Union are also developing specialized capacities for UN and regional peace operations. Hungary has several valuable specialized capacities that it plans to expand to make available for future NATO or EU missions, including a rapidly deployable engineering battalion that received praise for its work in the Balkans. It also has made available on short notice biological and water purification labs to the NATO Response Force (NRF), one of which was deployed to assist the International Security Assistance Force (ISAF) operation in Afghanistan. Additionally, the countries of Southeastern Europe are taking a regional approach to provide the UN, NATO, and the EU with a capacity for a rapidly deployable peacekeeping brigade, including a specialized capacity for engineering, within the South-East Europe Brigade, or SEEBRIG. SEEBRIG, headquartered in Constanta, Romania, includes participation from Albania, Bulgaria, Macedonia, Romania, Turkey, Greece, and Italy. Activated in September 1999, it is a brigade-sized force of about five thousand troops, which contains a mechanized infantry regiment, four infantry mechanized battalions, and an Engineer Task Force (ETF).

Search and Rescue, Demining and Unexploded Ordinance (UXO) Removal, and Logistics and Transport Capabilities

Niche capabilities beyond those addressed above include search and rescue capabilities, demining and unexploded ordinance clearance teams, and advanced logistical and transport abilities.

In Latin America, the Brazilian armed forces have extensive experience in search and rescue operations, particularly in the difficult Amazon terrain in the interior of the country. While Brazil is currently devoting the bulk of its peacekeeping efforts as the lead nation in the Haiti mission, it has also indicated a willingness to provide search and rescue in future missions, although likely only in operations in the Western Hemisphere.[15] In September 2006, the United States Department of Defense Security Cooperation Agency issued a news release indicating that the government of Brazil was in the process of procuring helicopters and other communications and support equipment to enhance its interoperability with U.S. and other forces during search and rescue training exercises, and specifically in support of these activities for peacekeeping operations.[16]

Also in the region, as part of the initial U.S., French, and Canadian intervention force in Haiti in early 2004, Chile exhibited some surprising specialized capacities. Within seventy-two hours, the Chilean armed forces and navy had deployed a fully sustainable company that included a medical unit able to immediately administer services. Chile's ability to respond rapidly to U.S.-led requests for assistance has been the result of focus, over the past five years, on the modernization of its armed and naval forces to the level of NATO compatibility. In doing so, the Chilean government has purchased F-16 fighter jets as well as C-130s and a variety of lift and transport equipment that has allowed Chile to rapidly deploy and sustain its forces in a theatre of operation.[17]

Chile also possesses critical expertise in two other areas: demining and unexploded ordinance removal, and the provision of judicial teams. After almost a decade of brinkmanship with Argentina over disputed territory between the two countries that ended with a peace treaty in 1984, the border between the two countries remained heavily mined. Over the past two decades, Chilean armed forces operating in the formerly disputed territories have gained significant training and experience in demining and unexploded ordinance removal, skills that the MOD has indicated might be a specialized capacity that could be exported to future peacekeeping operations. In addition, the Chilean Ministry of Foreign Affairs also sees an evolving role for Chilean judges, trained in war-crimes prosecution trials in the post-Pinochet era, to play a role in a quickly deployable "rule of law" kit that could be made available to the UN or through other multilateral arrangements as a standing capacity.

Because its national constitution limits the use of force to self-defense, Japan has increasingly become a provider of specialized capacities to peacekeeping operations in East Asia, although mainly through the use of its Self Defense Forces to deliver humanitarian aid and rebuild and restore destroyed infrastructures. Japanese experience in this capacity is fairly extensive. Additionally, Japan possesses the capacity to provide logistical support for peacekeeping missions, and it has contributed both humanitarian and logistical aid to support U.S. operations in Afghanistan and Iraq. Although these arrangements have been made bilaterally with the United States, Japan has also provided these services on a limited level to the UN in Namibia and East Timor.[18] Moreover, in their response to several regional crises, including the December 2004 tsunami disaster, the Japanese have proven highly adept at search and rescue missions and able to mobilize and react to natural emergencies quickly.

In Southeast Asia, both Thailand and Singapore also possess advanced search and rescue capacities that have been enhanced through bilateral and multilateral regional training exercises with the U.S. military's Pacific Command (PACOM). In addition to Thailand, Singapore was quite impressive in its command and performance in East Timor, particularly in its rapid mobilization for the mission. Within twelve hours, Singapore had helicopters and transport ships ready to provide support to the initial Australian-led intervention force. Singapore also possesses airlift capacities and has purchased C130s and KC135s from the United States, and it has an advanced maritime infrastructure that would potentially allow it to deploy in future operations without a heavy reliance on the United States or Australia.[19]

In Eastern Europe, several new NATO countries and NATO-aspirants are also lending specialized capacities to peacekeeping operations, particularly in the Balkans. Polish and Ukrainian troops have been highly praised for their professionalism and flexibility in Kosovo. During the March 2004 riots, and in other outbreaks of fighting in the province, Polish and Ukrainian special forces soldiers and police played critical roles in quelling the violence and restoring security. They have also been lauded for their abilities in crowd and riot control (CRC) and for their quick coordination with other troop-contributing countries. Furthermore, other than the United States and Russia, Ukraine is the only other country in the world that possesses critical strategic airlift capacities for large-scale troop deployments for peacekeeping operations. NATO currently has a standby arrangement with Ukraine to charter up to six planes in its fleet of Antonov An-124. Thus far, NATO has utilized the planes for large-scale troop deployments to the ISAF operation in Afghanistan, the African Union (AU) mission in Darfur, and in the delivery of earthquake relief supplies to Pakistan in 2005.[20] In addition to Poland and Ukraine, Slovakia and the Czech Republic are also developing, in coordination with NATO, specialized capacities for rapid deployment to peacekeeping operations, including medical and biological units and demining teams.

South Africa has both logistical and airlift resources and is able to deploy more rapidly to areas of operation in Africa than other countries on the continent, but lacks the capacities to deploy rapidly to missions outside of Africa. For the time being, however, South Africa retains the best-equipped, best-trained, and most easily deployable forces for peacekeeping in Sub-Saharan Africa, and it is able to sustain them for the longest amount of time without outside assistance.[21] South Africa, however, is unlikely to become a provider of specialized capacities per se. Smaller nations like Senegal, which provided a hospital/medical unit to Liberia and possesses a special police capacity that it is willing to deploy, may begin to fulfill that role on the continent.

African countries are also increasingly providing a valuable specialized capacity in peacekeeping operations that stems from experience gained in many of the conflicts that have plagued the continent over the past several decades: expertise in demining and unexploded ordinance removal (UXO). Several of the top U.S. and U.K.-based private security firms providing specialized services in demining and UXO removal have praised the skills of their Mozambican, Angolan, Ethiopian, and Eritrean demining teams.[22] Additionally, the British military, through the British Peace Support Team (BPST)—whose mission is to coordinate and monitor British military assistance to East African armed forces, as well as to increase peacekeeping capacity in Africa—has also been training Kenyan recruits for demining activities in Eritrea since 2002.[23] While most African contributions to demining and UXO clearance are currently found in the private security industry or through bilateral training initiatives such as those supported in East Africa by the BPST, the availability of this specialized capacity may well signal a trend in what will be available in the future.

Countries in the former Yugoslavia are also providing specialized capacities in the areas of demining and UXO removal to peace and stability operations globally. Bosnian demining teams have served in both Afghanistan and

Iraq in support of U.S. and Coalition efforts, while Bosnian, Croatian, and Serbian demining teams have recently provided a critical specialized capacity in global peacekeeping operations in the past decade.[24] As in Africa, the provision of these capacities for peace and stability operations is likely to increase in the coming years. This topic will be explored in more detail in the section below.

Current and Future Trends in the Provision of Specialized Requirements to Peacekeeping Operations

Factors conditioning current and future trends in national willingness to provide specialized requirements to peacekeeping operations vary greatly by region. In some cases, domestic politics have played the primary role in determining whether a country sees a future role for itself as a provider of specialized capacities while, in other cases, international policies have proven decisive. This section will examine these trends region by region, highlighting the current contributors and the factors conditioning their participation, as well as those factors that might encourage future contributions.

Africa

Apart from Europe, Africa remains the most forward-thinking region on developing military and political capacities to intervene in humanitarian crises and to participate in peacekeeping operations. What is generally lacking across the African continent however is the necessary resources—structurally, institutionally, and militarily—to mount a swift and comprehensive intervention without the aid of extra-continental actors. However, as noted in other chapters, Africa as a continent will still be one of the leaders in providing "boots on the ground" to peacekeeping operations for the foreseeable future.

In addition to contributing troops to peacekeeping missions, certain African countries, most notably Senegal and Rwanda, are also beginning to embrace roles as contributors of specialized capacities, such as gendarmerie forces, for future operations. African nations that provide demining and UXO teams are also on the rise, with several African countries, most notably Kenya, Angola, and Mozambique, deploying demining teams to operations in the Balkans and other African nations. What will continue to condition the willingness of African nations to contribute specialized capacities to peacekeeping operations will primarily be the training and support they receive from outside countries in deploying and sustaining these capacities abroad. Overall, internal support from within these nations for the development and enhancement of indigenous specialized capacities is high and therefore could create a valuable resource as a standing capacity for peacekeeping operations in the future. It is a capacity already being increasingly utilized by the private security industry, and one that should be enhanced through bilateral and multilateral training assistance programs.

Latin America

The factors and motivations that will condition the willingness of Latin American countries to continue to contribute specialized capacities to peacekeeping operations vary country by country, but they are generally trending downwards, particularly in regard to the provision of gendarmerie/specialized police capacities.

Argentina, long the region's leader in the provision of specialized police to peacekeeping operations, is still struggling with the effects of the 2001 financial crisis, which resulted in significant cutbacks in military spending, including for the national gendarmerie. In addition to financial constraints, changes in Argentinean law in 2004 took the decision-making power for the provision of Argentinean forces and gendarmerie away from the Ministries of Defense and Foreign Affairs and granted it to parliament, which has been much more conservative. National sentiment has also moved toward a more conservative approach about the deployment of the national gendarmerie to peacekeeping operations, despite its proud tradition; such sentiment has moved toward the view that these specialized forces are of more value at home.

A similar situation can be found in Chile, where, though the country has opened up more to the idea of Chilean contributions of specialized capacities to peacekeeping operations, there still remains the overarching principle that these missions should only be considered on a case-by-case basis. Although the Chilean MOD and Ministry of Foreign Affairs have occasionally voiced their willingness to contribute a standby specialized capacity, such as readily deployable rule-of-law teams, the country remains cautious about committing widely to future peacekeeping operations, particularly those that occur out of area.

Brazil remains a potentially greater contributor of specialized capacities to peacekeeping operations, although many of its future decisions may hinge on the eventual outcome of the mission in Haiti, where it has assumed the leadership role. Brazil, more than Argentina or Chile, seems determined to carve out a more robust place for itself in future peacekeeping missions, and it may look to become a provider of specialized capacities, particularly in the areas of search and rescue and the deployment of medical units.

East Asia

As in Africa and Latin America, the willingness of East Asian nations to provide specialized capacities for peacekeeping operations will continue to vary nation by nation. Certain countries, such as China, are trending upwards in their development of peacekeeping capacities overall, with specialized units such as engineer companies likely to be deployed to future operations. Particularly in Africa, a continent where China has deep economic interests, the provision of specialized assets such as engineering and other infrastructure development teams may serve the dual purpose of increasing Chinese participation in peacekeeping operations while simultaneously creating an environment conducive to future Chinese economic investment. Another motivating factor, as conveyed by a visiting Chinese scholar at an October 2006 Atlantic Council meeting in Washington, D.C., is Security Council pressure on China to "put up or shut up." In other words, there has been increasing pressure on China from within the Security Council since the end of the wars in the Balkans to match its willingness to use its veto power with a willingness to become more actively involved in both diplomatic resolution and peacekeeping mechanisms.[25]

In the case of Japan, continuing debate over whether to change the Japanese constitution to allow the Self Defense Forces a more proactive role in peacekeeping will condition that country's overall willingness and ability to contribute to future peacekeeping operations. In any case, in the provision of specialized capacities, particularly search and rescue and rapidly deployable medical units, the country is likely to continue or even increase its participation. As the response to the December 2004 tsunami demonstrated, Japan possesses some of the most advanced capabilities in these arenas and seems increasingly willing to use them, even in out-of-area, coalition-led operations such as Iraq. Although such operations will continue in the near term to be largely on an ad hoc or preexisting bilateral basis, it is likely that Japan will continue to fill a critical niche in the provision of specialized capacities for peacekeeping operations.

The nations of Southeast Asia are also, like Japan, apt to engage in the provision of specialized capacities on ad hoc, bilateral, or multilateral arrangements. As was the case in East Timor and Aceh, both Thai and Singaporean contributions were based on agreements with the lead nation, Australia, with additional arrangements reached with the U.S. Thailand, with a pre-identified medical unit for rapid deployment and trained engineers, is likely to continue to be a provider of specialized capacities in the region, although the country is also likely to remain reluctant toward increasing such requirements for future, out-of-area operations. The Philippines and Indonesia, while continuing to contribute troops and police to missions, have not shown strong trends in developing rapidly deployable specialized capacities for either UN or non-UN missions in the near term.

Europe

In Western Europe, the trend toward "training the trainers" has come to dominate these countries' attitudes about the provision of specialized requirements for peacekeeping. In France and Italy, in particular, the provision of indigenous national gendarmerie and special police units to peacekeeping operations has been supplanted in recent years by the desire to build training programs and facilities, like the CoESPU initiative and a current EU initiative aimed at training a national gendarmerie in the Democratic Republic of the Congo. Although both countries, along with Spain, the Netherlands, and Portugal, still provide gendarmes to peacekeeping operations, this role is likely to be filled in the future by the new member countries of the EU, in particular Romania and, to a certain extent, Poland.

In addition to Romanian and Polish special police contributions, other Eastern European NATO and EU members are increasingly willing to make up for a lack of ground forces with the provision of specialized capacities. Hungary, Slovakia, and the Czech Republic have all provided such capacities in engineering, landmine and UXO removal, and medical and biological units to various missions, most notably in the Balkans. The willingness of Eastern European countries to provide such capacities further afield remains questionable, however, due in part to financial constraints and to the reliance on other EU and NATO member states for logistical support, as well as to political pressures at home. It is more likely that for the foreseeable future new NATO and EU member states from Eastern Europe will continue to pool their specialized capacities in multilateral arrangements such as the South East Europe Brigade (SEEBRIG); this approach prevents both financial and logistical constraints from falling on one member nation alone.

In Southeastern Europe, however, the countries of the former Yugoslavia can be expected to begin to help fill the gap in specialized capacities for peacekeeping and in troop contributions. In Serbia, in particular, the need to downsize a costly and outdated military apparatus—and to improve the country's international standing—has made it one of the more willing contributors in the Balkans. In addition to the provision of troops for peacekeeping, the Serbian armed forces also contain specialized engineering units and chemical and biological capacities. They have also proven, along with Bosnian forces, to be extremely adept at landmine and UXO clearance, due to the history of wars in these countries. Both Serbia and Bosnia have indicated a willingness to provide specialized capacities to peacekeeping operations, both in their neighborhood and out of area; with EU and NATO assistance programs more specifically geared toward enhancing these indigenous capacities and modernizing outdated equipment, they could form a valuable resource for future missions.

Conclusion

As the missions of the past decade—from Bosnia to Liberia to Haiti—have shown, there is a growing need in today's complex peacekeeping environments for peace enforcement and capacity-building to occur simultaneously. Much of the international community's desire to maintain a "phased approach" to ending hostilities prior to engaging in rebuilding indigenous human and institutional capacities has resulted in a "public security gap" in the interim phase of peacekeeping missions—a gap that has sometimes severely crippled or even doomed a given mission to failure before reconstruction could begin. It has been in circumstances like these that the specialized skills that nations bring to peacekeeping operations, particularly in this interim phase when hostilities have not yet ceased but public order remains elusive, have come to be highly valued as critical capacities.

Overall, nations that are unwilling or unable to contribute large numbers of ground forces or provide overall strategic leadership are increasingly finding a role for themselves in the provision of specialized capacities. In some regions, such as Latin America and Southeast Asia, nations that have contributed specialized capacities, such as stability police and engineering battalions, are trending away from future deployments due to financial and political constraints, and they are likely to consider future operations on a case-by-case basis. Other regions, such as Eastern Europe, are demonstrating more positive trends in the provision of specialized capacities and, on their own or in partnership with neighboring countries, are attempting to institutionalize these capacities or make them available for rapid deployment under the leadership of the UN or other regional bodies. In some cases, nations that have traditionally contributed specialized capacities, particularly in Western Europe, have embraced the role of training and building indigenous skills in these areas. In addition, African nations, long-standing contributors of "boots on the ground," are also beginning to explore the roles that they can play in providing specialized capacities based on skills honed during the conflicts of the past several decades on their continent. In particular, several African nations are beginning to deploy increasing numbers of demining and UXO teams to missions as far afield as the Balkans, while other nations with indigenous gendarmerie forces are looking toward future contributions in this realm.

The growing importance of specialized requirements for peacekeeping operations coincides with the most painstaking lessons learned in the peacekeeping operations of the past decade: the failure to address the rule of law and the restoration of public safety and key infrastructure in the immediate aftermath of a military intervention. In this environment, nations and regions willing to provide such capacities are proving to be as critical as those that have traditionally been contributors of "boots on the ground," as well as those that have provided strategic leadership to peacekeeping operations. These developments, together with the increasing number of regions, nations, and coalitions of willing nations that are providing such capacities, will likely prove that the provision of specialized requirements for today's complex peacekeeping operations will continue in coming decades to move from the realm of capacities once deemed as "niche" to those increasingly viewed as "critical."

Part II
Micro View
Within Regions and Nations

Chapter 6

Africa: Building Institutions on the Run

Mark Malan

Since the mid-1990s, in the wake of the botched U.S. and UN interventions in Somalia and the failure to stop the genocide in Rwanda, there has been a concerted and ongoing effort by developed countries to assist Africans with a range of capacity-building programs aimed at developing continental security "mechanisms," especially peace operations capabilities. For example, there was a 1994 French proposal for an African Intervention Force to be mobilized under the auspices of the Organization of African Unity (OAU). In October 1996, the United States also came up with a proposal to set up an all-African military force—the African Crisis Response Force (ACRF)—to deal with regional crises where insurrections, civil war, or genocide threatened mass civilian casualties. It was hoped that the ACRF would be used for humanitarian intervention in Burundi. However, the French and American plans were met with widespread African skepticism, and in mid-1997 the United States transformed the ACRF idea into a longer-term capacity-building package—the African Crisis Response Initiative (ACRI).

The initial capacity-building initiatives envisaged the pre-positioning of equipment at bases in strategic points in Africa, with Europe, the United States, and others providing logistics while Africa supplied the troops. At the same time, the need was also felt for Africa to prepare to provide the bulk of a ready force package for utilization by the United Nations, and for Africa to be more assertive in placing its security issues on the UN agenda. At this point, Western nations were bogged down in peace operations in the Balkans, and it seemed unlikely that they would ever again deploy to Africa under a UN flag. However, if the UN remained unresponsive, it was felt that African organizations should be prepared to take action while continuing efforts to elicit a positive response from the Security Council.

The impetus for building African peace operations capabilities came from both the West and the continent itself. Underpinning the notion was an increasing determination to find "African solutions to African problems." In 1997, Salim Ahmed Salim, then secretary-general of the Organization of African Unity (currently the African Union Special Envoy on Sudan), declared:

OAU Member States can no longer afford to stand aloof and expect the International Community to care more for our problems than we do, or indeed to find solutions to those problems which in many instances, have been of our own making. The simple truth that we must confront today, is that the world does not owe us a living and we must remain in the forefront of efforts to act and act speedily, to prevent conflicts from getting out of control.[1]

This chapter takes stock of the progress that has been made to date in realizing this ideal: in building African institutions and capabilities for maintaining continental peace and security, and specifically in building the ability to react to violent conflict through the rapid deployment of effective peace operations. It focuses on African responses to regional and domestic conflicts from 1990 to date, and parallel attempts to create viable African security institutions to better plan for and manage such responses.

Regional Responses to Ubiquitous Conflicts

African regional organizations have been trying to build a fire brigade while the neighborhood burns. The idea of regional crisis responses is by no means a new one. The establishment of the African Union, its Peace and Security Council, and the African Standby Force was preceded by a number of African experiments with peacekeeping interventions. It is thirty years since an African multinational force first deployed to quell conflict in Zaire (in 1977, and again in 1978–79). Nigeria also sent a peacekeeping force to Chad, in 1979. Six African organizations have subsequently fielded multilateral peace operations. The Organization of African Unity (OAU) sent a force to Chad in the early 1980s, and deployed an additional ten operations—mostly small observer missions—before becoming the African Union.[2] In 1986 a small group of *Accord de Non Aggression et D'Assistance en Matiere de Defense* (ANAD) military observers were instrumental in resolving a border dispute between Burkina Faso and Mali.[3] In 1990 the Economic Community of West African States (ECOWAS) sent the ECOWAS Cease-fire Monitoring Group (ECOMOG) to Liberia, and it has subsequently authorized missions in four additional conflicts. In 1998 the Southern African Development Community (SADC) was used to justify interventions by regional forces in the Democratic Republic of the Congo (DRC) and Lesotho.[4] In January 2002 the Community of Saharan and Sahelian States (CEN-SAD) sent a small force to Central African Republic (CAR), and in November 2002 the Economic and Monetary Community of Central African States (CEMAC) also deployed a mission to Bangui, the capital of CAR.[5] Finally, the Intergovernmental Authority on Development (IGAD) tried unsuccessfully to mobilize and deploy a force to Somalia in 2006.

Other regional organizations, such as the Arab Maghreb Union (AMU), Common Market for Eastern and Southern Africa (COMESA), East African

Community (EAC), Economic Community of Central African States (EC-CAS), and Mano River Union (MRU), all have some level of aspiration to create structures designed to prevent, manage, or resolve conflicts.[6] While the conflict management capabilities of most of these organizations remained little more than an aspiration throughout the 1990s, ECOWAS proved capable of mounting and sustaining two large and robust missions. West Africa is therefore the focus of the discussion of regional "fire fighting" that follows, as a prelude to examining continental efforts at peacekeeping.

West African Experience

At the creation of ECOWAS in 1975, the agenda was to promote market integration through policy harmonization and coordination and to speed up the development of physical infrastructure. Fifteen years after its establishment, ECOWAS was confronted with its first major security challenge. In response to the Liberian civil war that broke out in December 1989, ECOWAS set up a five-member consultative group (the Standing Mediation Committee), which decided in August 1990 to establish a peacekeeping force called the ECOWAS Monitoring and Observer Group (ECOMOG).

ECOMOG was mandated to monitor a cease-fire, restore law and order, and create the necessary conditions for free and fair elections. It was also given the mandate to extend its stay in Liberia, if necessary, until a successful election was held and an elected government installed. ECOMOG was engaged in combat immediately after its insertion in Liberia, and often mutated from a peacekeeping force into a peace-enforcement force. The force was a rather spontaneous and unstructured response to a civil war that had, at the time, spawned no fewer than five armed factions and sixty thousand combatants, and that led to the death of tens of thousands of people. Nigeria contributed the largest contingent of troops and bore the brunt of the financial cost: operations in Liberia cost Nigeria about U.S.$5 billion and the lives of some five hundred troops.

While the ECOMOG operation in Liberia was winding down after the 1997 elections that installed Charles Taylor in the executive mansion, neighboring Sierra Leone (wracked by civil war since March 1991) erupted into renewed violence when rebels and rogue government troops collaborated to topple the elected government of President Ahmed Tejan Kabbah. ECOWAS extended ECOMOG's mandate to Sierra Leone and continued to systematically build up its forces. Troop strength reached ten thousand by January 1998, when ECOMOG successfully ousted the junta forces from Freetown and reinstated Kabbah. The following year, ECOMOG was replaced by a large UN operation (UNAMSIL) and its troops were "re-hatted" as UN peacekeepers.

ECOMOG operations were surrounded by controversy—some related to reported human rights abuses by the troops, but much of it around the legality and legitimacy of the regional mechanism. There was a lack of clear consensus among the region's political leaders about the role and mandate of the force. Some member states supplied Charles Taylor's National Patriotic Front for the Liberation of Liberia (NPFL) with arms and in some cases personnel; at the same time, ECOMOG forces were battling to contain the NPFL and force Taylor to the negotiating table. This severely undermined the force's effectiveness and badly splintered ECOWAS itself.

ECOMOG operations were run almost entirely by the military and were set up largely by military governments. There was little public understanding of the force's mandate, and Charles Taylor effectively utilized the international media to undermine ECOMOG and project himself as something of a victorious liberator. ECOMOG also faced serious problems with command and control at the operational level, especially after the unceremonious replacement of the force's first commander, General Quainoo of Ghana, with a Nigerian commander, General Dogonyaro. This followed the capture at ECOMOG's headquarters of the beleaguered Liberian President Samuel Doe and his murder by the rebel forces of Prince Yormie Johnson. Moreover, there were significant intercontingent differences regarding doctrine, capability, and equipment. It was in this context that the idea of an ECOWAS Standby Force was first discussed.[7]

The ECOWAS leadership responded to the lessons of ECOMOG by modifying the foundation charter and adopting a protocol relating to the Mechanism for Conflict Prevention, Management, Resolution, and Peacekeeping in 1999. The latter incorporates legal provision for building a collective military response capability within the subregion. However, implementation of the Mechanism had scarcely commenced when the renewal of war in Liberia again destabilized the Mano River Union. As efforts continued to consolidate peace in Sierra Leone during 2003, hundreds of former fighters in the Sierra Leonean civil war crossed into Liberia to fight as mercenaries either for the government or for the antigovernment rebellions.

ECOWAS quickly engaged in diplomatic efforts to address the crisis and, by July 18, 2003, had begun initial moves to deploy a vanguard force of peacekeepers into Liberia. Rebel forces fighting to topple President Charles Taylor had, by this stage, advanced to within seventeen kilometers of Monrovia. The ECOWAS operation was expected to resurrect a fragile cease-fire signed on June 17 by Taylor's government and the two rebel groups, the Liberians United for Reconciliation and Democracy (LURD) and the Movement for Democracy in Liberia (MODEL). The first contingent of Nigerians, a battalion redeployed from the UN Mission in Sierra Leone, arrived on August 4, 2003, and fighting around the capital came to a halt.

By mid-September, the ECOWAS Mission in Liberia (ECOMIL) had 3,500 soldiers from Benin, the Gambia, Ghana, Guinea-Bissau, Mali, Nigeria, Senegal, and Togo deployed in and around capital. However, ECOMIL lacked the capacity to deploy throughout the rebel-held northern and eastern parts of the country. The solution was for ECOMIL to become part of a much larger United Nations Mission in Liberia (UNMIL). After the warring parties signed a comprehensive peace agreement in Accra on August 18, 2003, the UN secretary-general recommended to the UN Security Council the authorization of a 15,000-strong operation for Liberia. In accordance with Resolution 1509,

UNMIL took over from ECOWAS forces on October 1, 2003, with ECOMIL troops "re-hatted" as UN peacekeepers.

ECOMIL involved troop commitments from eight ECOWAS member states and greater burden-sharing than in the 1990s missions. As the ECOWAS Secretariat had no planning capability, Ghanaian officers did the military planning. Although they had identified a need for a force of five thousand personnel for Liberia, only three thousand troops were pledged. The mission planners failed to identify some key capabilities; for example ECOMIL deployed on August 4 with the primary staff officers but with no "workers" for their staff sections. The deploying units also experienced time delays, mission changes, changing personnel and materiel requirements, and serious information deficits.[8]

ECOMIL did not have sufficient strength to deploy beyond the area immediately surrounding Monrovia and some key corridors, and even these limited deployments were executed at a much slower tempo than desired. The lack of a coherent logistics plan was a major impediment, and the lack of personnel with technical proficiency led to partner countries conducting air-load and sea-load planning. In short, ECOWAS and its member states lacked the basic logistical capability to conduct peace support operations without considerable assistance from partners.

ECOWAS played a similar peacekeeping role in Côte d'Ivoire, after a September 2002 military rebellion sparked an internal conflict that paralyzed the economy, split the political leadership, and illuminated the stark polarization of Ivorian society along ethnic, political, and religious lines. ECOWAS began mediation efforts within days. In October 2002 ECOWAS mediators brokered a cease-fire, and both the Ivorian government and the main rebel group, the Patriotic Movement of Côte d'Ivoire, agreed to the deployment of an ECOWAS monitoring mission.

However, the ECOWAS commitment to send troops was hampered by funding constraints and stalled for more than two months after it was made. In the interim, France agreed to fill the gap, expanding its longstanding military presence and extending its mandate from protection and extraction of French nationals and members of the international community to cease-fire monitoring. ECOWAS military engagement remained minimal until early 2003, while France's contributions increased on both the military and political fronts. There were over 3,000 French troops in Côte d'Ivoire working in conjunction with only 500 ECOWAS peacekeepers in February 2003, when a comprehensive peace agreement was signed at Linas-Marcoussis by the Ivorian government and the rebel groups.

Although the authorized strength of the ECOWAS Mission in Côte d'Ivoire (ECOMICI) was 2,386, by late May 2003 there were only 1,300 ECOWAS troops in place, with hopelessly insufficient resources. The cease-fire was thus policed mainly by the French troops, operating under the name *Force Licorne*, which had expanded to 4,000 troops. Additional cease-fire agreements and negotiations led to an officially proclaimed end to the conflict in July 2003, but there was little progress with implementation of the Linas-Marcoussis accords. On February 27, 2004, the Security Council authorized a UN peace-keeping operation for Côte d'Ivoire, with a strength of nearly seven thousand troops. On April 4, 2004, ECOMICI forces were subsumed under the UN flag as part of the UN Operation in Côte d'Ivoire (UNOCI).

As in Liberia, there were many lessons for ECOWAS from this experience. ECOWAS planners underestimated the gravity of the military situation in Côte d'Ivoire, and the number of troops pledged was far too small to execute the mission. At the operational level, the French presence was essential to the implementation of the mandate. Although the ECOMICI force commander's concept of operations envisaged four phases, the operation stalled at phase one (monitoring of the cease-fire line and the provision of VIP protection) because of a lack of human, financial, and other resources. The advance party, which deployed at very short notice, had to rely on the French for mobility and support, and there was a lengthy delay before the first contingents of troops arrived. The force commander had very little support from ECOWAS HQ, and it took more than one hundred days to set up a basic force head-quarters. When the main body of Detachment South deployed to Abidjan in March 2003, it had no vehicles and no place to work.

The entire logistic "system" was ad hoc and incoherent. For example, the French provided support to some countries, Britain supplied support to Ghana, and Belgium supplied support to Benin. U.S. equipment was supplied to the force via Pacific Architects and Engineers (PAE). The lack of integrated logistic support resulted in a laborious build-up of the force, which was further delayed by the need to await the arrival of radios and communications equipment from France. Delays in force generation were also caused by incoherent donor support. For example, the ECOMICI contingent from Benin arrived late in the mission area because they were waiting for the Belgians to provide the logistical support they had promised.

The ECOWAS Executive Secretariat was not organizationally prepared to handle the Liberian and Ivorian crises of 2002–3. The deputy executive secretary for political affairs, defense, and security, charged with the responsibility for assisting the executive secretary to implement the Mechanism, assumed duty in April 2001. By September 2002, when the Ivorian crisis erupted, his professional staff consisted of only two people: a principal program officer for peacekeeping, and a principal officer for political affairs. This small team worked almost around the clock to implement the Mechanism in conjunction with responding to the crisis in Côte d'Ivoire.

The team had to devise ad hoc methods for planning and coordinating the deployment of ECOMICI. Officers from member states were invited to assist, and the UN DPKO and United States European Command also provided planning assistance. An advance team was dispatched to Côte d'Ivoire on November 17, 2002, to undertake preliminary work on operational and logistics issues, but the force commander was only nominated and confirmed on December 18, 2002.[9]

The net result of all these deficiencies was that a transition to a UN operation in Côte d'Ivoire was essential. This trend toward African regional organizations handing over unfinished and underresourced operations to the UN continued with the African Union's mission in Burundi and is set to continue in Darfur and Somalia.

The African Union Experience

Three substantive peacekeeping operations have been launched by the African Union since the inaugural summit meeting of the AU in July 2002: in Burundi (2003), the Darfur region of Sudan (2006), and Somalia (2007).

Burundi

The first full-fledged peacekeeping mission for the African Union was in Burundi. After a protracted civil war that began in 1994, a peace process led by the late Julius Nyerere, President of Tanzania—and later by former President Nelson Mandela of South Africa—culminated in the signing of the Arusha Agreement for Peace and Reconciliation for Burundi on August 28, 2000. The Arusha Agreement provided that "immediately following the signature of the Agreement, the Burundian Government shall submit to the United Nations (UN) a request for an international peacekeeping force."[10] Implementation was very slow, and hostilities continued.

Given that the UN would not mandate the deployment of a peacekeeping mission in the absence of a comprehensive cease-fire, South Africa deployed a Protection Support Detachment in October 2000 to provide protection to select exiled leaders who returned to participate in the agreed-upon political process. Two cease-fire agreements followed much later—the first signed on October 7, 2002, by the Transitional Government of Burundi (TGoB) and the Burundi Armed Political Parties and Movements (APPMs); the second agreement signed on December 2, 2002, by the TGoB and the *Conseil national pour la defense de la democratie-Forces pour la defense de la democratie* (CNDD-FDD) of Pierre Nkurunziza. The Palipehutu–*Forces nationales de liberation* (FNL) of Agathon Rwasa remained outside these processes, and it continued to use force of arms.

Under Article III of the October 2002 cease-fire agreement, the TGoB and the APPMs agreed that the "verification and control of the ceasefire may be conducted by a UN mandated mission, or an African Union (AU) [mission]." In contrast, Article III of the cease-fire agreement of December 2002 provided that the "verification and control of the ceasefire agreement shall be conducted by an African Mission." In April 2003, the AU authorized the deployment of the African Mission in Burundi (AMIB), with a mandate to oversee the implementation of the cease-fire agreements; support disarmament, demobilization, and reintegration (DDR) of ex-combatants; create conditions conducive for the establishment of a UN peacekeeping mission; and contribute to political and economic stability in Burundi.

AMIB had a maximum strength of 3,335 troops, with military contingents from South Africa (1,600), Ethiopia (858), and Mozambique (228), as well as the AU observer element (43) drawn from Burkina Faso, Gabon, Mali, Togo, and Tunisia. AMIB started the establishment of its headquarters on April 27, 2003. However, it was not until the arrival of the contingents from Ethiopia and Mozambique (September 27 to October 23, 2003) that the force became fully operational. The force was concentrated in Bujumbura, with the South African and Ethiopian contingents expected to establish demobilization centers in the provinces to canton and disarm an estimated total of 20,000 ex-combatants.

The budget for the deployment, operations, and support of AMIB was estimated at about U.S.$110 million for the first year; at the end of its fourteen-month mandate, the total budget of AMIB amounted to U.S.$134 million. Lacking adequate funds, the AU expected to cover AMIB's budget with redeemed pledges and donations from its Western partners. The pledges from the partners, amounting to some U.S.$50 million, fell far short of what was needed, and actual donations into the trust fund amounted to just U.S.$10 million, though this figure excludes in-kind assistance from the United States (U.S.$6.1 million) and United Kingdom (U.S.$6 million), to support the deployment of the Ethiopian and Mozambican contingents, respectively.[11]

AMIB was not able to fully facilitate the implementation of the cease-fire agreements, nor was it able to ensure security in Burundi in collaboration with newly created national defense and security structures. Failure to reach agreement with the TGoB on the designation and security of identified pre-assembly and disarmament centers, combined with the lack of full cooperation from the APPMs, resulted in the inability of the mission to make much headway with the DDR process. As with ECOMIL and ECOMICI, AMIB faced considerable challenges at both the strategic and operational levels. The mission's logistical support and funding was particularly problematic, due to a lack of substantive support from within Africa, as well as from the UN and the international community. Moreover, the civilian leadership of AMIB did not have the capacity for effective administrative and technical management.[12]

From the outset, the AU had worked on the premise that AMIB was a holding operation pending the deployment of a UN peacekeeping mission. The mandate of AMIB came to an end on May 31, 2004. Effective June 1, 2004, the responsibility for peace operations in Burundi was assumed by the UN Operation in Burundi (ONUB), which was mandated on May 21, 2004, by Security Council Resolution 1545 (2004).

Darfur

In February 2003, a horrific humanitarian disaster began to unfold in Sudan's western region of Darfur. Within a year, tens of thousands of civilians had been killed and more than a million displaced in a well-coordinated campaign of ethnic cleansing by government-supported militia. In July 2004, the U.S. Congress passed a nonbinding resolution labeling the Darfur crisis "genocide"; in September 2004 then Secretary of State Colin Powell also called the consistent and widespread patterns of killings, dislocations, and rapes in Darfur "genocide," and he blamed the situation on the government of Sudan and the Janjawiid militia. No concrete steps were taken to halt the atrocities, but the AU had been putting pressure on the Sudanese government to halt the militias, and it had started negotiations with Khartoum to accept an African peacekeeping force of two thousand to oversee security in Darfur, protect civilians, and facilitate the delivery of humanitarian aid. On August 15, 2004, 150 Rwandan troops arrived in Darfur as the vanguard of this force. Nigeria's parliament voted a week later to send in 1,500 troops. By the end of August 2004, the AU had 305 soldiers in Darfur as part of a cease-fire monitoring mechanism, and the UN was working with the AU on plans to raise force levels.[13] By early 2006, the African Mission in Sudan (AMIS) had almost 6,000 military and 1,500 police in the field.

Stepping into the Darfur conflict was a bold step for the AU and reflected its commitment to nonindifference to intrastate conflicts on the continent. However, the mission was poorly conceived from the outset: "AMIS was never planned: it just happened."[14] The enlarged AMIS deployment (AMIS II, October 2004) was put together in a rush because of political imperatives. Mission staff members were given minimal guidance, and the strategic goals were not clearly articulated. The special representative of the chairman of the [AU] commission (SRCC), responsible for overall coordination of the mission, was nominated several months into the operation. Logistics constraints also had a major impact on the pace and format of the deployment. This was due largely to the fact that there was no structure for strategic guidance in place when the mission was initially launched in May–June 2004: the AU Peace Support Operations Division (PSOD) had hardly been formed at the time, and the Darfur Integrated Task Force (DITF) was only created in January 2005. The gap was bridged by a virtual planning team that did have some African members, but was "partner heavy." Successive changes were made later in the mandate without proper examination of the availability of resources and agreement with the partners.

The fact that the mission deployed at all, and that it was able to expand from a force of less than four hundred to over seven thousand in a short time, is a credit to the AU, but there was a fundamental lack of capacity to set goals; integrate police, civilian, and military planning; sequence deployment; provide logistic support; and generally to develop the mission in a coherent way. Partners have played a key support role in AMIS, technically and financially. The downside of this extensive engagement, however, is that it has created a lasting dependence, making the prospect of African "ownership" of African operations ever more remote.

The net result of severely limited AU and AMIS capacity is that the mission's deterrent effect has been very limited. An AU Joint Assessment Mission (JAM)—with EU, U.S., and UN participation—conducted in March 2005 concluded: AMIS made a significant difference where it was present, but large areas of Darfur remained beyond its reach; neither the assumptions on which the mission was planned nor those on which the Humanitarian Cease-fire Agreement was based had been borne out; and AMIS had not succeeded in creating a secure environment.

The African Union Mission in Sudan is clearly not effective, and it is widely recognized as being unsustainable. A recent International Peace Academy (IPA) report on a workshop—with top officials from the AU, the UN, AMIS, and the Darfur Integrated Task Force—lists the mission's glaring weaknesses: lack of clarity on the mission structure at field level, and its inadequacy for the purpose of integrated management of the mission; lack of strategic management capacity; the absence of effective mechanisms for operational level management; lack of tools and know-how to handle the relations of the mission with a variety of external actors—including the Government of Sudan and external partners and agencies; insufficient logistic support and ability to manage logistics; insufficient capacity in communication and information systems, compounded by unclear reporting lines from the field to the AU Commission; problems in force generation and personnel management; and total dependence on external partners to finance the mission and provide technical advice and support.[15]

The most obvious solution would be the "re-hatting" of AMIS and the deployment of a full-blown multidimensional United Nations peace operation in Darfur. On August 31, 2006, the Security Council adopted Resolution 1706 (2006), in which it authorized the expansion of the extant United Nations Mission in Sudan (UNMIS) into Darfur. When the government of the Sudan refused to consent to this expansion, the idea of a hybrid mission emerged, on November 16, 2006, from a high-level consultation in Addis Ababa that was cochaired by the UN secretary-general and the chairperson of the African Union Commission, and that included the P5, the government of the Sudan, the European Union, and the League of Arab States.

The meeting produced the outline of a three-phase approach to UN support for AMIS, consisting of a light support package, and a heavy support package that would help AMIS hold the line and enable it to transition to an AU-UN hybrid operation. The support packages were conceived as enablers, necessary for the third phase—the mounting of a hybrid operation that would be logistically and financially sustainable, and capable of contributing meaningfully to the restoration of security and the protection of civilians in Darfur. On November 30, 2006, the AU Peace and Security Council approved the Addis plan and further decided that the hybrid mission should benefit from UN "backstopping" and command and control structures. On December 19, 2006, the Security Council endorsed the Addis Ababa conclusions and the AU communiqué, called for their implementation without delay, and also called on all parties to facilitate the immediate deployment of the UN light and heavy support packages as well as a hybrid operation in Darfur. In a letter to the secretary-general dated December 23, 2006, President Al-Bashir reaffirmed the readiness of the government of the Sudan to implement the Addis Ababa conclusions and the Abuja communiqué. The government of the Sudan also informed the African Union of its acceptance of the decision of the Peace and Security Council.

However, deployment of both the heavy support package and the AU-UN force remains stalled, and it is unlikely that the hybrid force will materialize before 2008. This is due to the perennial problems of force generation and of finding UN member states that are willing and able to volunteer the quantity and quality of personnel and equipment required for an effective mission of this size in a hostile operational environment.

Somalia

The killing of seventeen U.S. troops in Somalia in late 1993 marked the beginning of the end for a U.S.–UN peacekeeping force that eventually left Somalia in 1995. The mission withdrew with few of its mandate objectives achieved, leaving Somalia in a state of anarchy. The latest round of civil war began in May 2006 with the Union of Islamic Courts' (ICU) conquest of Mogadishu from the Alliance for the Restoration of Peace and Counter-Terrorism (ARPCT), and it continued with further ICU expansion in the country. In July 2006 Ethiopian forces intervened in support of the Transitional Federal Government.[16]

Between December 24, 2006, and early January 2007, the UIC—which had gained control of eight of Somalia's eighteen administrative regions—was dislodged by Transitional Federal Government troops and Ethiopian forces. Remnants of the UIC militia were aggressively pursued in southern Somalia. The semblance of order and security that the UIC had created began to fall apart, and public resentment of the continued presence of Ethiopian troops in Somalia created a volatile situation that constrained humanitarian emergency operations in the central and southern portions of the country.

Amidst widespread concern that the withdrawal of Ethiopian forces would create a security vacuum and undermine the ongoing process of an all-inclusive national dialogue on the political future of Somalia, the UN Security Council responded by authorizing the deployment of an IGAD force to protect the Transitional Federal Government in Baidoa. The Transitional Federal Government welcomed the idea of an IGAD Peace Support Mission to Somalia (IGASOM), which had been proposed by IGAD and approved by the AU on September 14, 2006. The UIC opposed plans for IGASOM, claiming that the deployment of foreign forces in the country was tantamount to an invasion of Somalia by Ethiopia. According to UN Security Council Resolution 1725, states bordering Somalia would not be eligible to deploy troops under IGASOM.[17] The remaining (nonbordering) IGAD member nations include Sudan, Eritrea, and Uganda. Because of an objection to the burden falling on these three nations alone (including the rivals Ethiopia and Eritrea), the mission was expanded to include other AU nations.

When it became clear that IGAD could not generate a force, the AU decided to deploy an African Union Mission in Somalia (AMISOM). The AU Peace and Security Council approved the deployment of AMISOM for six months to contribute to initial stabilization in Somalia. At the same time, it requested that the United Nations provide all the financial and other support necessary for speedy mission deployment. The AU also urged the Security Council to consider authorizing a UN operation in Somalia that would take over from AMISOM within six months.

On February 20, 2007, the UN Security Council, acting under Chapter VII of the Charter, authorized the deployment of AMISOM to support dialogue and reconciliation in Somalia by assisting with the security of all those involved with the process; to provide protection to Transitional Federal Government institutions and security for key infrastructure; to assist as appropriate with implementation of the National Security and Stabilization Plan, in particular the reestablishment of national Somali security forces; and to provide security as appropriate for humanitarian assistance.[18]

Uganda agreed to provide two battalions for the operation, with Burundi, Ghana, and Nigeria also expressing interest in contributing forces. The United States announced that it would provide $14 million toward AMISOM, as well as strategic airlift support. On January 22, 2007, the EU foreign ministers signaled support to the tune of 15 million euros from the African Peace Facility. UN DPKO technical experts arrived in Addis Ababa in early February to help assess the planning support and other requirements of the AU for the establishment and management of AMISOM. They concluded, unsurprisingly, that the AU will need to considerably augment its headquarters capacity in Addis Ababa with a number of planning specialists—something that should have been obvious in light of the AMIS experience. And again the AU is turning to the UN and its donors to resolve the issue. According to the UN secretary-general, the "AU is currently exploring how its partners, including the United Nations, could support it in this regard, including ways to source staff and generate funding."[19]

AMISOM is to comprise an initial three battalions, growing to a total of nine battalions of 850 troops each. Uganda began troop deployment in March 2007. By June the two Ugandan battalions—approximately 1,600 troops—were the only AMISOM troops in Somalia. Burundi indicated that it could be ready to deploy troops to Somalia in late July—five months after Security Council authorization and shortly before AMISOM's six-month mandate expires. As with AMIS and the planned hybrid mission for Darfur, there is a dearth of African countries that are willing to provide troops and equipment for an AU mission in a nonbenign security environment.

In Somalia, as it was and is in Darfur, the African Union remains totally reliant on donor funding and on external technical support for mission planning and management. The latter aspect was emphasized as a critical shortcoming at the IPA workshop on AMIS last October, and it was acknowledged during the Africa–G8 meeting in Evian in June 2003. The Joint Plan clearly identified an underdeveloped strategic management capacity for multidimensional peace operations within both the AU and regional organizations as a major obstacle to achieving the requisite peace operations capabilities. Yet the UN and the concerned international community—Africa's "donor partners"—continue to authorize and promote new AU missions such as AMISOM with seemingly scant regard for the fact that Africa only began creating modest regional peace and security structures and capabilities during the past decade, while the vastly more capable UN has had nearly sixty years of experience in peacekeeping.

Regional Attitudes toward African Security Mechanisms

The controversial beginnings of ECOMOG in the early 1990s ignited a debate among African scholars. Some felt that ECOMOG was a bold attempt at peacekeeping, offering strong lessons in regional conflict management at a time when the international community had progressively disengaged from Africa.[20] Others thought ECOMOG was an ill-conceived and regionally divisive intervention exercise by autocratic leaders, with disastrous consequences for regional cohesion and sustainable democracy.[21] A third school of thought held that Africa first had to make significant progress with state-building at the national level before viable regional security organizations could emerge.[22]

Nevertheless, the conventional wisdom of the time was that an African capacity for conducting peace operations would eventually allow for multinational intervention where the UN lacks the will to act. It was thought that subregional organizations could play an important conflict management role—either independently, or as a building block for a greater African effort. These ideas were linked to the concept of "layered responses" to conflict in Africa, whereby local and national organizations respond initially, followed by responses at the subregional and regional levels, and finally by those of the broader international community.

The advantage of this type of approach to conflict management in Africa is that neighbors are more familiar with each other's problems than outsiders. Neighbors usually have a fairly common culture, a common social identity, a common history, and similar experiences. The disadvantage, however, is that close proximity often generates tension and reduces the spirit of impartiality between neighbors—to the extent that they sometimes become part of the problem, rather than part of the solution, as has been the case in West Africa and the Great Lakes region.

Moreover, African regional organizations are made up of weak states with economies based on the export of primary commodities. In most of the successful examples of regionalism, states that are already partners to solid economic and political processes (based on shared and complimentary values) pass on collective decisions to structures that supplement, rather than supplant, strong national institutions. While regionalism may over time lead to the creation of new political organizations, states remain the essential building blocks from which such arrangements are constructed, and it has been felt that there are limits to what can reasonably be expected of nascent regional economic communities and security mechanisms.

Linked to this have been fears of the "ghettoization" of peacekeeping in Africa, and consequently of removing African problems from the UN agenda. Eboe Hutchful raised the issue of "lean peacekeeping" operations in Africa—missions that operate under suboptimal conditions that would not be acceptable to military contingents from developed countries.[23] African military officers themselves expressed doubts about capabilities for directing, supplying, and financing operations; of doctrinal disparity and equipment incompatibility; and of partiality in the absence of a broad international spread of troop-contributing nations.

While there is now broad agreement—at least at the governmental level— on the need for an African peace operations capability, African leaders remain skeptical of donor assistance. At times, skepticism has turned to resentment toward foreign capacity-building initiatives. For example, at an OAU Council of Ministers meeting in 1998, Nigeria led three other states in strongly opposing Western initiatives for enhancing African peacekeeping capabilities, arguing that they constituted an attempt to divide Africa and weaken its efforts to take charge of its own security. The previous year France, Britain, and the United States had tried to address African sensitivities to the lack of coordination in external capacity-building initiatives by announcing a P3 initiative, which was supposed to coordinate ongoing and future capacity-building efforts by the three powers. To date, however, there has been little evidence of effective coordination among the P3, as well as among additional players like Germany and Canada.

Donor Support for African "Capacity-Building"

Donor-sponsored capacity-building programs have consisted mainly of classroom education, field training exercises, and provision of some equipment. Initially only France's RECAMP program provided weaponry and nonlethal equipment, and only on a very modest scale. ACRI's long-term objective was to build a peacekeeping and humanitarian assistance capacity in Africa of about 12,000 trained military personnel. The standard ACRI package consisted of six one-month training modules, presented over a three-year period and culminating in a multinational training exercise. ACRI provided training and nonlethal equipment (including uniforms, boots, generators, mine detectors, night vision devices, and water purification units).[24] Three years after the launch of ACRI, the virtual collapse of UN peacekeeping operations in Sierra Leone prompted U.S. policymakers to develop an additional training initiative parallel to ACRI—Operation Focus Relief (OFR). The program was rushed into existence in 2000, after the Revolutionary United Front in Sierra Leone took 500 UN peacekeepers hostage.

Under OFR, the United States committed some $90 million to train seven battalions from ECOWAS member states, on the understanding that these battalions would join UNAMSIL upon completion of the program. The OFR equipment package included the provision of personal weapons as well as crew-served weapons.[25] The OFR initiative essentially did what the defunct ACRF set out to do—it trained and equipped African troops to respond robustly to an African crisis—but under the auspices of the UN rather than an African regional organization.

The follow-on program to ACRI was announced by the U.S. State Department in July 2002. The Africa Contingency Operations Training Assistance (ACOTA) program includes training, technical and maintenance assistance, and the provision of some field equipment. The idea is to provide a more tailored program than the ACRI model. In its FY 2003 budget request, the U.S. administration confirmed that ACOTA also provides "the basis for lethal peace enforcement training."[26]

The centerpiece of French capacity-building policy remains RECAMP (*Renforcement des capacités Africaines de maintien de la paix*), which sponsors a series of regional peacekeeping field exercises, but without any obvious linkage to U.S. or U.K. capacity-building strategies. The initial U.K. policy, the African Peacekeeping Training Support Program, has been subsumed within a large program known as the Conflict Prevention Pool (CPP), which combines resources from the Ministry of Defense (MOD), the Foreign and Commonwealth Office (FCO), and the Department for International Development (DFID).

While the P3+ (the United Kingdom, United States, and France plus Germany, Canada, the Nordic countries, and others) support a potpourri of peacekeeping capacity-building programs, the most recent and ambitious is the U.S.-sponsored Global Peace Operations Initiative (GPOI). Launched at Sea Island in 2004 in response to the stated goals of the G8's Africa Action Plan, GPOI is a five-year program designed to train 75,000 foreign peacekeepers—40,000 of them African—and to assist the AU and other regional organizations with developing their headquarters capability for preparation and implementation of peace operations. The U.S.$660 million initiative also aims to "support Italy in establishing a centre to train international gendarme (constabulary) forces to participate in peacekeeping operations," and to "foster an international deployment and logistics support system to transport peacekeepers to the field and maintain them there."[27] ACOTA has been subsumed as the GPOI's training component in Africa.

The policy agenda behind GPOI is two-fold: "to allow nations to contribute more and better-trained troops to UN peacekeeping operations, and to increase the potential of regional and subregional organizations to conduct peace operations in their own neighborhoods should the need arise."[28] However, some African states continue to view the U.S. initiative with skepticism—as little more than an instrument to promote U.S. strategic interests. There is little doubt that the United States's peacekeeping capacity-building programs are motivated to a large degree by self-interest. The United States's preferred method of delivering assistance to the AU, for example, is through in-kind contributions—a method that enables it to give money to U.S. contractors and to maintain heavy influence over the regional organization. A self-interested approach may also account for the relatively minor role that the U.S. plays in the field of donor coordination.

While one of GPOI's purported goals is to promote "the exchange of information among donors on peace operations training and exercises in Africa," the United States nevertheless has not aligned its efforts with European training and support programs.[29] The "common P3 approach to capacity-building" has therefore resulted in little more than mutual noninterference, rather than harmonization. As Berman notes, "the three partners have created little in the way of synergy. Few countries are willing to co-operate with any enthusiasm if they do not get sufficient credit and have control of the situation. France, the UK and the US are no exception."[30]

The United States has also had internal interagency coordination difficulties, with discrepancies between the African capacity-building approaches of the Bureau of African Affairs within the State Department, and the Department of Defense, for instance.[31] Inconsistency has also characterized U.S. capacity-building assistance in a more general sense. According to the Council on Foreign Relations, on the whole, "funding is sporadic, heavily dependent upon supplemental appropriations, and more responsive to immediate crises than longer-term capacity-building."[32]

The acid test is whether or not the combined weight of all donor initiatives has been sufficient to empower African regional organizations to launch and sustain effective peace operations. Ramsbotham et al. answer in the negative: "The fact that the UN . . . has taken over African-led missions in Liberia, Burundi and Côte d'Ivoire during 2003/2004 suggests that ten years of Western capacity-building programs in Africa have, to date, had a relatively moderate effect, while African regional organizations' capacity to undertake and sustain [peace operations] remains similarly limited."[33]

Major differences persist between African and donor perspectives on priorities for capacity-building, not least regarding training. Donors continue to push training, but Africans are more interested in logistics, equipment, and sustainability. Perhaps this accounts for why African countries are not willing to fund their own centers of excellence for peacekeeping training.

Centers of Excellence

There are five institutions in Africa that claim to be centers of excellence for peacekeeping training. The oldest, the SADC Regional Peacekeeping Training Centre (RPTC) in Harare, Zimbabwe, was opened in October 1996, adjacent to the Zimbabwe Staff College. It was financed almost entirely by the Government of Denmark between 1997 and 2002. For a number of years the RPTC nominally fell under the SADC Inter-State Defense and Security Committee (ISDSC), but it was managed by the Zimbabwe Ministry of Defense under guidance of a resident Danish army colonel. In 2001 six SADC countries contributed staff members to the RPTC, but shortly thereafter the policies of the Zimbabwe government led to a withdrawal of support from Denmark and other European partners, and the Center effectively became moribund. Neither the SADC nor its member states were willing to provide funding for RPTC training courses. The 2003 SADC summit meeting decided that the RPTC should be "mainstreamed" into a SADC institution and the government of Zimbabwe, and the SADC Secretariat subsequently signed the Host Agreement on May 11, 2005, transferring "ownership" of the Center to the SADC Secretariat and formalizing its regional character. It now reports to the SADC Secretariat and is supposed to be funded by contributions from member states. However, it is doubtful that any such contributions will materialize, and discussions with donors are continuing.

The first course to be run at the "SADC-owned" center—and the first since the Danish withdrew their funding in 2002—was presented to thirty officers in April 2006. Throughout its existence, the training output of the RPTC has been modest in content and the number of students.[34] Courses were delivered mainly by external faculty and were based on the UN's standardized training courses. No real regional capacity was developed for delivering relevant training, and the center is seen by many as a white elephant.

The Defense Staff College of Kenya plays host to the Peace Support Training Centre (PSTC), which was established in August 2001. The PSTC's vision is to provide East Africa with a regional school for the training of peacekeepers. The PSTC is supported by trainers from the UN DPKO and funding from the governments of the United Kingdom, the United States, and Germany. The Center hosts about forty students at a time, with the focus on midlevel officers responsible for training their units. The PSTC is a relatively modest initiative, but it has presented some meaningful training—particularly predeployment training for Kenyan armed forces.

The newest African center of excellence, the Peacekeeping School at Bamako, Mali, was inaugurated on March 26, 2007. Initially founded by France in 1999 in Côte d'Ivoire, and located temporarily since 2002 in very modest facilities in Koulikoro (Mali), the Peacekeeping School claims to be a Malian establishment serving the West African region. The large new facility in Bamako is the result of France's efforts since 2004 to create a multilateral partnership that would give the school greater visibility and credibility. The entire cost of the building project, estimated at 8 million euros, was provided by France, Germany Canada, Denmark, the United States, the Netherlands, Britain, and Switzerland.[35] It is too early to assess the quality, quantity, and relevance of the training provided at the school, as the first course began only in April 2007. However, training is supposed to be pitched at the tactical level for junior military leaders, in accordance with an agreement within ECOWAS that operational-level training is to be conducted in Ghana and strategic level training in Nigeria.

The National War College in Abuja, Nigeria, is host to the African Center for Strategic Research and Studies (ACSRS), a new creation that was formerly known as the Centre for Peace Research and Conflict Resolution. The name change was approved by the governing board of the NWC in August 2004, probably to give credence to the notion that a "strategic-level center of excellence" actually exists. The ACSRS has an impressive structure and program—at least on paper. It is headed by a dean (a civilian academic) and has six departments: Defense and Security Studies; Conflict Studies; Peacekeeping and Humanitarian Affairs; Regional and Area Studies; Governance and Public Policy; and Science and Technology. However, the institution is by no means adequately staffed, and its research and teaching output has been minimal to date. Although the ACSRS lists nine core functions on its official website, only one relates vaguely to the notion that it is a regional center of excellence for peacekeeping: to "serve as organ for coordination of strategic level peacekeeping training and research in West Africa."[36]

The largest and most expensive African center of excellence is undoubt-
edly the Kofi Annan International Peacekeeping Training Centre (KAIPTC),
located in Accra, Ghana. The KAIPTC ostensibly operates on behalf of
ECOWAS to provide operational-level training for personnel involved in
global, regional, and subregional peace support operations (PSOs). Work on
the building began in 2002, with the final phase completed in mid-2006, well
after the official opening of KAIPTC in January 2004.

KAIPTC is officially a Ghanaian-led institution, with administrative support provided by the Ghanaian Ministries of Defense, Foreign Affairs, and
Interior. It is heavily supported by the international community through the
provision of staff, and especially through funding for building and for sponsoring all peacekeeping training and education that takes place. By 2006
KAIPTC has received over U.S.$16.5 million in direct funding and in-kind
support, mainly from Canada, France, Germany, Italy, the Netherlands, and
the United Kingdom.

The Centre's mission is ostensibly to provide mission-oriented peacekeeping training at the operational level for military and police officers, as well as
for civilians, prior to deployment on peacekeeping operations. KAIPTC has,
since opening in January 2004, hosted an impressive number of courses and
events for well over three thousand participants. However, with the exception
of training presented by UN DPKO staff for the headquarters of the UN mission in Côte d'Ivoire, there has been no predeployment training conducted at
the Centre.

The current curriculum includes an international peace support operations
(basically "Peacekeeping 101") course (four weeks), sponsored by the United
Kingdom and utilizing mainly U.K. expertise at an enormous cost; three
courses sponsored and presented by Canada through the Pearson Peacekeeping Center on disarmament, demobilization, and reintegration (two weeks);
UN logistics (two weeks); negotiations (two weeks); and "Civilian Police in
PSO" (two weeks). Other donor-funded courses are in media operations (two
weeks), election monitoring (two weeks), and CIMIC (one week).[37]

The KAIPTC strategy for training delivery relies on foreign institutions,
such as the Pearson Peacekeeping Centre (Canada), the Centre for International Peace Operations (Germany), the Africa Center for Strategic Studies,
and the Center for Defense Studies at King's College (U.K.). All courses and
events (including seminars and workshops) have been funded externally by
donors, and the Centre often has little say (and little to say) about what is
presented as KAIPTC training and education. For about 80–90 percent of
the activities, the Centre acts as little more than a conference facility and
service provider. This situation is not so much donor imposed, as it is due to
an astounding ongoing lack of in-house knowledge and expertise for a center
of excellence.

Most of the teaching staff at KAIPTC was originally envisaged as being
military officers; it was intended to employ them as course directors and
lecturers in both the Peacekeeping Studies and the Training departments.
For individuals who are not already expert in one of the core subject areas,

a progressive staff training regime was envisaged, after which individuals could take increasing ownership of activities. However, the majority of posts identified for Ghanaian officers remain unfilled; and those that have been appointed to these posts have moved on within a year or so. Nigeria is the only other ECOWAS country that has contributed staff (one lieutenant colonel), and the Centre's course directors—whether international or regional—act primarily as course clerks, handling course administration rather than shaping the curriculum and presenting instruction.

According to a KAIPTC report, "the only genuine [peacekeeping] expertise lies amongst the few seconded international officers but they have no opportunity to inculcate that expertise into African officers."[38] However, many of the international staff contributed to the Centre have no peacekeeping experience and no experience in Africa whatsoever. This includes the head of the Peacekeeping Studies Department (a German colonel) and the head of doctrine and training development (a U.K. Royal Navy commander). There are also vast discrepancies in remuneration and conditions of service within the various categories of employees at the Centre: those employed as Ministry of Defense civilian workers, Ghana armed forces personnel, seconded international military personnel, and those appointed on contract and remunerated directly by donor-funding to KAIPTC. For example, the salary of a British lieutenant colonel serving at KAIPTC is approximately eighteen times that of the commandant of the Centre—a Ghanaian two-star general. It should therefore not be surprising that local leadership is weak, and that the Centre is not so much managed as it is directed by a variety of external forces.

The primary weakness of the Centre is the lack of cohesion and authoritative strategic direction to be pursued by all staff members and stakeholders. The vision, mission, and objectives of KAIPTC have never been discussed at senior management level, nor have they been adopted and officially promulgated as such. On the one hand, KAIPTC is structured and commanded like a unit of the Ghana Armed Forces; on the other, it relies as heavily on donor support as any NGO. Compounding this dichotomy are the various national, regional, and international interests that need to be reconciled, including those of Ghana, the United Kingdom, Germany, Canada, France, the United States, the ECOWAS member states, the ECOWAS Commission, the UN DPKO, and the AU Commission. Sadly, true West African leadership and ownership of the Centre is likely to remain a myth, simply because "the KAIPTC is dependent on external funds for all that it does but the delivery of such funds is dependent on the prevailing global political and economic climate. The KAIPTC will never be self-funding, therefore the long-term engagement and commitment of donors is a pre-requisite for the Centre's sustained success."[39]

The Nascent Institutional Framework and the ASF

Article 52 of the UN Charter allows states to form regional organizations for dealing with such matters of peace and security "as are appropriate for regional action." The notion of subregional organizations seems fairly unique to the African security debate, and usage of the term can be confusing. According to the AU, there are five regions in Africa—North, East, Southern, West, and Central Africa. However, the UN regards Africa as a region of the world; as a result, it refers to West Africa, for example, as a subregion. The issue goes beyond semantics, however, since the notion of subregions underpins attempts to create a security architecture in Africa that is hierarchical, with the AU presiding over a number of subordinate regional conflict-management mechanisms.[40]

In the 1990s, the OAU, SADC, and ECOWAS all created new conflict resolution mechanisms. In 1993, the OAU adopted its Mechanism for Conflict Prevention, Management and Resolution. In 1996, SADC established its Organ on Politics, Defense and Security. And in 1999, ECOWAS passed its Mechanism for Conflict Prevention, Management, Resolution, Peace and Security. Nothing comparable has developed in the North African region. The AMU (Union of Arab Maghreb) should arguably be taking the lead, but the organization overlaps with the Community of Sahelian-Saharan States, and three of the latter's members would see their primary responsibility as contributing to the ECOWAS Standby Force. Progress on the establishment of a Central African standby brigade has been much slower than that in West, the Horn, or Southern Africa. Nevertheless, the Economic Community of Central African States (ECCAS) held six meetings at the levels of experts, Chiefs of Defense Staff and Ministers of Peace, and Security Council of ECCAS (COPAX) from July 2003 to December 2004, and new impetus can be expected in 2007, with an EU-sponsored project to assist the ECCAS conflict-management mechanism.

As previously noted, the initial efforts to build continental peace operations capabilities were inspired and driven by outsiders—most notably the P3 (the United Kingdom, United States, and France). While donor initiatives all concentrated on peacekeeping training, little attention was paid to building regional institutional capacity to mount and manage large and complex operations. It was African military officers, expressing deep concern about the uncoordinated and unstructured nature of these initiatives, who began thinking about an institutional framework for mobilizing, preparing, and deploying continental peacekeeping forces.

The roots of the present concept of an African Standby Force (ASF)—the envisaged primary instrument for implementing resolutions of the African Union Peace and Security Council—can be traced back to 1997. A group of military experts and observers from forty-five African nations met in Harare, from October 21–23, 1997, to draft peacekeeping proposals for consideration by the second meeting of the African Chiefs of Defense Staff. No fewer than fifty substantive and specific recommendations were approved at this meeting.

It was decided in Harare that the OAU concept for peace operations should be firmly linked to the operationalization of its Early Warning System within the Conflict Management Division, which would include a network linking the early warning cells of the various subregional organizations in Africa. The proposed concept for the conduct of OAU peace operations included the use of subregional organizations as a possible first line of reaction. The Chiefs of Defense Staff also recommended a brigade-sized contribution from each of the five African subregions as a starting point for a standby arrangements system.

However, Africa's political leaders did not act on these recommendations for nearly six years, until after the African Union had been established and there was need to give effect to the Constitutive Act and the July 2002 Protocol Relating to the Establishment of the Peace and Security Council of the African Union.[41] It was not until 2003 that a third meeting of African Chiefs of Defense Staff (ACDS) took the Harare ideas forward, largely in response to urging by the G8 countries. At the Kananaskis Summit in 2002, the G8 leaders agreed to an Africa Action Plan that committed them to providing technical and financial assistance, so that by 2010 African countries and regional organizations will be able to engage more effectively to prevent and resolve violent conflicts on the continent. Specific assistance that was promised included the following: working with African partners to deliver a joint plan, by 2003, for the development of African capability to undertake peace support operations; and providing training for African peace support forces—including through the development of regional centers of excellence.

The third meeting of the ACDS, held in May 2003, was convened in order to sign off on a draft policy framework document on the establishment of the African Standby Force.[42] This document subsequently served as the common African position during the Africa-G8 meeting in Evian in June 2003, during which the G8 and African partners agreed on a Joint Plan to implement commitments made in the Africa Action Plan.[43]

The ASF was conceptualized as a system of five regionally managed brigades, located in Central, North, Southern, East, and West Africa—as well as a sixth continental contingent centered at the AU's headquarters in Addis Ababa, Ethiopia.[44] Each brigade is to be composed of police units, civilian specialists, 300–500 military observers, and 3,000–4,000 troops, bringing the proposed total stand-up capacity of the force to between 15,000 and 20,000 peacekeepers. The ASF is supposed to be capable by 2010 of undertaking a variety of operations, ranging from simpler observation, monitoring, and humanitarian assistance operations to more complex disarmament, demobilization, and peace-building missions, as well as interventions to halt ethnic cleansing or genocide.

The latter mission types have profound political implications, but the ACDS has received little in the way of policy direction from their political masters. For example, at the first meeting of African Ministers of Defense, in January 2004, the ministers simply made the point that Africa should not be unduly dependent on external resources for the ASF, as such dependence could jeopardize ownership of the process and could limit the scope of action of the AU and its member states. Paradoxically, the ministers also agreed that the AU was to pursue efforts with the EU on the African Peace Facility, as agreed to during the Maputo Summit in July 2003.[45] In effect, the African defense ministers were urging African solutions to African problems—with EU help.[46]

There is therefore an immense gap between the ideals of African owner-ship and the logic of ongoing dependency, and between aspiration and imple-mentation. This gulf has not yet come into sharp focus. Rather, it has been fudged by both donors and the AU due to the AU's utter dependence on donor support to cope with extant missions such as AMIS and AMISOM, and the donors' desire to have Africa take care of its own conflicts, way ahead of the establishment timelines for the ASF and the development of viable AU peace support capabilities. The result has been floundering African missions, and a lack of true progress toward the capability planned for 2010.

Obstacles to Creating Effective Regional Mechanisms and Forces

The current African security architecture implies a set of hierarchical bureau-cratic relationships between the UN, the AU, and African subregional organi-zations—or Regional Economic Communities (RECs), as they are often called. This is extremely problematic, for all three levels of organization are made up of member states that belong simultaneously to these (and often many other) intergovernmental organizations. For example, East Africa has overlapping regional arrangements that include members from organizations as diverse as IGAD, the Common Market for East and Southern Africa (COMESA), and the East African Community. Despite the fact that the African Union defines East Africa as a region composed of some thirteen countries, it does not have an overarching and integrated conflict prevention, management, and mitiga-tion framework similar to those in West or Southern Africa. As a result, the African Union mandated IGAD, on an interim basis, to coordinate the efforts of the region toward the establishment of an East African Standby Brigade (EASBRIG). Whereas IGAD itself is composed of seven countries, the discus-sions on EASBRIG initially included all thirteen countries included in the AU definition of the region, until Tanzania and Mauritius decided to con-tribute to the ASF as part of SADC. EASBRIG will therefore be composed of contributions from Djibouti, Ethiopia, Kenya, Madagascar, Rwanda, Uganda, Sudan, Eritrea, and Seychelles. This configuration proved totally inadequate and inappropriate for generating the requisite forces to deploy IGASOM, and it calls into question the logic and viability of extant architecture.

Moreover, it appears that AU/REC relations have been addressed only at a generic level and as a largely legal issue in the process of creating the ASF, rather than at a conceptual level incorporating the political and operational dimensions of peace operations.[47] There remain many unanswered questions about AU/REC cooperation in peace operations. For example, it is unclear what the procedure would be for a REC (such as ECOWAS) to transfer com-mand and control over its regional standby brigade (the ESF) to the AU.

There has also been little deliberation on reporting channels and the kind of liaison and coordination that would have to occur between the AU PSC and Commission and, for example, the ECOWAS Mediation and Security Council and Commission prior to and during an ASF operation. Likewise, the political, operational, and financial implications of a REC providing the planning and operational headquarters for an AU-mandated mission have not been investigated.

African states' ubiquitous failure to finance their own regional institutions—from conflict management mechanisms to peacekeeping training centers—undermines both African leadership of the capacity-building process and donor faith in those institutions. Operationally, neither the AU nor regional bodies have provided funding for troop contributors to operations that they have mandated, and AU commitments to establish African funding sources have not yet been implemented. The issue of standardizing operational costing among regions, the AU, and the UN has not been addressed; nor has consideration been given to how long donors will be willing to sustain African missions—and how reliably they can do so given their own domestic political constituencies and pressures. The fact is that donors' budgets for supporting African capacity-building are small in comparison to the scale of the task; this suggests the need for a hard and long-overdue look at African peacekeeping ambitions versus real and potential African capabilities.

While it is difficult to generalize about fifty-three countries of vastly differing shapes and sizes, all African countries are poor, and all are recipients of development aid and donor assistance. Maintaining properly trained and equipped security forces is simply beyond the reach of most of these nations. Since 1999, there has been a sharp increase in the demand for both UN and regional peacekeepers in Africa. African military capabilities are very limited, and few countries have the capacity to contribute more personnel and equipment than they already are providing to a number of UN and regional missions in Africa (and further abroad in some cases). Ghana, for example, is currently the sixth largest contributor of troops and police to UN missions (out of 117 countries). With armed forces totaling under ten thousand, it needs to rotate approximately seven thousand troops annually for its existing commitments to UN operations. It is difficult to see how Ghana could at the same time significantly increase its contribution to ECOWAS and/ or AU operations, and many other African troop contributors are similarly overstretched.

Inherently weak and poor African states are also the building blocks of the AU and the RECs—organizations that were born of a need for economic cooperation, and that have only relatively recently been expected to play a role in security cooperation and conflict management. This has resulted in a very poor fit between institutional roles and structures, as evidenced in the SADC's inability to "operationalize" its Organ for Politics, Defense and Security. At the continental level, the AU still lacks a comprehensive and realistic multidimensional peace operations strategy, and the necessary structures to plan operations and implement this strategy.

According to the preamble to the PSC Protocol, the heads of state and government are "desirous of establishing an operational structure for the effective implementation of decisions taken in the areas of conflict prevention,
peace-making, peace support operations and intervention . . . in accordance
with the authority conferred in that regard by Article 5(2) of the Constitutive
Act of the Union." At the strategic level, the authority for mandating and terminating AU peace missions rests with the Peace and Security Council, and
responsibility for implementing mandates rests with the chairperson of the
Commission—acting largely though the commissioner for peace and security. Article 7 of the PSC Protocol states that the Peace and Security Council,
in conjunction with the chairperson of the Commission, may authorize the
mounting and deployment of peace support missions. However, the Protocol
is silent on the issue of strategic and operational-level planning and management of such missions. While the main burden of responsibility for the establishment of the ASF has been delegated to the commissioner for peace
and security, it is clear that there should also be roles for the other commissioners in the strategic-level planning and management of multidimensional
ASF operations—most obviously for the commissioners assigned to conflict
prevention, management and resolution, political affairs, and human rights,
democracy, good governance, elections, civil society, humanitarian affairs,
and refugees.

However, to provide for multidimensional strategic-level management
capability, the ASF Policy Framework simply requires the establishment of
fifteen-person planning elements at the AU headquarters and at each of the
RECs/Regional HQs. According to the Roadmap for the Operationalization
of the African Standby Force, drafted in March 2005, strategic-level planning
will be conducted by an AU headquarter-level planning element, to be established through a request by the AU Commission to member states to second
five "experienced" officers to the AU Commission in Addis Ababa.[48]

In Addis Ababa, the AU's Peace and Security Department can be considered as the rough equivalent of the UN Department of Peacekeeping Operations. However, within this department, the AU has created both a Conflict
Management Division and a Peace Support Operations Division (PSOD); this
complicates the lines of authority and responsibility for multidimensional
mission planning and management. According to extant AU organizational
charts, the sole function of the Conflict Management Division is to house the
Continental Early Warning System, and there are no direct lines of interaction between this division and the PSOD. Moreover, the PSC Protocol specifies that "a Peace and Security Council Secretariat shall be established within
the Directorate dealing with conflict prevention, management and resolution."[49] It remains unclear as to how the Conflict Management Division, the
PSOD, and the Peace and Security Council Secretariat relate to one another,
and what roles they have in the mission planning and management process.

Mission management at the operational level is addressed very briefly in
the PSC Protocol, under the rubric of "Chain of Command":

For each operation undertaken by the African Standby Force, the Chairperson of the Commission shall appoint a Special Representative and a Force Commander, whose detailed roles and functions shall be spelt out in appropriate directives, in accordance with the Peace Support Standing Operating Procedures. The Special Representative shall, through appropriate channels, report to the Chairperson of the Commission. The Force Commander shall report to the Special Representative. Contingent Commanders shall report to the Force Commander, while the civilian components shall report to the Special Representative.[50]

This chain of command is essentially the same as that for UN missions, but the procedure for spelling out the roles and functions of the special representative—"in appropriate directives, in accordance with the Peace Support Standing Operating Procedures"—is patently flawed. The Standing Operating Procedures (SOPs) have been developed by meetings of mid-ranking military officers, without any clear strategic or operational-level guidance.

Such tasks have been delegated to ad hoc meetings of officials nominated to attend by member states, in part because of the consultative nature of the AU—and in large part because there is no headquarters capacity to deal with them. Operational pressures on the AU, ECOWAS, and more recently IGAD have exacerbated already weak HQ capacity for strategic, long-term planning and have hindered the development of a stable African peace and security architecture. For example, responding to the Darfur crisis has seriously impeded the capacity-building process at the AU. The AU Commission simply does not have the staff and the expertise to plan and conduct missions, and it certainly lacks the institutional capacity to absorb at the same time a confusing array of donor capacity-building assistance packages and schemes. The donor-led drive for demonstrable operational capability has led to unrealistic goals being demanded of the AU in Darfur, in Somalia, and in the process of standing up the ASF. Failure to deliver against these goals then undermines donor support for longer-term capacity-building. Moreover, overemphasis by donors on tangible results leads to a narrow focus on "visible" military capacity at the expense of other essential elements of planning and mission success: political analysis, public information capabilities, police capacity, and so forth. Perhaps this is deliberate; if the AU had adequate analytic capability and strong policy advisors heeded by their political masters, the AU would probably not have tried to establish a multidimensional mission in Darfur nor authorized the mission in Somalia.

Prospects for the Standby Brigades and the ASF

There is a real need for creating an independent African capability for peace operations; however, there is still a remarkable lack of clarity and policy direction as to the exact nature and scope of such operations. Is the intention to create regional "fire brigade" forces that can intervene in conflicts as stop-gap measures, until such time as the UN can launch a full-blown multidimensional mission capable of supporting the full range of peacekeeping and peace-building activities? Or is the intent rather to create African capabilities in order to independently engage in multidimensional missions on the African continent?

Common wisdom points to the former interpretation, since the AU and the subregional organizations cannot mobilize the full range of UN agencies and international partners in the same way as the UN can. Indeed, UN operations are increasingly being conceived and managed as integrated missions, in which the UN seeks to help countries in transition from war to lasting peace by mobilizing and coordinating a systemwide UN response, subsuming various actors and approaches within an overall political-strategic crisis management framework. In establishing the African Peace Facility, the EU apparently envisaged a far more limited mission capability for Africa—one that could stabilize and temporize a conflict situation until such time as the UN is ready and able to take over responsibility for peace-building:

> Today the UN faces two main challenges in accomplishing its mission. First, the number of peace keeping missions throughout the world continues to grow, risking to overstretch the UN's ability to intervene quickly: this is particularly true of Africa, at present the theatre of the greatest number of conflicts. Secondly, the UN's mandate to send peace keeping troops is often dependent on the agreement of all parties to a conflict. The African Peace Facility will support AU initiatives designed to promote and accelerate the establishment of the appropriate conditions for the UN to intervene and fulfill its international responsibilities.[51]

On the other hand, the African Union seems to be aspiring toward the creation of full-range, multidimensional mission capabilities—at least in terms of the AU's broad legal and policy framework for peace operations. For example, in the Protocol Relating to the Establishment of the Peace and Security Council of the African Union, Article 13 (3), the African Standby Force is mandated to conduct the full range of operations and tasks associated with contemporary multidimensional UN operations, including intervention in a member state, postconflict disarmament and demobilization, and peace-building.

There is strong logic to the argument that energies could be better devoted to making the UN system work, rather than attempting to create an entirely alternative system for multidimensional peacekeeping in Africa. Maintaining and enhancing the quality and quantity of African troop and police contributions to UN missions on the continent would certainly be a cheaper option, and all 192 UN member states would get to share in the financial cost—and African countries would pay proportionally for peacekeeping, rather than relying entirely on donor hand-outs. When ECOMOG was doing "lean peacekeeping" in West Africa, it was thought that African organizations could keep the peace better and at a far lower cost than the UN. But this thinking has proved unsound. Not only have African missions proved to be ineffective and unsustainable; they are also proving to be more expensive. For example, the U.S. contribution to an African Union mission such as AMIS is twice that which it would be to a UN mission of similar size and scope.[52]

While a return to Hutchful's notion of "lean peacekeeping" is obviously not desirable, a "leaner and meaner" AU capability makes a lot of sense, especially in the context of Article 4 of the AU Constitutive Act and UN acceptance of the Responsibility to Protect. As noted in 1995: "The arguments for such a force . . . have their basis in the horrific inter-tribal slaughters in Rwanda and Burundi. If the UN had at its disposal even a small, rapidly-deployable constabulary force of lightly-armed troops, it might have been able to prevent this new chapter in man's cruelty to man. Indeed, the speed with which such a force could be deployed may be more important than its tactical proficiency, which may need to be only marginally better than rag-tag local forces to have a profound effect."[53]

In this context, the 6th ASF brigade—the one to be stationed in Addis Ababa, on high alert—may well have been the most useful tool in the box for the AU Peace and Security Council. As noted earlier, however, plans for establishing this brigade were scrapped by the African defense chiefs in May 2003.

Conclusion

At the same time as fielding extremely challenging missions in Burundi, Darfur, and Somalia, the AU is expected to establish a viable on-call regional peace support capability, based on joined-up capabilities provided by the five regions of Africa. Most donors are implementing their capacity-building initiatives with the expectation that African peace operations will not only be able to transition into UN missions, but also on the premise that the AU will develop the competence to undertake wholly independent, multidimensional missions. There seems to be neither adequate appreciation of just how enormous a task this is, nor much thought given to the possibility of prioritizing AU objectives—that is, concentrating on those areas of the AU that are most capable of being properly developed (for example, its rapid reaction capabilities), and leaving its patently more limited and immature capacities (such as for humanitarian assistance and postconflict reconstruction) for management by the UN. Nor has there been a serious effort to first build the AU's absorptive capacity and mission planning and management capabilities before mustering and training a bunch of battalions and pushing them into places like Darfur and Somalia.

The global-regional relationship underpinning African peacekeeping capacity-building programs has not been built on an understanding of the comparative advantages and disadvantages of the UN and African regional organizations. Donor partners have done little to temper African ambitions that have been lofty and unrealistic, with a proposed operational capacity that far exceeds extant capabilities as well as capabilities than can realistically be built in the foreseeable future. AMIS has clearly demonstrated the folly of putting the cart before the horse—of not disaggregating the specific peacekeeping strengths and weaknesses of the AU—and it points to the importance of pushing in more practical directions, such as international-regional collaborative missions (like the planned hybrid UN-AU mission for Darfur).

Moreover, there has been little attention paid to the strategic planning gap. This is evident in the policy framework and other documents underpinning the ASF, which all lack finesse, depth, and coherence. They resemble a potpourri of ideas borrowed from a variety of sources, rather than authoritative policy documents based on clear political guidance. Considerable donor support is being provided to implement this framework, without any concerted effort being made to clarify the inherent ambiguities in this framework. At this stage, the development of the ASF remains largely a preserve of the PSOD and, to some extent, of the Defense and Security Division, with very limited buy-in from the other parts of the Commission. The PSOD is hopelessly understaffed and lacking in core capacities for planning and analysis. Providing donor staff to fill African capacity gaps (as with the DITF and AMIS) is not useful in the medium-to-long term. It does not help build African capacity, and it implies African incompetence. The size and shape of future missions should rather take into account existing African expertise available for pursuit of the mandate, and enough time should be given for a realistic build-up of continental capacity.

Capacity-building is a long-term undertaking and should cover the full spectrum of support to Africans. Better training and education are essential elements of capacity, but of little use without the equipment and resources to put them to good use. Training initiatives will not build true capacity if programs are not designed with long-term, even generational, timelines in mind. Moreover, donor support to diverse peacekeeping training centers with overlapping mandates is clearly counterproductive. If KAIPTC, the biggest and best of the regional centers, is hostage to the vagaries of donor interest and support, then it makes little sense to establish two more regional peacekeeping centers in West Africa. No region in Africa has been prepared to fund one, never mind three centers. There needs to be more honesty and coordination between donors; there are still too many competing agendas, and too much wasting of time and resources in argument or duplication of effort. One focused project, based on very clear regional needs and seen through from inception to fruition, would provide a lot more credibility to the capacity-building enterprise.

Peacekeeping capacity-building, as applied to Africa since the mid-1990s, has not led to success. It is time to move beyond the politically correct—yet practically flawed—rhetorical call for "African ownership" of peacekeeping, and move instead toward a feasible division of labor. It is recommended that donor partners grasp the nettle and, together with the relevant AU Commissioners, confront squarely the challenge of developing a common, realistic political-military vision of peace operations and an organizational structure capable of leading and executing effective AU/ASF missions. In the process, the leadership of the Commission should establish appropriate linkages between the PSOD and the Crisis Management Division on the one hand, and other components of the AU Secretariat on the other to define their respective roles in peace operations—especially the Political Department.

Finally, no matter what the size and shape of the ASF that the AU eventually manages to create, the African member states will have to agree to make a financial contribution to providing troops (and police), together with minimal equipment and logistic support, if they intend to attain a degree of autonomy in peacekeeping. He who pays the piper generally calls the tune.

Chapter 7

Europe: Looking Near and Far

BASTIAN GIEGERICH

European forces are deployed to peace support operations (PSO) around the globe, both as part of various multilateral frameworks and as part of coalitions of the willing. Because of its prosperity, military capacity, and values, the transatlantic community, including Europe, has been singled out as having a strong obligation to contribute.[1]

Europe is home to some countries that have engaged in UN missions for approximately five decades, whereas others, such as Germany, have participated in PSOs only since the end of the cold war. At the same time, Europe is home to the two most sophisticated regional institutions with peace support functions, namely NATO and the European Union (EU). Both institutions have branched out into the business of military peace support operations, the former by expanding its scope beyond collective defense and the latter by building up a Common Foreign and Security Policy (CFSP) that includes a European Security and Defence Policy (ESDP). Overlap between the two is high, with Austria, Cyprus, Finland, Ireland, Malta, and Sweden being the only EU member states, out of a current total of twenty-five, that are not members of NATO. Iceland, Norway, and Turkey are the only European members of NATO not currently in the EU. For most European countries, these two regional frameworks are available so that they can conduct peace support operations. The situation in Europe is thus characterized by a mix of high institutional sophistication and complexity on the one hand, and high military capacity and a tradition of participation in PSOs on the other.

NATO, the European Union, and PSOs

NATO, founded to defend its members against aggression and the threat of aggression, continues to be the world's most powerful military alliance. Its core principle, laid out in Article 5 of the 1949 Washington Treaty, is that an armed attack against one or more NATO members will be considered an attack against all. Article 5 has only been invoked once in NATO's history, following the September 11, 2001, terrorist attacks in the United States. Collective defense remains the core task according to the treaty even today. However, the actual focus of NATO activities has undergone fundamental change since the end of the cold war.

With regard to NATO's involvement in PSOs, the adaptation, begun in 1991 with the approval of a new strategic concept, proceeded in three crucial steps. First, the 1991 strategic concept committed the Alliance to work for the security of Europe as a whole through partnership and cooperation. Second, the unfolding Balkans crises committed NATO to conducting PSOs within the Euro-Atlantic area but beyond Alliance territory. This was recognized in the revised strategic concept adopted at the Washington Summit in 1999, which committed NATO to maintaining peace and stability in the wider Euro-Atlantic area. However, in the wake of the 9/11 attacks, and driven by the realization that contemporary security threats cannot be contained geographically, NATO member states in 2002 made it clear that they were willing to engage in PSOs beyond the Euro-Atlantic area, which hitherto had been the Alliance's accepted realm of responsibilities.[2] Thus, at least as a matter of policy, at the end of this adaptation process NATO stands ready to conduct PSOs across the globe.

The European Union is first and foremost the institutional manifestation of a political and economic process of regional integration. Begun in the 1950s as the European Coal and Steel Community (ECSC), the European Atomic Energy Community (EURATOM), and the European Economic Community (EEC), it always had a security dimension to it but it was inward looking. Economic and political integration were, at least in part, means to help European countries overcome their security problems and stop being the breeding grounds for global military confrontations. In this sense, European integration has been a huge success. During the cold war, security and defense as a policy area was by and large left to NATO.

Only with the enactment of the Treaty on European Union (TEU) have member states engaged in the building of CFSP. The EU foray into military crisis management did not begin until 1999 with the launch of ESDP. At the EU's Cologne Summit of June 1999, member governments decided that "the [European] Union must have the capacity for autonomous action, backed up by credible military forces, the means to decide to use them, and a readiness to do so, in order to respond to international crises without prejudice to actions by NATO."[3] The operational remits of EU military crisis management are the so-called Petersberg tasks, originally defined at the meeting of the Western European Union (WEU) in 1992. The TEU lists them in Article 17.2 as humanitarian and rescue tasks, peacekeeping tasks, and tasks of combat forces in crisis management, including peacemaking.[4]

Institutional Set-up for Military Operations

The core institutional set-up to launch and run military crisis management missions through ESDP was established in 2000, when the European Council created three major bodies residing permanently in Brussels. They are the Political and Security Committee (PSC), the EU Military Committee (EUMC), and the EU Military Staff (EUMS). The PSC replaces the Political Committee (PoCo) and meets on the ambassadorial level. In noncrisis situations, the PSC takes over PoCo's tasks of tracking international developments as they relate to CFSP. In crisis situations, the PSC turns within limits from a decision-shaping into a decision-making body: the TEU states that the PSC shall exercise "political control and strategic direction of crisis management operations" (Article 25).

The PSC is the "linchpin" of ESDP and CFSP; in crisis situations it is the body that "examines all the options that might be considered as the Union's response." In preparing the EU's response to a crisis, the PSC proposes to the Council "the political objectives to be pursued by the Union" and recommends "a cohesive set of options aimed at the settlement of the crisis."[5] The 2000 Presidency Report on ESDP further defined a four-step mechanism that enables the PSC to take political and strategic direction of a military EU crisis management operation. The PSC, based on the advice of the EUMC, sends a recommendation to the Council. The Council then decides to launch a military operation within the framework of a joint action. The joint action defines the role of the secretary-general of the Council, who is also the EU's High Representative for CFSP (SG/HR). Throughout the duration of the operation, the Council will be kept informed by PSC reports presented by the SG/HR in his capacity as PSC chairman.

The EUMC is composed of the member states' chiefs of defense (CHODs), represented by their military representatives (MILREPs). Its chairman, a four-star flag officer appointed by the Council on recommendation of the CHODs, attends Council meetings if decisions with defense implications are on the agenda. The general functions of the EUMC are to provide direction for the EUMS, to provide consensual military advice to the PSC, and to make recommendations to the PSC either on its own initiative or on the PSC's request.

In crisis situations, the EUMC, upon the PSC's request, tasks the director general of the EUMS to define and present military options for an EU operation. The EUMC evaluates these options and forwards them to the PSC. Based on the option chosen by the Council, the EUMC authorizes an Initial Planning Directive for the operational commander. The Concept of Operations and the draft Operations Plan defined by the operational commander are evaluated by the EUMS, after which the EUMC provides advice and recommendations to the PSC based on these evaluations. During the course of the operation, the EUMC monitors the proper execution of the military operations. Finally the EUMC advises the PSC on the termination option of any military operation.

The EUMS—mostly seconded from the member states—is about two hundred strong. It is the EU's source of military expertise and performs three main functions: early warning, situation assessment, and strategic planning for the Petersberg tasks. The EUMS works under the direction of the EUMC, but it is organized as a department of the Council Secretariat and thus attached to the SG/HR. Since the EUMS identifies European national and multinational forces for Petersberg tasks, its staff ensures that the EUMC is aware of the available military resources. Overall, it is important to recall that ESDP remains a purely intergovernmental part of the EU—thus, other bodies such as the European Commission, the European Parliament, or the European Court of Justice have virtually no authority in this field.

NATO, given its origin as a military alliance and its persistent focus on the defense and security of its member states, is an intergovernmental organization par excellence. Decisions at every level within the Alliance are made according to the principle of consensus. The North Atlantic Council (NAC) has the overall political authority and decision-making power. It meets at the ambassadorial level or higher (ministers of foreign affairs; ministers of defense; or heads of state and government). The NAC is supported by its international staff and the NATO Military Committee (NMC), which is the highest military authority in the Alliance and charged with the conduct of operations. It is, in turn, supported in its tasks by the international military staff.

Once the NAC decides to take on an operation, the Supreme Allied Commander Europe (SACEUR), who heads Allied Command Operations based at Mons, Belgium, nominates a joint force commander, who in turn drafts a Concept of Operations (CONOPS) and a Statement of Military Requirements (SOR). This takes place within the limits set by political guidance as defined by the NAC. Once the NAC approves the CONOPS, the Supreme Headquarters Allied Powers Europe (SHAPE) releases an Activation Warning (ACT-WARN), which formally notifies NATO member countries of the fact that a force is needed and also outlines the mission. ACTWARN is followed by an Activation Requirement (ACTREQ), which is a request directed at Alliance members to pledge forces against the SOR. Once the joint force commander is content that the forces committed meet the military requirements, SHAPE issues an Activation Order (ACTORD), which releases the national forces provided to the NATO joint force commander. At all stages during the operation, the NAC maintains overall political control. As the NAC is the only body deriving its authority directly from the Washington Treaty, all other bodies of NATO are subordinated to the NAC (which established them in the first place). As the discussion of the processes in both the EU and NATO shows, the EU institutional crisis management set up is in part modeled on NATO.

Precrisis Military Cooperation within NATO and the EU

In many ways, constant precrisis military cooperation on all levels is one of the greatest strengths of NATO. The fact that NATO member countries and their forces exercise together, train together, plan together, and use standardized procedures and equipment is an enormous advantage, contributing to the operational effectiveness of NATO forces. Multinational operations always present challenges to the participating forces, but the continuous and repeated interaction through NATO means that its forces know how to work together.

For example, NATO regularly conducts military exercises. Recently, NATO conducted Steadfast Jaguar on the islands of Cape Verde in the Atlantic to test the capacity of the NATO Response Force (NRF) to operate outside the immediate geographical realm of Alliance responsibilities. A total of about 7,700 troops were deployed over a distance that equals that between Paris and New York. The basic lesson is that the NRF is ready to deploy, although it cannot yet handle the full spectrum of assigned missions, as forced entry remained problematic. Senior NATO leaders were able to identify a range of more specific lessons learned; for example, they learned about the effectiveness of seaborne command and control assets, which cannot be replicated completely in a computer-assisted exercise.

Defense planning through NATO remains the basis for all Alliance operations, whether they have a collective defense dimension or not. It provides an important framework for the harmonization of national efforts by defining political guidance and a NATO-level of ambition, and also by setting planning targets for the member states and then reviewing their progress in meeting these targets, all defined under the principle of consensus. Aside from setting planning targets and force goals, NATO uses SHAPE to plan and conduct operations.

Yet another aspect of precrisis military cooperation is the standardization process. NATO has an organization that coordinates and defines standardization efforts throughout the alliance in order to increase interoperability of NATO forces and ensure the effective use of resources. In essence, the NATO Standardization Organization (NSO) aims to eliminate duplication and fragmentation in all aspects relevant to the Alliance, including operational tasks, procurement, and research.

NATO also has a wide range of educational facilities, the most significant being the NATO Defense College and the NATO School. At the Defense College senior military leaders from Alliance and partner countries take courses on politico-military affairs that help establish a coherent perspective throughout the various military establishments. The NATO school educates both civilian and military personnel on central aspects of Alliance policy, strategy, and operations. Together with other facilities, the educational institutions of NATO make a crucial contribution to common training.

Within the EU the level of precrisis military cooperation is significantly lower than within NATO. Obviously, as is the case with NATO, permanent institutions such as the EUMS, in which personnel seconded from member states continuously interact in a European framework, can be expected to socialize participating individuals through that interaction, thereby contributing over time to a shared "European" view of security affairs.

The EU has undertaken several crisis management exercises—one in 2003 that was conducted jointly with NATO—to test the EU's structures and procedures in both the military and civilian realms. Using fictional scenarios, the complete set of politico-military and operational structures were involved. Late in 2005 the EU conducted its first computer-assisted military exercise, which focused on the interaction between an EU operations headquarters and an EU force headquarters on a simulated EU-led PSO mission. In June 2007 the EU conducted a military exercise that tested and evaluated the interaction between the EU Operations Center and an EU force headquarters (provided by Sweden) during an EU-led mission. So far, the EU has not conducted any live military exercises.

At the EU Summit in June 2004, member governments agreed to create a limited military planning capability within the EU. In essence, this capability consists of three parts: an autonomous EU planning cell at SHAPE, a NATO liaison presence at the EUMS, and a civilian/military cell within the EUMS, which also serves as the nucleus for an operations center. The December 2005 Presidency Report on ESDP stated that the civil-military cell was fully staffed. Meanwhile the civil-military cell had already assisted in the planning of the civilian ESDP mission in Aceh. Since March 2006 the EU Cell at SHAPE (EUCS) has been up and running.[6] In 2005, the EU established the so-called European Security and Defense College. For the time being, the College is a network of national institutions within EU member states rather than a central entity. Within these national institutions ESDP modules are taught, and orientation courses for personnel from non-EU countries are given. Overall, there is a growing degree of precrisis military cooperation by means of ESDP, although it is far below the level found in NATO.

There are also cooperative arrangements between the EU and NATO, with regard to both precrisis and crisis situations. In 2002–03 the EU and NATO agreed on modalities for the so-called Berlin Plus agreement, which gives the EU assured access to NATO assets and capabilities for operations in which the Alliance as a whole is not engaged. As will become clear in the next section, this agreement has already been used several times in support of EU-led PSOs. Although military cooperation is working to a satisfactory degree, the political bodies find it difficult to strengthen their strategic dialog despite the NATO-EU Declaration on ESDP, upon which a strategic partnership is supposed to rest. Agreements governing the exchange of classified information have been signed, but, apart from matters of operational planning, the EU-NATO partnership remains limited.[7]

Organizational Record of PSOs

NATO got involved in military crisis management in operational terms during the summer of 1995. The Alliance conducted a two-week air campaign against Bosnian Serb forces; the campaign prepared the ground for the Dayton peace accord of the same year, which ended the Bosnian War. Following the Dayton agreement, NATO led an Implementation Force (IFOR) of sixty thousand soldiers; this was later succeeded by the NATO Stabilization Force (SFOR), which in turn was replaced by an EU mission at the end of 2004.

During 1999 the Alliance launched the controversial seventy-eight-day air war against Serbia, which followed a year of fighting and gross human rights violations in Kosovo. The Kosovo War was followed by another significant NATO-led PSO deployment, when the UN-mandated Kosovo Force (KFOR) arrived. KFOR remains in-theater until today. Whereas at its peak KFOR was comprised of more than 40,000 troops in Kosovo and another 6,000 support troops based in FYROM, its strength at the time of writing was some 16,000 troops.

In its first truly preventive military deployment, NATO helped in 2001 to avoid civil war in the former Yugoslav Republic of Macedonia (FYROM). A NATO team helped broker the Ohrid Agreement between the Skopje-based government and the so-called National Liberation Army (NLA). Crucially this agreement was followed by the deployment of a 4,000-strong force, Operation Essential Harvest, which oversaw the NLA's disarmament during September and October 2001. Upon the request of the government of FYROM, NATO kept follow-on forces until early 2003 in FYROM, deployed in operations Amber Fox and Allied Harmony, to minimize the risk of instability. The size of these forces was gradually reduced from approximately 1,000 to about 350.

Since August 2003, NATO has been in charge of the UN-mandated International Security Assistance Force (ISAF) in Afghanistan. Having NATO take over has solved the problem of finding new lead nations for ISAF every six months and has ensured smooth handovers. Initially limited to Kabul, ISAF has been gradually expanding, and as of October 2006 its area of responsibility covers all of Afghanistan. As of February 2007, ISAF's total strength was some 35,000 troops, 14,000 of which were American. A total of thirty-seven countries contributed troops at the time of writing. While ISAF and the U.S.-led coalition forces (Operation Enduring Freedom) will continue to have separate mandates, ISAF has expanded into parts of Afghanistan where the distinction between stabilization and security missions, on the one hand, and counterterrorism operations, on the other, is blurred. ISAF is the first NATO PSO that operates beyond the Euro-Atlantic area.

NATO launched a military training mission to help the Iraqi authorities develop effective security structures and headquarters personnel in August 2004. This mission has been expanded from some fifty personnel to about three hundred as the pace of training has been stepped up during 2005. The Iraqi training mission is distinct in the sense that it does not involve any operational aspects.

In coordination with the European Union, NATO has also been assisting the African Union (AU) in its peacekeeping mission in Darfur, Sudan, since 2005. NATO has provided airlift to AU troops and civilian police and has trained AU peacekeepers in intelligence management and command and control for multinational headquarters.

Just as with NATO, the European Union has been active in various locations. [8] On the invitation of the authorities in the FYROM and backed by UN Security Council Resolution 1371, it took over for NATO's Allied Harmony. The EU's first military operation, *Concordia*, began on March 31, 2003, and consisted of about 350 military personnel from all EU member states, except Ireland and Denmark, with France serving as the framework nation. Fourteen nonmember states have also contributed, with the biggest contingent, seventeen soldiers, coming from Poland. Concordia was implemented using the Berlin-Plus arrangements between the EU and NATO. After its mandate expired, Concordia was succeeded by an EU-run police operation launched in December 2003.

The EU-led Operation Artemis in the Democratic Republic of the Congo (DRC) represented the most significant test of the military dimension of ESDP during 2003. Following an appeal by the UN secretary-general and based on the mandate defined in UN Security Council Resolution 1484, the EU launched Artemis on June 12, 2003. The force protected refugee camps housing internally displaced persons, secured the airport in Bunia, and was responsible for the overall safety of the civilian population and personnel of organizations—including the UN—that were trying to deliver humanitarian aid. As planned, Artemis filled a crucial gap before a larger and more robust UN mission could step in. The EU force handed over responsibilities on September 1, 2003. Artemis encompassed about 2,200 soldiers, with France acting as the framework nation. Artemis, like Concordia, also included personnel from non-EU states (Brazil, Canada, and South Africa).

Artemis made the EU cross the military-crisis-management Rubicon in several ways. For the first time, it engaged in military-crisis management beyond Europe. The EU chose not to make use of the Berlin Plus agreement, thus conducting the mission without NATO support. Finally, troops had to be deployed over a long distance and had to operate in a demanding environment. Nonetheless, the big qualification is that only five EU member states contributed troops to this EU operation. Hence, the political will was limited to a small group within the EU.

On December 2, 2004, the EU launched operation Althea, which took over responsibilities for a safe and stable environment in Bosnia and Herzegovina from NATO's SFOR. The force, initially numbering more than 7,000, has since been reduced to about 6,000 soldiers, which operate under a Chapter VII UN mandate. In terms of sheer numbers, Althea remains the largest EU operation to date. The transition from NATO to EU forces proved relatively unproblematic, and the EU force is using NATO assets and capabilities under the Berlin Plus agreement.

During 2006, the EU further strengthened its engagement in the DRC. After a request by the UN in December 2005, the EU launched an approximately 2,000-strong military mission to help secure the DRC during the 2006 elections. Germany was the lead nation in this effort, contributing about 780 troops, which were joined by a French contingent of similar size and further contributions by sixteen other nations. The force, EUFOR RD Congo, supported the 17,000-strong UN force MONUC already in the country. EUFOR was in the DRC for four months beginning on July 30, 2006. Deployment and redeployment phases are not included in these four months.

Even with less than four years of EU-led PSOs, it is clear that ESDP has outgrown its initial focus on the Balkans. Nonetheless, the EU is gradually taking over military responsibilities for the Balkans from NATO. Another trend is that both the EU and NATO act in support and sometimes on behalf of the UN, but their member states seem to prefer to organize their PSOs through the regional organizations rather than the world body. It is not clear yet, however, whether this latter trend will hold. After the crisis of July and August 2006, which saw armed conflict between Hezbollah in Lebanon and the Israeli defense forces, EU member state forces built the backbone of the reinforced UN mission UNIFIL; an EU operation in support of the UN, as in the DRC, was apparently never discussed as a serious option. On the other hand, the unique nature of the conflict, combined with its geographic location and regional context, may suggest that EU members simply saw the UN as a more appropriate framework in this case.

Regional Attitudes and Their Drivers

Virtually all European governments have begun military reform processes, which aim at improving their militaries' force projection capabilities. This process is driven by a threat assessment, which does not foresee a conventional military threat, but rather a range of threats that are connected, deterritorialized, asymmetric, and involve a multitude of state and nonstate actors. There is a general consensus that PSO operations are a much-needed element of a comprehensive security policy that encompasses both civilian and military-crisis-management instruments. There is also general agreement that Europe cannot limit its efforts to Europe in a geographical sense. The overarching conceptual framework for all governments is cooperative security, as the assessment is that no state can fight contemporary threats on its own.

In December 2003, the European Council adopted a paper titled "A secure Europe in a better world," which contains the EU's first-ever European security strategy (ESS). The strategy paper argued that the European Union had to take on global responsibility in the security realm:

> We need to develop a strategic culture that fosters early, rapid, and when necessary, robust intervention. . . . Preventive engagement can avoid more serious problems in the future. A European Union which takes greater responsibility and which is more active will be one which carries greater political weight.[9]

The draft document listed international terrorism aimed at maximum fatalities, the proliferation of weapons of mass destruction, and failed states—sometimes exploited by organized crime—as the three central threats facing Europe, and it acknowledged that there is a danger that these threats might connect with each other. Its clear focus made the paper a useful starting point, since the three listed threats would rank among the prime concerns of all EU member states' governments. In fact, when the ESS was adopted in December 2003, the list of threats in the Solana draft had grown to five, as organized crime and regional conflicts were added as key threats.

However, just beneath the surface of a shared threat assessment and a basic consensus about the necessity for participation in PSOs, there is a wide range of divisions. The most significant ones include, first, uncertainty over whether the EU and NATO should accept truly global responsibilities. While the logic of the threat assessment leads to a global perspective, this does not yet translate into a strategy for global engagement. Not all European members of NATO support the U.S. agenda of transforming the Alliance into a global intervention force.

Second, the robustness of the military element in the comprehensive security concept favored by European governments is an issue of unmistakable divergence. Whereas for some governments the use of military force as an instrument of foreign policy, even under demanding and dangerous circumstances, is an accepted reality, for others it is still the exception to the rule.

Finally, although the differences have been narrowed down, there is still disagreement about what the relationship between NATO and the EU should look like in practice. Can and should there be a geographical or functional division of labor with regard to crisis management? Both organizations have different comparative advantages: the EU's is able to bring the full range of instruments—civilian and military—to the table, whereas NATO remains the only European security organization that can guarantee U.S. involvement and a truly global and robust force projection capacity.

A complex set of factors—some domestic, some international—explain these divisions. First, there is a latent dissatisfaction with the current global power distribution. Those Europeans who want to check U.S. power see NATO as an important venue for that undertaking. However, those who are prepared to actively resist the United States, and who would find it acceptable to weaken NATO, are a tiny minority. It is generally understood that Europe and the United States need to cooperate and work together to address pressing international security questions. A different matter, yet again, is that for some the real question is what to do if the United States begins to disengage from crisis regions around the world in response to policy failures of the recent past. If this were to happen it would strengthen the argument for a stronger EU capacity, since the original selling point of ESDP was to be able to act in case NATO (as led by the United States) does not want to or for some reason cannot act.

There are important domestic political constraints aside from the resource challenges analyzed in the next section. The situation varies considerably across European countries, but the first domestic driver of governments' decisions to participate in PSOs is their political vulnerability. Many countries are ruled by coalition governments, and many heads of state and government need parliamentary approval in order to send soldiers abroad. The resulting need to maintain a governing coalition and the parliamentary majority that is supporting it, paired with sometimes less than enthusiastic public support for PSOs, can create complex debates that to the outsider may look like wavering and indecisiveness. For example, during the debate in the run-up to the 2003 EU operation in the DRC, there was a widespread debate in Germany about whether German soldiers could and should be put in a position where they might have to confront child soldiers. In a similar vein, since most European governments send their troops to PSOs with limited objectives, their (and their electorates') willingness to accept casualties is limited.[10]

Both diverging agendas in coalition governments and the necessity to convince a majority in parliament to support deployments constrain leaders.[11] For example, whereas the French president and the British prime minister have relative autonomy in the decision to deploy troops, the German chancellor usually is the head of a coalition government and needs parliamentary approval for every deployment and every extension of a mandate. In Austria a new *Entsendegestz*—the law regulating the deployment of Austrian forces abroad—was adopted in 1997. Its major innovation was that Austrian participation was no longer limited to UN missions. The executive does not need approval from the parliamentary plenum, nor does it have to put deployments on the parliamentary agenda. The executive merely needs approval of the *Nationalrat's* main committee (*Hauptausschuss*), which brings together some thirty MP's from all parties in parliament.

In Spain a new law (*Ley Orgánica 5/2005 de la Defensa Nacional*) was enacted in November 2005 that gives the Spanish lower house, the *Cortes Generales*, a marginally stronger say in the decision to use the military abroad. Before passage of the law, parliamentary consent was only necessary for the use of force based on a declaration of war. Against the background of the Spanish participation in the 2003 invasion of Iraq—which did not have popular support, and which was not put to a vote in parliament—and the 2004 Madrid bombings, calls for a revision of the status quo grew louder. The November 2005 law was justified by the government in light of the new international missions the military had to take on. The stipulations of the law were watered down significantly when compared to earlier ideas. In the end, Article 17 states that the government has to consult and obtain permission for the external use of force from parliament for operations "which are not directly related to the defense of Spain or national interests."

Other factors driving attitudes in the region are foreign policy traditions and strategic culture. Strategic culture is best understood as an ideational milieu that limits choices of states in relation to the use of military force, including questions of when, under which circumstances, and in which contexts military force is to be used as a political tool. This ideational milieu is based on the historically unique experiences of a given society, which generates persistent preferences that are only open to gradual change through policymaking elites, particularly in times of perceived crisis.[12]

This means that on crucial dimensions, European governments will continue to have diverging understandings of what is appropriate behavior in certain situations. The classic divide is between Atlanticists and Europeanists, with Britain leading the former and France the latter camp. In practical terms, this means that for Atlanticists NATO remains the default framework for PSOs, whereas for Europeanists European autonomy in this field as embodied through ESDP is an overriding concern. Similar divisions exist regarding the acceptance of military force as a foreign policy tool. Whereas both France and the United Kingdom have a long history of extrovert behaviour in this regard, for some, such as Germany, armed forces during the cold war solely served the purpose of territorial defense. In general, external pressures and a growing body of shared experiences in PSOs can be expected to grind down these differences over time and expand the area of overlaps. However, it remains important to understand that it is more appropriate to speak of increasing levels of overlap and increasing levels of compatibility of different attitudes in the region, rather than of true convergence and the emergence of a coherent outlook on these questions across Europe.

Resource Challenges

With few exceptions, economic growth in Europe is still proceeding at a slow rate, increasing the pressure on defense expenditures as governments try to come to terms with overall budget priorities. Hence, it is not surprising that aggregated data show defense spending on a continued downward slope. In the ten-year period from 1995 to 2004, NATO defense expenditures as a percentage of GDP, not including the United States, have declined from 2.42 percent to 1.87 percent. For non-NATO Europe the figures are 2.10 percent and 1.48 percent, respectively. There is every indication that this downward trend continued during 2005 and 2006.[13] The European Defense Agency reported that its twenty-four member states spent a total of EUR 193 billion in 2005. Only 18.4 percent of this total is invested in equipment procurement and research and development efforts. The top three spenders on research and development—France, the United Kingdom, and Germany—account for 80 percent of all spending on research and development. Only 18 percent of equipment procurement spending happens in a collaborative framework, counting cooperation both among EU members and with non-EU members. For spending on research and development, the figure is even lower at 12.4 percent.[14] As markets are still fragmented—as is the case for customers and suppliers in Europe—limited budgets are spent inefficiently. This overall situation is unlikely to change.

Spending on research and development as well as on equipment procurement are crucial indicators of the ability to transform military capabilities. Furthermore, equipment costs rise much faster than other costs.[15] The issue is therefore not simply how much countries are spending, but also what they are spending on. Here the picture is mixed again, but overall, as the following examples indicate, many European countries have not adopted the right spending mix to significantly improve their force projection capacity, nor have they arrived at satisfactory overall spending levels.

For example, the Swedish defense budget has been cut significantly in the 2005–07 defense bill, which was approved by parliament in December 2004. The total budgetary envelope for 2005 was set at SKr 40.68 billion (EUR 4.37 billion) excluding contingency measures against accidents and severe emergencies. The proposed budget for 2006 was set at SKr 40.01 billion, which the government estimates will shrink further to 39.34 billion by 2007. Defense spending is thus slipping below 1.5 percent of GDP. More cuts may yet be introduced, as the government has indicated that it plans to return to the issue of defense spending. While funding for operations is set to increase, a positive fact is that personnel costs are comparatively low. According to figures presented in the 2005–07 defense bill, they amount to approximately 30 percent of the total defense budget.

The Danish defense budget is established in five-year cycles as part of the nation's Defense Agreements, a practice that provides relative planning security. At 2004 prices, the budget for 2005 has been set at DKK18.6 billion (about EUR 2.50 billion) and is due to rise to DKK19.1 billion (about EUR 2.56 billion) by 2009 after peaking at DKK19.3 billion in 2006 and 2007. Hence, as it has in the past few years, defense expenditure will continue to hover at around 1.5 percent of GDP. Within the five-year budget cycle, funding allocated for the investment into new equipment varies significantly. For example, the 2006 and 2007 budgets earmark around 25 percent of the total for new equipment. However, no funds for new equipment are allocated for 2009. According to NATO estimates, total expenditures on equipment amounted to about 18 percent in 2005, as opposed to more than 52 percent for personnel.

For some countries, such as Spain, the overall size of defense expenditures is difficult to assess. Some research and development funding, and some procurement funding, is hidden in the budgets of other ministries, such as Spain's Ministry of Science and Industry (which has been split into two parts by the incoming Zapatero government). Furthermore, other government ministries routinely give loans to the MoD, for example for acquisitions. This practice, referred to as "pre-financing," means that some costs appear in the defense budgets with delays. Each of the last two Spanish budgets saw a slight increase, with the 2005 version standing at EUR 6.98 billion, which amounts to about 1.3 percent of GDP. According to NATO data, 54 percent of the total is spent on personnel, whereas between 21 and 22 percent is spent on equipment. It should be noted, however, that between 2003 and 2005 Spanish governments signed up for re-equipment programs costing more than EUR 6.6 billion in total.

Austria has one of the smallest defense budgets in Europe when measured as a percentage of GDP. The 2005 budget establishes an overall envelope of EUR 1.8 billion, which amounts to approximately 0.8 percent of GDP. While the *Bundesheer* reform documents acknowledge the need for increased defense spending, no overall recommendation has been made. The exception is a proposed increase of investment to one-third of the budget; currently, investment is dwarfed by personnel costs. In the 2005 budget personnel costs swallowed EUR 1.05 billion, or 58 percent, whereas procurement and acquisition was limited to EUR 373 million, or about 21 percent. In the absence of a political consensus to increase defense spending significantly, the Austrian government has begun to streamline service activities and has embarked on a comprehensive restructuring of military infrastructure. Particularly the latter effort is supposed to generate the necessary funds to sustain the reform effort.

The German defense budget has been stagnant as the country struggles to increase economic growth rates. The budget for 2005 establishes an envelope of EUR 23.9 billion, which is due to increase to EUR 24.7 billion by 2007. The overall defense expenditure has slipped below 1.5 percent of GDP. The percentage of overall investment, including equipment, is supposed to slowly increase from the current 25 percent to about 30 percent by the end of the decade. Spending on equipment amounts to less than 15 percent. Furthermore, according to NATO, German defense expenditures are plagued by high personnel costs. In 2004, they were estimated to account for almost 60 percent of total defense spending, compared to about 35 percent and 39 percent, respectively, for the United States and the United Kingdom. The German government has attempted to free funds by outsourcing various service activities and putting unused property on the market. However, savings and profits generated this way in the past have only been partially reinvested in the defense budget, with considerable amounts being diverted to other portfolios by the finance ministry; this reflects the overall budgetary problems Germany is facing.

Both the EU and NATO have recently launched capabilities development initiatives, which aim at increasing their member states' ability to project military force for crisis management purposes. In December 2003, the EU's military headline goal, defined at Helsinki in 1999, was supposed to be met. EU member governments tiptoed past this deadline in spite of obvious capabilities shortcomings. They chose to define a new aspiration, the Headline Goal 2010, declaring in May 2004 that they are committed "to be able by 2010 to respond with rapid and decisive action applying a fully coherent approach to the whole spectrum of crisis management operations covered by the Treaty on European Union."[16] A crucial element in the new headline goal is the military instrument of the so-called battlegroups. They are a rapid reaction force package, up to 1,500 strong, deployable for up to 120 days, and equipped for tasks at the upper end of the Petersberg spectrum. In November 2004 the EU member states committed to establishing thirteen of these Battlegroups, with full operational capability of two simultaneously deployable Battlegroups reached as of 2007.[17] During 2005, the EU organized two Battle Group Coordination conferences. As a result the initial pledge of thirteen, dating back to November 2004, has been increased to eighteen. With the Battlegroups on six-month rotation schedules, all slots up to 2010 have been filled, although some of the pledged force packages will not become operational until 2012. The Battlegroups as a key element of the Headline Goal 2010 were a clear indicator that the EU has switched its capabilities improvement activities from quantity (the 1999 Headline Goal) to the quality of the force packages.

For NATO, the key engine for transformation is the NRF, which was declared operational in November 2006. The fully operational NRF is an approximately 25,000-strong, permanently available, multinational and joint force at extremely high readiness. It is supposed to be deployable in five days and sustainable for thirty. Its missions, to be determined by the NAC on a case-by-case basis, can comprise Article 5 and non–Article 5 crisis management tasks without any geographical limits. Thus, the NRF can be deployed as a stand-alone force, an initial entry force facilitating the deployment of larger follow-on contingents, or serve as an instrument to support diplomacy if resolve needs to be demonstrated. As should be clear from this wide spectrum of options, the NRF has to be able to engage in high-intensity combat.[18]

The force is intended to be a catalyst for the development of advanced network-centric capabilities among NATO member countries. The key instruments to achieve this within the NRF are rotation and certification. Directly before the multinational units are deployed or put on standby for six months, they undergo a rigorous six-month joint training period. They will be evaluated by SHAPE, which certifies whether the units brought together by the member states are combat ready. The training and deployment phase, usually followed by a six-month refitting phase, make up a full NRF cycle for the units involved. The trick is that certification requirements will become more demanding with each cycle.[19] Hence, as NATO member governments are forced to rotate units through the NRF, transformation supposedly spreads through the Alliance's forces as units struggle to meet certification requirements.

Most forces participating in the NRF are "double-" or even "triple-hatted," the latter meaning that in principle they are available for NATO, EU, and national missions. So far, rotation schedules have been drawn up that deconflict the NRF and EU battlegroups. No units will be assigned to both forces at the same time. The number of troops pledged by contributing states should thus be available even during parallel deployments of the NRF and EU battlegroups. However, whether the same holds true for critical enablers such as airlift remains to be seen.

An additional important challenge is that the rules of engagement the different national contingents bring to international operations are peppered with restrictions on what they can do. These so-called caveats—for example, prohibiting night flights by transport planes—undermine an operation's effectiveness and can endanger its success if a multinational force is paralyzed as a result. ISAF in Afghanistan reportedly has had to function with some six dozen different national caveats. The issue of caveats and rules of engagement highlights the fact that, in today's security environment, different national priorities do not necessarily support overarching international interests. Reconciling these differences is an important step toward operational effectiveness.

There is also a tendency among European nations to try to secure political influence through symbolic contributions to PSOs. A recent example is the 2006 EU mission to the DRC, which despite its moderate size of about 2,000 soldiers, and despite the fact that Germany and France together provided some 1,600 of these, consisted of 18 contributors in all.[20] The 2003 EU-led operation Concordia in FYROM, which was 350 soldiers strong, consisted of at least 27 national contingents. There is a clear tendency to exploit the symbolism of these encompassing coalitions from both directions: for contributing states, even the smallest contingent buys them a seat at the table; for the EU as a whole, to get as many countries involved as possible provides legitimacy and also demonstrates a capacity for common action. It has to be understood, however, that there is a trade-off between symbolism and political legitimacy on the one hand, and operational effectiveness on the other.

Prospects

In Europe, both necessary capabilities as well as sophisticated regional organizations exist for the conduct of PSOs. Furthermore, many countries have a long tradition of being involved in these operations, and the recent activities of both NATO and the EU demonstrate the region's political will to continue being involved. The central question is whether European nations will be willing and able to do more in the future?

Several observations can be drawn from the survey presented in this chapter. First, political attitudes—related to the use of force or organizational competition—will continue to pose obstacles for improved operational effectiveness. However, such political attitudes are unlikely to stand in the way of action as such. These issues affect the "how we do it" rather than the "should we do it" dimensions of PSOs.

Second, resource and capabilities limitations remain key problems. For both NATO and the EU, the initiatives of recent years have not met expectations. Thus, both organizations have learned to maximize the benefits of what they have. However, over the next five years there is a real chance of some of the more long-term initiatives yielding results. If they are matched with the necessary political will, increased capacity should be the result. On the financial side, however, there is no indication that defense budgets will rise or that spending will become significantly more efficient. The costs of peace support operations are problematic, since for most activities both NATO and the EU operate with the costs-lie-where-they-fall principle, which means that those nations that contribute most assets and troops also have to pay for them. Hence, there is a debate about common funding for these operations, although progress on this issue has been marginal so far.

Third, European governments pursue limited objectives in peace support operations, since their territorial security is not perceived to be directly jeopardized by the various crisis situations. Therefore, the deployment of troops is discretionary and affected by political vulnerabilities. This also opens the door to debates about burden-sharing among European countries. In particular demanding missions, such as in Afghanistan, have a tendency to lead to squabbles if a country is perceived as not pulling its weight or is seen as being unwilling to share the risks.

Finally, perhaps the greatest promise—so far not realized—is the development of the EU into a truly comprehensive actor in the security and defense field. The EU has the unique potential to be able to combine economic, political, civilian, and military crisis management tools. Given that contemporary crises demand this diverse mix of means, a European Union guided by a coherent vision and equipped with the necessary capabilities could play a significant global role. Barring drastic and unforeseen developments, Europe will provide a significant PSO capacity. Its willingness and ability to do more than it is already doing, however, will only change gradually.

Chapter 8

Peace Support in the New Independent States: Different from the Rest?

ALEXANDER I. NIKITIN AND MARK A. LOUCAS

The collapse of the Soviet Union in 1991 led to the emergence of a group of new independent states (NIS) on its former territory. The NIS have a history of deploying peace operations within their own communities in addition to sending troops to missions abroad. While Russia and Ukraine have sent sizable forces to the Balkans and Iraq, respectively, as well as observers to other United Nations missions, this chapter restricts itself to operations within the NIS boundaries. The regional operations are common among the NIS because out-of-region states and organizations have consciously avoided authorizing or engaging in significant peace operations within the region. The NIS take care of their own, so to speak, and they have launched four major regional operations in the last decade and a half under the auspices of either the regional interstate organization, the Commonwealth of Independent States (CIS), or of subregional agreements negotiated by individual NIS governments on bilateral or trilateral bases.[1] Questions have been raised outside the region as to whether these NIS engagements meet international standards for peace operations. Of the regional chapters in this volume, this one is unique in that it is the only one that addresses disagreements about the conceptual definition of a peace operation.

This chapter begins by briefly analyzing why outsiders leave NIS operations to the governments and organizations of the NIS themselves. It then turns to the doctrinal legal and regulatory background that underpins Russian and CIS peace operations activities, and it describes CIS experiments with multinational peacekeeping in Tajikistan, the two operations in Georgia, and the Moldova (Transdnestrian) mission. Due to questions that have arisen about whether NIS operations can be properly described as international peace missions, the next two sections focus on their legal aspects and compare them to international standards. The chapter then shifts its focus to the recent formation of new institutions that could (but do not yet) serve as mechanisms for NIS operations. They include the intraregional Collective Security Treaty Organization (CSTO), the Shanghai Cooperation Organization

(SCO), the GUAM (Georgia, Ukraine, Azerbaijan, and Moldova) group, and the Community of Democratic Choice. The chapter ends by assessing the prospects for peace support within the CIS.[2]

A Region Largely on Its Own

Historically, the UN's international peace support and crisis response operations have largely been influenced by the interests of major powers. Thus, the international community was not prepared for the conflicts that erupted in the very heart of a former superpower, as was the case in post-Soviet territories during the 1990s. Apprehension about the political situation of the former Soviet Union was so high that not one of the four major intra-CIS peace operations conducted in Tajikistan, Georgia, and Moldova received a UN mandate. The level of UN involvement was limited to relatively passive observation missions.

Broader regional organizations were also reluctant to enter into NIS internal affairs. The most ambitious was the Organization for Security and Cooperation in Europe (OSCE), which in 1993 approved a mandate for a full-scale OSCE peace support operation in Nagorno-Karabakh. For the first time in history, an OSCE operation containing a strong military element was planned for deployment in a conflict area. However, the shaky cease-fire in Nagorno-Karabakh was broken as the focus shifted to securing finances and negotiating national military contributions. Subsequently, the conflict returned to a stage of armed confrontation, and consensus within the OSCE regarding the peacekeeping operation dissolved. The operation was aborted before it even started. The OSCE ultimately placed some small observation missions in post-Soviet areas. The most prominent of these missions was undertaken in Transdnestria/Moldova with the support of the European Union.

Although NATO immediately invited the fifteen new states to join the North-Atlantic Cooperation Council, a forum for potential interaction with the NIS, the Alliance remained reluctant to get involved in post-Soviet conflicts.[3] During the course of bilateral contacts and high-level meetings with leaders from Georgia, Azerbaijan, Armenia, and Moldova, the issue of conflict resolution was constantly on the table, yet only Georgia from time to time—beginning as early as the first half of the 1990s—seemed interested in learning whether NATO might carry out certain peacekeeping functions in its territory. In the mid-2000s, after Mikhail Saakashvili's government came to power in Tbilisi, the nature of NATO–Georgian negotiations changed. Georgian authorities announced their interest in becoming a member of NATO in the future. On the one hand, this was an invitation for NATO to get more involved in Georgian affairs; on the other hand, it complicated Georgia's application for NATO membership, since NATO's Charter states that no future NATO member state can, at the moment of its entrance into the organization, be a party to either an internal or external conflict.

Thus, the conflict resolution role that outsiders played in the NIS remained low in the decade and a half following the dissolution of the Soviet Union. Far more influential were the internal actors, including Russia, the key regional power.

A CIS Experiment with Multinational Peacekeeping: The Case of Tajikistan

A full-scale international peacekeeping operation was launched in Tajikistan in October 1993, following one of the bloodiest stages of the Tajik civil war. After months of armed conflict between different clans and ethnic groups, resulting in the loss of tens of thousands of lives, a new leadership was installed in Dushanbe, the capital city. In response to formal appeals for assistance from Dushanbe, the heads of the CIS states adopted joint statements on the situation in Tajikistan in October 1992 and January 1993. In September 1993, after a serious increase in tensions inside Tajikistan and on the Tajik-Afghan border, the CIS finally agreed to organize a multilateral peacekeeping force for Tajikistan.

Initially it was decided that military contingents from Russia, Kazakhstan, Kyrgyzstan, and Uzbekistan, together with Tajik governmental units, would form the force. However, the Tajik forces were later excluded due to alleged political prejudice. The majority of the forces were provided by Russia: around six thousand troops of the 201st motorized infantry division, which had been located in the area since Soviet times, were strengthened by rotating Russian contingents. Small contingents also came from Uzbekistan and Kazakhstan, but the Kyrgyz parliament objected to the participation of its soldiers in operations outside national borders, limiting Kyrgyz participation to staff liaison officers. In the end, there were fewer than ten thousand troops in the operation, as opposed to the planned number of twenty-five thousand. While these forces were overseeing the disengagement and disarmament of the belligerents, the key task of sealing the border between Tajikistan and Afghanistan was carried out by Russian troops. The Russians guarded the border as a result of a formal request by the Tajik government. A peace settlement was reached in 1997, but the situation is still volatile and could flare up again.

A small number of United Nations military observers were located in the area. The presidents of five CIS states—including Russia, Tajikistan, and Kazakhstan—appealed to the UN secretary-general in 1995 to launch a full-scale, UN-mandated peacekeeping operation in Tajikistan. The request was turned down: neither the UN nor any other international organization expressed any readiness to undertake efforts to stabilize the situation and reestablish peace in the Central Asian area. As a result, the CIS took matters into its own hands, created a peacekeeping operation, and played an important stabilizing role.

The operation was formally completed in 2000. Collective peacekeeping forces were dismissed, and most of them were reorganized into a CIS rapid deployment force (RDF) for the Central Asian region. In 2003 the RDF came under CSTO leadership after that organization was put in charge of former CIS military-integrative responsibilities.

The Operation in South Ossetia/Georgia

Since 1992, when South Ossetian authorities expressed their desire for independence from Georgia, long-standing historical frictions between Ossetians and Georgians were reawakened. The situation was complicated by the involvement of numerous armed volunteers from North Ossetia, a territory belonging to the Russian Federation, who actively supported their "southern compatriots" and favored a "reunited Ossetia." Negotiations between Russia and Georgia were arranged in Dagomys, Russia, and the Dagomys Agreement on Governing the Peaceful Settlement of the Conflict in South Ossetia was produced on June 24, 1992. The operation was mandated by the Russian-Georgian interstate agreement.

The conflict parties and Russia make up the Joint Control Commission: essentially a civilian political organ that is responsible for the settlement of the conflict and that coordinates with the governments of Georgia, Russia, and the authorities of South Ossetia. The conflict parties and Russia each provide a component to the peacekeeping, or "patrolling," force that is guided by the commission. As the third party, Russia and its forces played a critical role. Since the beginning of trilateral patrolling, the cease-fire has mostly held. Between 1996 and 2004, the operation was considered a reasonably successful example of international peacekeeping.

Since 2004, after the so-called "Rose Revolution" in Georgia and the election of Mikhail Saakashvili as the new president, the central authorities in Tbilisi changed their policy concerning attempts to reestablish full control over secessionist regions of Georgia, warning that, if required, force would be used. A subsequent armed operation led to the reestablishment of full state control over the semi-autonomous region of Adjaria, demonstrating the seriousness of the Georgian authorities' intentions.

Since then, a shaky balance of forces has existed in the South Ossetian region. The results of a referendum in 2006 demonstrated the willingness of most South Ossetians to become independent of both Russia and Georgia. It was dismissed by the Georgian government. Ossetian authorities insist on the continuation of the presence of Russian peacekeepers in contested areas. Georgian authorities, however, have said that the Russians should withdraw as soon as possible, with the EU and NATO possibly providing a disengagement contingent until the initiation of new negotiations over the political status of the area. At present, the contingent force includes a Russian military component of five hundred Russian soldiers from a regiment of the 45th Guard motorized rifle division. However, the postrevolution Georgian authorities no longer endorse their presence. As a consequence, the ongoing peace operation that initially started on the basis of a Russian-

Georgian interstate agreement can no longer be seen as possessing de jure status.

Stalemate in Abkhazia/Georgia

While armed hostilities in the Abkhazian territory of Georgia had been under way for three years, there was no peacekeeping involvement until a Georgian–Abkhazian agreement called for a cease-fire and disengagement on May 14, 1994, and for multinational CIS supervision. The agreement centered on the disengagement of Georgian and Abkhazian forces clashing along the Inguri river. The mandate, agreed to by Georgia, Abkhazia, and Russia, provided for the creation of a twelve-kilometer-wide "security zone" along the Inguri. The Georgian troops were to withdraw, and troops from Russia were to protect the river and guard numerous returning refugees, specifically in the Galsky district, who had left the Abkhazian area during the violent stage of the civil war.

The peacekeeping force received its mandate from the CIS. Around 1,100 Russian military personnel were deployed to the area for the duration of the conflict. Their mission was to protect military installations and humanitarian bases without interfering in hostilities between the conflict parties.

The operation in Abkhazia has not yet resulted in a stable peace. The inability to resolve the refugee problem has hindered efforts toward peace. In addition, attempts from both the Georgian and Abkhazian parties to burden peacekeepers with tasks outside their mandates as impartial mediators have slowed the process. Nevertheless, the peacekeeping force did manage to contribute to the stabilization of the region: Five thousand tons of humanitarian assistance from the UN and OSCE were distributed to the population, as well as 200,000 tons of economic and humanitarian assistance from Russia and Georgia; nine thousand refugees returned to their native areas; ninety-two pieces of armored vehicles and heavy military equipment with five thousand rounds of ammunition were confiscated from the warring parties; seventy unauthorized military groupings were disarmed; and over eight hundred factories, schools, hospitals, and other public sites were cleared of mines.

The post–2004 situation in Abkhazia resembles that in South Ossetia. In accordance with a 1994 agreement, Georgia is calling for the full withdrawal of the two remaining Russian military contingents. A significant portion of the Abkhazian population, however, requested and received Russian passports upon expiration of their former Soviet passports, rather than apply for Georgian documents. Thus, Moscow established a relatively legitimate reason for insisting on the protection of Russian "semicitizens" in Abkhazia on the basis of international law.

The Georgian government recognizes that if the Russian military forces were to leave, some intermediate peacekeeping force would still be required. Georgia has expressed an interest in having either a UN-mandated international force or a NATO contingent fulfill this role.

Limited Success Freezing an Awkward Equilibrium:
The Trilateral Operation in Moldova/Transdnestria

The roots of another conflict where multinational forces have been involved in the NIS can be traced back to 1992, when the Transdnestrian area of independent Moldova, formerly the Soviet Republic of Moldova, rejected subordination to the Moldovan government. A separate Transdnestrian Moldavian Republic was proclaimed in the region.

Tensions exploded in the summer of 1992, resulting in mass armed violence between supporters of the Chisinau central authorities and proponents of Transdnestrian separation. A chain reaction of uncontrolled mass clashes spread, and much civilian blood was spilled. Under these circumstances, a trilateral preliminary political agreement was achieved between Russian, Moldovan, and Transdnestrian leaders. On July 21, 1992, the Russian President Boris Yeltsin and the Moldovan President Mircea Snegur signed a basic document titled "Agreements on the principles of peaceful settlement of the armed conflict in the Transdnestria region of the Republic of Moldova." The third signatory was the Transdnestrian leader Smirnov. This agreement called for quick disengagement operations to be performed jointly by Russian, Moldovan, and Transdnestrian contingents, and it was followed by trilateral patrolling of the area to prevent both the unauthorized use of arms and further population clashes. It is important to stress that locally involved and biased military contingents of the former 14th Soviet army, which had been stationed in Moldova for decades, were not used in this disengagement stage. Instead, battalions of the 45th motorized division of the Leningrad military district and the 106th airborne division were relocated to the area. After disengagement and a cease-fire were reached, the trilateral peacekeeping forces (around 1,800 men) were composed of troops from four Russian battalions, three Moldovan battalions, and three Transdnestrian battalions.

A United Control Commission was created as the main multilateral political organ to supervise peacekeeping efforts and to be responsible for further diplomatic negotiations. Formally, all military authorities involved in the peacekeeping came under its jurisdiction. Although the negotiations did not deal with the full political settlement of the Transdnestrian separatists, the peacekeeping stage of the operations effectively achieved its goals. The trilateral military contingent patrolled the area, and no significant cases of armed violence were reported in the region.

In 2006, the European Union, by invitation of Moldovan authorities, introduced a small observation mission on the border of Moldova and Ukraine in the Transdnestria region. Russia faced increased international pressure to withdraw its residual contingents from the area. As was the case in Georgian secessionist areas, the two parties to the Transdnestria-Moldovan conflict insisted on the deployment of different peacekeepers. The nonrecognized Transdnestrian Moldavian Republic insisted on the continuation of the mission by Russian peacekeepers, while the central Moldovan authorities welcomed the growing readiness of the EU to step in as the chief conflict moderator.

Is It "Peace Support"? Debates over Legal Aspects of Peace Support Operations in the NIS

Clarifications should be made concerning the character of conflict resolution actions undertaken by Russia and the other CIS states. The UN Charter states that regional organizations or agreements may deal with matters relating to regional and local conflicts if enforcement on a state-level does not work. Moreover, mediation, peacekeeping, peace building, and preventive diplomacy activities can be undertaken not only under a UN Security Council mandate, but also under the provisions of regional interstate structures. However, coercive peace enforcement that goes against the will of the conflict parties cannot be arranged by states or groups of states without the appropriate decision and mandate from the UN Security Council.

Chapter VII of the UN Charter defines enforcement as actions including the use of armed force as authorized by the Security Council against the will of the target state. When actions are undertaken in accordance with a formal request, the agreement of the state on whose territory the conflict takes place, or with the consent of several states involved in the conflict, international involvement is not considered enforcement.

It is important to realize that the use of armed forces per se is not necessarily a feature of enforcement actions. All peacekeeping operations initiated by requests or with the consent of the conflicting parties involve the presence or use of armed forces. During peacekeeping operations, for example, armed violence could be used by peacekeepers against unauthorized local armed groupings or as a self-defense measure against local forces refusing to observe a cease-fire. Such uses of force do not change the legal nature of an operation. If undertaken with the agreement of the conflicting sides, including above all the legitimate authorities of the state on whose territory the conflict takes place, it does not constitute enforcement under the UN Charter.

As a result, none of the known collective operations initiated on the territories of NIS states between 1992 and 1995 can be considered enforcement according to Chapter VII. Legal agreements between the conflicting sides were decided upon prior to the start of the actions, and the actions were undertaken with the consent of the parties on whose territories the conflicts emerged. The agreement for South Ossetia involved all interested parties: Georgia, South Ossetia, North Ossetia, and Russia. Representatives from each of these parties were included in the multilateral Political Control Commission. Nevertheless, this operation remains in legal limbo today due to Georgia's request that Russia withdraw its forces. In Moldova/Transdnestria, the initial agreement was between the Presidents of Moldova and Russia. The agreement to start force disengagement was also cosigned by the highest political leader of the nonstate party to the conflict—President Smirnov of the unrecognized Transdnestrian Moldovan Republic. The other two operations, in Abkhazia/Georgia and Tajikistan, were mandated by the CIS after the agreement of each CIS head of state. However, the request of the Georgian authorities that the Russian forces withdraw means that the Abkhazia operation may also be open to legal questioning.

Comparing Peacekeeping Efforts of Russia in the New Independent States with International Standards

Within the political circles of Russia and CIS countries themselves, there are different basic approaches to the definition of operations in CIS conflict areas involving the use of force. Some politicians and analysts refer to the provisions of the CIS Charter, which provide that CIS decisions can be agreed among the "interested member states" while other member states can stay outside the agreement. More specifically, the latter states can remain outside the agreement if they do not oppose the decision in principle, but simply have no significant interests involved. The proponents of this approach argue that the notion of "regional agreements" in Chapter VIII of the UN Charter covers both nonuniversal agreements that are not necessarily signed by every country in the region as well as agreements on matters of regional conflicts signed by the interested parties. Under such provisions, the Georgian/Abkhazian/Russian operation or the operation in Tajikistan could be considered collectively as "CIS authorized operations."

However, such an approach goes too far, and the CIS administrators in Minsk and the Moscow-based Staff for CIS Military Cooperation adopted a different approach for years. Accordingly, only the multilateral operation in Tajikistan was considered a full-scale CIS peacekeeping operation, with the operation in Abkhazia/Georgia being almost purely Russian despite CIS approval. The operation in Tajikistan had a clear CIS mandate signed by the heads of all CIS states. It is the only operation in which command was subordinated directly to the CIS Council of Heads of State, the Council of Foreign Affairs Ministers, and the Council of Defense Ministers. The operation was administrated not by national ministries of defense, but by the international Staff for CIS Military Cooperation, which appointed commanders on a rotating basis. From this point of view, only this operation and, to a lesser degree, the Abkhazian case can be legally regarded as regional peacekeeping CIS operations. The other cases—in the territories of Georgia (in South Ossetia) and Moldova (in Transdnestria)—are considered trilateral operations on the basis of interstate agreements.

The aggressive operations carried out internally by the decision of Russian authorities and with the use of Russian forces on the territory of the Russian Federation in North Ossetia/Ingushetia and in Chechnya were formally considered domestic police type operations aimed at reestablishing internal civil order. These actions do not have an international, interstate character. They were neither peacekeeping nor peace enforcement by definition or action.

From the perspective of Russian and CIS/CSTO authorities, there have been no cases of peace enforcement in the NIS till now, and thus no need for a UN mandate. Chapter VIII credentials legitimized the CIS, and now the CSTO, as regional security organizations able to provide peacekeeping based upon regional mandates. Nevertheless, politicians and analysts in Western and CIS countries constantly disagree over the nature and character of armed actions in conflict areas within the CIS territories. Several factors common to most of these operations influence the attitudes of the international community toward CIS conflict resolution activities.

One factor is the lack of external authorization, especially from the UN Security Council. This lack of external authorization exists in spite of the fact that the NIS states, including Russia, remain in principle in favor of the internationalization of conflict resolution in the NIS. They regularly inform the UN about the status of the operations in Tajikistan, Georgia, and Moldova. Nevertheless, UN circles continue to express great doubts about UN readiness to undertake any formal international peacekeeping missions on NIS territory that go beyond the deployment of small numbers of unarmed observers.

A second factor is the seemingly obvious violation of the international requirement that mediators and peacekeepers should not represent countries or forces that have vested or selfish interests in the region of conflict. That is the reason why, for example, peacekeepers from Scandinavia, Canada, and Japan are considered highly suitable for deployment in Africa or other regions where their countries do not have any direct current interests or a historic record of involvement. According to this rule, all of the peace operations within the NIS violate this tradition, since all of the participants in these operations have had vested interests in their outcomes as well as a record of historic involvements in Georgia, Tajikistan, and Moldova.

Nonetheless, recent practice indicates that reliance on organizations and forces from within the region of an operation is generally becoming more acceptable, particularly as the UN has strained to find the manpower to embark on its own missions. This has become the standard for missions throughout Africa, and it was and remains the case for the missions in the former Yugoslavia.

NIS conflict resolution practices are innovative because they involve the opposing sides in the peacekeeping processes. For example, in the case of South Ossetia both Georgian and South Ossetian military battalions patrolled together with the Russian troops. In Transdnestria, three Moldovan and three Transdnestrian battalions compose the peacekeeping force in collaboration with four Russian battalions. Reports show that joint patrolling with opposing parties has been successful, although in the early stages effectively combining the multinational contingents required a significant amount of effort. (In the case of Tajikistan, where the participating sides and CIS officials abided by international standards, the Tajik contingents supplied to international peacekeeping forces were excluded from the operation during the later stages.)

A third source of debates is whether NIS operations conform to international standards regarding rules of engagement. NIS operations are often criticized for their use of heavy weapons, war-like tactics, and standard armed forces in civilian areas instead of specially trained and equipped "purely peacekeeper" contingents. In earlier years, when there was a notable lack of specifically trained soldiers and officers, such practices were extremely common. After 1994, the situation changed: special training facilities were expanded, and Russian conscripts were no longer sent to external conflict zones. Throughout the 2000s, all Russian military peacekeeping troops have been assembled on a contractual basis and have undergone training comparable to that received by Russian peacekeepers deployed to Yugoslavia by the UN.

As for the tactical and technical characteristics of NIS operations, they have begun to resemble patterns used by the UN and NATO in areas such as the former Yugoslavia. Such UN and NATO peace operations use a set number of practices that have evolved during the 1990s and early 2000s:

- a shift toward earlier involvement so as to prevent mass violence entirely;
- the use of force beyond self-defense to cause belligerents to disengage, push them out of conflict areas, coerce them to obey cease-fires, and pressure them to give up their weaponry and missions;
- the deployment of troops with more advanced or heavy weapons, including tanks, artillery, air support, radio frequency jamming, and means of technical reconnaissance; such weaponry provides UN forces with real combat capabilities in addition to their diplomatic skills.

Practically all of the aforementioned practices are applicable to the operations involving Russian armed forces in the NIS conflict regions. Western operations in the Balkans (Bosnia, Kosovo) and Russian operations in the NIS, regardless of legal and political differences, have demonstrated similar peacekeeping tactics in ethnically motivated conflicts.

Nevertheless, Russia and the West have always engaged in mutual criticism and nonrecognition of the other's peace support practices, and there is little reason to believe the situation will significantly improve with the establishment of the Collective Security Treaty Organization (CSTO), other regional arrangements in the CIS, and international arrangements such as the Shanghai Cooperation Organization. These developments may only serve to further complicate matters and arouse old contradictions and problems concerning the NIS and Russian peace support efforts.

The CSTO Creates New Instruments for Regional Collective Security

In September 2002, the charter documents for a new organization came into effect, marking a significant change in the geostrategic situation of the NIS region. The conversion of the Collective Security Treaty into the Collective Security Treaty Organization (CSTO), a full-scale international organization, began during the Moscow session of the CIS Collective Security Council on May 14, 2002.[4] After the initiation of the CSTO, the military and security integration of the participating NIS was essentially taken out of the CIS framework, and the CSTO became a self-supporting mechanism of integration placed under the CSTO framework. The Staff for the Coordination of CIS Military Cooperation, which formerly supervised operations in Tajikistan and Abkhazia, passed their responsibilities to the CSTO Military Staff.

The CSTO has claimed three regions of collective security under its protection: Eastern (Belarus-Russia), Caucasian (Armenia-Russia) and Central Asian. While the first two are familiar areas of concern, conflict resolution in Central Asia is growing in importance. The very formation of the CSTO was expedited because of a common threat to the security of Russia and Central Asia posed by Taliban-dominated Afghanistan in 2000–1. In May 2001, before the creation of the CSTO, a decision was made to form a Collective Rapid Deployment Force (CDRF) for the Central Asian Region of Collective Security under the CIS aegis. In the summer of 2001, before the events of September 11, the force consisted of fifteen hundred troops, with battalions from Kazakhstan, Kyrgyzstan, Russia, and Tajikistan. In 2004, the CRDF was upgraded to eleven battalions, with military headquarters in Bishkek and the air force base in Kant. The base in Kant contains an international staff of up to eight hundred people, which greatly contributes to the deployability of the CDRF during potential violent outbreaks that must be immediately pacified. The CSTO secretary-general explained that "the time for decision-making concerning the use of the CRDF does not exceed hour-and-a half to two hours in case of a sharpening of the local situation. Just several more hours would be required by the military to relocate the contingent into the conflict region."[5]

Since 2005 the CSTO has fully replaced the CIS as the mechanism for military-political integration and peace support among the new independent states. One of its major goals is to establish a full-scale, collective CSTO force that integrates elements from each of the seven CSTO countries into a coordinated military and security machine. However, this is a strategic goal to be achieved in the second decade of the twenty-first century. Currently the CSTO contains a system of political and military command structures that can coordinate security and defense efforts of member states in real time. This system includes regular CSTO summits, which have taken the place of CIS summits. It also includes operation of the CSTO Council of Foreign Affairs Ministers, Defense Ministers, Secretaries of Security Councils, and Commanders of Border Guard Services. The CSTO Military Staff in Moscow is well connected to the general staff of the Russian armed forces.[6]

As noted above, the first operational element of the CSTO security system inherited from the CIS was the Rapid Deployment Forces for Central Asia. They have been drastically upgraded under CSTO guidance, and currently the CSTO is working on the creation of two more regional "fire brigades": a collective Russian-Belarusian force, and a Russian-Armenian crisis response force intended for the Southern Caucasus.

Since June 2005 military cadres from CSTO states can train and be certified in Russian defense academies and institutions at no cost, or at extremely reduced costs to their governments. Joint programs for the training of peacekeepers, antiterror, and antidrug specialists from all CSTO countries have also been organized.

In 2006, the process of elaborating a doctrine for the joint CSTO peace support system was finished. The system foresees the creation of Collective CSTO Peace Support Forces to be used under a UN mandate or a mandate of regional organizations.[7] An additional instrument under construction is the Collective Emergency Reaction Forces, which will be used in the territories of the CSTO during natural disasters and social emergencies.

One of the proposals debated in CSTO circles is the possibility of obtaining a UN mandate for the postconflict stabilization of the Tajik-Afghan border. A UN mandate would enable the CSTO to carry out this task in legal and practical conjunction with NATO. Since the mobile NATO Response Forces (NRF) reached full operational capability with twenty thousand men in 2006, it would be timely to coordinate a mode of potential interaction between NATO's NRF and CSTO Rapid Deployment Forces.

Other Regional Patterns in NIS Area with Peace Support Potential

The potential to engage in combined conflict resolution and peace operations may be extended by involving the Shanghai Cooperation Organization (SCO). The SCO arose out of a series of talks in 1996–2000 on the delineation of the border between China and a group of its post–Soviet neighbors (Russia, Kazakhstan, Kyrgyzstan, and Tajikistan).[8] After the initial security task was fulfilled, it was decided that the Shanghai group should remain in existence but that its efforts be redirected into a broader political and economic dialogue. In 2001, the "Shanghai five" group was converted into a political interstate organization, and it later adopted Uzbekistan as its sixth member.[9] But in the mid-2000s, a new "wave of observer's enlargement" took place, and Mongolia, Iran, Afghanistan, Pakistan, and India were all given observer status in the SCO. As the Chinese Xinhua News Agency proudly stated in connection with the SCO's fifth anniversary, the SCO member and observer states now cover one-fourth of the planet's landmass, and one out of three people on the globe lives in a SCO member or observer country.

Today, the SCO does not focus on security dilemmas as often as it emphasizes general political and diplomatic dialogue as well as economic and social issues. Thus, no serious integration of military infrastructures is envisaged. Nevertheless, meetings of defense ministers do take place, and joint military exercises have been conducted. The first was held in 2003 under a peace-keeping scenario, with one phase taking place in Kazakhstan and a second in China.

The former GUUAM (Georgia-Ukraine-Uzbekistan-Azerbaijan-Moldova) consortium, established in the 1990s as a counterforce against the CIS, lost Uzbekistan in 2006 after it shifted back to the Moscow-centered CSTO. Also in 2006 the smaller GUAM group announced that it would create a collective peacekeeping force, and that a corresponding legal framework would soon be adopted. As of June 2007 there is nothing of significance to report with regards to their progress.

Finally, at the peak of the "color revolutions," Kiev and Tbilisi initiated the creation of the CDC, the Community of Democratic Choice. In addition to Ukraine and Georgia, the CDC includes the Baltic states (all three of which would be in favor of an anti-Moscow posture for the alliance) plus Moldova, Romania, Slovenia, and Macedonia.[10] The CDC Alliance is formally registered as an interstate organization, but is not viewed as having any serious influence apart from supporting an "away-from-the-Post–Soviet Space" mentality in the three Baltic states. However, on multiple occasions CDC leaders have announced that the organization may develop its potential for conflict resolution and, subsequently, capacity to carry out peace operations.

Prospects for Future Peace Support

In the NIS at least three different sets of conflicts, or political situations, need to be addressed with regard to peace operations requirements. First, despite an effort lasting a decade and a half, four NIS conflicts remain unresolved and may require the continuation of old arrangements or new peacekeeping operations in the near future. Solutions in political, interethnic, and territorial integrity have not yet been found between Nagorno-Karabakh, Abkhazia and Georgia, South Ossetia and Georgia, and Transdnestria and Moldova. Nonrecognized, self-proclaimed states that have emerged during the course of all four of these secessionist conflicts now possess several strong characteristics of statehood. The recognized states on whose territory they have emerged—Azerbaijan, Georgia, and Moldova, respectively—continuously express political and economic interest in their reabsorption.

Second, there are residual postconflict problems in areas such as Chechnya and Dagestan in Russia, as well as in Tajikistan, Kyrgyzstan, and Uzbekistan. But in these cases, the conflict-hosting state is relatively willing to oversee or facilitate postconflict reconstruction. While sporadic eruption of hostilities is possible, especially because these conflicts have deep roots, there seems to be no direct need for international peacekeeping operations.

Third, the phenomenon of "color revolutions"—internally motivated regime changes with elements of civil disobedience—may create new precedents in the NIS and foster situations that might require international interference to avoid human losses and social chaos. It is too early to predict whether countries like Belarus, Turkmenistan (which happens to be entering a period of political turnover amongst the ruling elite), Uzbekistan, and Kyrgyzstan will experience social upheaval that may require international involvement in the future. In past conflicts in Ukraine, Georgia, and Kyrgyzstan from 2000–05, the international community, as well as the narrower NIS community, were caught unprepared and were not able to propose any mediated solutions. In the future, the international community must be more wary of those transitional states in the NIS that are susceptible to "color revolutions."

The above residual conflicts or situations are sources of instability in the NIS, but the region is still not yet fully prepared to cope with them collectively. Russia-centric or Russia-dominated mechanisms for regional conflict mediation were adopted by the NIS throughout the 1990s instead of truly comprehensive CIS schemes. In addition, Russia's efforts in Tajikistan, Georgia, and Moldova were never tied into one unified and centrally planned system. Russian efforts over the last few years to provide better integration have run afoul of the rising independence and self-assertion of the elites in Georgia, Moldova, and some Central Asian states.

Although it does not yet have a concrete record of successfully implemented peace support solutions, the CSTO has more potential to serve as an integrating regional peacekeeping organization than did the CIS. The CSTO's combined forces are preparing for operations that could occur under a UN or possibly OSCE mandate, if not under the CSTO's own authority.

The CSTO's readiness to serve under external mandate runs parallel with another important change: the self-imposed restrictions on outsiders who wish to enter the post–Soviet territories have been, for the most part, removed. The EU, NATO, and extraregional powers such as the United States, China, Iran, and Turkey are gradually getting more involved in conflict resolution, economic projects, and politics in the post–Soviet territories. Russian public opinion has increasingly recognized the South Caucasus and Central Asia as "not being ours" or, to be more precise, "not necessarily being fully ours." Simultaneously, the Russian ruling establishment is not yet interested in political, military, and economic withdrawal from these areas, or at least not to the extent that it withdrew from the Baltic states.

Although "grand security architecture" issues remain under the control of Russia as the biggest actor in post–Soviet military infrastructure, it has become impossible for the West to negotiate or resolve military and security issues solely with Moscow. Some security issues have been relocated into the "CSTO basket," with Russia-dominated yet multilateral diplomatic procedures and mechanisms.

The time has come for Moscow to recognize that the conflict resolution process in Moldova and Transdnestria, Georgia and Abkhazia, and Georgia and South Ossetia can no longer be conducted without participation from the European Union, NATO, and the Council of Europe. At the same time, Western institutions seeking a role involving mediation in the NIS should recognize that peacekeeping must proceed in cooperation with Russia—not "instead of Russia."

Thus, the NIS has gained both specific and broad experience with respect to peace support in the 1990s and 2000s. There is still much debate as to whether some missions fall in the category of peace support practices. Obviously, extensive thought must go into qualifying and classifying the stages of conflict resolution, and there have been several discrepancies concerning the NIS cases. While some of these cases really do not qualify as peace support operations, others fit UN standards even though a formal UN mandate was not applied. At the same time, if we compare NIS activities to all varieties of UN-mandated operations, "coalition operations," NATO missions, and unilateral and unmandated U.S. actions in conflict areas, they do not seem so different after all.

Mutual recognition of general peace support practices between the West and NIS—with meticulous critiques, analytical approaches, and respect for legitimacy—will be essential to future cooperation within the international community and for achieving effective international peace support.

Chapter 9

Latin America: Haiti and Beyond

JOHN T. FISHEL

Latin American states have a long and distinguished history of participation in peacekeeping operations, and they have also been major players in developments related to international law and institutions. This chapter looks at Latin American peacekeeping efforts from the 1940s to the 1990s, and then it examines Latin American peacekeeping training institutions and activities.[1] The rest of the chapter gives a detailed account of Latin American countries' contributions to the ongoing United Nations Stabilization Mission in Haiti, or MINUSTAH. This case study illustrates factors that can influence Latin American participation in peacekeeping operations and how the MINUSTAH experience has in turn shaped current trends in Latin American governments' approaches to peacekeeping.

The Latin American Role in Peacekeeping and Other Peace Operations

Latin Americans trace their involvement in international organizations to the Congress of Panama organized by Simón Bolívar—known as the Liberator—in 1826.[2] The Latin American countries were strong supporters of the League of Nations during the interwar years, and several were among the most active of the founding members of the United Nations in 1945. The Americas' own regional international organization traces its origins back to the Commercial Bureau of the American Republics, which was established as the Secretariat of the International Union of American Republics on April 14, 1890, at the first International Conference of the American States in Washington, D.C. This organization became the Bureau of the American Republics in 1902, the Pan-American Union in 1910, and the Secretariat of the Organization of American States (OAS) in 1948 (following the OAS's establishment on April 30, 1948).[3]

The first specific instance of Latin American militaries engaging in peacekeeping came in the wake of the Chaco War, fought between Bolivia and Paraguay from 1932 to 1935. Latin American troops were provided to monitor the ceasefire, disengagement, and establishment of permanent borders called for in the peace treaty. Uruguay proudly lists this action as its first formal participation in peacekeeping operations. It thus has more than seventy years of PKO experience.[4]

In 1941 Ecuador and Peru went to war over their disputed boundary in the Amazon region. The war ended with the signing of the Protocol of Peace, Friendship and Boundaries between Peru and Ecuador (Rio Protocol) in 1942; the peace was guaranteed by four American powers: Argentina, Brazil, Chile, and the United States. The guarantor powers assisted in the demarcation of the border and in terminating the several flare-ups of fighting in subsequent years, most significantly in 1981.

As Paul Kennedy points out, the Latin American states have been major contributors to UN PKOs since Argentinean and Latin American military observers joined the first two UN PKOs: Argentine and Chilean observers in the United Nations Truce Supervision Organization (UNTSO) in the Middle East, deployed in 1948; and Chilean and Uruguayan observers in the United Nations Military Observer Group in India and Pakistan (UNMOGIP), deployed in 1949.[5] Since that time, Latin American states have been prominent among the peacekeepers in nearly all of the UN's PKOs. Brazil played leading roles in the United Nations Angola Verification Missions (UNAVEM I-III) and in the United Nations Operation in Mozambique (ONUMOZ) in the early 1990s, and again in East Timor starting with the United Nations Transitional Administration in East Timor (UNTAET). Uruguay was also a major player in ONUMOZ and has been actively involved in the current mission to the Congo (United Nations Organization Mission in the Democratic Republic of Congo, MONUC). Brigadier General Luis Block Urban of Peru was acting forces commander of the United Nations Mission for the Referendum in Western Sahara (MINURSO) in 1992. On a larger scale, Argentina has contributed two force commanders to the United Nations Peacekeeping Force in Cyprus (UNFICYP), after having contributed a battalion to the United Nations Protection Force (UNPROFOR) in Bosnia and Herzegovina.

The First Major Latin American PKO: Dominican Republic

Perhaps the most significant PKO mission for Latin America prior to the 1990s was the Inter-American Peace Force (IAPF), created in 1965 for deployment in the Dominican Republic.[6] Of particular interest to this study is the fact that the IAPF's mission was conducted under the auspices of the OAS. The mission grew out of the unilateral U.S. intervention to terminate an internal conflict between the Constitutionalist (rebel) and the Loyalist (provisional government) forces. Dominating the intervention was the American fear that Fidel Castro and the Communists controlled the Constitutionalist movement, a fear shared by most of the American republics—even some of those that ultimately voted against OAS involvement.

The OAS resolution that authorized the mission passed by fourteen votes to five. Brazil, Honduras, Nicaragua, Paraguay, Costa Rica, and El Salvador agreed to provide personnel to the mission. Implicit to the passage of the resolution was the quid pro quo that a Latin American officer would be the force commander. This role fell to Brazil since it contributed the largest number of troops—1,130 men. In addition to the countries that voted against the resolution (Chile, Ecuador, Mexico, Peru, and Uruguay), other potential contributors decided against supplying forces, either for internal political reasons or, in Argentina's case, due to dissatisfaction with the prominence of Brazil's role.

Although the American diplomats and military on the ground had desired U.S. command of the IAPF, they had been overruled by the president on the advice of the U.S. ambassador to the OAS, Ellsworth Bunker, who, as the leading member of the three-man OAS negotiating team, was the de facto head of the political mission to the Dominican Republic. The Brazilian force commander, Lt. Gen. Hugo Panasco Alvim, was given a staff that was dominated by Americans, although he was able to overrule his deputy commander, U.S. Lt. Gen. Bruce Palmer, and select a Latin American officer as his chief of staff. Thus, the staff of the IAPF included a Brazilian commander, an American deputy commander, and Latin Americans as chief of staff and as staff secretaries of personnel and administration (C-1), information and security (intelligence) (C-2), and plans and operations (C-3). Americans headed logistics and services (C-4) and communications (C-5). The deputies to the Latin Americans were from the United States, while the deputies to the American staff principals were from Latin America. The bulk of each staff section, however, was drawn from the U.S. military—in particular from Palmer's U.S. Forces Joint Staff Directorate for Military Affairs of the Inter-American Armed Force (Inter-American Armed Force was an earlier name for the IAPF).

The IAPF forces were divided into U.S. Forces, Dominican Republic—under the command of General Palmer—and the Latin American Brigade. The latter was under the command of a Latin American officer selected by General Alvim and consisted of a Brazilian battalion and the Fraternity Battalion, which was made up of a Brazilian marine company and troops from Honduras, Nicaragua, and Paraguay, along with Costa Rican police.[7]

What is significant about this structure is that it (a) set a precedent for Latin American command of a PKO force that included U.S. forces and finessed the argument about subordination of U.S. military to non-U.S. command; (b) demonstrated that the Latin Americans in general, and the Brazilians in particular, were fully capable of providing both command of forces and staff principals to control those forces; and (c) that the Latin American militaries were able to resist U.S. demands for certain leading staff positions.

Grenada and the Regional Security System (RSS)

In 1983 a bloody coup d'état was mounted by one faction of the Marxist government of the anglophone Caribbean island of Grenada. The Organization of Eastern Caribbean States (OECS), along with Caribbean Community (CARICOM) member Barbados, appealed to the United States to assist in restoring order. The Reagan administration, already concerned about the Communist threat as well as the safety of medical students at St. George's Medical School on Grenada, leaped at the request and mounted a military operation to accomplish the multiple objectives of rescuing the mostly American medical students, restoring order, and eliminating Communist influence on the island. Along with the U.S. forces went a composite battalion of military and police from the OECS states and Barbados under the command of Barbados Defense Force Brigadier Rudyard Lewis.

Out of that composite battalion grew the Regional Security System (RSS)—a land/sea military and police force with a permanent staff and headquarters in Barbados.[8] The RSS has conducted numerous disaster-relief and counter-narcotics operations, and it has assisted its members in putting down several prison riots. It has been advised, trained, and equipped by the United States and United Kingdom since its inception. It has also conducted a variety of exercises with other anglophone Caribbean forces, and it has held discussions with the Dominican Republic about the latter joining the RSS. Its current members are Antigua and Barbuda, Barbados, Dominica, Grenada, St. Kitts and Nevis, St. Lucia, and St. Vincent and the Grenadines.

The Multinational Force and Observers in the Sinai and MOMEP

The 1979 Treaty of Peace signed by Egypt and Israel called for deployment of a UN peacekeeping force and observers in the Sinai.[9] It was envisaged in the treaty that the Second United Nations Emergency Force (UNEF II), deployed in the wake of the 1973 Arab–Israeli War, would provide the peacekeeping forces. However, the mandate of UNEF II lapsed in July 1979 and was not renewed. The existing U.S. Sinai Field Mission took over the verification functions. After two years of unsuccessful efforts to deploy a new UN force, a protocol to the Treaty of Peace was signed that established a new non-UN mission, the Multinational Force and Observers (MFO), to carry out the security provisions of the 1979 treaty. The MFO was given the status of an international organization, with its headquarters in Rome.

Among the initial force providers to the MFO were Colombia and Uruguay.[10] Today Colombia continues to provide an infantry battalion while Uruguay provides a unit of eighty-seven engineers. Approximately half the Uruguayan troops have had previous PKO experience in the MFO, and most have served in UN PKO missions. All have been trained in the Uruguayan Army Peace Keeping Operations School (Escuela de Operaciones de Paz del Ejército).

The guarantors of the Rio Protocol of 1942 established the Military Observer Mission Ecuador-Peru (MOMEP) to supervise the disengagement of Ecuadorian and Peruvian forces after the Itamaraty Declaration of Peace of February 17, 1995, ended the January 1995 border conflict.[11] As noted above, the guarantor powers were Argentina, Brazil, Chile, and the United States. Argentina tended to support Peru, while Chile leaned toward Ecuador. Brazil and the United States were more the honest brokers. Political leadership of MOMEP was largely in the hands of senior diplomats from the guarantors and the parties (Ecuador and Peru) and generally worked out of Brasília. The military mission on the ground was lean and operated with an international staff made up of officers from both the guarantors and the parties.

MOMEP proper included ten officers from each of the guarantor powers. They operated under a Superior Consultative Committee "coordinated" by a Brazilian general. The Committee also included two senior officers from the parties (either generals or colonels) and colonels from each of the four guarantors. Together they performed key traditional staff functions. The colonels were "dual hatted" as commanders of the national contingents, which were composed of sixteen observers, four from each of the guarantors. In addition, each party provided eight observers. The United States provided logistics and transportation support with a Joint Task Force (JTF-Safe Borders) of sixty personnel and four helicopters. The unique feature of MOMEP was the full integration of the parties into the operation. Even more important is the fact that MOMEP showed the full capabilities of the Latin American participants, including the parties, to command and control a difficult and complex PKO. It is of interest that in the latter stages of the operation, which ended in 1999, the support task force was transferred from the United States to Brazil.

An Interim Summation of the Latin American PKO Experience

For more than seventy years the Latin American states have been engaged actively in peace operations—primarily PKOs. They have provided contingents that have ranged from military observers to force commanders, and they have provided the primary political leadership in numerous cases. Latin American troop units—typically infantry companies or battalions—have been generally well trained and militarily competent. Although the three traditional South American powers—Argentina, Brazil, and Chile—have often been the leaders, others, including Uruguay, the small Central American states, and some of the microstates of the anglophone Caribbean, have also made significant contributions to peace operations.

An additional aspect of the Latin American peace operations experience is the existence of a regional organizational infrastructure, including not fewer than three international organizations that can authorize and support such missions. Preeminent among these is the OAS, which provided the mandate for the IAPF in the Dominican Republic. Although it has been reluctant in subsequent years to authorize similar operations, the OAS has played a diplomatic role in many regional conflicts and has cosponsored action in Haiti with the UN. The other regional organizations that can and have provided a framework for peace operations are found in the Caribbean among the anglophone states. CARICOM and the OECS were instrumental in the Grenada intervention and in the formation of the RSS.

Latin American PKO Training Centers and Exercises

Although PKO training centers became common after the establishment of the Pearson Peacekeeping Centre (PPC) in Canada in 1994, Uruguay's two schools for the Army and Navy predate the founding of the PPC. The major difference is that the Uruguayan schools exist primarily to train Uruguayan peacekeepers (although the class in session in November 2005 had two students from Paraguay).[12] Argentina founded the Centro Argentino de Entrenamiento Conjunto para Operaciones de Paz (CAECOPAZ) in June 1995. CAECOPAZ offers courses for high-level Argentinean forces personnel and coordinates closely with the PPC and other centers. In July 2002 Chile established the Centro de Entrenamiento Conjunto de Operaciones de Paz de Chile (CECOPAC). Although its courses are primarily for Chilean military, police, and civilians, they are open to other nations for a fee. Brazil has also established an internal PKO training center, while Guatemala is in the process of setting up a center for the Conferencia de Fuerzas Armadas de Centro-America (CFAC). CFAC is planning to train and field a multinational Central American battalion for peace operations, and the Guatemala center will be the training institution.[13] Other countries in the region, such as Peru and Paraguay, provide ad hoc training courses for those of their forces that are scheduled for participation in a PKO.

In addition to the national training centers and schools, organizations like the RSS and various subregional groups of countries conduct peacekeeping training exercises, mostly with the support of the U.S. Southern Command (USSOUTHCOM). For over two decades USSOUTHCOM has conducted multiple series of joint and combined exercises in Central and South America.[14] In recent years SOUTHCOM has sponsored command-post exercises (CPX), called PKO-North and PKO-South, focusing on peacekeeping operations.[15] According to Colonel Rosales, these exercises have been of significant benefit in training multinational Latin American and U.S. staffs to work together using common procedures.[16] In recent years SOUTHCOM's annual Cabañas series of field training exercises (FTX) have focused on PKO as well as disaster relief. Rosales reiterates his commendation of the utility of the FTX both as stand-alones and in conjunction with the CPX.[17]

Closely related to the USSOUTHCOM-sponsored exercises are those organized under the auspices of the Conference of American Armies (CAA).[18] The CAA has chosen to focus its meetings for the current and previous cycles on PKOs and disaster assistance, and it has addressed both with practical projects relating to such issues as common terminology, common staff procedures, and combined exercises, all of which are ongoing.[19] As Rosales makes clear, the value of both the CPX and FTX is the development of interoperability among the participating military forces. That interoperability is easily interchangeable between peacekeeping and disaster assistance operations. Most of the skills required are the same; the others come from common roots; few are classic war fighting skills, and both are more closely related to aspects of policing than they are to infantry combat. Nevertheless, combat skills remain essential as a deterrent in traditional peacekeeping and to meet violent threats in wider peacekeeping and peace enforcement operations.

In sum, the Latin American states have a long history of participation in peace operations, and Latin American regional institutions have provided political direction for those operations on several occasions. They also maintain—at times with support from their hemispheric partners the United States and Canada—the training and educational institutions and regimes to sustain their involvement in PKOs. These include the various national and multinational centers, epitomized by CAECOPAZ and CECOPAC, as well as USSOUTHCOM-sponsored exercises and the developing role of the CAA.

Haiti: The Case of a Failed State

Since 1994 Haiti has been the subject of two major peace operations that occurred in a number of installments. Haiti achieved independence from France in 1804 following a slave rebellion, and it developed what many modern authors have called a predatory culture.[20] Between 1843 and 1915 Haiti had twenty-two heads of state, "with fourteen removed by force, two with fates unknown, and only one completing the term of office."[21]

In 1915, when President Jean Vilbrun Guillaume Sam was literally torn limb from limb, the United States intervened to restore order and to secure the Windward Passage (a strategically important strait lying between Haiti and Cuba) from Imperial Germany's U-boats. American Marines stayed for nineteen years. They built up Haiti's physical infrastructure, did much to improve the health of the people, and created a relatively effective governmental institution, the Gendarmerie d'Haïti, later renamed the Garde d'Haïti; after the departure of the Americans in 1934, it became the core of the national army, the Force Armée d'Haiti. This armed force helped to keep the mulatto elite securely in power until François "Papa Doc" Duvalier was elected president in 1957 (the first nonmulatto black to hold office). Papa Doc created a personal police force called the Tonton Macoutes to use as a counterweight to the armed forces and to buttress his own regime. When he died in 1971 the life presidency passed to his son, Jean Claude "Baby Doc" Duvalier, who ruled until he fled the country in 1986. Baby Doc essentially made common cause with the equally predatory mulatto elite that his father had kept at bay.

In 1990 Haiti held a free election and Father Jean-Bertrand Aristide was elected president. His populist actions frightened the mulatto elite, and the army under the command of Lt. Gen. Raoul Cédras overthrew him. "Numerous acts of barbarism marked the Cedras regime," and this triggered OAS and UN sanctions and resulted in negotiations that culminated in the Governors Island Accord, which stated that Aristide should return as president by October 30, 1993, and that the junta should be granted amnesty.[22] To facilitate the accords a UN peacekeeping operation, the United Nations Mission in Haiti (UNMIH), was created in September 1993.[23] When the USS *Harlan County* arrived in Port-au-Prince with another 220 military personnel on October 11, the junta orchestrated a potentially violent demonstration, and the *Harlan County* sailed away without having landed the force.[24]

After nine months of dithering, the UN Security Council passed Resolution 940 on July 31, 1994, which authorized deployment of a multinational force that could use "all means necessary" to facilitate the junta's departure and Aristide's return to power, permitting the implementation of the Governors Island Agreement and invoking Chapter VII of the UN Charter. Once a secure and stable environment was established, UNMIH would be deployed with an expanded mandate.[25]

Operation Uphold Democracy and UNMIH

Between July 31 and September 18, 1994, the United States put together a twenty-eight-nation coalition multinational force (MNF) to restore President Aristide and oust the junta. The MNF was very heavily American, but it included a battalion of Caribbean Community (CARICOM) forces as well as units from other American states. On September 19, as the troops were en route to Haiti, the negotiating team led by former U.S. President Jimmy Carter reached agreement with General Cédras, averting a military confrontation and allowing the MNF to enter the country in a permissive—more or less peaceful—environment. The MNF conducted operations in Haiti to secure a stable and peaceful environment and oversee the return to office and power of President Aristide (on October 15, 1994). It succeeded in getting government ministries established with significant assistance from U.S. Army Civil Affairs Ministry Support Teams and began the training of both Haitian interim police and the permanent Haitian National Police (Police Nationale D'Haiti). The two major cities were controlled by brigades of the Tenth Mountain Division. The rest of the country was divided among units of the CARICOM battalion and U.S. Army Special Forces.

On March 31, 1995, the MNF transferred responsibility to the UN, and UNMIH became a reality.[26] Like the MNF, UNMIH's military force was commanded by U.S. Major General Joseph Kinzer, and it was heavy with U.S. (and Bangladeshi and Pakistani) troops. However, CARICOM and several Latin American states, especially Guatemala and Honduras, also contributed forces. Kinzer saw his mission as holding an election and transferring authority to the newly elected Haitian government. In December 1995 René Préval was elected President. In March 1996, military command of UNMIH was handed over to Canadian Brigadier General J. R. Pierre Daigle, and most of the U.S. forces left, including the Special Forces teams that had controlled much of the countryside. Thus began the deterioration of the security situation in Haiti, coinciding with the failure of the Haitian state to effectively govern the country. The government of President Préval was paralyzed by a congress controlled by supporters of former President Aristide (who wanted Préval to fail so that Aristide could recover the reins of power).

After several years of governmental stalemate and a number of iterations of UNMIH by other names and with fewer troops, Aristide was elected president for the second time in November 2000. During this period, the Haitian National Police became both more corrupt and politicized, while the opposition to Aristide—made up of the mulatto elite; former members of the Force Armée d'Haiti, who had never surrendered their weapons; armed paramilitaries in civilian clothing known as "attaches"; and elements of Aristide's own

Lavalas political movement—significantly raised the level of political violence. By early 2004 many believed that the threat to Aristide's life was of the same order as that to President Guillaume Sam in 1915. On February 29, Aristide resigned; many believed, and Aristide himself later argued, that the United States had forced him out. He fled the country on a U.S. military transport airplane. The president of the Supreme Court, Boniface Alexander, assumed the presidency and requested UN support to stabilize the situation.[27]

The Multinational Interim Force

The UN Security Council passed Resolution 1529 on February 29, 2004. Once again invoking Chapter VII of the UN Charter, it authorized deployment of a Multinational Interim Force (MIF) for up to three months, to be followed by a longer-term UN stabilization force. The resolution specified that the OAS should be consulted regarding the size, structure, and mandate of the stabilization force.

Forces for the MIF were provided by the United States, France, Canada, and Chile.[28] Of particular interest in this chapter is the Chilean participation. Although Di Nocera and Benavente argue, with reason, that Chile has been involved in PKOs since 1947, it had a very narrow view of what constituted its appropriate role until the late 1990s.[29] However, by the time Chile established CECOPAC in 2002, it had made a conscious decision to participate fully in peace operations, including wider peacekeeping and peace enforcement efforts under Chapter VII of the UN Charter, and to do so in the most professional way possible. This was evident in its response to UNSCR 1529: the Chilean contingent of 336 soldiers and officers for the MIF deployed by using the country's own assets within three days of the resolution's adoption.

MINUSTAH

The follow-on mission, known as MINUSTAH—the French acronym for the United Nations Stabilization Mission in Haiti—was authorized by UNSCR 1542, passed on April 30, 2004. Heading the mission as special representative to the secretary-general (SRSG) was the Chilean diplomat Juan Gabriel Valdés, with Brazilian General Augusto Heleno Ribeiro Pereira as force commander and an Argentine as his deputy. In addition, seven of the twelve initial military force contributors were from Latin America, and by May 31, 2007, nine of nineteen troop-contributing countries were from Latin America: Argentina (562), Bolivia (220), Brazil (1,217), Chile (499), Ecuador (67), Guatemala (105), Paraguay (31), Peru (210), and Uruguay (1,140).[30] These numbers are likely to remain relatively constant so long as the contributors remain committed to supporting the mission, since these numbers reflect the relative strength levels that the individual countries are willing and able to contribute to peace operations. In general they are infantry units with organic equipment and transport.

Also in May 2007, six Latin American countries were contributing police personnel to MINUSTAH: Argentina (four), Brazil (three), Chile (fifteen), Colombia (two), El Salvador (two), and Uruguay (one).[31] Grenada has also contributed police to MINUSTAH, making it the only anglophone Caribbean country to participate in MINUSTAH.[32] The other CARICOM countries objected to the manner in which Aristide left the presidency. The relatively small numbers of police contributed by each country reflect the nature of policing: most active police forces are fully committed to the domestic public safety mission and do not have the manpower to spare for large PKO deployments. Police units like Chile's Carabineros or Argentina's Gendarmería Nacional do have a larger deployment capability, but it is nonetheless more limited than that of the military.

In September 2005 there was a change of military command in the mission: Ribeiro was replaced by another Brazilian, Lieutenant General Urano Teixeira da Matta Bacellar, whose deputy was General Eduardo Aldunate Herman of Chile. When Urano committed suicide in January 2006, Aldunate briefly became acting commander until the Brazilians named Lieutenant General José Elito Carvalho Siqueira as a replacement.[33] In May 2006, Valdés was replaced as SRSG by Ambassador Edmond Mulet of Guatemala. Siqueira was replaced in January 2007 by the current MINUSTAH commander, Major General Carlos Alberto Dos Santos Cruz of Brazil.

Factors Influencing Latin American Participation in MINUSTAH

Given the centrality of Latin American participants in MINUSTAH, it is useful to consider the factors influencing their willingness to participate. The critical capacity in this regard is political will.[34] Factors driving political will include prestige, sense of international obligation, feeling of hemispheric solidarity, and national interest/national agenda.

PRESTIGE

In some respects, prestige is the single most powerful factor affecting political will.[35] Each of the Latin American participants in MINUSTAH has believed that participation significantly enhances their prestige both at home and in the world. Brazil provided the largest contingent of forces and was made the force commander. It is believed, according to Eugenio Diniz, that Brazil's participation and military leadership as the force commander would, at best, enhance its chances of attaining a permanent seat on the UN Security Council. At the least, it would give Brazil an increased voice in world affairs. Partly as a reward for its rapid deployment of forces both to the MIF and to MINUSTAH, Chile was assigned initial political leadership of MINUSTAH, with the appointment of a Chilean as the first SRSG. For Chile, participation alongside Brazil and Argentina sent a strong signal of cooperation and leadership within the region. Argentina's sense of competition with both Brazil and Chile influenced (both positively and negatively) its perception of the prestige attached to participating in MINUSTAH. Because the Argentine Congress spent so long debating whether to participate or not, Argentina was not offered either of the two principal leadership positions—SRSG or force commander—and was forced to settle for the deputy force commander post. Nevertheless, Chile's political leadership—and Brazil's military leadership—of MINUSTAH made participation mandatory for Argentina in order to avoid a major loss of prestige. For the other Latin American countries, participation in a UN PKO in the hemisphere was also seen as a source of prestige. Commenting on Latin American participation in MINUSTAH, Argentine Defense Minister José Pampuro remarked, "Es tiempo de que América Latina muestre que tiene puestos los pantalones largos" ("It is time that Latin America shows that it has put on long pants").[36]

SENSE OF INTERNATIONAL OBLIGATION COUPLED WITH A SENSE OF HEMISPHERIC SOLIDARITY

A second factor affecting the willingness to participate in MINUSTAH and other PKOs seems to be a sense of international obligation felt by most Latin American nations. This is particularly relevant with respect to UN PKOs. All of the Latin American participants in MINUSTAH attach great significance to their national obligations under the UN Charter. Paraguay, for example, treats an international treaty not only as having the force of domestic law but as hierarchically superior to conflicting domestic laws. Most other Latin American countries have adopted similar interpretations. For them, the Charter is a treaty of this sort.[37] There is every reason to believe that this interpretation is likely to remain dominant throughout Latin America for the foreseeable future.

A related factor is the sense of hemispheric solidarity. As noted above, the Americas have a long history of regional relationships and international organizations that date back at least to the International Union of American Republics of 1890. They also have a love–hate relationship with the United States and an accompanying need to demonstrate independence from Washington. PKOs, in general, and UN PKOs in particular, give Latin American states the opportunity to support U.S. positions internationally while at the same time emphasizing their preference for multinational action.

NATIONAL INTERESTS AND POLITICAL AGENDAS

The late Speaker of the U.S. House of Representatives, Thomas P. "Tip" O'Neill, once remarked that all politics is local. This aphorism certainly applies to the decision of the Latin American states to participate in MINUSTAH. As noted above, the Argentine Congress debated for a long time—some might say that it dithered while its neighbors and rivals acted—before it decided to take part in the mission. The local political issue was that in previous cases of Argentine participation, such as in Kosovo, the president had not bothered to consult the Congress as required by law. In this case, the Congress exercised its prerogative vis-a-vis the executive.[38] The consequences were a somewhat less visible position (i.e., of deputy force commander) than Argentina might have expected otherwise.

While there was little conflict in Brazil over participating in a UN PKO, the Brazilians have become wary of Chapter VII operations. Nevertheless, Brazil agreed to provide the largest national military contingent and the force commander to MINUSTAH, even though UNSCR 1542 clearly identified it as a Chapter VII operation. Given opposition in Congress, the executive sought to obscure the issue and treat Brazilian participation as if it were a Chapter VI mission. This confusion carried over into the army itself, creating the potential for conflict between the force command and the Brazilian contingent command.

For Chile, the only political issue was the commitment of a detachment of Carabineros to the civilian police component of MINUSTAH. Opposition to their deployment existed but was overcome with relative ease. Guatemala's civilian political leadership chose to use the MINUSTAH request for forces to gain some control over the decision-making process in the armed forces. Prior to this—and especially during the period of the Guatemalan civil wars of the twentieth century—the armed forces had completely excluded civilian political leaders from any involvement in decisions affecting the military. "In fact, Guatemala introduced the PKO participation concept as one objective of a more ambitious defense transformation program that envisions new roles and rules for the Guatemalan Army in the post internal conflict period."[39] That role, as noted above, focuses on peace operations and includes the new Central American PKO training center. In 2006, Guatemala announced that it would participate in the expanded United Nations Interim Force in Lebanon (UNIFIL) PKO in Lebanon, partly to support its bid for a nonpermanent seat on the Security Council but also as a token of its commitment to UN peacekeeping.

According to the former director of policy and strategy of the Peruvian Ministry of Defense, Enrique Obando, Peru's decision to restructure its armed forces for PKOs had important civil–military relations goals.[40] The issues raised by this decision were played out in discussions between Peru's political leaders and the Armed Forces Joint Command, which resisted the deployment on economic grounds. The Joint Command had the support of the Finance Ministry, which resisted spending the money due to Peru's stabilization agreement with the IMF. Nevertheless, the Ministry of Defense saw significant economic incentives to participation in MINUSTAH, since the UN provided resources based on the number of soldiers in the national contingent. This amounted to an increase in resources for the military as an institution. In the end, a compromise solution was worked out that reduced Peru's planned contribution from an infantry battalion to two companies.[41]

The Peruvian compromise illustrates what some countries have known for a long time and others are just beginning to learn: that while a relatively small national investment can net a positive return for the armed forces, the investment must be made. Uruguay has long made use of UN monies to multiply the effectiveness and capacity of its armed forces. In this sense, Haiti was just another mission that the government as a whole supported, in part because it enhanced a military oriented toward peacekeeping and funded to a significant degree by the UN. Paraguay, by contrast, desired to gain the same benefits as Uruguay, but it had not budgeted the funds for the investment and, therefore, was left somewhat embarrassed by the fact that it could only send a few staff officers to Haiti and not the two hundred soldiers it had originally committed to the operation. Political choices, in the broadest sense, constrain the political will of countries to participate in a PKO.

CAPACITY

Several factors can contribute to a nation's overall capacity to participate in peacekeeping operations. One is whether a nation possesses a well-developed diplomatic capability. This is an area of real strength for Latin Americans when one considers that the former secretary-general of the UN, Javier Pérez de Cuéllar, was Peruvian, that the UN special representative killed in Iraq in August 2003, Sérgio Vieira de Mello, was Brazilian, and that the SRSGs of MINUSTAH, Juan Gabriel Valdés and Edmond Mulet, were from Chile and Guatemala, respectively.

A second factor is whether a nation's government is characterized by smooth interministerial operations and coordination. This cannot be said to be an area of strength for Latin American nations. The case of Peru, noted above, illustrates this particularly well, as internal struggles developed between the Ministries of Defense and Foreign Affairs on one side and the Ministry of Finance and the Joint Command of the Armed Forces on the other. Argentina and Brazil both experienced significant differences between their congresses and executives when deciding whether and how to participate in Haiti. It should be noted here that few, if any, countries can take much pride in their interministerial (or interagency) capabilities. Governments simply do not deal very easily with competition among ministries or branches—that, after all, is what politics within a government is all about.

A third factor is the availability of a nation's military and police personnel. As seen in table 9.1, the nine Latin American countries that currently participate militarily in MINUSTAH have significant military capabilities for peace operations. Most have long experience as well. While force sizes are being reduced in many of these countries, the contributions should not change very much. Guatemala is an exception to the experience factor, as it is just now taking its place as a major participant. Many Latin American countries, however, find their participation constrained by a lack of funding. This was the case in Paraguay and Peru, both of which had to reduce their participation in MINUSTAH for budgetary reasons.

Although nearly all Latin American states have national police forces, only a few have demonstrated the capacity to contribute to peacekeeping civilian police operations. Of the nine military force contributors to MINUSTAH, less than half—Argentina, Brazil, Chile, and Uruguay—also contribute civilian police. El Salvador and Colombia contribute police but no military (this was also true of Grenada). The Argentine Gendarmeria and the Chilean Carabineros have excellent reputations with regard to their capability for CIVPOL missions, and like the Italian Carabinieri they are paramilitary institutions— forces that have a reserve capacity that allows more easily for international PKO deployment than for more traditional civilian police deployment.

Table 9.1. Latin American Armed Forces/Police

State	Total Military	Army	Equipment	Navy	Equipment	Air Force	Equipment	Paramilitary Police
Argentina	71,400	41,400	IFV APC, HELO	17,500	PC, AMPH SPT, HELO	12,500	TPT, HELO	31,240
Bolivia	31,500	25,000	APC	3,500	PC (RIVER)	3,000	TPT, HELO	37,100
Brazil	287,600	189,000	RECON APC, HELO	48,600	CV, PC, AMPH SPT, HELO	50,000	SAR, HELO, COIN ACFT	385,600
Columbia	77,300	47,700	IFV APC, RECON APC, HELO	19,000	PC, AMPH SPT, HELO	10,600	TPT, HELO COIN ACFT	36,800 APC, HELO
Ecuador	59,500	50,000	APC, HELO	5,500	PC, AMPH SPT	4,000	TPT, HELO	270 (CG) PC
Guatemala	31,400	29,200	APC	1,500	PC	700	TPT, HELO, MP	19,000
Paraguay	18,800	14,900	RECON APC	2,000	PC (RIVER)	1,700	TPT, HELO	14,800
Peru	100,000	60,000	RECON APC, HELO	25,000	PC, AMPH SPT	15,000	TPT, HELO	77,000 (NP, CG)
Uruguay	24,000	15,200	IFV APC RECON APC	5,700	PC, AMPH SPT	3,100	TPT, HELO	920

Source: IISS, *The Military Balance, 2003–4.*

However, they are a highly valued commodity domestically, and politicians face pressure not to deploy them abroad. That said, the willingness of Colombia, El Salvador, and Grenada to contribute police to CIVPOL harkens back to the sense of obligation that these countries feel to the Charter of the United Nations.

The Future of Latin American Involvement in Peace Operations

As noted at the beginning of this chapter, some Latin American countries have considerable experience in peace operations, both as force contributors and as providers of political leadership. During the last decade, Argentina, Chile, and (to a lesser extent) Uruguay have established international training centers that are part of a community that includes Canada's PPC. They have now been joined by Guatemala, with its center for Central America. Closely related to the Guatemala center, the Central American subregion is in the process of developing a multinational peace operations battalion under the auspices of CFAC for standby use on UN deployments. This CFAC battalion has the potential for making significant contributions to UN operations over the next decade.

Moreover, the Americas is a region particularly rich in the institutions of international cooperation. These include the OAS, CARICOM, OECS, RSS, CFAC, the Inter-American Defense Board (which in 2006 was finally brought wholly under the OAS), and the regimes of combined exercises in PKOs sponsored by the U.S. Southern Command. Together, these institutions provide mechanisms for regional peace operations.

The degree to which each Latin American country is willing to support a wider peacekeeping or peace enforcement mission depends on both international circumstances and domestic politics, and it is reflected in their varying national policies. Thus, Chile has been very willing to participate fully in Chapter VII peace operations, while Brazil has agonized and equivocated over its participation in Haiti.

Some Latin American countries that have not been so deeply involved in PKOs have decided in recent years to focus their militaries on this mission. They have done so for many reasons, most of which have been addressed here in the section on the MINUSTAH mission. One reason that has not yet been discussed involves "taming" the armed forces in countries where the military has long dominated politics. If a state is not going to disband its military—the choice of Costa Rica (in 1948), Panama (in 1994), and Haiti (in 1994)—then a legitimate role must be found for it. Many Latin American states found that role to be peace operations.

Given this history, MINUSTAH is hardly a watershed. Rather, it is one more episode in a long history of Latin American involvement in peace operations. MINUSTAH does offer some lessons for the future, however. First, the modern state cannot undertake a peace enforcement mission without being willing to invest in the capabilities required to do so. Moreover, it must do so in advance of the operation. Second, it cannot count on others to pay the entire cost. This, too, is part of the necessary prior investment. But not all of the costs are financial. A major weakness for all states that wish to engage in peace operations is the lack of sufficient interagency/interministerial capacity. Bureaucratic politics will always be an obstacle to successful missions. This can be compounded by the politics of competition between the separate branches of government.

For Latin America, such competition is a good thing. In the past no Latin American state allowed the legislative branch to intrude on executive decision making. What we saw in the Argentine debate leading to commitment to MINUSTAH was the Argentine Congress exercising its power in foreign affairs for nearly the first time. The debate in the Brazilian Congress over Chapter VI versus Chapter VII had a similar origin. Even the mild debate in Chile over participation by the *Carabineros* was similar in a number of ways. Perhaps the real impact of MINUSTAH has been in the perception of many outside the region that, to echo the words of the Argentine Defense Minister, Latin America has put on long pants.

Chapter 10

Rethinking Peace Operations in East Asia: Problems and Prospects

MELY CABALLERO-ANTHONY

Any analysis of regional peace operations must bear in mind two things. First is the need to have an informed knowledge of the kinds of security structures found in the region; second is the need to have a clear understanding of the regional security approaches that have been established to respond to security threats and challenges.

These two factors are critical in examining regional capacities for peace operations in East Asia, especially in light of current developments both within and outside the region. In the case of the Association of Southeast Asian Nations (ASEAN), traditional security practices have been challenged by new strategies for managing and resolving conflict in order to make the organization more effective. Many of the ideas that have begun to percolate call for more proactive conflict prevention and conflict resolution, including even the possibility of building a regional peacekeeping force. There has also been a growing desire within the region to establish institutions and mechanisms that could respond expeditiously to crisis situations instead of relying on ad hoc responses. In other parts of East Asia, significant shifts have taken place in the attitudes of major powers like China and Japan, leading to increased participation in peacekeeping missions.

The push for rethinking norms and practices did not simply happen in a vacuum; rather, it was shaped by the series of crises that hit the region in the last ten years. The region's experience with the 1996–98 political turmoil in Cambodia, and with the troubled transition to independence of East Timor beginning in 1999, forced ASEAN member states to reassess regional modalities in responding to crises, particularly those that are humanitarian in nature. Since the 1997–98 Asian financial crisis, a slow and calibrated recrafting of regional institutional structures is occurring, and new mechanisms are emerging that are geared to build regional institutional capacities for responding to a host of security challenges confronting the region. These would include the introduction of the ASEAN Troika—a mechanism, described below, intended to allow ASEAN quicker response to crises—and the participation in UN peacekeeping operations in East Timor, albeit on an individual basis. There are also new initiatives to introduce more defined elements of conflict prevention, resolution, and peace-building for ASEAN within the broad framework of forming an ASEAN Security Community by 2020.[1]

At the level of the ASEAN Regional Forum (ARF), which includes all of the East Asian countries plus the United States, Russia, the European Union, and other South Asian and Pacific Rim countries (see below), ideas are also abounding, particularly within the debate about moving beyond confidence-building activities and toward measures for advancing an agenda of preventive diplomacy. This can be seen in ARF discussions on an enhanced role for the ARF chair, on the need for early warning mechanisms, and on the establishment of the Friends of the ARF Chair and/or Experts and Eminent Persons Group.[2]

In sum, we are seeing dynamic developments in the region defined increasingly by proactive rather than reactive attitudes. Such changes are extremely significant for the evolving conceptualization of security in East Asia, which in turn has salient implications for the broader prospects of regionalization of peace operations. Against this background, the objectives of this chapter are twofold. First, it provides a review of the current state of peace operations in East Asia by examining critical events that have become "tipping points" in the reassessment of regional modalities for conflict resolution. Second, it looks at some new ideas and initiatives that have been introduced in the region and examines how these multiple intraregional processes could lead to a more progressive attitude about building regional capacities for peace operations.

The chapter adopts a broad definition of peace operation that goes beyond peacekeeping, and it encompasses a multifunctional and multidimensional range of activities that include conflict prevention, peacemaking, and peace-building.[3] With the aforementioned definition, this chapter addresses how peace operations fit within the broader topic of regional security cooperation in East Asia.

Revisiting Regional Security Structures and Approaches toward Peace Operations

Before assessing the capacity of East Asia to undertake any of the multifunctional tasks involved in today's peace operations, it is useful to examine the two regional security structures through which East Asian security cooperation takes place: ASEAN and the ASEAN Regional Forum.

ASEAN was established in 1967 with the long-term objective of establishing a "security community" in Southeast Asia.[4] Although its foundational declarations were not very explicit about its security role, ASEAN's establishment represented a decision by its member states to provide themselves with an overall framework for managing antagonistic relations, evidenced at the time by the *Konfrontation* (confrontation) between Indonesia and Malaysia and the bilateral dispute between Malaysia and the Philippines over Sabah.[5] As described succinctly by the late foremost authority of ASEAN studies,

Michael Leifer, ASEAN had for all intents and purposes become a "diplomatic device" for subregional reconciliation.[6] Bringing together a region that was once described as the Balkans of the East, ASEAN has been credited with maintaining peace and security in Southeast Asia for the last forty years. As a result, it has often been described as one of the most successful regional organizations in the developing world.

Until 1997, ASEAN's success was largely defined by the ability of its founding members (Indonesia, Malaysia, the Philippines, Singapore, and Thailand) to manage their relations by preventing conflicts and avoiding the escalation of potential flashpoints. The organization did so by embodying basic principles and norms for interstate conduct. These key norms are found in a series of ASEAN documents, most notably the Bangkok Declaration of 1967 that established ASEAN; the Zone of Peace, Freedom and Neutrality Declaration of 1971; and the Treaty of Amity and Cooperation in Southeast Asia of 1976.[7] Within these documents are three key aspects of the "ASEAN Way" that are of direct relevance to this chapter's discussion of peace operations. First, sovereignty was to be respected, and the norm of noninterference in the internal affairs of another state was to be adhered to. Second, ASEAN clearly stresses the non-use of force in dispute settlements, as evident from its appearance in many key ASEAN documents. This norm reflected the desire of the member states to avoid the numerous conflicts that occurred prior to ASEAN's formation. As described by Michael Antolik, the member states "still had mutual suspicions; yet, they were compelled to promise restraint because competition had proved costly, futile, and foolish."[8] Third, ASEAN cultivated the norm of "good neighbourliness and cooperation" characterized by member states' practice of decision making through consultation and consensus. This practice was marked by informality and accommodation and was linked to *musyawarah* (consultation) and *mufakat* (consensus), customs of the Malay culture.[9] The approach, while time consuming, provides opportunities for officials from different member states to socialize and to know one another well, thereby developing sensitivity to each others' political, economic, and security issues.[10]

It is important to note that these are the same approaches that ASEAN embodied when it helped to establish the ASEAN Regional Forum in 1994.[11] The creation of the ARF—which is the other regional security organization in East Asia—was in fact seen as ASEAN's attempt to extend to the Asia–Pacific region its processes of conflict avoidance writ large through fostering constructive dialogue and consultation on political and security issues. Hence, the process of regional reconciliation that had earlier been confined to ASEAN was expanded to become an "inclusive" form of regionalism with the establishment of a security forum covering the vast expanse of the Asia Pacific region. In bringing together like-minded and non-like-minded states, the ARF aspired to become a building block of several "islands of peace." And like ASEAN, this security orientation is underpinned by the promotion of norms of interstate conduct found in the Treaty of Amity and Cooperation.

It is useful to briefly examine the motivations behind such institutional innovation, which had brought together twenty-six states from the Asia-

Pacific region. During that period, the ASEAN members that formed the core of the ARF believed that an inclusive approach to regionalism would allow ASEAN to lock in the interest of major powers (the United States, China, and Japan) in maintaining regional peace. By doing so, ASEAN countries sought to reduce the prevailing strategic uncertainty brought about by the structural changes in the international security environment following the end of the cold war. The other salient objective was to make the ARF a useful venue and mechanism to socialize China when it was still wary about multilateralism.[12] As an important confidence-building mechanism, the ARF focused most of its efforts on promoting dialogue by facilitating the flow of information and regular consultation.

The security structures in the region—ASEAN and the ARF—are less institutionalized than, for example, the European Union; they are characteristically process-oriented and geared toward conflict prevention and mediation. We do not see any alliance-type arrangements among the Asian states, unlike in Europe or Africa. In fact, the Asian security lexicon does not include collective and common security. Instead, the concepts of comprehensive and cooperative security dominate the discourse in both ASEAN and the ARF. ASEAN has emphasized the comprehensive nature of security in promoting political and economic cooperation in the region. Within the context of the ARF, the objective of cooperative security was seen "as replacing the Cold War security structure (characterised by bilateral military relations) with a multilateral process and framework . . . geared towards reassurance rather than deterrence."[13] In the Asian context, "cooperative security" has been translated to denote the principle of inclusiveness, dialogue, and multilateral cooperation among state and nonstate actors.[14]

In brief, at least until the Asian financial crisis of 1997–98, it appeared that the loosely structured "security community" of ASEAN and the ARF had served its members well. In July 1997, when ASEAN expanded from seven to nine members, representing nearly all the states in Southeast Asia (Cambodia's accession, also scheduled for July 1997, was postponed until 1999), it was hailed for its success in maintaining regional peace and security. However, a series of regional crises sparked by the regionwide economic crisis in 1997 cast a lot of doubt over the role and future of the organization. Much has been written about the impact of the financial crisis on ASEAN.[15] It was the first in a series of crises that exposed gaping inadequacies in the region's ability to deal with new threats to stability.[16] The most difficult to contend with was the crisis in East Timor surrounding the August 1999 referendum on independence from Indonesia. ASEAN and the ARF came under severe criticism for their inability to stem the violence and gross violations of human rights that occurred. As noted in many accounts, ASEAN could not initiate any form of concerted action to prevent the conflict. Among the many reasons for this inability was the member states' strict observation of the norm of noninterference in the domestic affairs of member states (in this case, Indonesia). It was not until the deployment in late September 1999 of an Australian-led, UN-sanctioned peacekeeping mission, the International Force for East Timor

(INTERFET), that violence was controlled and large-scale humanitarian relief operations were carried out.

The series of crises highlighted two important aspects about the kinds of regional arrangements within the region. First, since ASEAN (and, by extension, the ARF) had been mainly a regional cooperative mechanism for conflict prevention, the nature of its institutional development had been parsimonious. Whatever institutions were established, particularly in the case of ASEAN, had been geared mainly for engendering an environment for building trust and confidence among members, particularly during its formation. Over the past four decades, ASEAN has chosen to take a very conservative path to ensure a stable transition and peaceful relationships among its members. The same holds true for the ARF, which continues to emphasize a wide range of confidence-building measures. As a consequence, when certain crises occurred that needed specialized expertise to respond to financial meltdowns, humanitarian emergencies, and peacekeeping operations, ASEAN and the ARF were more often than not unprepared. As experience has shown, the nature of the crises and challenges that confront the region today requires much more than what the loosely structured organizations have been able to provide. Second, given the lack of (regional) institutional capacity and expertise, the responses of regional institutions to crises have also been mostly ad hoc in nature. These points are discussed further in the later section of this chapter.

Emerging Shifts in the Global Structural and Normative Terrain: Finding Convergence with Regional Dynamics

The crises faced by East Asia during the last decade were not unique to the region. As argued by many, the kinds of conflicts that emerged in the early 1990s reflected broader developments that defined the post–cold war era. Many conflicts were internal in nature and threatened to spill over into neighboring states, thus posing serious threats to regional and international security. Implicit in the new thinking that accompanied this era was the notion that national sovereignty and security should be exercised in line with international responsibility and international order. As a consequence, the United Nations found itself having to cope with more security challenges than it could manage.[17] This is seen in the dramatic increase in the number of peace operations conducted by the UN in various parts of the world.[18]

Thus began a series of global initiatives highlighting the need for the UN to seek partners in peace operations. One appeared in 1992 when then UN Secretary-General Boutros Boutros-Ghali launched his report *An Agenda for Peace*.[19] In it he argued for a task-sharing arrangement between the UN and regional organizations to advance regional, as well as global, order. *An Agenda for Peace* essentially called for a revisiting of Chapter VIII of the UN Charter, which had ascribed to "regional arrangements and agencies" the task of dealing with "matters in relation to the maintenance of international peace and security as are appropriate for regional action." A second initiative was the *Report of the Panel on United Nations Peace Operations*, also known as the Brahimi Report, issued in August 2000, which outlined the intricate nexus between peace-building and peacekeeping and presented a number of key recommendations that were essential to achieving success in these efforts.[20] Relevant to the conduct of peace operations, it identified three key requirements (aside from the provision of financial support and resources) for success: clear organizational structures, achievable mandates, and strong leadership. A third initiative was Kofi Annan's report of June 7, 2001, *The Prevention of Armed Conflicts*.[21] Its aim, said Annan, was to "move the United Nations from a culture of reaction to a culture of prevention." A fourth initiative, closely linked to the UN agenda of developing a global culture of conflict prevention, was the Responsibility to Protect Report of September 2001.[22] Drafted by the International Commission on Intervention and State Sovereignty (ICISS), a salient feature of this report was the attempt to reframe the concept of sovereignty from "sovereignty as control to sovereignty as a responsibility."[23] Finally, despite the lack of consensus on many of the issues identified in these earlier reports, Annan rode the momentum of debates about their recommendations to introduce yet another report, titled *In Larger Freedom*, in March 2005.[24] It proposed groundbreaking recommendations for restructuring and improving the UN in order to effectively respond to the global challenges of development, security, and human rights.

Against the backdrop of these initiatives at the global level, we now turn to examine what impact these developments have had on East Asia—and more specifically, on where to locate their experiences in managing and resolving conflicts against these ongoing endeavors to maintain peace and security in the wider international community. In this regard, the key question we need to ask is whether there is an emerging congruence of views between the UN and East Asia on how the new demands for peace operations might be met. In addition, we will consider the "new" role of the regional states in improving prospects for peace operations at the regional and global levels.

Nature of Peace Operations in East Asia: More of the Old Tools and a Bit of the New?

In light of the fact that East Asia is underinstitutionalized to respond robustly to the new initiatives proffered by the United Nations, it is useful to examine the regional mechanisms that are available and to assess the extent to which they are being recalibrated to respond to new security challenges. It is also appropriate to examine whether wholly new mechanisms are being created to strengthen the region's capacity to meet emerging security threats and undertake peace operations.

This section discusses these possibilities within the framework of an expanded concept of peace operations, noting that the multifunctional tasks now associated with the concept involve tasks that go beyond the traditional interposition operations to include modalities for conflict prevention and peacemaking. The discussion is divided into two parts. The first begins by re-visiting how regional institutions like ASEAN, through the use of a variety of "innovative" conflict prevention mechanisms, have helped promote regional peace and stability. These mechanisms are discussed in reference to their spe-cific applicable cases. The second part moves beyond Southeast Asia to exam-ine the emerging role of regional powers like China and Japan in the broadly defined context of peace operations.

ASEAN and the Conflicts of the 1990s

A trio of crises in Southeast Asia highlighted the institutional development of ASEAN. These were the Cambodian election controversy, the UN interven-tion in East Timor, and the monitoring of the conflict in Aceh. Each scenario exhibits a step in the evolution of ASEAN as regional body committed to pro-moting good governance and regional cooperation

The ASEAN Troika and the 1997–98 Cambodian Crisis

Events in Cambodia in 1997 spurred ASEAN to create an important new per-manent mechanism, the Troika. This instrument allows ASEAN to respond to crises with greater flexibility. The crisis began when the shaky coalition government, formed after the May 1993 Cambodian elections, was caught in a power struggle. Hun Sen, leader of the Cambodian People's Party (CPP), refused to accept the election result and pressured Prince Norodom Rana-riddh, the leader of the victorious FUNCINPEC party, into sharing power. Beginning in September 1993, Cambodia had two prime ministers: Prince Ranariddh (the "first prime minister") and Hun Sen (the "second prime min-ister"). In July 1997, Hun Sen staged a coup to oust Prince Ranariddh. The coup took place less than three weeks before Cambodia's scheduled formal entry into ASEAN. As a result, ASEAN decided to delay Cambodia's admis-sion until the crisis was resolved. (Cambodia eventually joined ASEAN in April 1999.) ASEAN insisted that Cambodia meet certain conditions before it could be admitted. However, to keep ASEAN engaged in Cambodia, the ASEAN Troika was created to assist in efforts to restore political stability in Cambodia. The Troika was to be composed of three ASEAN foreign ministers: Domingo Siazon of the Philippines (which at that time chaired ASEAN), Ali Alatas of Indonesia (because of Indonesia's prominent role in the negotiations that culminated in a 1991 peace treaty between warring factions in Cambo-dia), and Prachuab Chaiyasan of Thailand (because of Thailand's geographical proximity to Cambodia, and because it was hosting Ranariddh and several other Cambodian political exiles).[25]

The Troika took responsibility to mediate in the political crisis and set into motion "shuttle diplomacy" between King Norodom Sihanouk, Hun Sen, Prince Ranariddh, and Ung Huot, who Hun Sen had appointed as "first prime minister" in Ranariddh's place. The Troika conveyed ASEAN's position on various issues to the Cambodian interlocutors, particularly on the need to hold a credible election. Meanwhile ASEAN members offered their technical expertise in facilitating the holding of elections in the country, including sending representatives to serve as electoral observers for the general election in July 1998.[26]

Despite teething problems, the Troika initiative was generally considered a successful exercise in preventive diplomacy. The 1998 election was held in a relatively successful manner, and Cambodia was finally admitted into ASEAN in 1999. As observed by a Cambodian scholar, Sorpong Peou, ASEAN's intervention was significant in that it was confined to diplomatic mediation without any material or military support to either faction, and without any imposition of sanctions. These measures helped in preventing any escalation of the conflict.[27] The other salient factor for its success was the consent that the Troika received from the Cambodian government for ASEAN to play a mediating role in the crisis. As a Filipino diplomat argued, without such a mandate ASEAN's initiative would have quickly failed since it was a stark departure from the regional norm of noninterference in the domestic affairs of states.[28]

ASEAN's experience with the Troika in Cambodia eventually led to the formal establishment of the ASEAN Troika in 1999.[29] As defined by its Cambodian experience, the Troika was to be an ad hoc body comprising the foreign ministers of the present, past, and future chairs of the ASEAN Standing Committee. The positions would rotate in accordance with the ASEAN practice of rotating the chairmanship of the Standing Committee based on alphabetical order. The ASEAN paper on the Troika set as its purpose to enable ASEAN to address urgent and important political and security issues in a timely manner. By the time the Terms of Reference of the Troika were completed, however, the role of the Troika had become highly circumscribed, since it had to be compatible with the principles enshrined in the Treaty of Amity and Cooperation in Southeast Asia, particularly the "core principles of consensus and non-interference" in domestic affairs of states.[30] Thus, its constrained mandate reflected the controversies that emerged as a result of the new security challenges that confronted the region, including the dilemma over the Myanmar imbroglio.

Ad Hoc Volunteerism in Peace Operations and the East Timor Crisis (1999)

In contrast to ASEAN's active role in Cambodia, the East Timor crisis proved to be one of the most difficult challenges to ASEAN's approach to conflict prevention. Since Indonesia's annexation of East Timor in 1975, ASEAN had effectively stayed away from the controversy surrounding its biggest neighbor's occupation of the territory. ASEAN had staunchly maintained that the East Timor issue was an internal affair of Indonesia.

The situation took a dramatic turn in 1999 when the government of Indonesia under President Bacharuddin Jusuf Habibie decided to allow the people in East Timor to hold a referendum on the territory's future status—to become either an autonomous province of Indonesia or an independent state.

Indonesia, in consultation with the UN, agreed to the establishment of a UN mission to oversee preparations for the referendum. The UN Mission in East Timor (UNAMET) was established for this purpose on June 11, 1999. Four ASEAN members—Malaysia, the Philippines, Singapore, and Thailand—contributed to UNAMET by sending civilian police, staff members, and electoral volunteers.

The referendum was held in August 1999. A majority of 78.5 percent voted against the proposed "special autonomy" within Indonesia.[31] Despite the presence of UNAMET, violence erupted when anti-independence militia, reportedly backed by the Indonesian army, carried out systematic killing, sexual abuse, and destruction of property.[32] The atrocities drew strong reaction from around the world, with many governments, either individually or collectively, urging Indonesia to enforce law and order within the territory. The Indonesian government accepted an offer of international assistance on September 12, 1999, and the UN authorized a peacekeeping mission. The International Force in East Timor (INTERFET), led by Australia, was consequently deployed to restore peace and stability in East Timor. By then a significant number of people had been killed in East Timor, and the area had suffered massive property destruction and witnessed the forced displacement of thousands of people.

After Indonesia consented to international assistance, ASEAN officials began to discuss their countries' participation in INTERFET.[33] These discussions took place at the sidelines of the APEC Summit held in Auckland, New Zealand, from September 9 to 13, 1999. Prior to the APEC Summit, no ad hoc ASEAN meeting had been convened to address what was at that time a spiraling humanitarian crisis in the region.

While some ASEAN members participated in INTERFET and the UN Transitional Authority in East Timor (UNTAET) that was established in October 1999, their contributions became less visible in the barrage of criticisms against ASEAN's belated response and meager participation.[34] ASEAN officials responded to the criticisms by declaring that only the UN had the legitimacy and capabilities to undertake a preventive deployment or peacekeeping mission. As explained by ASEAN's former secretary-general, ASEAN "undertook consultations, arrived at consensus, and let individual members decide what specific contributions to make to the UN effort. Any other course would not have been possible, desirable or effective."[35]

Although it could be argued that ASEAN's response was consistent with its usual processes and modalities of conflict management, the crisis in East Timor nevertheless exposed ASEAN's inadequacy to respond to crises that required military intervention. It also highlighted the dilemma faced by an organization in responding to an internal problem of one of its member states. As pointed out by analyst Alan Dupont, ASEAN's deference to Indonesia over the issue of East Timor was essentially for pragmatic reasons since "maintaining good relations with Indonesia must take priority over self-determination for the East Timorese."[36] Furthermore, the reluctance to act was also due to the underlying concern among some ASEAN states that a similar kind of international response could be directed against them if and when the international community deemed it justifiable to carry out a humanitarian intervention.

While ASEAN did fail to take any preventive diplomatic measures to stem the crisis in East Timor, it was not completely passive. As noted earlier, a number of ASEAN members played significant parts in multilateral efforts to contain the conflict, albeit under the UN framework. This included the consecutive designation of Filipino and Thai officers as force commanders of UNTAET.[37] Moreover, the indirect role of ASEAN in Indonesia's decision to allow humanitarian intervention to take place must also be recognized. Although it is not widely acknowledged, Indonesia's consent to the humanitarian intervention was made possible when it received assurances from its ASEAN partners (including Thailand and the Philippines) that the Australian force would not be given a dominant role in the peace operation and that ASEAN would be involved in the mission. As explained by Thailand's former foreign minister, Surin Pitsuwan, President Habibie had wanted ASEAN to conduct the entire peacekeeping mission, but since ASEAN had no peacekeeping force he intimated to ASEAN officials that he was willing to accept humanitarian intervention as long as ASEAN led it. Thus, as has been pointed out by Pitsuwan, without ASEAN the crisis in East Timor could have been worse.[38]

ASEAN's involvement in the Cambodian and East Timor crises reveals a number of points relevant to our discussion of current initiatives in ASEAN. First, the absence of ASEAN institutional structures to manage and resolve conflicts did not preclude regional actors from undertaking elements of preventive diplomacy in order to lessen tensions and deal with conflicts in the region. Second, these preventive diplomacy measures were at best ad hoc. Third, given the ad hoc nature of these efforts, the results achieved were in turn either considered modest, relatively successful, or not sustainable. However, these preventive diplomacy measures did have the consent of the parties involved; without that consent, the preventive diplomatic efforts would not have had any effect whatsoever.

It was against this checkered experience that the proposal for an ASEAN Security Community (ASC) was introduced at the Ninth ASEAN Summit in Bali, Indonesia, in 2003. Regarded as an idea whose time had finally come, the ASC was seen by many as ASEAN's attempt at addressing the lack of institutional capacity in the region so that it could respond to new, emerging security challenges. The ASC and its components will be discussed at the end of this chapter.

ASEAN and the EU Aceh Monitoring Mission

The European Union's civilian Aceh Monitoring Mission (AMM) was established in August 2005 shortly after the Indonesian government and the Free Aceh Movement (GAM) concluded a peace agreement to end the thirty-year conflict in Aceh, which had claimed fifteen thousand lives and displaced thousands of people. Although the AMM largely consisted of personnel from EU member states, five ASEAN members also contributed: Singapore, Malaysia, Thailand, the Philippines, and Brunei Darussalam. The main objectives of the AMM were to assist the Indonesian government and GAM in implementing their memorandum of understanding (MOU), which focused largely on the demobilization of GAM and the decommissioning of its armaments.[39]

The AMM has already completed its first mandate of facilitating implementation of the MOU. It has been commended for its success in facilitating the peace agreement between the Indonesian government and GAM and in laying down the foundations for future work on reconstruction and peace-building in what was once a war-torn province of Indonesia. What is perhaps most salient in the establishment of the AMM and the participation of ASEAN, however, is that this was the second time that the state in conflict (in this case, Indonesia) had welcomed the involvement of ASEAN countries and the international community in assisting with its peace operation. It is also significant that the regional efforts undertaken under the broad rubric of peace operations were now being led and initiated by Indonesia—ASEAN's largest country. It was in fact Jakarta that conceptualized and advanced the idea of the ASEAN Security Community.

Developments beyond ASEAN: Regional Powers and Peace Operations

The developments taking place in Southeast Asia were, in a way, reinforced by changes occurring in the wider East Asian region, in particular the emerging role of China in regional and international affairs. As mentioned earlier, a strong motivation by ASEAN states to establish the ARF was to engage China and in the process reduce the strategic uncertainties prevalent during the immediate post–cold war period.

China's departure from its isolationist stance was welcomed in the region. Its growing interest in global affairs and regional multilateralism was demonstrated by China's increasingly robust participation in various UN peacekeeping missions. This change in attitude can be traced back to the mid-1980s, when China embarked on its economic reforms and adopted an open-door policy. Prior to this, China had generally been wary of UN peacekeeping operations, regarding them as illegitimate and a gross interference in a country's internal affairs.

As explained by Pang Zhongying, China's move toward a more market-oriented economy compelled Beijing to make major foreign policy shifts, and one of its first steps in this direction was to participate in UN peacekeeping missions.[40] In 1999 China sent its first group of military observers to serve in the UN Truce Supervision Organization (UNTSO), which monitored the cease-fire agreements in the Middle East.[41] China has participated in sixteen UN peacekeeping operations to date and has deployed approximately seven thousand peacekeeping soldiers and civilian police.[42] As of May 31, 2007, China was contributing 1,828 peacekeepers to twelve UN operations.[43] China has become one of the top troop-contributing countries to UN peacekeeping missions. With PKO troops spread across four continents, it provides more troops, military observers, and civilian police than all the other permanent members of the UN Security Council apart from France.

China's desire to be seen as a "normal" state and a responsible power in the region has led Beijing to be more committed to multilateralism. Participation in UN PKOs has been seen as an integral part of this new Chinese thinking, which has also been articulated in China's new security concept.[44] Peacekeeping has provided China the platform to demonstrate its emerging role as a regional and international actor.

These trends are politically important, especially when one also looks at the increasing participation of Japan in PKOs over the last decade. Japan's desire also to be seen as a "normal" nation has caused it to increase its profile in the international arena and become more active in multilateral peace operations. Despite the fact that the country's pacifist constitution may have hampered its more robust participation in past missions, this hurdle is now being addressed through incremental amendments to constitutional restrictions. In particular, the 2001 revision of the country's International Peace Cooperation Law has allowed for increased participation of Japan's Self Defense Force (SDF) in peacekeeping operations.[45]

It is interesting to note that Japan made its first significant foray into peacekeeping operations in East Asia. Following the enactment of its 1992 International Peace Cooperation Law, Tokyo dispatched 724 observers, civilian police officers, and logistic support staff to the UN mission in Cambodia (UNTAC) in the early 1990s.[46] It deployed 680 troops when it participated in UNTAET.[47] As of March 2005, Japan's cumulative contribution to UN peacekeeping operations totaled 4,633 personnel in eight missions.[48] Aside from Tokyo's field contribution, it has also been active in international humanitarian relief operations in places like Afghanistan and Iraq. Yet, despite having assumed the chairmanship of the UN Security Council Working Group on Peacekeeping Operations, Japan notably lags behind other countries in providing more troops. In addition to its residual constitutional constraints, Japan remains conscious of the way other countries in the region might perceive a more robust Japanese participation in PKOs. One senior Japanese foreign ministry official has nonetheless lamented Japan's lagging behind other countries, especially in light of its position as the largest economy in the region.[49]

Notwithstanding nagging concerns about an increased Japanese participation in peacekeeping operations and its reemergence as a military power—along with the realization that China's growing role in peacekeeping is indicative of rising power—the trend toward increased participation by these two regional powers should be regarded positively. China and Japan bring considerable assets to the region. Their continued willingness to cooperate and participate in peacekeeping operations should be a major contribution toward maintaining regional peace and stability.

From the foregoing discussions, one could surmise that there is an evolving congruence of views between the UN and the region on the need to enhance international and regional capacity in addressing security issues more effectively. It also follows that for this objective to be realized, efforts will have to be mutually constituted at various levels to allow for a task-sharing arrangement between the global, the regional, and the national actors. With this in mind, we now examine whether requirements for new peacekeeping or peace operations fit within the overall approaches to and mechanisms for regional peace and multilateral security cooperation.

The ASEAN Security Community: Advancing the Agenda of Peace Operations in East Asia

As observed by Yasushi Akashi, former UN undersecretary for humanitarian affairs, Asia has no regional framework "with [the] high integrity of a European Union or a NATO." However, he also expressed the hope that the ARF could "become such a high-integrity organization in the future, [although it is] still in its infancy period."[50]

In light of recent trends in regional security, however, it appears that one should look not to the ARF but to ASEAN when seeking an institution that, at the very least, might offer some semblance of a regional framework for managing peace. In this regard, we should examine ongoing efforts by ASEAN to establish a security community in Southeast Asia.

Bali Concord II and the ASEAN Security Community: An Idea Whose Time Has Come?

Despite the region's uneven record on peace operations, as exemplified by ASEAN's efforts in preventive diplomacy, it is noteworthy that the ASEAN Security Community (ASC) was adopted. In essence, the concept of a security community "was meant to provide a sense of purpose, a practical goal, and a future condition that all [ASEAN] members should strive for."[51] It was also about "raising political and security cooperation in ASEAN to a higher plane."[52] Since its launch in 2003, the ideas and modalities of the ASC have been the subject of intense deliberations by many parties in the region, including nonstate actors. The proposals for improving security cooperation in ASEAN are reflected in the 2004 Vientiene Plan of Action, which identifies the areas—or strategic thrusts—to realize the idea of a security community. These are political development, shaping and sharing of norms, conflict prevention, conflict resolution, and postconflict peace-building.[53]

To many observers of ASEAN, the mechanisms being proposed under the areas of conflict prevention and conflict resolution are remarkably progressive. In particular, the subheading "developing regional cooperation for maintenance of peace and stability" calls for the following activities:

- Promoting technical cooperation with the UN and relevant regional organizations in order to benefit from their expertise and experiences;
- Establishing/assigning national focal points for regional cooperation for maintenance of peace and stability;

- Utilizing national peacekeeping centers (which currently exist, or are being planned in some ASEAN Member Countries) to establish regional arrangements for the maintenance of peace and stability;
- Establishing a network among existing ASEAN Member Countries' peacekeeping centers to conduct joint planning, training, and sharing of experiences, with a view to establishing an ASEAN arrangement for the maintenance of peace and stability.

The desire to develop greater capabilities to participate in peacekeeping operations—which had formerly been politically "taboo"—is clearly stated. Moreover, the regional mechanisms that are being proposed for conflict prevention and conflict resolution (and even postconflict peace-building) are not only more proactive but indicate some shifts in attitudes on issues of state sovereignty and noninterference. These measures encourage a wider and deeper type of security cooperation that, in the past, would have been considered far too intrusive in the domestic affairs of states.

These ideas about peace operations are quite new for ASEAN and for the wider region. In fact, it was Indonesia that originally proposed that ASEAN consider having its own peacekeeping force. In explaining the rationale for this proposal, a spokesperson for the Indonesian government remarked that "ASEAN countries should know one another better than anyone else and therefore [we] should have the option . . . to take advantage of an ASEAN peacekeeping force to be deployed if they so wish."[54] While some ASEAN states had objected to the peacekeeping force proposal on the grounds that it was "too early" to consider setting up a force—and that it was highly problematic because "each country has its own policy about politics and the military,"[55] this proposal obviously has not been completely rejected, at least if one goes by what is outlined in the 2004 Action Plan. In fact, one of the alternatives that has been put forward in lieu of a regional peacekeeping force is the idea of setting up a regional peacekeeping training center. Moreover, military officials attached to peacekeeping units in some ASEAN states, such as Thailand, have already openly endorsed the similar idea of having regional coordinating centers for regional peacekeeping units—centers that would offer joint training exercises and joint PKO courses.

Aside from earlier reservations by ASEAN members about having peacekeeping troops, there was also the unspoken concern that this might send the wrong signal to countries outside the region, particularly China and Japan. Moreover, until some ASEAN countries started to contribute PKO forces to selected UN missions, such operations had not been part of the miliary doctrines of these states. Hence, the prospect of starting modestly by establishing peacekeeping centers is indeed a step in the right direction. Given the experience of ASEAN states (Thailand, Malaysia, the Philippines, Singapore) in peacekeeping operations within the region—in Cambodia and East Timor—one can be cautiously optimistic about its prospects in the medium term.

Moreover, if one examines the compatibility of this proposal on peacekeeping training centers with capacities outside the region, one would note that this dovetails well with the different training centers found in China and India. As argued in a study by the Council for Security Cooperation in the Asian Pacific, the region's various peacekeeping capacities should be better networked in order to minimize training inconsistencies and to benefit from others' practical experiences and "lessons learned." In addition, better net-working would forge greater intraregional cross-training in skills, doctrine, and applicable law. It would also permit others within the region who have an interest in developing greater peacekeeping capacity to draw upon the exist-ing skills and experiences of other regional members.[56]

Wider Remit of Security Cooperation in the ASC
In the meantime, while discussions continue about translating the ideas in the ASC into more concrete regional mechanisms, a number of significant events have also occurred that are indicative of changing attitudes about adopting more proactive solutions to security challenges and the resolution of conflict in East Asia. They involve not only ASEAN, but also other states in East Asia.

One area of cooperation identified by the ASC is in addressing threats to maritime security. The Straits of Malacca between Malaysia and Indonesia is a major sea lane of communication (SLOCS) that is not only essential for seaborne traffic of energy supplies but also for naval vessels from within and outside East Asia. The threat of piracy has increased at an alarming rate. Ac-cording to the International Maritime Bureau (IMB), the Strait of Malacca is the most piracy-infested channel in the world, and more than two-thirds of attacks reported to the IMB are in Asian waters.[57] In response to this growing threat, a trilateral arrangement among ASEAN's littoral states of Malaysia, Indonesia, and Singapore (MALSINDO) has been formed to conduct joint pa-trols along the Straits to beef up maritime security in the region. Since then, Thailand, the Philippines, and Japan have joined in many of MALSINDO's training activities in antipiracy, antiterrorism, and coast guard patrols.

There is also the recently launched Regional Cooperation Agreement on Combating Piracy and Armed Robbery against Ships in Asia (ReCAAP). Fi-nalized in November 2004, ReCAAP is the first government-to-government agreement to enhance the security of regional waters beyond Southeast Asia. The initiative, which was originally proposed by the Japanese prime minis-ter in October 2001, aims to enhance multilateral cooperation among sixteen regional countries (the ASEAN nations plus Japan, China, Korea, India, Sri Lanka, and Bangladesh) to combat sea piracy and armed robbery against ships in the region. The ReCAAP Agreement was finalized in November 2004 in Tokyo.[58]

Military Cooperation in Providing Disaster Relief and Rehabilitation
The devastation wrought by the 2004 Asian tsunami reflected the lack of any regional capacity to respond to natural disasters and provide emergency re-lief, rehabilitation, and reconstruction. In its aftermath, however, ASEAN embarked on a Regional Disaster Emergency Response Simulation Exercise (ARDEX-05), which commenced in 2005.[59] The simulation is to be an annual

exercise, bringing together personnel and mobilizing light-to-medium equipment geared toward providing immediate humanitarian assistance to affected countries in times of natural disaster.

Beyond ASEAN, ARF ministers have also decided to address natural disasters by working together on emergency relief, rehabilitation, and reconstruction measures, as well as on prevention and mitigation efforts.[60] More significantly, at the July 2006 ARF Ministerial Meeting, officials from member states (including the United States, China, Japan, and Russia) discussed possible guidelines for improving civilian and military cooperation in humanitarian operations including those in response to natural disasters. Improvements would involve standard operating procedures on civilian-military cooperation in disaster relief operations, and would entail developing a database of military assets of ARF members for disaster relief.[61]

Moving the ASC Agenda Forward and Prospects for Regionalization of Peace Operations

In assessing the prospects of the ASC and whether these might augur well for the regionalization of peace operations in East Asia, one should also keep an eye on other key developments that have a significant bearing on institutional developments in the region. Foremost among these is the decision by ASEAN leaders to work toward the creation of an ASEAN Charter. At the Eleventh ASEAN Summit in Kuala Lumpur, Malaysia, in 2005, the ASEAN's Eminent Persons Group (EPG) was convened and mandated to provide ASEAN leaders with broad policy guidelines on the drafting of such a Charter.[62] At this time the EPG has submitted its recommendations, and the ASEAN Summit of January 2007 has endorsed its report and tasked a High Level Task Force to commence drafting the Charter, which was adopted at the Thirteenth ASEAN Summit in Singapore in November 2007.

Why is the Charter important? Aiming to provide, among other things, a constitutional framework for ASEAN, the drafters of the Charter will have to navigate the tenacious waters of the ASEAN's norm on noninterference in internal affairs and address issues pertaining to conflict prevention and conflict resolution. Thus, the implications of the Charter on ASEAN's modalities in general and efforts related to peace operations in particular are enormous. ASEAN truly stands at a crossroads. It has to choose between maintaining the status quo or drastically altering the nature of interstate relations. To the extent that the Charter is meant to enshrine the operating principles of ASEAN in intra- and interregional relations, the EPG drafters of the Charter had to contend with prevailing sensitivities in the region and struggle with how the ideas of "flexible engagement" and "enhanced interaction" might be applied and incorporated as part of the regional modalities for conflict prevention.

Despite significant developments in ASEAN in building regional capacity and institutional development, considerable challenges remain. These involve the commitment of member states, shared interests, and institutional capacity. Such matters are indeed fundamental in determining whether ASEAN can effectively meet the increasing demands of responding to a host of new and emerging security challenges, which include undertaking more robust forms of peace operations in the region.

ASEAN has indeed come a long way toward maintaining and, if necessary, restoring peace and security in the region of Asia and the Pacific. From its initial efforts at building confidence among its member countries, it has increased its ability to promote norms and mechanisms for conflict prevention within the wider region, including among members of the ARF. The ASC initiative is an ambitious yet logical step toward furthering regional peace and security. The ASC has also come at a time when the region is in the throes of significant changes. It has been said that ASEAN cooperates best under pressure; hence the timing of the ASC could not have been better. The current security agenda of ASEAN is therefore well-suited to support current security strategies covering a number of functions, including peace operations to maintain international peace and security in the wider Asia.

Chapter 11

South Asia: Contributors of Global Significance

Dipankar Banerjee

The challenge of finding sufficient and effective forces for peace-keeping is a pressing concern in the world today. The potential of peace operations in a large number of conflicts that are ripe for solution may be sty-mied if the requisite forces are not available—a concern shared by Jean-Marie Guéhenno, UN undersecretary-general for peacekeeping operations: "A large number of conflicts are moving towards resolution, and millions of lives are being saved. To ensure that some of these conflicts really do have a chance of ending completely, the UN Security Council is creating a number of new peacekeeping missions. . . . There is a paradox, though, in this growing peace: The military resources needed to help keep the peace are being strained by so much peace to keep."[1] This was reinforced in November 2006, when then Secretary-General Kofi Annan said, "Today, half a century after launching the first peacekeeping mission, UN peacekeeping again faces another enormous challenge. With 18 current operations, a historic high of 93,000 personnel in the field, and a total that may reach 140,000 in 2007, UN peacekeeping is stretched as never before."[2]

Does South Asia have the potential to contribute substantially to a possible solution? The answer is yes: it has both the capacity and competence to provide more soldiers to undertake the complex integrated missions that are required to keep the peace in the world today. Whether its states will actually do so, however, is going to depend on a host of factors.

South Asia has been on the forefront of UN peace operations since the United Nations Operation in the Congo (ONUC), which started in 1960. In-dia's experience of peacekeeping began even earlier with its participation in the Neutral Nations Repatriation Commission in Korea in 1952. Pakistan's contribution to UN peacekeeping started when it joined ONUC in 1961. Bangladeshi personnel were first deployed in 1988 to a UN peace mission, the Iran-Iraq Military Observation Group (UNIIMOG). Nepal joined its first UN peacekeeping mission, the United Nations Observation Group in Lebanon (UNOGIL), in 1958, and since then it has provided substantial forces in spite of its own recent internal turmoil. Sri Lanka was little involved in UN peace-keeping until 2004, but it has participated in at least eight missions since. Together these five countries contribute about 40 percent of the total UN peace operations forces today. It would not be an exaggeration to assert that without this contribution, peace operations under the UN would not be as effective and could even collapse. A summary of this contribution as of the end of May 2007 and of the region's share of global peacekeeping can be found in tables 11.1 and 11.2.

The high competence of South Asian diplomatic and military leadership ensured that the region received adequate representation in top positions within UN peace operations. Names such as Indarjit Rikhye, Dewan Premchand, and Satish Nambiar call to mind the significant contributions to global peace by these stalwarts.[3]

This chapter will examine the potential of force contributions from South Asia for UN peace operations by analyzing existing military forces and their capabilities. It will then examine the contributions of these countries to UN peace operations in the past and their effectiveness. It will also examine the peace training institutions in South Asia, and the role they have played in sustaining these operations. The chapter will conclude by examining the future possibilities of force contributions from South Asia.

South Asian Armed Forces and Their Capabilities

Before providing an overview of peacekeeping participation from South Asia, it is necessary first to outline the history, nature, and composition of the armies of South Asia and to assess their capabilities. Present-day armies of South Asia (apart from Sri Lanka) have a long history. Whether in the ancient Hindu period or later Mughal era, the bearing of arms has always been an

Table 11.1. South Asia's Contribution to Global Peacekeeping (as of May 31, 2007)

Countries	Troops	Military observers	Civilian police	Total	World ranking[a]
Pakistan	9,659	130	830	10,619	1
Bangladesh	8,796	103	778	9,677	2
India	8,772	89	481	9,342	3
Nepal	3,054	44	537	3,635	4
Sri Lanka	953	7	88	1,048	22
Total	31,234	373	2,714	34,321	
Rest of the world	39,833	2,331	6,827	48,991	
World total	71,067	2,704	9,541	83,312	
South Asia's share (%)	43.95	13.79	28.45	41.20	

Sources: UN Department of Public Information, "Contributors to United Nations peacekeeping operations: monthly summary of contributions as of 31 May 2007," http://www.un.org/Depts/dpko/dpko/contributors/2007/may07_1.pdf; and UN Department of Peacekeeping Operations, "Ranking of military and police contributions to UN operations," May 31, 2007, www.un.org/Depts/dpko/dpko/contributors/2007/may07_2.pdf.

[a] World ranking refers to the country's standing among contributors to UN peacekeeping operations, as judged by numbers of personnel currently deployed.

Table 11.2. South Asia's Contributions to UN
Peacekeeping Operations since 2001

Year	Numbers	Share of total UN forces (%)
2001	15,600	33.11
2002	12,590	31.75
2003	16,161	35.27
2004	24,305	37.55
2005	30,290	43.37
2006	32,637	39.74

Source: UN Department of Public Information, "Monthly summaries of contributors to peacekeeping operations, Nations Peacekeeping," available at www.un.org/Depts/dpko/dpko/contributors/95-0.htm and www.un.org/Depts/dpko/dpko/contributors/.

Note: Force numbers include troops, military observers, and civilian police. They are calculated from the total contributions in December of the year indicated.

important duty of citizens and has entitled them to a higher status in society. This tradition of military service has continued to this day, and it has been reinforced by its direct lineage from the British Indian Army, where it was seen as an honorable and respectable profession. The Indian and Pakistani armies as they exist today have imbibed the military traditions, regimental affiliations, and professionalism of the British Indian Army, with its tradition of service going back to the eighteenth century.[4]

Under the British colonial rule, military service was voluntary. This tradition has continued in all the armies of South Asia to this day. Soldiers have assured income and a pension after retirement; hence, service in the military is coveted and volunteers far outnumber vacancies. Also continuing is a tradition of high discipline initially instilled in the British Indian Army. This army was responsible for maintaining law and order at home, and it did so through the early twentieth century. Its actions were based on the principle of "minimum force," since they were being undertaken against fellow citizens. The principle called for maintaining friendly interactions with civilians, a policy that is vital in any peace operation. This practice contrasts with the "warrior" ethos that is prevalent in many other armies, and that calls for seeking out and destroying the enemy with maximum force, preferably from a distance.

The British Indian Army was also employed in expeditionary campaigns in Iraq, Afghanistan, Burma, Southeast Asia, and China in the nineteenth and early twentieth centuries. In World War II a united India contributed well over two million soldiers to the Allied war effort, all volunteers; in no small measure, they helped determine the final outcome of that global conflict. Such campaigns inculcated a tradition of overseas service that also remains alive to this day.

With the end of British imperial rule in South Asia in 1947–48, the new state of Pakistan inherited one-third of the united Indian military, and India inherited the rest. Both maintained the traditions and professionalism of earlier times. Postindependence wars in South Asia, including the brief border war between India and China in 1962 and several border skirmishes between India and Pakistan, ensured that their military capabilities were enhanced and maintained at a highly professional level.

Both nations have competent armed forces, with a full range of military capabilities. In numbers alone India and Pakistan have the world's third and sixth largest armed forces, respectively. In military equipment and combat training their armies fare well by international standards. In a decade of joint military training with the United States the Indian armed forces of all three services—particularly the air force, in exercises in Indian skies as well as over Alaska—proved that they were comparable at least in training and effectiveness, if not in weaponry, to the U.S. armed forces.[5] Pakistan too has been exposed to western military training and doctrine as a member of the Southeast Asia Treaty Organization (SEATO) and Central Treaty Organization (CENTO) since the 1950s and 1960s and, more recently, as a non-NATO military partner of the United States.[6]

Bangladesh separated from Pakistan and emerged as an independent country in December 1971. Its officer corps, if not its rank and file, retains some links to the British period through its earlier affiliation with the Pakistani army.[7] Compared with either India or Pakistan, Bangladesh has a substantially less capable military. Nevertheless, it is fairly large in absolute numbers, especially in view of its limited operational deployment and the absence of a perceived military threat.

Sri Lanka's relative isolation provided it security and less reason to maintain an army in the past. In the colonial era security was provided by the British Royal Navy and a small military garrison. At independence it had only a few thousand soldiers in a volunteer force, whose main function was to assist the police in maintaining public order. It has thus lacked what may be defined as a military tradition. However, ethnic conflict on the island has necessitated a fairly large standing army today.

Nepal never came under direct British rule, and the king needed only a small force for the security of his household. Yet the king was allowed to maintain a larger army, so that in a case of urgent need, such as in support of the British during the Indian Army mutiny in 1857, it could come to its aid. Since the 1980s the army has steadily expanded and is today a significantly larger force.

Historically then, a certain military capability existed in all countries of South Asia. South Asian states never quite had to address the issue after the Second World War of whether an army was necessary or not. The newly emerged countries of South Asia needed armies both for external security and to protect the nation from internal challenges. All these factors have ensured that South Asia continues to have very substantial military capabilities and thus the potential for contributing to UN peace operations. This is precisely what has been recognized by the UN and is reflected in tables 11.1 and 11.2. A summary of current military strengths in South Asia is provided in table 11.3.

Table 11.3. South Asian Military Strengths

Countries	Total Armed Forces on Active Service	Paramilitaries (including reserves)
Bangladesh	126,500	63,200
India	1,316,000	1,293,229
Nepal	69,000	62,000
Pakistan	619,000	302,000
Sri Lanka	150,900	88,600

Source: James Hackett, ed., *The Military Balance 2007* (London: Routledge, January 2007).

UN Peace Operations Participation by South Asian Forces

India, Pakistan, Bangladesh, and Nepal have traditionally contributed substantial forces for UN peacekeeping. Sri Lanka too provided forces in the 1950s and again since 2000. Brief remarks on their contributions are described below.

India

India has been historically the largest troop contributor to UN peace operations, including forty-one missions and over eighty thousand soldiers.[8] As all Indian soldiers serve for a minimum of one year under the UN, rather than the more usual six-month tour of duty by many Western peacekeepers, the overall contribution is larger than these numbers might suggest. One hundred twenty-three Indian soldiers have died on peacekeeping duty since 1961, the largest number for any country to date, and over forty officers and soldiers have been decorated or have received commendations.[9] India also provided the bulk of the personnel for the three international control commissions (ICC) in Indochina after the 1954 Geneva Agreements, and it provided both the chair of the Neutral Nations Repatriation Commission in Korea and the custodian force (numbering 434 officers and 5,696 other soldiers) responsible for separating and repatriating the prisoners of war.[10]

Indian armed forces take immense pride in this participation. It is seen both as the nation's commitment to international peace and as a showcase of its military proficiency.[11] The principal motivation for participation, however, comes from India's determination to be seen as an international player. Peace operations are India's major contribution to the world and the showpiece of its global role. In its bid for permanent membership on the Security Council in 2004 and 2005, its contribution to peace operations was repeatedly mentioned as one of its principal justifications.

India's international responsibility is enshrined in its Constitution. In the section devoted to the "promotion of international peace and security," Article 51 specifically calls on the State to:

- promote international peace and security;
- maintain just and honorable relations between nations;
- foster respect for international law and treaty obligations in the deal-ings of organized peoples with one another; and
- encourage settlement of international disputes by arbitration.[12]

India has been popular as a peacekeeper for three principal reasons: the size and professionalism of its armed forces; the lack of such forces in most other developing countries, particularly in the early years after World War II; and India's neutral stance during the cold war—a position that made it acceptable to most sides in a conflict as an independent actor. The principle of equitable geographic and geopolitical representation in the UN system and the absence of well-trained militaries in the developing world made India doubly attractive.[13]

India's participation in peacekeeping operations (PKOs) declined in the post–cold war period. This is true both in absolute numbers and in proportion to the contribution of other countries to UN peace operations in the 1990s. This was due not so much to the absence of interest in India as to the fact that other developing countries acquired the capacity to participate. It also re-flected Indian reservations about the new types of PKOs that were initiated in this period. India was particularly troubled by the use of force to ensure com-pliance with UN decisions and by the trend to subcontract enforcement op-erations to standing or ad hoc military coalitions.[14] India was also troubled by the emerging concept of humanitarian intervention. This was later couched in more acceptable terms by the UN Commission report titled "Responsibility to Protect."[15] Nonetheless, India's experience with colonialism, under which aggression was often justified by various "civilized" objectives, meant that it could not accept such unilateral interventions even when sanctioned by the UN Security Council.[16]

The early years of the twenty-first century again witnessed active participa-tion from India in UN peace operations. Its overall numbers in 2007 hovered around ten thousand. An overwhelming majority have been in different hot spots in Africa. Two high-powered appointments in the UN's Department of Peacekeeping Operations were also held by Indians. The first was the UN ci-vilian police adviser from 2003–05, held by Ms. Kiran Bedi, an Indian police officer.[17] The other was military adviser, held by Lieutenant General Randhir Kumar Mehta from 2005.[18]

India's Peacekeeping Experience beyond the UN
A description of India's efforts at peacekeeping cannot be complete without a brief mention of the two efforts that were not UN operations. Both took place in the 1980s. The first was the Indian peacekeeping force dispatched to Sri Lanka in July 1987 as part of a bilateral agreement signed with Colombo.[19] Three characteristics of this intervention set it apart. The first is that it took place without any international agreement or under the United Nations Charter; instead, it was conducted as part of a bilateral accord. Second, it

took place within South Asia and was influenced by India's strategic concerns. A third characteristic was India's very substantial force participation: it deployed four infantry divisions and exceeded fifty thousand soldiers.

After two and a half years of intense counterinsurgency operations against a daring and suicidal enemy, the Indian peacekeeping force withdrew, leaving over one thousand soldiers dead and more than three times that number wounded, without having achieved anything substantial. It did not ensure peace for the island as hostilities resumed soon afterwards. Nevertheless, the experience imparted some very valuable lesson; these were internalized and have influenced subsequent participation in peace operations by India:

- Particularly in ethnic conflicts or civil wars, unless there is a peace to keep, foreign forces would find it very difficult to end the violence.
- Sovereignty remained a powerful force in most countries even in the late twentieth century, particularly against external interventions, and even when intended to maintain peace or for humanitarian assistance.
- The aim of counterinsurgency operations is limited to creating a positive environment to allow a peace process to begin. In the absence of a political dialogue, no substantive developments are likely. Armed forces alone cannot induce this learning.
- Finally, complex peacekeeping operations are perhaps even more difficult to launch than war and require no less preparation or resource.

Maldives 1988–89

The only other peacekeeping intervention by India apart from UN operations was in the Maldives, a tiny archipelago in the Indian Ocean and a member of the South Asian Association of Regional Cooperation (SAARC). Suddenly on the morning of November 3, 1988, the international community received frantic calls from the Maldivian government—including calls to the United States and India—for immediate military help against an attack by mercenary forces. Within eighteen hours of the call, the Indian air force landed two companies of troops at the Maldivian airport at Hulule after a nonstop flight from India of over two thousand kilometers. The Indian troops restored government rule at Male within hours. The fleeing mercenaries were apprehended in the Indian Ocean by Indian naval vessels patrolling the area. The brief, bloodless operation was completely successful.[20] The most important lesson from this operation was that a rapid response by well-trained soldiers with necessary resources could decisively rectify an adverse military situation that might otherwise destabilize a country for years.

Pakistan

According to its Inter Service Public Relations Office, "Pakistan, has always endeavoured to provide maximum possible support to maintain peace and stability around the world and has been at the forefront in international peacekeeping. Pakistan firmly believes in the purpose and principles of the UN Charter and its contribution to UN peacekeeping has been as wide ranging as the varied cultural, geographic, political and security conditions in which it had to operate."[21] The Pakistani armed forces are well trained and well equipped and are fully capable of conducting complex peace operations, as they have successfully demonstrated over the years. Pakistan has participated in sixteen peacekeeping missions and sent observers to many others. It remains one of the largest and most consistent troop contributors to UN peacekeeping missions in Africa, Asia, and Europe, and it has also sent detachments to Haiti. At the end of May 2007, around 9,920 Pakistani troops were deployed in twelve UN peacekeeping operations in Burundi, Côte D'Ivoire, the Democratic Republic of Congo, Ethiopia and Eritrea, Georgia, Haiti, Kosovo, Liberia, Sierra Leone, Sudan, Timor-Leste, and Western Sahara.[22] Pakistan has suffered ninety-six fatalities in UN peacekeeping operations as of May 31, 2007.[23]

The UN Operation in Somalia (UNOSOM) was Pakistan's most deadly, dangerous, and complex UN peace operation. Its prolonged commitment and presence in war-ravaged Somalia arguably qualifies Pakistan as one of the UN's most reliable peacekeepers. It also led to some debate and criticism within the country, particularly over one incident. On June 5, 1993, as part of aggressive actions against warring factions, Pakistani forces were sent to secure weapons and inspect the arms storage sites of the warlord leader Muhammad Aideed. This force was ambushed and lost twenty-four soldiers.[24] Overall in UNOSOM, Pakistan lost forty soldiers with another seventy-one wounded.[25] The June 5 incident was the greatest setback that Pakistan has suffered in a UN operation, and it raised some serious questions at home. Domestic opposition leaders criticized the government for actions against a Muslim "freedom fighter" (Mohammad Aideed) in another country and called for the withdrawal of its forces. The Pakistani government, however, persevered in Somalia and later, acceding to President Bush's request, even contributed another 2,500 soldiers, bringing its total force strength there to 7,500. This determination and support helped enhance Pakistan's image as a responsible peacekeeper. A withdrawal from Somalia might have also inspired unflattering comparisons with India, which had deployed five thousand soldiers in the western part of the country and had performed very creditably, earning the respect of all rebel factions with their conduct and humanitarian support.[26]

Indeed, rivalry and competition with India has been an important motivation for Pakistan in supporting UN peace operations. Consistently, the total forces provided by Pakistan and India have been comparable in size. At the same time there has been very good cooperation between Indian and Pakistani forces in the field (as well as with those from Bangladesh). Indian and Pakistani forces have served under each other's command. All manner of logistics and combat support tasks have been provided by one to the other, and these too have been very successful.

Two other important motivational factors for Pakistan are its desire to be seen as a country with strong military capabilities and its determination to be recognized as a responsible Muslim nation willing to fulfill its international commitments (its military potential has never been in doubt). As an Islamic nation, moreover, its forces have a symbolic value while peacekeeping in Islamic countries.

Bangladesh

Bangladesh has emerged in recent years as a lead country in contributing to UN peace operations. It should be recalled that the country itself became independent only in 1971. Less than four years after independence there was a military coup, and the army led the country for nearly fifteen years in two successive regimes. In spite of this turbulent beginning and the creation of an army virtually from scratch, Bangladesh has built an enviable reputation as a UN peacekeeper. Its first mission was in 1988 with the Iran-Iraq Military Observation Group (UNIIMOG), where it provided thirty-one military observers including the deputy chief military observer. By 1996, in barely eight years, it topped the list of UN troop contributing nations.[27]

It has several motives for participation:

- First, it sees participation in UN peace operations as a way of fulfilling its international obligations. As a "least developed country," its other options to contribute to the UN are limited.
- Bangladesh is also heavily dependent on international aid from international financial institutions and donor countries. Participating in UN peace operations helps project a positive image of the nation to its donors.
- Given its very high population density and its limited resources, economic opportunities within the nation are limited. Hence exporting surplus labor has long been a state policy, and contributing soldiers is an honorable way of achieving this. It also helps keep the military engaged and profitably employed—a powerful reason why there has been no military rule in recent years. Even today, when a civilian administration is running the country, it is the military that keeps the administration in office; nonetheless, it does so in a very limited and unobtrusive way, remaining in the background. The military is determined not to assume power openly; this would be to sully its image and deprive itself of peacekeeping opportunities.
- Long military rule allowed Bangladesh the luxury of creating a significant army of over 100,000 well-equipped soldiers. This has provided a very large pool from which to draw forces for UN operations. There is no perception of a major external threat; therefore, the personnel on UN duty are not missed in the country. This allows the country to contribute to UN operations on every occasion without any undue constraints.
- Finally, Bangladesh may well qualify as the ultimate source of "per diem" soldiers. The salary and allowances that its forces earn go a

long way toward supporting the economy. A portion of the amount is put in to an army welfare kitty, helping those who may be left out of participation. On average, every soldier gets a chance to serve on a UN operation once during his career. An officer would probably have an opportunity to serve twice.[28]

Nor should one underrate the contributions of Bangladesh. It provides an excellent example of an army that has evolved and matured through its participation in UN peace operations. Today its forces are as well equipped and trained as those from other developing countries. Its military observers, civil police contingents, and staff officers are competent and capable. There will always be doubts about how it will fare on missions with robust mandates and where major conflict is likely. But, even in such cases, Bangladesh has a good record. It participated in the highly dangerous UN Protection Force (UNPROFOR) in Bosnia in the first half of the 1990s, provided troops in the first Gulf War, and participated in the UN Transitional Authority in Cambodia (UNTAC) as part of the effort to establish democracy there in 1992–93.

Nepal

Nepal is another South Asian country that has consistently contributed to UN peace operations. It commenced participation in 1958. Out of a total of sixty-one peacekeeping operations authorized by the UN to February 2006, Nepal had participated in twenty-nine, contributing 50,167 military personnel. Forty-nine Nepalese peacekeepers had laid down their lives, and forty-eight had suffered serious injuries by that date.[29] The Nepalese Ministry of Foreign Affairs cites the inclusion of a Nepalese peacekeeper, Mr. Ratna Gurung, in the entourage of the UN team that received the Nobel Peace Prize in Oslo in 1988 as a sign of Nepal's widely recognized contribution to the maintenance of international peace and security.[30] Three Royal Nepalese Army officers have served as force commanders of UN peacekeeping operations: Lieutenant General Krishna Narayan Singh Thapa, in the United Nations Iraq-Kuwait Observation Mission (UNIKOM), from 1994 to 1995; Lieutenant General Victory Rana, in the United Nations Peacekeeping Force in Cyprus (UNFICYP), from 1999 to 2001; and Lieutenant General Balananda Sharma, in the United Nations Disengagement Observer Force (UNDOF) in the Golan Heights from 2004 to January 2007.

Nepal's forces have successfully lived up to the reputation of "Gurkha" soldiers, exemplifying bravery, courage, and steadfastness in battle. The legend was vindicated on numerous battlefields throughout the world, fighting under the British Indian army. The Nepal army, however, is patently different. It is not as well trained, equipped, or potent as its counterparts serving in both the Indian and British armies today. Yet all the character qualities associated with good soldiers are to be found in the Nepalese, and this is what has led to their general acceptance in UN peace operations. The Nepal army has never let this high reputation be devalued.

Nepal faces no external threat of consequence. However, since the internal Maoist uprising in 1996—and the military's direct involvement in countering this uprising after 2001—the availability of forces has understandably gone down. This situation may well change now that there has been a calm year following the peaceful uprising in April 2006 that led to the restoration of democratic rule after more than a year of direct rule by King Gyanendra.

Sri Lanka

As mentioned briefly earlier, Sri Lanka has perhaps had the least military exposure of all South Asian countries prior to independence. Its first involvement in a UN peacekeeping operation was in 1960, when a group of six service personnel from the Sri Lankan army led by Brigadier General C. T. Caldera deployed to the ONUC mission in Congo. This first group was replaced in 1961 by a contingent led by Brigadier General J. G. Balthazar. Thereafter, there was no involvement in peacekeeping missions by Sri Lanka for around four decades.[31] This can be explained both by domestic political developments and, since 1983, by ethnic civil war with the Liberation Tigers of Tamil Eelam.

In the last seven years, however, Sri Lanka has provided the services of military and police personnel for UN peacekeeping operations in different conflict zones around the world: the UN Transitional Administration in East Timor (UNTAET), the UN Mission of Support in East Timor (UNMISET), the UN Office in Timor-Leste (UNOTIL); the UN Integrated Mission in Timor-Leste (UNMIT); the UN Stabilization Mission in Haiti (MINUSTAH); the UN Organization Mission in the Democratic Republic of Congo (MONUC); the UN Advance Mission in Sudan (UNAMIS); the UN Mission in the Sudan (UNMIS); the UN Mission for the Referendum in Western Sahara (MINURSO); the UN Operation in Burundi (ONUB); the UN Operation in Côte d'Ivoire (UNOCI); the UN Mission in Liberia (UNMIL); and the UN Mission in Sierra Leone (UNAMSIL).[32] According to Sri Lankan Army records, about 1,602 military personnel had already completed their tours of duty with UN peacekeeping missions by 2006.[33] They had served in different capacities, including as military observers and staff officers. As of May 31, 2007, there were 1,048 Sri Lankan service personnel serving in UN peacekeeping missions, but it is difficult to see how long this can be sustained since the nation, as of early 2007, has returned to a state of undeclared internal war with the Tamil Tigers.[34]

South Asian Peace Operations Training Institutions

Training centers specifically for peacekeeping are relatively new in South Asia, as they are elsewhere in the world. Training for peacekeeping was initially provided in all armies in existing military training schools. Special courses were developed keeping in mind the requirements of a theater for specific peace operation missions. Special capsules or training workshops were held

to train personnel for these tasks. This began to change in the early 1990s
when the surge in peacekeeping operations called for special training facilities to be created for a much larger number of personnel.

Bangladesh was the first South Asian country to set up a separate institution, initially called the Peace Keeping Operation Training Centre (PKOTC)
in 1999; it became the Bangladesh Institute for Peace Support Operation
Training (BIPSOT) in 2002.[35] The Institute is located some forty-five kilometers from the capital Dhaka at Rajendrapur. The stated objectives of the
Institute are to provide tactical and operational training for UN peace support
operations and to develop faculty for research on peace and conflict studies.
Since UN peace operations are by far the most important activity of the Bangladesh army, the Institute enjoys high priority and sufficient resources are
allotted to it. Currently the Institute conducts the following courses for the
military, police, and civilians, of the Bangladesh army, as well as for a number
of other armies:

- Potential Observers and Staff Officers Course (POSOC)
- Contingent Members' Course (CMC)
- Predeployment Training (PDT)
- CIVPOL Training
- Special Training peculiar to different missions, or operations-
  related tasks.

The BIPSOT has hosted international symposia with the support of the
U.S. Pacific Command, and it has trained a large number of personnel from
its armed forces and a few from selected countries of Asia and Africa. The
institute has contributed in a significant manner in meeting the pressing requirement of instructors for its large peacekeeping commitments. BIPSOT
has plans to upgrade its existing facilities further to meet domestic peacekeeping training requirements as well, but also to train foreign peacekeepers.

India's peace operations training center is part of the United Service Institution of India in New Delhi; it is called the USI-Centre of UN Peacekeeping
(USI-CUNPK).[36] It conducts international training capsules for military contingent officers, military observers, and staff and logistics officers.

The USI-CUNPK is a member of the International Association of Peacekeeping Training Centres (IAPTC). The presidency of IAPTC, along with its
secretariat, was recently handed over to the USI-CUNPK. While the presidency changes every year, the secretariat remains at a selected institute for a
much longer period. Since its inception ten years ago, the IAPTC secretariat
was provided by the Pearson Peacekeeping Centre in Canada. With the secretariat now in India, it will facilitate the coordination of institutes, particularly
those in the developing world and especially in South Asia. It is also a high
recognition of the USI-CUNPK, and it should allow it a greater role in future
peacekeeping activities around the world.

On June 15, 2005, Pakistan's then minister of state for defense, Za-
hin Hamid, said that his country was "actively considering" setting up a

peacekeeping training center.[37] Even though it remains one of the most active peacekeepers in the world, Pakistan has not hitherto felt the need for a separate training center for peacekeeping. This task continues to be performed by its existing military schools.

Sri Lanka too has an institution for peacekeeping training. Set up in 2004, it is called the Institute of Peace Support Operations Training Sri Lanka (IPSOTSL) and is located at Kukule Ganga, in southern Sri Lanka. The main objective of the institute is to conduct pre- and postdeployment training for UN peacekeepers.[38]

These peacekeeping training centers seem to suggest that there is a lot of interaction and coordination in peace operations among South Asian countries. In reality, this is far from true. These are not regional peace training centers in any thoroughgoing sense of the term; in fact, they function mainly to train national forces. India trains some Sri Lankan peacekeepers on request and, of course, holds frequent annual training conferences. Pakistan, however, is excluded from this. It is only the U.S. Pacific Command that occasionally brings South Asian countries together in joint peacekeeping seminars.

The enormous potential to develop a joint South Asian capability to conduct large-scale peace operations by an integrated South Asian force is not likely to evolve in the near future. This is a great pity, for if this were possible, South Asia could provide forces of sufficient strength and capability to conduct numerous complex missions with high capability and success. For now this must remain hostage to the geopolitical concerns of the region.

Motivation and Support for Peace Operations

What is it that has allowed South Asia to emerge as a major force-contributing region in UN peace operations today? Many of the reasons have been examined separately under respective national examinations. There are both common threads that run through all of these countries, and others that are specific to particular nations.

Among the common points are a commitment to advancing international peace efforts, earning international goodwill, showcasing national military capabilities, and upholding norms of humanitarian support to prevent suffering and casualties in internal conflicts. There is little that is different in South Asia in these senses than in most other countries. What is different, however, is the availability of surplus military capabilities to accomplish these tasks. If the two major internal conflicts in South Asia—the Maoist insurgency in Nepal and the civil war in Sri Lanka—were to end, there might be little motivation to retain large military forces in these countries, particularly if the South Asian Association of Regional Cooperation (SAARC) were to really move toward closer regional integration. However, while the situation in Nepal seems to be more promising, Sri Lanka is again entering a state of civil war from which there seems to be no early end. In the interim, there will be sufficient forces available for participation in UN peace operations.

Bangladesh in particular provides an interesting case. A casual observation may well suggest that it maintains an army for the sole purpose of participating in international peace operations. Certainly the massive per diem subvention plays a large role in its decision to contribute to peacekeeping operations. The goodwill it generates internationally may be considered a bonus effect. The whole venture is an effective outsourcing operation with win-win outcomes for both the developing as well as the developed world, including the UN. We are perhaps not quite prepared to accept peace operations as a purely commercial proposition and outsourcing phenomenon, but in reality that is what it has come to be in Bangladesh's case. For Pakistan and India, the cash for peacekeeping soldiers may well be an added incentive to individuals, but as a factor for national motivation it is likely to be marginal.

For India especially, participation in UN peace operations is a particularly honorable activity. Units are selected for their outstanding performance in operations. Individual officers are carefully selected based on their records of service. Therefore, being selected for UN peace operations is recognition of one's performance and is a high reward in itself. Given the large size of the Indian army, only a small fraction of soldiers get to participate, and there is great competition. The Indian government has a set of policies for participation in such operations, and it has in the past refused to contribute forces where these did not meet the criteria.

Future Participation from South Asia

Given the above considerations, what is the future of South Asian force contribution to UN peacekeeping operations? Quite obviously South Asia, despite already being the leading contributor to peace operations, still has surplus capacity; provided there is no further conflict within the region, this capacity can be utilized for greater international good. Yet, some conditions must be addressed to translate this possibility into reality:

- One is a need for greater international recognition of the role being played by South Asia. This needs to be met by allowing a higher degree of participation by South Asian countries in international decision making, particularly in areas of peace support operations.
- A second is allowing greater representation of South Asia in contracts for logistics and communications support.
- Third, the present rates of subventions for allowances and pay for soldiers should continue, and the terms should be revised as necessary.
- Finally, efforts should continue to end South Asian conflicts. Two UN missions are currently in South Asia (apart from Afghanistan)—in Kashmir and Nepal—and it is to be hoped that another may be established for Sri Lanka. Should these conflicts come to an end (particularly the one in Jammu and Kashmir), conditions in the region could be transformed. In turn this could lead to a situation where

much greater effort from the region would be possible without any strain on resources.

Conclusion

South Asia has consistently been in the forefront of UN peace operations for about five decades. Even as these operations enter a new stage, with global commitments on a scale not perhaps visualized by the original framers of the UN Charter, the challenge can be met. South Asian countries are perhaps uniquely placed to contribute to this effort. With their belief in internationalism and commitment to the UN Charter and its ideals, they also have the ability to provide forces that have demonstrated their competence and capability in a wide variety of integrated peace operations around the world for over five decades.

Appendix 11.1 United Nations Force Commanders from South Asia

Peacekeeping Operations	Force Commanders	Duration
UNSF	Maj. Gen. Saiduddin Khan (Pakistan)	Oct. 1962 – Apr. 1963
UNYOM	Lt. Gen. P.S. Gyani (India)	July 1963 – Sep. 1964
UNEF I	Lt. Gen. P.S. Gyani (India)	Dec. 1959 – June 1967
	Maj. Gen. Indar J. Rikhye (India)	Jan. 1966 – June 1967
UNTAG	Lt. Gen. Dewan Prem Chand (India)	Jan. 1980 – Mar. 1990
UNPROFOR	Lt. Gen. Satish Nambiar (India)	Mar. 1992 – Mar. 1993
UNOSOM I	Brig. Gen. Imtiaz Shaheen (Bangladesh)	June 1992 – Apr. 1993
ONUMOZ	Maj. Gen. Mohammad Abdus Salam (Bangladesh)	Mar. – Dec. 1994
UNIKOM	Maj. Gen. Krishna N.S. Thapa (Nepal)	Jan. 1994 – Dec. 1995
	Brig. Gen. Upinder Singh Klair (India)	Aug. – Oct. 2003
UNAMIR	Brig. Gen. Shiv Kumar (India) (*Acting*)	Dec. 1995 – Mar. 1996
UNAMSIL	Maj. Gen. Vijay Kumar Jetley (India)	Dec. 1999 – Sep. 2000
	Maj. Gen. Sajjad Akram (Pakistan)	Oct. 2003 – Sep. 2005
UNIFIL	Maj. Gen. Lalit Mohan Tewari (India)	Aug. 2001 – Feb. 2004
UNDOF	Lt. Gen. Bala Nanda Sharma (Nepal)	Jan. 2004 – Mar. 2007
UNMIS	Lt. Gen. Jasbir Singh Lidder (India)	Mar. 2005 – Present

Source: UN Department of Peacekeeping Operations, http://www.un.org/Depts/dpko/dpko/index .asp

Chapter 12

The Greater Middle East: Problems of Priorities and Agendas

PAUL R. PILLAR

No region would appear to be in greater need of effective peace operations than the Middle East. Long-running conflicts fester, giving rise to bouts of warfare and insurgency, which in turn raise legitimate fears about escalation and violence spinning out of control. Not only do the prevalence and virulence of armed conflict in the region make the need for a robust and effective regional capability for peace operations evident; the region has financial resources—in the form of the petroleum-based wealth of several states in the region—that could help to bankroll such a capability. Moreover, regionally based peace operations presumably would have the support and encouragement of outside powers that have expended many of their own resources in the Middle East and that worry about the prospects for escalation and expansion. Nonetheless, up till now the Middle East has been one of the least successful regions in developing or deploying a regional capacity for peace operations.

The explanation for this failure lies mainly in the structure of conflict within the Middle East, the extent to which Middle Eastern governments view themselves as parties to those conflicts, and the lenses through which most Middle Easterners view the conflicts. There are too many who believe they have a direct stake on a particular side of a dispute, and too few who have the disinterested outlook of a peacemaker or peacekeeper.

Impact of the Arab–Israeli Conflict

The conflict that has overshadowed all others in the region for more than half a century, and that has been mainly responsible for the unfertile ground that has precluded growth of a regional capability for peace operations, is that between Israelis and Arabs. This includes especially the dispute between Israelis and Palestinian Arabs over land and statehood in Palestine. It also includes the wider conflicts between Israel and neighboring Arab states, some of which still are formally in a state of war with Israel. The Arab–Israeli conflict has been so salient, so laden with emotion, and so much of a defining dimension for generations of Middle Easterners that it colors and constrains thinking about all security issues, including any thought that might be given to peace operations. By cutting such a strong and seemingly permanent divide through the region, it has been the largest impediment to the development of the kind of regional consensus that would be necessary for an effective peace operations structure.

Because of the ethnic dimension of this conflict, all Arabs feel themselves, to varying degrees, to be parties to it. It is a conflict that pits Israel against not just Palestinians or Syrians, but against all Arabs. This largely negates the benefit that might otherwise flow—for peace operations as for any other cooperative regional endeavor—from the common ethnicity that most of the region's people share. Arabs cannot be neutral peacemakers or peacekeepers in any specific conflict that is an extension of the Arab–Israeli conflict. Moreover, the conflict—as an all-purpose reference point, distraction, and excuse for inaction—has inhibited any initiative that might otherwise have been taken to address peace operations for other conflicts in the region, just as it has inhibited the forthright addressing of many other problems within the Arab world.

The religious dimension of the conflict—seen as largely Jew versus Muslim—provides an additional basis for Middle Easterners to identify with one or the other side rather than with a disinterested regional interest in keeping the peace. This is evident, for example, in the emphasis that Saudi leaders place on the disposition of holy places in Jerusalem. Saudi King Abdullah Ibn Abdulaziz Al-Saud—author of a peace plan that gained the endorsement of other Arab governments in 2002 and became known as the Arab Peace Initiative—has indicated that, although it is up to the Palestinians to decide what is acceptable on other issues that divide them from Israel, all Muslims have a stake in control of the holy sites.

Israel's status as an outcast within a largely Arab region makes it unacceptable to Israelis to entrust any aspect of their security to any mission dominated by their neighbors. The same outcast status also rules out Israeli involvement in any peace operations elsewhere in the Middle East. As a result, the militarily strongest state in the region can play no role either as a consumer or as a provider of regionally based peace operations.

Other Divisions

To lesser degrees, other fault lines in the region also work against the consensus and cooperation needed for effective security operations. One is the line between Arabs and Persians, across which the bloodiest war in the region in recent decades was fought—the Iran–Iraq war of 1980–88, in which perhaps a million died, although estimates of casualties in the war are uncertain. Here again, shared ethnicity makes all Arabs parties to the conflict. That was a major basis of support for Saddam Hussein in sustaining his folly.

Among Arab governments, the shared ethnicity that could be the basis for enhanced security cooperation has underlain a sort of intramural rivalry that is all the more intense to the extent that each Arab regime is seen as an alternative model—and thus a threat—to other regimes. Conservative monarchies regard socialist republics this way. And among the latter, the Syrian and Iraqi wings of the Ba'athist movement have illustrated how ethnic brethren who also are ideological soul mates can be bitter rivals because each purports to be a model and leader for the rest of the Arab world.

In short, the ethnic and political map of the Middle East fosters attitudes that are less those of neighbors interested in the stability of their neighborhood and more those of participants in family feuds. It is an inhospitable environment in which to build a standing capacity for peace operations.

The Arab League

The international organization whose membership is closest to being coterminous with the Middle East is the League of Arab States. The League, currently with twenty-two members, is one of the oldest of the current regional organizations, having been established in the closing months of World War II.[1] According to its charter, the League was to protect Arab independence and sovereignty, to promote Arab interests in general, and to enhance political, economic, social, and military cooperation among member states.[2] The founding of the League was accompanied by hopes that it would be a vehicle for deeper Arab unity—aspirations that later found voice in the Arab nationalism of Egyptian President Gamal Abdel Nasser, and in a variety of merger and unity schemes involving Nasser's Egypt and other Arab states. The League's charter, however, was phrased in the more modest terms of cooperation and amity rather than unification, and its work has never put it on a track to be a major security player in its own right.[3]

Although the Arab League's founding predates that of the United Nations by three months, its founders shaped it partly with an eye toward the impending creation of the new world organization. Some of the vagueness and dearth of specific procedures in the League's charter reflected a deliberate effort to keep it flexible enough to be able to adapt to the UN.[4] The earlier League of Nations' covenant also served as a model for some of the language in the Arab League's charter.[5]

The Arab League's organization and procedures make it more of a forum for discussion and debate among members, and a means for coordinating what member states would be inclined to do anyway, than an instrument for impelling members to take action they would not otherwise take. The highest body of the League is its Council, which has some declared functions that sound much like those of the UN Security Council, such as coordinating defensive measures in the event of aggression. It also is assigned other roles, such as supervising the execution of agreements between member states and determining how the League will cooperate with the UN. The Council meets semiannually and may be convened in extraordinary session at the request of any two member states.

Unlike the UN Security Council, however, the Council of the Arab League is not a specialized body with a select membership. Instead, all members of the League are represented, each having an equal vote. Council decisions are binding on all members only if they are unanimous. Other decisions are considered binding only on those member states that supported them.

A variety of technical and specialized committees support the Council on such matters as finance, administration, and legal issues. In addition, the League has specialized ministerial councils to promote cooperation and common policies on information, home affairs, legal affairs, health, housing, social affairs, transport, youth and sports, telecommunications, and the environment.

A secretariat is headed by a secretary-general, whose appointment requires a two-thirds vote of the League's Council. The secretariat has been located in Cairo for all of the League's history, except for a decade when it was in Tunis—a consequence of Egypt's membership in the League being temporarily suspended following its conclusion of a peace treaty with Israel. All but one of the League's secretaries-general have been Egyptians. The secretariat is divided into several departments, some of which correspond to departments in the UN Secretariat, but there is no department for peacekeeping operations.

The Arab League's most significant departure—at least on paper—into military matters was the signing of a collective defense pact in 1950.[6] The agreement established a joint defense council, comprising foreign and defense ministers, to address collective security and preparation of joint defenses. The pact also created a permanent military commission, comprising representatives from the general staffs of member states, to construct plans for joint defense, coordinate their implementation, and study the application of resources to joint military efforts. Despite the apparently sweeping functions of these bodies, however, there has been little or no military cooperation at the level of the Arab League since the 1973 Arab–Israeli war.[7] The League also has had no permanent military institutions devoted to peace operations, such as a regional training center.

The Arab League's current secretary-general—a dynamic and charismatic Egyptian diplomat and former foreign minister, Amre Moussa—has pushed a package of proposals intended to make the League stronger and more effective. He achieved a breakthrough in December 2005 with the convening in Cairo of the first-ever Arab regional parliament. (The Arab League hitherto lacked any sort of assembly comparable to the UN General Assembly.) The Arab parliament consists of four representatives from the legislature of each member state (or, for states that lack elected legislatures, from their appointed advisory councils). It is to be based in Damascus, Syria, and to meet twice a year. The current parliament is considered interim and has five years to draft arrangements for a permanent successor. Some Arab League officials have expressed hope that the permanent parliament will have powers comparable to those of the European parliament, perhaps with direct election of representatives.[8] For now, however, the Arab parliament has no legislative authority and is empowered only to give its opinion on matters referred to it by the Council of the Arab League.

Some of Amre Moussa's other ideas could have even more significance, especially for peace operations. One would be creation of an Arab security council to address regional disputes.[9] That proposal evidently has not yet gained traction among Arab heads of state. It no doubt gives them far more reason for pause—and for worrying about how it could affect their own national interests—than does the creation of a talking shop for parliamentarians.

Peace Operations by the Arab League

The Arab League twice has deployed under its auspices a joint Arab military force to perform a peacekeeping operation. The first was in newly independent Kuwait in 1961, as an indirect response to fears of war arising from Iraq's claims that Kuwait was rightfully part of Iraq.[10] The crisis began with the signing of an agreement between the United Kingdom and Kuwait in June 1961, reaffirming Kuwait's independence and sovereignty. Within days, Baghdad declared its sovereignty over Kuwaiti territory. Less than a week later, amid rumors that Iraq would forcefully exercise its claim, Britain deployed six thousand troops to Kuwait.

Although the new Kuwaiti government had invited the British troops, members of the Arab League denounced the deployment as external interference in the affairs of an Arab state. The Council of the League agreed to grant Kuwait's request for membership, but only in exchange for its pledge to ask the British to leave and to accept in their place an Arab League force. The Iraqi representative did not participate in the Council's vote, and Iraq refused to give up its claims.

The Arab League force that was assembled over the next three months totaled 3,300 troops, mostly from Saudi Arabia and Egypt with smaller contributions from Jordan and Sudan. A Saudi officer commanded the force. Shortly after the deployment was complete, however, Egyptian President Nasser reversed course and pulled his country's troops out, his rationale being that he did not want to be seen as interfering in Kuwaiti affairs. Later in 1962 the Kuwaiti government requested that the Arab force be drawn down to only a token element. The Saudi and Jordanian contingents left in early 1963, with the Sudanese element being the last to leave. The crisis abated when a coup in February 1963 brought a different Iraqi government to power and Kuwait made overtures to the new regime in the hope of better relations.

The operation in Kuwait illustrated some of the principal attributes of Arab thinking about actual or potential peace operations in the region. One is the emphasis on removing, or keeping out, non-Arab and non–Middle Eastern forces. The direct, immediate reason for deployment of the Arab League force in Kuwait was to get the British troops out, and in that regard it succeeded.

A second feature is the major part that conflicts of interest among Arab states played—in this instance, both in the function that a multilateral force served and in the complications and constraints that it faced. The deployment of the Arab force was not really peacekeeping in the sense of a neutral intercession but rather—to the extent it might have served a purpose beyond getting the British out—a tripwire to deter any Iraqi aggression against Kuwait. Taking sides in a dispute over sovereignty that involved one of the larger and stronger Arab states was, ipso facto, a source of discomfort to other Arab states, including Egypt as a principal contributor and Kuwait as the host state for the force.

A third attribute of the Kuwait operation is that it did nothing to resolve the underlying dispute, as demonstrated by Saddam Hussein's invasion of Kuwait three decades later. It was a stopgap response to an immediate need involving a non-Arab force and not an investment in long-term peace and stability.

The other, more challenging, experience of the Arab League in deploying a multinational force involved the Lebanese civil war in the late 1970s and early 1980s.[11] The complexities of the multifaceted disorder in Lebanon, overlaid with elements of the Arab–Israeli conflict, the statelessness of the Palestinians, and the regional ambitions of an Arab state such as Syria, would have made any peacekeeping effort there extremely difficult. Many of the same challenges bedeviled the later Western, U.S.-led multinational force, whose experience in Lebanon was in large part a failure. The Arab League faced, in addition to these challenges, sharp divisions among its own members.

The League's Council first tried to address the fighting in Lebanon in the latter half of 1975, but Lebanon, Syria, and the Palestine Liberation Organization (PLO) boycotted the proceedings, and nothing was decided. Further escalation of combat in the first half of 1976 led to Syrian military intervention in June 1976. In response, the Arab League resolved to create an Arab Security Force with the stated intention of replacing Syrian forces and with the proviso that it would stay in Lebanon only as long as the Lebanese president so requested. Lebanese acceptance of the Arab force was grudging but finally came after a pledge that the force would be under the Lebanese president's control.

All Arab League members except Iraq eventually endorsed the Arab Security Force, with a mandate to "maintain security and stability" in Lebanon.[12] Libya, Saudi Arabia, South Yemen, Sudan, and the United Arab Emirates contributed troops—not in place of, but in addition to, the larger Syrian presence. Later deliberations of the League called for further augmentation of the force, which was renamed the Arab Deterrent Force (ADF). Some member states (and the PLO) objected to the size of the Syrian contingent, but no agreement was reached on what to do about it. The ADF had some positive effects in stabilizing parts of the country, but it did not manage to disarm the militias that were the main protagonists in the violence. It also never ventured into the part of Lebanon that is closest to Israel (south of the Litani River), leaving Palestinian guerillas free to operate in that area.

When escalating Israeli–Palestinian violence led to Israel's seizure of almost all Lebanese territory south of the Litani in March 1978, the Arab League Council condemned the action, called for further mobilization of Arab resources, and extended the mandate of the ADF. However, the Egyptian peace initiative, in connection with which President Anwar Sadat had traveled to Jerusalem, introduced new and sharp divisions within the League. In protest against Sadat's initiative, Algeria, Iraq, Libya, South Yemen, and Syria all boycotted a summit meeting intended to deal with the latest phase in the Lebanese crisis.

By then, the non-Syrian participants already were feeling uneasy about their position in Lebanon and had begun to pull out, beginning with the Libyans and South Yemenis. Christian Lebanese leaders—against the background of heavy fighting between Christian militias and the Syrian contingent of the ADF—also became opposed to renewal of the ADF's mandate. By mid-1978 Lebanese President Elias Sarkis acknowledged that he had no control over the force. Less than two years later, further withdrawals by the minor troop contributors left only the Syrians.

Following the full-scale Israeli invasion of Lebanon in June 1982, the Lebanese government called for withdrawal of all non-Lebanese forces. In August Lebanon agreed to the deployment of a U.S.-led, non-UN multinational force comprising U.S., French, and Italian troops. British troops joined this force in 1983. An Arab League summit in September 1982 acknowledged a request from the Lebanese government to end the ADF's mission. New Lebanese President Bashir Gemayel formally declared the dissolution of the ADF in March 1983, although Syrian troops remained in the country.

Some of the patterns first seen in the Arab League's deployment to Kuwait in 1961 arose, albeit in a somewhat different form, in this later mission in Lebanon. The idea of an Arab force as an alternative to intervention by Western or other non-Arab forces was again present, although in Lebanon it was a Western force that took the place of the Arab one rather than vice versa. Divisions among Arab governments were even more intense during the Lebanon crisis than they had been in the Kuwait case. Syria played the previous Iraqi role of a dominating, and in some eyes threatening, local power, but with the added dimension that it actually invaded the country in dispute and began a decades-long military domination of it. The divisions among Arab states were mirrored in the lines of conflict among Lebanese parties and militias. The divisions among Arab regimes were further exacerbated by Sadat's peace initiative toward Israel, which led to a decade-long ostracism of Cairo in Arab circles.

By almost any measure the Arab League's military mission in Lebanon was a failure. Unlike in Kuwait, the Arab League's force in Lebanon did not even succeed in keeping a Western force out. Terrorist attacks by Hezbollah, not substitution of an Arab peacekeeping element, eventually drove the Western multinational force out of Lebanon in 1984. The Lebanese civil war would continue for several more years until the Saudis and Syrians succeeded in brokering a new political formula, the Taif Accords, in 1989.[13] The issue of the Syrian military presence in Lebanon was left to fester for more than two decades, until the assassination of the popular Lebanese politician Rafiq al-Hariri in 2005 generated enough pressure on Damascus to withdraw its troops.

In the wake of the experience in Lebanon, it was not surprising that the Arab League demonstrated neither the confidence nor the competence to mount effective peace operations when future opportunities to do so arose. The biggest test of the League's ability to address seriously a security problem within the Arab world was the naked aggression committed by one of its members against another: Iraq's invasion and annexation of Kuwait in 1990. The Arab League quickly convened an emergency summit. An irreparable split paralyzed it. Twelve members (Egypt, Syria, Lebanon, Morocco, Somalia, Djibouti, and the six Persian Gulf monarchies) condemned the invasion, demanded Iraqi withdrawal, expressed support for the Saudis' invitation to the United States to send forces to defend Saudi Arabia, and agreed to impose sanctions on Iraq and to provide troops for an Arab defensive force in Saudi Arabia. The other members, however—including not just Iraq but states sympathetic to it, such as Jordan and Yemen—condemned the presence of foreign troops in Saudi Arabia and refused to participate in further discussion of the crisis.

Following the 1990–91 crisis over Iraq and Kuwait, divisions within the Arab League were reflected in significant difficulties in collecting members' dues. By the mid-1990s several member states were delinquent in their payments. Some had not paid dues for years, making them vulnerable to suspension of their voting rights. Bahrain, Kuwait, Libya, Morocco, and Yemen all objected to the size of their assessments.[14] Today, most members of the Arab League regard it more as a forum for debate and an expression of long-standing aspirations for unity than as an effective instrument for practical cooperation on security matters.

The Gulf Cooperation Council

The other Middle Eastern international organization that plays a security role is the Gulf Cooperation Council (GCC)—or to use its official name, the Cooperation Council for the Arab States of the Gulf. The GCC, founded in May 1981, owes its existence to the shared security concerns of its six members— Bahrain, Kuwait, Oman, Qatar, Saudi Arabia, and the United Arab Emirates— all of which are conservative Arab monarchies with economies dependent on their region's vast petroleum reserves. The security dilemmas of these states had long centered on their relationship with the other two—much more militarily powerful—states of the Persian Gulf: Iraq and Iran. The Gulf monarchies feared and distrusted these two powers and had reason to try to reduce their own military vulnerabilities by cooperating among themselves. They also worried, however, about how the Iraqis and Iranians would react to any creation of a Persian Gulf security organization that excluded them. The Iranian revolution in 1979 added to the monarchies' fears by creating a regime that seemed intent on fomenting revolutionary change elsewhere in the region and on agitating among the Shia, who constitute significant minorities (or in Bahrain, a majority) of their populations.

The outbreak in 1980 of the Iran–Iraq war, by preoccupying those two powers and increasing Iraqi dependence on its Arab neighbors, gave the Gulf monarchies the opening they needed to institutionalize their felt need for greater cooperation. Establishment of the new organization stimulated complaints from some other Arab governments, which charged that a subregional grouping of this sort would undermine what hope there was for the Arab League to operate more effectively in providing for regionwide security. In the face of those criticisms, the GCC states downplayed the security mission of their new organization and emphasized its other functions.

In line with that emphasis, the structure of the GCC and the stated purposes in its charter resemble those of other general-purpose regional organizations. Its highest authority is a Supreme Council consisting of the heads of state of the six members, who meet annually and, if requested by any two members, in additional extraordinary sessions. A council of foreign ministers meets quarterly, again with possible additional sessions. A Consultative Commission consisting of five citizens appointed from each state studies matters that the Supreme Council refers to it. A secretary-general heads a secretariat that is divided into sections for political, economic, military, environmental, and legal affairs, as well as units covering patents, telecommunications, administrative matters, and representation to the European Union. The GCC's public statements stress its economic role as a regional common market.

Notwithstanding the GCC's deliberate downplaying of its military dimensions, its security-oriented origins were reflected in on-the-ground military cooperation beginning shortly after the organization's founding. The six states held a series of multilateral military exercises through the mid-1980s that involved thousands of troops.[15] Defense ministers and military chiefs of staff also held a series of meetings aimed at developing plans for joint defense.

Potentially the most significant departure for regional security was agreement by the defense ministers in 1984 to create a GCC strike force, known as Peninsula Shield; it was conceived to be the size of two brigades, based in Saudi Arabia, and commanded by a Saudi officer. The agreement was at least partially implemented, to the extent of establishing a headquarters staff and seeing all six members contribute elements to one infantry brigade. Questions remained, however, about whether the brigade could function as a cohesive military force. Other questions concerned the mission of the force, the deployment of which would require a unanimous decision of the GCC Supreme Council.[16] It was never clear, for example, whether the force could ever intervene to deal with a domestic emergency. Concern among the smaller member states about Saudi dominance has served as a brake on further development of Peninsula Shield.[17]

The GCC did not play a significant role in the greatest security crisis it faced since its creation: the invasion of one of its members, Kuwait, by Iraq in 1990. The Peninsula Shield force evidently was reinforced prior to the U.S.-led Operation Desert Storm to expel the Iraqis from Kuwait, but it did not participate in the war as a unit. Shortly after the war Egyptian President Mubarak raised again the issue of whether security in the Gulf should be the concern not just of the GCC but of all Arab states acting through the Arab League.[18] Egypt, Syria, and the GCC members subsequently announced a plan for an Arab deterrent force to protect Kuwait, with Egypt and Syria to provide

most of the troops and the GCC to finance it. The proposal was never implemented, probably mainly because of second thoughts among the Gulf Arabs
about having the troops of these other Arab states on their territories. Neither
Egypt, with its earlier involvement in the Yemeni civil war in the 1960s, nor
Syria, with its more recent domination of Lebanon, offered reassuring histo-
ries in this regard.

The GCC states have since taken some additional steps toward military
cooperation, such as an agreement in 1997 to link the militaries of all member
states in a communications network that could be used for warnings. The
greater potential for multilateral security cooperation that the GCC's creation
had seemed to offer in the 1980s, however, has never been realized. The same
fundamental problem—the Gulf Arabs' military weaknesses amid stronger
neighboring states—that motivated them to explore together the possibilities
for greater security cooperation also has led them to conclude individually
that their security must ultimately depend on other arrangements. Since the
1991 Gulf War this has meant, for the most part, bilateral arrangements with
the United States.

What cooperation has occurred has focused on deterrence and security
against threats from outside the GCC countries, not on peace operations. The
GCC does not have institutions or procedures specifically designed for peace
operations. The organization's charter does provide for ad hoc activation of a
commission for the settlement of disputes among members, but there is no
indication that a role for peacekeeping forces was ever envisioned, and in any
case the GCC has not compiled a record of resolving disputes.

Perhaps the sharpest dispute with military dimensions that has divided
GCC members during the quarter century of the organization's existence is
one between Bahrain and Qatar concerning sovereignty over some islands
and reefs off the Qatar peninsula. The dispute heated up in 1986 when a Qatari gunboat fired shots and briefly took some Bahraini prisoners on the Fasht
al-Dibal reef. The GCC has not had a role in settling the dispute. The Saudis
long tried to mediate it. Bahrain welcomed the Saudi role, but Qatar, which
has had its own squabbles with Riyadh, did not. Qatar referred the case to the
International Court of Justice in 1991, and after several years of resistance
the Bahrainis finally agreed to accept the court's jurisdiction on the matter.
The court's ruling in March 2001 awarded the principal islands in question to
Bahrain but said other disputed territory belonged to Qatar.[19]

The next most intense recent quarrel between members, after the Bahraini-
Qatari conflict, has been the aforementioned one between Qatar and Saudi
Arabia. It has partly involved a border dispute; a shooting incident at a border post in 1992 led Qatar to withdraw temporarily its contingent from the
Peninsula Shield force and to boycott GCC ministerial meetings. Progress in
resolving the border question was made through mediation by Kuwait and
later by Egypt's Mubarak. The acrimony between Doha and Riyadh is much
broader than specific territorial or military matters, however, and includes
such irritants as commentary on the Qatar-based al-Jazeera satellite television
station that the Saudis find objectionable.

The GCC, with smaller membership and more tightly focused interests than the Arab League, has greater potential than the League for effective security-related cooperation. But any major role in peace operations appears precluded by the limited military capacity of the group's members and by the divisions and different perspectives among the members.

Other Organizations

Other Middle Eastern international organizations have had almost nothing to offer in dispute resolution, let alone peace operations. Egypt, Iraq, Jordan, and Yemen created in 1989 an Arab Cooperation Council (ACC), largely in reaction to the development of the GCC. Iraq's role in the 1990–91 Persian Gulf crisis dealt a major blow to the ACC's ability to function, and the organization has seemed moribund ever since. An active body with a membership at least as broad as that of the Arab League is the Organization of the Islamic Conference (OIC). However, the OIC's membership actually extends beyond the Middle East to Muslim countries worldwide. Although the OIC has its headquarters in Saudi Arabia and a special interest in Middle Eastern issues such as the disputed holy places in Jerusalem, it is not strictly speaking a regional organization. Moreover, neither its structure nor its stated mission has a military dimension.

Subregional Perspectives

The creation of competing subregional groups such as the GCC and ACC reflects the weakness—despite long-standing rhetoric about Arab unity—of any shared sense of responsibility for security and stability of the entire Middle East, or even for the Arab-inhabited portion of it. Opposition to Israel has been the one unifying cause, strong enough to motivate a state as distant as Morocco, for example, to send troops to participate in the 1973 Middle East war. Beyond the anti-Israeli theme, however, security concerns tend to be defined along more limited geographic lines. The combination of understandably strong security worries close to home and little interest in comparable security problems in more distant parts of the region provides little foundation for any effort to develop a regional capability for peace operations.

The Arab states that have supported most vigorously the strengthening of a regionwide institution such as the Arab League have been the ones most directly involved in the Arab–Israeli conflict, including Egypt—the most populous Arab state and the birthplace of pan-Arabism—and Syria. For these frontline states, Arab unity has meant strategic depth and support in a conflict in which they have borne the heaviest burden. For Egypt, it also has been a vehicle for continued leadership among Arabs.

The same intensity of feeling about the conflict with Israel that has helped the frontline states to claim attention and support also has multiplied the consequences when differences have arisen over policies toward that conflict.

The Arab response to Sadat's peace initiative in the late 1970s was a major blow to any endeavor that required Arab comity and cooperation, since it turned the putative leader of the Arab world into a pariah. With only Jordan having followed suit in making peace with Israel, the effects of divisions created in the 1970s are still being felt.

Syria's place within the Arab ranks has been upset by its own policies, which have been subjects of controversy and resentment among other Arabs, particularly its support for Iran in the war with Iraq and its occupation in Lebanon that long outlasted the civil war there. A similar observation can be made about Saddam Hussein's Iraq, which, though not literally a frontline state, viewed itself in similar terms and made pan-Arabism a theme of its foreign policy. The complications involving Iraq's status revolved around its initiation of two wars, particularly one against a fellow Arab state, Kuwait, in 1990.

Besides the frontline states and the Gulf monarchies of the GCC, the other major subregional grouping of Arab states is in the Maghreb, or North Africa. The Maghreb regimes have said and done the expected things regarding the confrontation with Israel, including the aforementioned dispatch of troops in previous wars. And, especially because they are largely Arab, most mental and policy maps of the world group them with the Middle East. But the interests and attention of the Maghreb states also are oriented in two other directions. One is to the north, toward Europe, with which they share the Mediterranean Sea. The other is to the south, to the states of Africa, with which they share a continent. The Maghreb states are members of the African Union, except that Morocco has declined full membership in protest against the separate representation of the disputed Western Sahara.

Algeria, Libya, Mauritania, Morocco, and Tunisia formed their own subregional organization, the Arab Maghreb Union, in 1989. The principal objectives were economic, including the establishment of a common market and a united front in negotiating with the European Union. However, discord between Algeria and Morocco over the Western Sahara has virtually paralyzed the group since the early 1990s. Since then most of the Maghreb states have pursued their own bilateral ties with Europe, especially France, and with the United States.

The orientation toward Africa has been displayed most clearly by Libya's Muammar Qadhafi, who once was one of the most vocal champions of unity of the Arab world from the Atlantic to the Persian Gulf. In more recent years Qadhafi has turned his back on Arabs and the Arab League and has made it clear that he is focusing much more on Africa. That turn has come amid increased acrimony between Qadhafi and other Arab leaders, highlighted by shouting matches at Arab summits and a reported Libyan plot to assassinate the crown prince of Saudi Arabia.

Capabilities

The issue of capabilities within the Middle East for peace operations—of the availability of forces that could be contributed to multilateral operations—cannot be separated from the various political issues and intraregional divisions discussed above. The principal constraints on contributions have less to do with budgets and force levels than with the political acceptability of the troops of particular countries being deployed elsewhere within the region. The Middle East is by some measures a heavily militarized region, but when one considers each country individually and the limits that would apply to each as a potential donor, the effective pool of available forces is small.

An additional limitation on the ability of Middle Eastern military forces to perform effectively in peace operations—or in any other external mission—is that many of them have been organized with a primary focus on their own nations' internal politics. Regimes use such features as intrusive political controls, limitations on the judgment and initiative of commanders, and parallel and duplicative military structures to maintain tight control over their militaries and reduce the chance of coups.[20] Middle Eastern regimes have largely succeeded over the past three decades in achieving the desired control and stability, but at the price, in many instances, of lowered military effectiveness and professionalism.

The largest armed forces in the region belong to Iran, with ground forces that number about 350,000 in the regular army and another 125,000 or so in the separately organized Revolutionary Guard Corps.[21] Two Iranian observers are currently deployed with the UN Mission in Ethiopia and Eritrea (UNMEE).[22] It is difficult to imagine any scenario for peace operations in the Middle East, however, for which Iranian troops would even be considered. Tehran's outspoken anti-Israel posture and support for terrorism against Israel clearly disqualify it for participation in any peacekeeping missions related to the Arab–Israeli conflict. The fact that Persian–Arab suspicions and animosities continue to flourish, well after the end of the Iran-Iraq war, also makes it unlikely that Iranian troops would be accepted for a mission anywhere on Arab territory. Deployment in the Middle East of troops from another of the region's largest—and the most modern and effective—armed forces, that of Israel (125,000 ground forces), would for obvious reasons be even more of a nonstarter.

The largest Arab army, with ground forces numbering about 340,000, belongs to Egypt. Egypt has made contributions in recent years to UN peace operations, most recently in the UN Mission in Sudan (UNMIS), to which 817 troops are currently deployed. If there were to be a leader around which regional peace operations might be organized, it would have to be Egypt. But a potential role for Cairo in this regard has three main limitations. One is that, even though Egypt no longer faces the more extreme ostracism from other Arabs that greeted Sadat immediately after his peace initiative, the distinction between those who have made peace with Israel and those who have not still complicates inter-Arab affairs. Second, distrust and resentment among other Arabs over Egypt's earlier record of throwing its weight around in places such as Yemen have not entirely disappeared. Third, the Egyptian army's ability, in terms of skills and professionalism, to contribute effectively to multilateral peace operations must be questioned. The army's stature and appeal within Egypt have declined in the years since making peace with Israel. Without the prospect of another Egyptian–Israeli war, members of the better-educated classes who earlier might have welcomed military service due to patriotic feelings now tend to shun it.

The Arab state with the next largest military force, Syria (ground forces numbering 200,000), would be an unwelcome contributor in most of the region for reasons already mentioned, particularly the experience in Lebanon. Moreover, Damascus probably would be reluctant to dispatch troops outside its immediate neighborhood while it is in what it still considers a state of war with militarily superior Israel.

Perusal of the list of other Arab states finds one reason or another to question the ability of each state to contribute to peace operations in the Middle East. States with medium-sized armies (in the range 60,000–75,000 troops) include Lebanon, whose own internal instability makes it more of a recipient than a contributor of peacekeeping forces; Yemen, whose armed forces are subject to even more questions about their professionalism and effectiveness than are Egypt's; and Saudi Arabia, which like Egypt is subject to suspicions and resentments by smaller neighbors (Saudi Arabia was the other interloper in the Yemeni civil war), and which probably considers its hands to be full with security concerns in its immediate neighborhood.[23] The other GCC states, with the possible exceptions of Oman and the United Arab Emirates, have forces that simply are too small to make more than token contributions. The gradual rehabilitation of Libya (45,000 ground forces) may someday make it suitable for a role in peace operations, but for the time being its relations with other regional states are simply too rocky for it to assume such a role. Tunisia, like Egypt, has contributed forces to UN peace operations, and it currently has 495 troops and military observers in the UN Organization Mission in the Democratic Republic of Congo (MONUC), along with small contingents in UNMEE and the United Nations Operation in Côte d'Ivoire. However, its pool of troops (with ground forces numbering 27,000) is too small to expect a great deal more.

Algeria currently contributes a total of thirteen military observers to MONUC and UNMEE. However, it is the Arab state that has perhaps the greatest potential to contribute more to peacekeeping missions. Algeria has 120,000 ground troops. It still has its differences with Morocco over the Western Sahara, but that conflict long ago subsided from the status of a shooting war. Most important, its own internal violence, which in the 1990s escalated into abhorrent bloodshed, has subsided as well.

The two Greater Middle Eastern states that could be said to have contributed significantly to peace operations in recent years are Morocco and Jordan. Morocco has one of the larger armies in the region, with 180,000 troops. It has been participating in UN missions in Bosnia, Kosovo, and Haiti, and it currently has large troop contingents in MONUC and UNOCI. Jordan has a smaller (85,000 ground troops) but well-trained and highly professional army. It currently contributes 2,666 troops and military observers to nine UN missions, including MONUC, UNMEE, UNMIS, UNOCI, and the UN Stabilization Mission in Haiti (MINUSTAH).

A combination of four characteristics probably helps to explain Morocco and Jordan's exceptional—by Middle Eastern standards—willingness to furnish forces for international peace operations. First, both regimes have foreign policies that stress the importance of relations with nonregional powers and particularly with the West. They place high value on being good international citizens. Second, both countries lack the petroleum-based wealth of many of their neighbors, and so the extraregional ties are important for economic as well as security reasons. The economic benefit of participating in peace operations can be both direct, in securing what amounts to a partial subsidy for their armed forces, and indirect, in gaining whatever considerations may flow from being a good international citizen. Third, armed conflict is close enough to both countries in time and space that their militaries are still important and respected parts of their political and social structures, and they still have skills and experience that come from involvement in previous combat. But fourth, the armed conflicts that have directly affected each country have de-escalated enough that they have forces to spare for multilateral missions abroad. For Morocco, de-escalation has involved the evolution of what had been an active insurgency in the Western Sahara into a diplomatic dispute. For Jordan, it involved the conclusion of its peace treaty with Israel. Participation in peacekeeping operations may even be a way to keep gainfully employed forces that might otherwise, because of the subsidence of immediate conflicts, become unemployed and therefore a political as well as economic liability. This last point might be especially important for Morocco, which faces the challenge of reintegrating many troops into civilian society if the Western Sahara conflict is completely settled.[24]

The regionwide pattern, with the conspicuous exceptions of Jordan and Morocco, of minimal contributions to peace operations suggests there is a broader attitudinal phenomenon involved, in addition to the more specific factors discussed above. The weaknesses of regional organizations, after all, are irrelevant to the unwillingness to contribute troops to UN-organized peace operations. The Middle East lacks a pro-peacekeeping ethos that is in evidence in other regions such as South Asia. Whatever the original reason for a different ethos to have developed in the Middle East—most likely, the belief that military resources must be reserved to deal with conflicts within the Middle East itself—the ethos persists as an impediment and an additional reason for meager contributions of forces.

Susceptibility of Middle Eastern Conflicts to Peace Operations

Despite the unhelpful regional ethos, the contributions of Morocco and Jordan to UN peace operations would seem to raise the possibility that they at least, and possibly other Middle Eastern states such as Algeria, could provide the core of a standing capability for regional peace operations. But just as a more detailed look at the supply side (i.e., the availability and acceptability of forces from specific countries) reveals less potential than first meets the eye, a similarly detailed appraisal of the demand side—the specific conflicts, or types of conflicts, within the Middle East in which a multilateral Middle Eastern force could feasibly serve a peacekeeping role—also shows very limited potential.

The pattern of UN peace operations in the Greater Middle East provides a sense of the overall place that peace operations can play in the region. Several of the UN operations in the region have been created to observe truces after rounds of Arab–Israeli fighting. The first peacekeeping operation in the history of the United Nations was the United Nations Truce Supervision Organization (UNTSO), which was created to oversee the truce in Palestine in 1948 and remains in existence. Other UN operations in the Arab–Israeli theater have included a United Nations Emergency Force (UNEF I) after the Suez war of 1956 and a similar mission (UNEF II) after the 1973 war. Besides UNTSO, ongoing peace operations that are related to the Arab–Israeli conflict are the United Nations Disengagement Observer Force (UNDOF) in the Golan Heights and the United Nations Interim Force in Lebanon (UNIFIL) in Southern Lebanon.

Outside the Arab–Israeli conflict, past UN peace operations in the Greater Middle East have observed armistices and disengagements following the Yemeni civil war in the 1960s, the Iran–Iraq war in the 1980s, and the war in Kuwait in 1991. An existing operation is the United Nations Mission for the Referendum in Western Sahara (MINURSO).

The nature of these UN operations—and the identities of the parties to the conflicts they have been designed to control—makes it infeasible for the missions to be performed by a regional force. The neutrality needed for supervision of truces along any front of the Arab–Israeli conflict is not to be found in the region. The same has been true of conflict between Iraq and Iran, given the Arab-versus-Persian coloration of that confrontation. Perhaps there has been somewhat greater potential for a regional contribution to peace operations focusing on Arab-versus-Arab conflicts, but even there the search for neutral parties is apt to be difficult due to the direct involvement of major Arab states or the relevance of other lines of contention with wider relevance, such as the royalist-versus-republican dimension of the Yemeni civil war. The Western Sahara conflict pits the two most populous Maghreb states, Morocco and Algeria, against each other.

Beyond the truce supervision missions that the United Nations has deployed to the region, the Middle East has presented few occasions for the kind of major, state-building multilateral operations that have operated in turmoil-stricken lands elsewhere, such as Kosovo or East Timor, where international intervention has provided the only apparent route out of domestic disorder. Insecurity and strife in the Middle East have tended to take other forms, including interstate warfare and extremism that leads to terrorism. Lebanon has come closest to the model of general domestic disorder. But the Arab League earlier tried and largely failed to make a significant contribution to peace there, for reasons described above. Following the outbreak of a new round of hostilities between Israel and Hezbollah in southern Lebanon in mid-2006, all discussions about insertion of a beefed-up peacekeeping force envisioned a UN force made up of troop contributions from states outside the region—not a force under the Arab League or any other regional organization.

Two other members of the Arab League have had plenty of internal disorder and turmoil in recent years: Sudan and Somalia. Despite their Arab affiliations, however, they are thought of mainly in African rather than Middle Eastern terms. Egypt, the one other Arab country with a special interest in Sudan, has made a modest contribution to the United Nations Mission in the Sudan (UNMIS), and in October 2006 the Arab League offered to dispatch Arab troops to the violence-wracked region of Darfur in western Sudan as part of an effort to break a stalemate over the proposed deployment there of UN peacekeepers.[25] There would be little interest, however, among Middle Eastern states to take either Sudan or Somalia under the wing of a Middle Eastern regional organization.

Since 2003 there has arisen a major and conspicuous case of apparently intractable internal turmoil in a Middle Eastern state: Iraq. But the provenance of this turmoil—a deeply unpopular invasion and occupation by the United States—has precluded Middle Eastern states from stepping forward to assume any burden of peacemaking or reconstruction. No Middle Eastern states have contributed troops to the "coalition of the willing" that the United States has led there, and any move by a regime to associate itself with the U.S. operation would make it vulnerable to criticism from its own population as well as other Arabs. An unspoken element of schadenfreude probably also influences the policies of Middle Eastern governments that have no desire to assume costs and risks to rescue the United States from its self-made quagmire. Several of those governments have serious security-related worries about spillover effects from Iraq, and someday Iraq could be the focus of a regionally based peace operation. But for now, this is out of the question with the United States still in charge.

Prospects

The prospects for more extensive, or more successful, regionally based peace operations in the Middle East are dim. All aspects of the political and ethnic geography of the region, the emotions surrounding the conflicts there, and distrust among neighbors that have impeded or precluded peace operations in the past will persist.

Crises will periodically give rise to discussion of what more Middle Eastern states could do to keep peace in their own neighborhoods. Proposals probably will be made from time to time for involvement of the Arab League in peace operations. Possible operations with the greatest chance of coming into existence, although they might involve some endorsement by the League, would more likely consist of ad hoc groupings of regional states with strong shared concerns about a particular hot spot. An eventual U.S. withdrawal from Iraq, by concentrating the minds of the neighboring states that have an interest in avoiding escalating and spreading disorder there, might give rise to such an ad hoc coalition. But these are still just remote possibilities in a part of the world in which the overall prospect for more effective regional peacekeeping remains poor.

The prospects for greater contributions by Middle Eastern states to global peacekeeping operations also remain dim, for the individual state-specific regions discussed earlier. Issues of reform of the United Nations, and particularly the structure of the Security Council, may affect the future willingness of Middle Eastern states to contribute troops to UN peace operations. Reforms that gave the Arab states a better sense of having a real stake, and a fair share of power, in the United Nations might at least marginally increase their inclination to contribute.

In some respects the most recent breaches of the peace, including the war between Israel and Hezbollah in mid-2006, have only heightened the impediments to regional peace operations. In addition to intensifying Arab rage against Israel and fueling extremist sentiment, this most recent chapter has demonstrated anew the apparent powerlessness of Middle Eastern regimes to keep their own neighborhood in order. Moreover, outside influence has hardly contributed to the development of a peacekeeping culture in the region, with the most conspicuous aspect of U.S. policy during the opening weeks of the crisis being active resistance to a cease-fire in the apparent hope that Israeli military action would deliver a crushing blow to Hezbollah.

The war in Iraq, in addition to shaping Arab views as described above, has exacerbated yet another fault line that impedes regionwide cooperation on security issues: that between Sunni and Shia. This division has long been a subtext to much of the violence in the region (as in Lebanon) and to security-related subregional cooperation (the underlying concerns of the GCC states being a case in point). As Iraqi Shia have been brought to a position of dominance within a fractured and violence-ridden society, the fears of Sunni regimes about a Shia encirclement have grown worse. The sharpening of this fault line will put effective regionwide security cooperation, including peace operations, even further out of reach.

The myth of Arab unity continues. The reality is a Middle East whose divisions still make it infertile ground for the development of effective regional peace operations.

Conclusion

Donald C. F. Daniel

This chapter highlights some of the major findings of this volume. The first section looks to conclusions drawn from the macro analyses that went across regions and nations, and the second to conclusions from the micro analyses that focused within regions and nations. The third section assesses the trends and prospects for peace operations.

Across Regions and Nations

Among its objectives, part 1 seeks to answer basic questions about trends in mission numbers, their breakdown by type (inter- and intrastate), troops totals, and the like. Birger Heldt's longitudinal analysis, covering nearly six decades, reveals three eras for most variables: a period of relatively low totals from 1948 to the late 1980s and early 1990s; a second period of rising totals through the mid-1990s; and the period since then with its new plateaus from which to measure year-to-year fluctuations. The trend lines for mission numbers and deployed troops in the third era are generally three to four times higher than for the first. The ratios are higher yet when one adds peace enforcement missions that Heldt's Folke Bernadotte Academy (FBA) database excludes. Eleven missions, rare in the first era but prominent in the third, are part of the Center for Peace and Security Studies (CPASS) database utilized by Daniel and assistants in chapter 2; when included, the 1948–2005 mission total is 136, and the troop totals for the last few years average about 140,000 to 150,000 personnel (as per the CPASS database) compared to FBA's 110,000 to 120,000.

Intrastate operations drove the mission number and troop increases in the second era and have sustained the plateaus established in the third. In the FBA database, there were up to three such operations ongoing at any point in the first era, and twenty or more at any give time in the third. The labor-intensive nature of these operations easily explains an equally substantial increase in deployed personnel numbers. Adding the eleven peace enforcement missions on the CPASS list, all of which were intrastate, to the third era totals further magnifies the difference. Instead of roughly ten times more intrastate operations at any point in the third era compared to the first, the ratio rises to thirteen or greater.

While these broad trends are well-known to students and practitioners of peace operations, the actual statistics are not. The numbers provide the bases for appreciating not only the substantial differences between the first and third eras but also the speed of change—that is, these dramatic changes occurred in only eight to ten years—between them. During those years peace operations went from being a modestly demanding, infrequently employed, collective response mainly to interstate conflicts to a mechanism regularly turned to when intrastate crises threatened a region's stability.

Heldt frames his analysis around the question of how to view the relation between the UN, on the one hand, and regional organizations and ad hoc coalitions on the other. The broad trends he identifies may not be as well known to students or practitioners. He concludes that the long-term pattern is one of coordination, complementarity, and coexistence rather than of competition. In a conclusion that may surprise some, he credits the UN with fewer overall operations (sixty) than non-UN missions (sixty-eight, of which twenty-eight received some form of UN Security Council approval). When one includes the eleven peace enforcement missions, the non-UN number rises to seventy-nine. Heldt accepts that the verdict is still out on the most recent period (1996 to 2005), during which time non-UN entities have conducted more intrastate operations, but he believes that it may be yet another cycle that is coming to an end.

The complementarity Heldt identifies is well illustrated in the geographic distribution of missions. Overall Africa has been by far the most frequent site for operations (forty-seven), followed by Asia and Europe (twenty-five each) and the Mideast and the Americas (seventeen and sixteen, respectively).[1] Contrary to fears that Africa would lose access to peace forces as other regions (Europe, the Americas, and Asia) experienced an increased need for them in the third era, Heldt argues that the UN has become better able to concentrate on Africa because non-UN actors have taken up the burden in other regions.

Heldt's data about comparative access to troop contributors is also worthy of note, since it indicates only two—and not three historical—eras. Consistent with earlier findings, he posits a first era of relatively few contributors to both UN and non-UN operations (about twenty for each, with overlaps between both sets), followed by an ongoing era of gradual increases (to highs of about one hundred for UN and eighty for non-UN operations, again in overlapping sets). Consistent with Heldt's findings are those of Daniel and his assistants for 2001 through 2006. While utilizing different counting rules (and having no overlaps), they recorded a better than one-third increase in designated contributors from the low fifties to the upper seventies over these six years.

Part I also looks at trends in contributor characteristics and their relation to the availability of troops for operations. Clear headlines emerge from the inquiry by Daniel and his assistants into the characteristics of contributors and the factors that affect troop contribution totals. One is that the majority profiles for the contributors are essentially the obverse of the majority profiles for the nominal and noncontributors. A second is that the majority of contributors possess high-quality social characteristics, especially in governance and stability. A third headline—one identified as well by Heldt in his analysis of wealth—is that quality has dropped somewhat as the number of contributors has increased. A fourth is that the high-impact states are also the highest-quality group, a conclusion that underscores even more thoroughly the link between quality and size of contribution. A fifth is that states that possess a high quantity of ground forces and/or high-quality armed forces are critical to providing the troop numbers necessary to man and sustain labor-intensive missions. A sixth headline is that states with high-quality armed forces are particularly critical for standing up non-UN missions. A final headline is that there may be a regional ethos in Europe and South Asia that encourages contributions, while such an ethos (if there is one) seems far weaker in the Middle East and the CIS (or, to adopt Nikitin's convention, the NIS).

At the end of his chapter Heldt offers an optimistic observation and a word of caution. The observation is that the global supply of troop contributors is as secure as it has ever been; the caution is that the UN would do well to diversify its donor base, since it may be reliant on too small a subset. In chapter 3, Daniel offers some context for this when he addresses factors that cause nations to deploy notably small percentages of their troops to operations. He argues (a) that the challenging nature of contemporary peace operations puts a premium on high troop numbers and quality; (b) that, against that backdrop, only about 40 percent of states possess the number or quality of forces critical to manning and sustaining such missions; and (c) that no matter how large or qualified a nation's forces, only a small percentage can be expected to deploy at any one time due to legal restrictions, the makeup of a nation's forces, and rotation cycles. He adds that when one also considers the political factors that enter into any national decision to deploy or not, it is not surprising that percentages are low and will probably remain so. Nevertheless, Daniel also notes that designated contributions have risen significantly, and that while many militaries will get smaller, a good subset of them should become more flexible, more rapidly deployable, and, with the increase in the number of peacekeeping training centers, better able to perform, especially in nonhazardous missions.

Finally, part I seeks to identify trends in the provision of capabilities that have surfaced in the last decade or so as critical to the success of challenging operations. In chapter 4, Gary Anderson draws on his military expertise to highlight representative military capabilities that will probably be required if highly hazardous missions are indeed undertaken. The broadest of these is a generic capacity for operational leadership in the run up to and the establishment of such missions. Anderson identifies only thirteen states at global or regional levels that might be able to plan a mission, organize the headquarters, and provide much of the initial core of troops that other contributors can fall in behind. In addition, Anderson highlights specific material capabilities and skill sets. These include helicopters, nonlethal weaponry, air protection and air defense systems, and troops that can operate at night and in urban environments where they must be prepared to transition from benign activities in some "blocks" to combating resistance in others.

Anderson's list is not exhaustive, and the significance of his chapter is in causing us to go back to a bottom-line question: What are peace operations really about today? Anderson is far more concerned with the war end of the military operations spectrum than with the classical peacekeeping end, where troops with weapons are forbidden to use them except when in extremis. Anderson's focus is on preparing for the worst, and the worst has been part of operations in the Congo in the 1960s and since the 1990s in Somalia, Sierra Leone, the Balkans, East Timor, Haiti, and other places (including again in the Congo). Yet, there are still states and observers that consider such forceful activities to be outside the peace operations pale. This difference in viewpoints is one reason why the FBA and CPASS databases are not identical. It is also a feature of Nikitin's chapter in this volume, when he underscores the significance of potential differences of opinion among states.

The final chapter in part I parallels that by Anderson, but its concern is not with the provision of robust military capacities but with nearly everything else required when peace enforcement and national capacity-building occur simultaneously. Patricia Taft's focus is on the specialized requirements of complex missions where public order remains elusive. These capabilities consist of units that assist in or undertake policing, the administration of justice, the restoration of infrastructures and social services, demining, explosive ordnance disposal, and the handling of chemical and biological agents and of incidents connected with them. There is considerable variance in the willingness of states to provide these capabilities, but on the whole Taft offers a positive picture. Although theirs is a resource-limited continent, African countries such as Senegal, Rwanda, Kenya, Angola, Mozambique, and South Africa are stepping forward in one or more areas, particularly in gendarmerie, demining, and ordnance disposal. Of the East Asian nations, two regional leaders, China and Japan, have become (or are becoming) notable contributors of specialized capabilities, including to out-of-area missions. Lesser roles can probably be expected from Thailand, Singapore, the Philippines, and Indonesia.

The Western European states (especially France, Italy, Spain, the Netherlands, and Portugal) are important for the specialized capabilities they bring to missions and also for the specialized police training they provide to nations in Africa and elsewhere. New members of the EU and NATO, such as Poland and Romania, also see the provision of specialized capabilities as one way they can establish themselves as regional citizens who do their share. Partly for financial reasons, the picture is not as upbeat for Latin America, but Brazil may buck the trend. More than Argentina or Chile, Brazil seems determined to carve out a recognized role for itself and may look to become a provider of specialized capacities, particularly in the areas of search and rescue and the deployment of medical units.

Within Regions and Nations

Part II focuses on how far each region has gone (or not gone) to institutionalize collective mechanisms and use them to conduct operations both within and outside of their own region. The authors provide insights into the regional political dynamics as well as cultural and ideational characteristics, such as a regional view on the use of force or the proper role of the United Nations. As part of their analyses, the authors also focus on the motivations of individual nations in such a way as to allow us to draw overall conclusions about them.

In chapter 6, Mark Malan describes both the dynamism and challenges of security cooperation on the continent of Africa. He examines ongoing work to build institutional mechanisms to make political decisions regarding such operations and the serious challenges to building the capabilities needed to train peacekeepers, plan operations, and sustain deployments.

Probably more than any other region, Africa possesses developed security organizations at both the continentwide and subregional levels. As a result, the relationship that emerges between the subregional bodies—such as ECOWAS, IGAD, and SADC—and the African Union will be a defining factor in the development of an effective security architecture in Africa. Another distinctive factor pertains to the significant role played by outside countries supporting capacity-building efforts of African national militaries and the continent's regional and subregional organizations. Bilateral support for African peacekeepers has largely come from France, the United Kingdom, and the United States. Support for African organizations has come from a broader group that includes Canada, Japan, the United Nations, and the concerted and individual efforts of European Union member countries.

Malan ends his chapter with a plea not to expect too much too soon from the African states. Highly dependent on the UN and other outsiders, the region has a very long way to go in developing the institutional prerequisites (for both political decision making and operational planning) as well as the military capacities to undertake challenging operations on its own. As Malan sees it, ad hoc initiatives and politically correct rhetoric about African ownership of peacekeeping are no substitutes for a realistic vision of what can be accomplished over time. With such a vision, he adds, donor partners and especially the Africans themselves can establish priorities for how African states will expend their very limited resources.

Along with Africa, Europe has been the focus of a significant amount of scholarly attention concerning the region's efforts to build and utilize regional security organizations. In his chapter Bastian Giegerich states that the fundamental issue is not whether Europeans will participate in operations, since that question has largely been answered in the affirmative; rather, the critical questions go to how the Europeans will organize themselves to do so and what level of burden they will be willing to take on. Whereas Africa has witnessed an evolving relationship between the continentwide African Union and several subregional bodies, Europeans have two regionwide bodies to work through: NATO (with twenty-four of its twenty-six members being European) and the EU. The relations between the two are complex, and their overlapping memberships have much to do to sort out which organization will do what and with which contributors and resources. Questions about what role the UN should play in specific cases add yet another level of institutional complexity. Ultimately, however, the two most significant factors shaping Europe's ability to play an increased role in peace operations may be decisions of governments and populations about how much they are willing to spend to build peacekeeping capabilities and how many casualties they are willing to sustain as peace operations become more dangerous. While not predicting how far the Europeans are willing to go in these respects, Geigrich does provide sobering observations about each. One is that there is no indication that defense budgets will rise or that spending will become more efficient. Another is that particularly demanding missions tend to lead to squabbles about burden-sharing.

Like Malan in his discussion of Africa, Giegerich calls on Europe both to develop a coherent vision of itself as an independent comprehensive actor and to marshal the necessary resources. Europe, however, is far wealthier than Africa. Giegerich writes that it already has a significant capacity to undertake operations, but he also sees only gradual change in its willingness and capability to do more than it is currently doing.

In chapter 8, Alexander Nikitin and Mark Loucas show that, while "peace operations" have been a feature of NIS intraregional relations since the end of the Soviet era, Russia's dominant role both laterally and in mechanisms such as the CIS has hindered the development of a truly regional framework for such operations. By the time Russia moved to establish a more integrated approach in this decade, it found that Georgia, Moldova, several Central Asian states, and the Baltic states (now members of NATO) had become more assertive. Nevertheless, Russia pushed ahead with the formation of the CSTO, whose potential for peace operations (including the proposed creation of Collective Peace Support Forces) is untested but considered promising by the authors. A number of unresolved regional conflicts, including in Moldova, Azerbaijan, and Georgia, may yet provide a test, but the authors believe that their resolution may now also require participation by the EU, NATO, or the Council of Europe. Should peace operations be part of the solution, however, Russia and the Western states will have to resolve their differences about the nature of peace support operations and the practices that are appropriate to them.

In chapter 9, John Fishel highlights the mechanisms for Latin American crisis management at regional (OAS) and subregional (CARICOM, and the OECS) levels that can authorize and support missions. He also addresses the state-to-state lateral option evidenced in MOMEP's establishment by the guarantors of the Rio Protocol. He reminds readers of the tradition for contributing to UN peacekeeping missions around the world and, as seen in MINUSTAH, within the region as well. He singles out Argentina, Brazil, Chile, and Uruguay, while adding that the next tier of Latin American countries from Central America and the Andes region have demonstrated in MINUSTAH that they too want to play a larger role. To do so they will have to do more to enable their militaries to deploy, but indicators of progress are there. Some of the small Caribbean and Central American states have formed the Regional Security System composite battalion to handle a variety of tasks, including regional peacekeeping, and plans are in hand for the CFAS group to stand up another battalion that would be kept on standby for UN missions. In addition, Latin America now has a number of peacekeeping training centers and promotes training across national divisions (including within a U.S. Southern Command framework).

Regionwide institutional peace operations initiatives, however, are rare in Latin America and probably will remain so. A reason may be that the venue for such initiatives most likely would be the OAS, an institution in which the United States has played a heavy hand and exhibited sometimes off-putting preoccupations with the internal and/or external policies of various Latin American governments. There has not been an OAS-sponsored peace operation since 1965 when, at the United States's urging, the OAS approved the Inter-American Peace Force for the Dominican Republic. Even that mission was characterized by considerable diplomatic finessing to accommodate Latin American sensitivities about who was seen to be in charge. As Fishel notes, the OAS has played a diplomatic role in other regional conflicts and cooperated with the UN on Haiti, but it may be a long while yet before the OAS itself sponsors a mission or puts in place planning, training, or force-generation mechanisms so as to be ready to undertake missions.

In chapter 10, Mely Caballero-Anthony discusses the changes taking place in East Asia. She does so against the backdrop of the region's time-honored preference for "quiet diplomacy" to resolve crises and the extreme value placed on national sovereignty and on the principle of not "infringing in the internal affairs" of regional neighbors. Developments over the last decade, however, have slowly generated some willingness to move away from such strictures. Incremental change can be seen in both Northeast and Southeast Asia. In Southeast Asia, as Caballero-Anthony explains, a series of political and economic crises in the past decade have prompted the region, and in particular a number of leading countries, to look for more extensive conflict and crisis management mechanisms. She examines ASEAN's evolving role as it slowly expands beyond the consensus-based and quiet-diplomacy methods that served the organization through its first three decades and now faces questions about how to respond to growing transnational and intrastate challenges. ASEAN has expressed in a number of documents its desire to build on the nascent peacekeeping capabilities of its member countries, which were displayed in contributions by Thailand, Singapore, Malaysia, and the Philippines to UN and other missions in the region, through the proposal for an ASEAN Security Community. This would take place through increased cooperation on peacekeeping training, greater sharing of information, and further discussions on establishing ASEAN mechanisms for maintaining peace and stability.

In Northeast Asia the realization by Japan and China that each needed to play a greater role in international peacekeeping derived not so much from a particular crisis, as from each country's determination to achieve greater prominence regionally and globally. That China has undergone a significant change in its approach to peace operations is clear. In the past three years it has gone from minimal involvement in peacekeeping to being on the cusp of joining the list of the top ten largest contributors to UN operations. As for Japan, constitutional provisions have served as a brake on its becoming a steady or major troop contributor. Yet these provisions are under review, and Japan has provided niche or specialized capabilities to UN missions and in Iraq. That it took the chairmanship of the UN Security Council Working Group on Peacekeeping Operations is an indication of Japan's willingness to consider increasing its profile.

In his chapter on South Asia Dipankar Banerjee describes the long-standing and storied peacekeeping efforts of four countries that consistently are at or near the top of UN peacekeeping contributors: Pakistan, Bangladesh, India, and Nepal. Without what Banerjee terms the "surplus military capacity" of these four countries and Sri Lanka, the UN would be at a great loss for peacekeepers. That the region consists of a small number of nations, some of which have lasting enmities, makes it difficult for it to establish regional institutions for collective action. India's experience in Sri Lanka, furthermore, though unilateral, is not at all encouraging for intraregional efforts in general. In short, one can expect that the South Asian states will continue to operate as major players in the global peace operations arena while probably also calling for a greater role in the decision-making processes leading to the creation and mandating of UN missions.

In chapter 12, Paul Pillar seeks to explain why most of the countries of the Middle East have generally played a small role in global peacekeeping. Pillar also examines the challenges that the region has faced in its attempts to establish regional security institutions. On both topics, the author argues that, because many countries of the Middle East view themselves as being affected (and aggrieved) parties to the region's major conflicts, it precludes them from valuing the role of a peacekeeping operation in specific cases, and to a great degree it undermines the concepts of peacekeeping in general. Most governments in the region view their own security situation as requiring that their armed forces be maintained solely for the purposes of traditional national security and defense. Moreover, so many divisions characterize relations among countries in the Middle East (religious, regime type, ethnic, etc.) that the trust necessary to empower the region's multilateral institutions (the Arab League, the Gulf Cooperation Council, and the Arab Cooperation Council) simply does not exist.

Finally, the regional chapters provide bases for plumbing national motivations for contributing to peace operations. There are no surprises in the list. Some states:

- seem to have a sense of international obligation;
- may be influenced by a regional ethos or "strategic culture";
- see peace operations as a way to enhance their prestige, polish their reputation, and/or portray themselves as responsible regional or global citizens;
- consider participation in some operations as a way to repay or curry favor with a major power;

- seek outlets for surplus military capacity as a way to "tame" their armed forces;
- rely on remunerations provided by the UN or others for use of their troops;
- desire the training and equipment support provided by developed states;
- see peace operations as a way to share the burden of responding to destabilizing developments, especially in their own region; and
- consider peace operations conducted under their own regional aegis or coalition as a way for the participants to better control their own destiny.

What is intriguing about the list is the extent to which the reasons or their underlying dynamics do not seem to be universal. Several examples are noteworthy. For example, only Fishel's chapter on Latin America and Banerjee's discussions of India, Pakistan, and Bangladesh make clear attribution to the international-obligation motive (with the added twist that Pakistan sees itself as a Muslim nation in that regard). In short, a sense of international obligation would seem at best very narrowly salient. A second example goes to the desire of states to respond to destabilizing developments in their own region. Instabilities in the Balkans, East Timor, in East and West Africa, the NIS, and in the Caribbean all prompted nations in each of those respective areas to augment (or to consider augmenting) their institutional or national capacities. Yet this trend did not occur in the greater Middle East or in South Asia. As noted above, South Asia may have too few states with too many reasons for mutual distrust, while the states of the Greater Middle East may simply be riven by too many national, subnational, and transnational factions, too self-absorbed by internal troubles, and, based on their regional experiences, too little impressed by the value of peacekeeping.

A third example is that of regional ethos or culture. An ethos in favor of participation in peace operations is clearly not universal, but the more interesting issue concerns the underlying dynamics. In Europe regional solidarity may be such that new or aspiring members of the EU or NATO see peace operations as something they should do to evidence their solidarity. In contrast, the lack of South Asian solidarity seems to be a factor encouraging troop contributions by Pakistan, India, and possibly Bangladesh. In other words, what ethos exists in South Asia may be based more on competition and "keeping up with the Joneses" than on solidarity. A fourth example is that of nations wanting to control their own destiny. Paradoxically, African states are most reliant on outside help, but their efforts to develop their capacities arise out of a sense that Africans must ultimately rely on themselves and that accepting outside help is a necessary step in doing so. While a different dynamic is at play, the same applies to European efforts to augment the EU rather than fall back on a US-led NATO. Similarly, in Latin America this motive may be a factor that discourages states from working through the regionwide OAS due to U.S. hegemonic concerns. It also seems a factor that has plagued Russian efforts to make the CSTO a strong union that could handle peace operations needs across the entire NIS region. Indeed, some states within the NIS (as well as some outside it) see the variant of peace operations sponsored by Russia more as a mechanism for intervention and control than of advancing the well-being of areas where the operations have taken place.

An Overall Assessment: Whither Peace Operations

This volume has identified numerous contemporary trends in peace operations—trends that make it clear that the prospects for the future are certainly mixed. Nations and organizations now regularly turn to peace operations as a tool of choice for contending with destabilizing events in all regions of the globe. Preparing for how to (better) undertake such operations is now a matter of course in the planning departments of many government agencies and on the agendas of organizations in Africa, Europe, Latin America, and East Asia. The plateaus in the number of operations and troops deployed are well established at unprecedented highs. The number of contributor nations has also been rising significantly and may soon plateau at a high level as well. Most of the countries that seem most capable of taking up peace operation burdens by virtue of their wealth, stability, and the size and quality of their militaries generally are consistent and high-impact contributors. The number of peace operations training centers has increased steadily, and many militaries are transforming themselves in ways that make them more readily deployable for peace operations. There is also a slow but gradual broadening in the majority profile of contributors and thus some lessening in overreliance on a particular subgroup of states. Finally, there seems to be a reasonable division of labor among the UN, regional organizations, and coalitions of the willing, with each taking the lead in different types of operations. The UN seems to be the instrument of choice for complex missions where there is some consent from the indigenous parties, and for some missions in Africa. Regional organizations and coalitions are usually the choice for the most challenging peace enforcement missions, and for missions that regional partners prefer to conduct themselves.

There are also negative trends of considerable significance. Labor-intensive and challenging intrastate operations have been the norm since the 1990s. That the trend seems irreversible probably means that the demand for ready core military and specialized units (including civilian police) will exceed supply. Most at risk of not taking place at all or of eluding success will be the hazardous missions that test not only the capabilities and resolve of potential contributors but also their conceptions of what constitutes a peace operation. There was a generally accepted view of what a peace operation consisted of prior to 1989, and that view did not include ONUC-type missions. Since then, international and national decision makers have mandated operations with little attention to how to define them. Their concerns involved, among other things, the quelling of instabilities—not the niceties of conceptual categories. Troop contributors, however, still get to choose where they will send their forces and what rules they will operate under when there. The global division of labor that characterizes peace operations is consistent with that reality, since most militarily robust organizations (e.g., NATO and EU) and states are the ones that take on the most hazardous or potentially violent missions. Those states and organizations are already overstretched, and they should remain so for many years to come. As more militaries and specialized units become more proficient, the benefits, so to speak, will probably go to the challenging but less hazardous missions—the missions that better fit within the conceptions of what many contributors consider to be a peace (as opposed to a close-to-war enforcement) operation.

Even for the less hazardous operations, however, increases in the proficiencies of the deployed units will come very slowly, due to national spending limitations and internal political struggles about whether to fund guns or butter. National debates will parallel regional ones as resource issues, political differences, and rivalries slow the development of regional institutional capacities. As in so many other areas of national and international life, rhetoric as to what should be done in peace operations exceeds in nearly all cases the reality of what will be accomplished.

It is sobering to consider that the bulk of troops that are contributed to operations come from a limited number of states, and that the major increases in troop contributions in this decade have been largely due to established providers increasing their contributions as opposed to many new states weighing in. States with the resolve to carry on will find it difficult to overcome internal structural limits on how many troops they can deploy at any one time. Any major global or regional financial crisis—and any major peace operations disaster resulting in the loss of many of the deployed—would almost surely guarantee backsliding and the reversal of positive trends.

In sum, no one systematically based judgment seems valid. The picture is very positive when one looks at the impressively upward trends of the past fifteen years or so. When one looks to the future, furthermore, it seems likely that the demand for easy or moderately challenging operations will generally be met. In contrast, cautionary or negative factors—in particular, heavy reliance on a limited number of countries to provide the vast bulk of deployed personnel, the fragile nature of political willingness, and the slow rates of growth in international and national capabilities—will be highly salient and possibly determinative for agenda-dominating, challenging, or hazardous missions. The missions most likely to occur will be those called for by global or regional hegemons that at the time in question will have available the military and political wherewithal to take on these missions and bring others along with them. Even when hegemons are involved, such operations may not necessarily be highly effective (as demonstrated in Darfur or Afghanistan today), and they surely will tie up forces that will not be available for use elsewhere, but they may be the best that can be expected. From such a perspective, one ironically is left to hope that more hegemons arise whose interests coincide with a larger global or regional interest to prevent humanitarian disasters or quell destabilizing conflicts.

Finally, there is always the temptation to end a volume such as this one on a positive note, but doing so may reflect less systematic analysis and more personal psychology: specifically, a proclivity to look at how the peace operations glass became half-full rather than dwelling on the half that yet remains stubbornly empty.

Notes

Introduction

1. Figures are based on the Stockholm International Peace Research Institute database on multilateral peace operations, http://conflict.sipri.org/SIPRI_Internet/.

2. UN Security Council Resolution 1674, April 28, 2006. The texts of UN Security Council resolutions can be accessed at www.un.org/Docs/sc/index.html.

3. See Sharon Wiharta, "Peacekeeping: Keeping Pace with Changes in Conflict," in *SIPRI Yearbook 2007: Armaments, Disarmament and International Security* (Oxford: Oxford University Press, 2007), 107–28.

4. See D. C. F. Daniel and B. C. Hayes, *Beyond Traditional Peacekeeping* (London: Macmillan, 1995) and D. C. F. Daniel and B. C. Hayes with Chantal de Jonge Oudraat, *Coercive Inducement and the Containment of International Crises* (Washington, D.C.: U.S. Institute of Peace, 1999), 7–40.

5. The breadth of concern is nicely highlighted in the final report of The Challenges Project. See The Challenges Project, *Meeting the Challenges of Peace Operations: Cooperation and Coordination—Executive Summary and Conclusions in the Official Languages of the United Nations* (Stockholm: Elanders Gotab, 2005). See also five papers published by New York University's Center on International Cooperation and available at www.cic.nyu.edu/internationalsecurity/globalpeace.html: Bruce Jones with Feyral Cherif, "Evolving Models of Peacekeeping" (2004); Ian Johnstone, "Recent Thinking on Peacekeeping Literature Review 1" (December 16, 2004); Ian Johnstone, "Recent Thinking on Peacekeeping Literature Review 2" (April 18, 2005); Ian Johnstone, "Recent Thinking on Peacekeeping Literature Review 3" (June 17, 2005); and Ian Johnstone, "Recent Thinking on Peacekeeping Literature Review 4" (August 2005).

6. The Fund for Peace sponsored regional meetings in order to determine views about humanitarian intervention. See Jason Ladnier, *Neighbors on Alert: Regional Views on Humanitarian Intervention* (Washington, D.C.: The Fund for Peace, 2003), and Patricia Taft and Jason Ladnier, *The Capacity to Protect: The Role of Civil Society—Perspectives from Africa, Asia, the Americas and Europe* (Washington, D.C.: The Fund for Peace, 2005).

7. See David S. Sorensen and P. C. Wood, eds., *The Politics of Peacekeeping in the Post–Cold War Era* (London and New York: Frank Cass, 2005); Michael E. O'Hanlon, *Expanding Global Military Capacity for Humanitarian Intervention* (Washington, D.C.: Brookings Institution Press, 2003); Michael O'Hanlon and P. W. Singer, "The Humanitarian Transformation: Expanding Global Intervention Capacity," *Survival* 46, no. 1 (2004): 77–100; and Patricia Taft with Jason Ladnier, *Realizing "Never Again": Regional Capacities to Protect Civilians in Violent Conflicts* (Washington, D.C.: The Fund for Peace, January 2006).

8. One of the best systematic efforts to date was written in 1986: see Ernst Haas, "The Collective Management of International Conflict, 1945–1984," in United Nations Institute for Training and Research, *The United Nations and the Maintenance of International Peace and Security* (Dordrecht and Boston: Martinus Nijhoff, 1987), 3–70. Haas coded for non-UN as well as UN operations.

9. The FBA project, for instance, does not include peace enforcement missions, but both the CPASS and SIPRI projects do. The SIPRI project included peacebuilding and special political missions; the CPASS project does not.

Chapter One

Helpful comments from Don Daniel and William Durch are gratefully acknowledged.

1. See Birger Heldt and Peter Wallensteen, *Peacekeeping Operations: Global Patterns of Intervention and Success, 1948–2004*, 3rd ed. (Stockholm: Folke Bernadotte Academy Publications, 2007).

2. Ibid.

3. For the UN's positions, see United Nations, *A More Secure World: Our Shared Responsibility. Report of the High-level Panel on Threats, Challenges and Change* (New York: United Nations, 2004); also United Nations, *In Larger Freedom: Towards Development, Security and Human Rights For All. Report of the Secretary-General* (New York: United Nations, 2005). The process is described in some detail at http://web.archive.org/web/20050210060300/www.un.org/Depts/dpa/prev_dip/fr_un_cooperation.htm. See also Oldrich Bures, "Regional Peacekeeping Operations: Complementing or Undermining the UN?" *International Peacekeeping* 18 (2006): 83–99; Björn Hettne and Fredrik Söderbaum, "The UN and Regional Organizations in Global Security: Competing or Complementary Logics?" *Global Governance* 12 (2006): 227–32; Hilaire McCoubrey and Justin Morris, *Regional Peacekeeping in the Post–Cold War Era* (The Hague: Kluwer Academic Publishers, 2000).

4. Alex J. Bellamy and Paul D. Williams, "Who's Keeping the Peace?" *International Peacekeeping* 29 (2005): 157–95.

5. Ibid.

6. The assumption is related to the old question of why nations participate in peacekeeping operations. The theoretical literature often refers to different forms of self-interest or motivations given a certain opportunity to participate, and to national characteristics (even idealism) that have a constant effect apart from any given opportunity to participate. The "crowding out" argument does not appear prominent in that literature. See Laura Neack, "UN Peace-Keeping: In the Interest of Community or Self?" *Journal of Peace Research* 32 (1995): 181–96; Peter V. Jacobsen, "National Interest, Humanitarianism or CNN: What Triggers UN Peace Enforcement after the Cold War?" *Journal of Peace Research* 33 (1996): 205–15; Andreas Andersson, "Democracies and UN Peacekeeping Operations, 1990–1996," *International Peacekeeping* 7 (2000): 1–22; Bruce Bueno de Mesquita and George W. Downs, "Intervention and Democracy," *International Organization* 3 (2006): 627–49; James H. Lebovic, "Uniting for Peace?" *Journal of Conflict Resolution* 48 (2004): 910–36.

7. Data for figures 1.1–1.3, and for table 1.1, are found at www.press.georgetown.edu. Data notes for all other figures are available from the author. Other attempts at institutional-level analysis include Paul F. Diehl and Young-Im Cho, "Passing the Buck? Regional Organizations and Conflict Management in the Post–Cold War Era," *Brown Journal of World Affairs* 12 (2006): 191–202; Bellamy and Williams, "Who's Keeping the Peace?" The latter study covers the twenty-first century and uses a wider definition of peacekeeping, whereas the former study excludes cases of non-UN operations in interstate conflicts and uses a partly different set of non-UN operations. Moreover, this chapter carries out a more detailed analysis of the dynamics across time and space.

8. Note that United Nations Peacekeeping Force in Cyprus (UNFICYP) is later counted twice, as it was an interstate operation from mid-1974 and onwards, and an intrastate operation before that. For the same reason, Multinational Force, Iraq (MNF I) is later counted twice, as it was an inter- as well as intrastate operation. This means that the number (130) of intra- and interstate operations presented later exceeds the aggregate (by name) number (128) of operations here mentioned.

9. Data compiled from the UN Security Council resolutions found at www.un.org/Docs/sc/unsc_resolutions05.htm.

10. The bivariate OLS regression coefficient is almost perfect at 0.96 when using the number of UN operations as dependent variable. The explained variance is 77 percent, indicating the amount of variation in the number of UN operations that is predicted accurately by the number of non-UN operations. Results and data notes for this and other statistical analyses found in this chapter are available upon request.

11. An indicator of this is the aforementioned degree to which non-UN operations have been approved or authorized by the UN Security Council. See Rosemary Durward, "Security Council Authorization for Regional Peace Operations: A Critical Analysis," *International Peacekeeping* 13 (2006): 350–65.

12. It is also interesting to note that these two non-UN operations—the Neutral Nations Supervisory Commission (NNSC) between the two Koreas, and the Multinational Force and Observers (MFO) in the Middle East—are so-called out-of-area operations, in that they are carried out by countries from other regions. We thus have a situation where it is never countries from the region of conflict that try to manage their interstate conflicts.

13. The bivariate OLS regression coefficient is -0.20 when one uses the number of interstate UN operations as dependent variable. The explained variance is a mere 1.5 percent.

14. The bivariate OLS regression coefficient is 0.7 when one uses the number of intrastate UN operations as dependent variable. The explained variance is 82 percent.

15. The operations in question are the Symbolic (Token) Arab Security Force, Arab Deterrent Force, the Arab Ceasefire Observer Mission, and the Multinational Force (I).

16. The four operations in question are the OAS Committee of Military Experts (Advisors), OAS Committee of Military Experts (Observers), OAS Military Observers I, and OAS Military Observers II.

17. Inertia is a common phenomenon. For militarized interstate disputes (MID) the magnitude of inertia is extremely large, in that using the state (dispute/no dispute) a certain year to predict the state the following year results in a prediction accuracy of 96.5 percent over a time span of 175 years. See Simon Jackman, *In and Out of War: The Statistical Analysis of Discrete Serial Data on International Conflict* (unpublished manuscript, Department of Political Science, Stanford University, 1999).

18. The operations in question are the International Commission for Control and Supervision (ICCS), International Commission for Supervision and Control—Cambodia (ICC—Cambodia), International Commission for Supervision and Control—Laos (ICC—Laos), International Commission for Supervision and Control—Laos II (ICC—Laos II), International Commission for Supervision and Control—Vietnam (ICC—Vietnam), Neutral Nations Supervision Commission (NNSC), Multinational Force and Observers (MFO), Multinational Force I (MNF I) and Multinational Force II (MNF II), Artemis, Licorne, Joint Monitoring Mission/Joint Military Commission, and the Multinational Interim Force in Haiti.

19. Niclas Swanström, ed., *Conflict Management and Conflict Prevention in Asia* (Uppsala: Uppsala University, Silk Road Studies Program, 2005).

20. The bivariate OLS regression coefficient is 0.36 when one uses the number of UN peacekeepers as dependent variable. The explained variance is 22 percent.

21. Data are from the UN Department of Peacekeeping website. See Peace and Security Section of the Department of Public Information, *Monthly Summary of Contributors to UN Peacekeeping Operations*, UN Department of Peacekeeping Operations. www.un.org/Depts/dpko/dpko/contributors/95-05.htm.

22. This insight is similar to findings reported in Gilligan and Stedman (2003). The study attempts to identify the conditions under which the UN establishes peacekeeping operations in civil wars. It reports a positive relationship between, on the one hand, civil war duration and

number of casualties, and, on the other hand, the probability of a UN operation. This finding supports the argument that it is need rather than great power interests that conditions UN decisions. The UN does thus not avoid serious (in terms of casualties) or intractable (in terms of duration) conflicts, but rather focuses on them. See Michael Gilligan and Stephen J. Stedman, "Where Do the Peacekeepers Go?" *International Studies Review* 5 (2003): 37–54.

23. The bivariate OLS regression explained variance is 65 percent when one uses the number of TCCs in UN operations as dependent variable.

24. The bivariate OLS regression explained variance is 54 percent when one uses the number of TCCs in non-UN operations as dependent variable.

25. The bivariate OLS regression relationship is very strong, with 78 percent of the variance explained.

26. The findings build on a multivariate Probit regression run on monthly data covering 1970–2004 and all the countries of the world. Control variables include regime type (democracy versus nondemocracy), GDP per capita, size of armed forces, and presence of armed conflicts within or between countries.

27. The bivariate OLS regression explained variance is 7 percent and 15 percent, respectively, when one uses the wealth of UN TCCs as dependent variable.

28. The findings build on a multivariate Probit regression run on annual data covering all the countries of the world. Control variables include regime type (democracy versus nondemocracy), GDP per capita, size of armed forces, and presence of armed conflicts within or between countries.

29. See chapter 3 (Daniel, "Why So Few Troops from among So Many?") in this volume.

Chapter Two

This chapter has benefited from comments made by the principals at the Yale-Folke Bernadotte Academy workshop on peacekeeping research held in New Haven, December 1–2, 2006.

1. The profiling of countries in the extant literature is done in the context of UN operations and focuses particularly on democratic governance. The broadest work (and the one that comes closest to what we have attempted) is by James H. Lebovic, "Uniting for Peace? Democracies and United Nations Peace Operations after the Cold War," *Journal of Conflict Resolution* 48, no. 6 (December 2004): 910–36. See also Andreas Andersson, "Democracies and UN Peacekeeping Operations, 1990–1996," *International Peacekeeping* 7, no. 2 (Summer 2000), 1–22; and Davis Bobrow and Mark A. Boyer, "Maintaining System Stability: Contributions to Peacekeeping Operations, " *Journal of Conflict Resolution* 41, no. 6 (December 1997): 723–48. See also Michael E. O'Hanlon, *Expanding Global Capacity for Humanitarian Intervention* (Washington, D.C.: Brookings Institution, 2003), chaps. 3 and 4. The principal author of this chapter has earlier published on this subject. See D. C. F. Daniel and Leigh C. Caraher, "Characteristics of Troop Contributors to Peace Operations and Implications for Global Capacity," *International Peacekeeping* 13, no. 3 (September 2006): 297–315. This chapter builds upon and goes beyond that earlier piece.

2. Special political, peacebuilding, and police missions are excluded from our analysis since they are comprised mainly or exclusively of civilians.

3. We accept that undersized companies may have some measurable impact on the success of small missions, but we had no way to systematically capture which contributions of less than one hundred were formed units. We also suspect that some contributions of under one hundred represented the deployment of niche capabilities, such as engineers or medical personnel, but again we had no way to systematically capture such facts. On niche capabilities, however, see chapter 5 of this volume.

4. Ground forces data were for 2003 and was drawn from the International Institute of Strategic Studies, Military Balance for 2003–2004.

5. Transfers or "rollovers" included Task Force Fox succeeding Task Force Harvest in September 2001, UNMISET's taking over for UNTAET in May 2002, Concordia's taking over from Allied Harmony in March 2003, UNMIL's integration of ECOMIL on 1 October 2003, UNOCI's integration of ECOMICI on 4 April 2004, AMIB's incorporation of SAPSD in April 2003, ECOMIL's integration into UNMIL in October 2003, Task Force Allied Harmony taking over from Task Force Fox in December 2003, JONUB's integration of AMIB on 1 June 2004, MINUSTAH's taking over for MFO-Haiti on 1 June 2004, Althea-BiH taking over from SFOR in July 2004.

6. *Freedom in the World* country ratings, 2005, www.freedomhouse.org/research/free world/2005/tables.htm. The ratings reflect global events from December 1, 2003, to November 30, 2004.

7. 2003 Quick Reference Table, issued in 2004, www.worldbank.org/data/quickreference/ quickref.html. The World Bank did not include statistics for Afghanistan, Brunei, Cuba, Myanmar, North Korea, and Taiwan. For these states we used gross domestic product per capita data found either in *The Military Balance* or in the UNDP, *Human Development Report, 2004*. On the latter, see note 9 below.

8. High-income countries have a GNI per capita of U.S.$9,386 and above; middle-income countries range from U.S.$766 to U.S.$9,385; and low-income countries have less than U.S.$766.

9. UNDP, *Human Development Report 2004* Statistics, Table 1, Human Development Index, http://hdr.undp.org/reports/global/2004. While the adjusted real income portion of the index, based on GDP per capita, overlaps with the GNI per capita variable mentioned earlier in the text, we contend that it does not invalidate the use of both income and development indicators. UNDP uses high, medium, and low development categories.

10. Monty Marshall and Ted Robert Gurr, *Peace and Conflict 2005* (College Park, MD: University of Maryland, Department of Government and Politics, CIDCM, 2005). Belize, Brunei, Cape Verde, Luxembourg, Malta, and Suriname were absent from the ledger but judged to be stable after we consulted various other sources, such as U.S. State Department Country Reports, the CIA Factbook, and other unclassified data.

11. Data from 2001 through 2004 were obtained from the WDI databases for 2004 through 2006, found at http://o-devdata.worldbank.org.library.lausys.georgetown.edu/dataonline/old -default.htm. As much as possible, 2003 were used as the base year, with data from other years being used to fill gaps. UNCTAD data came from its Handbook of Statistics for 2005, as found at http://stats.unctad.org/Handbook/TableViewer/tableView.aspx?ReportId=147.

12. This is true for all categories except governance, where the G2-6 score is .42 less than the G7-9 score, and it is .43 better than the G7o score.

13. Most other European contributors probably had little scope to be notable rising contributors because of their prior high level of contribution.

14. They are Belize, Cape Verde, Estonia, Guyana, Jamaica, Luxembourg, Malta, Suriname, and Trinidad-Tobago.

15. Only four states fully fit the higher-impact profile. Latvia, New Zealand, and Switzerland were eliminated since their ground forces did not meet the 4000 personnel threshold suggested above as a probable bottom line. Slovenia was eliminated because it did not meet the trajectory criterion.

16. The four South Asian states are Bangladesh, India, Nepal, and Pakistan. The six African states are Ethiopia, Ghana, Kenya, Nigeria, Senegal, and Zambia.

Chapter Three

1. See chapter 2 in this volume for the definition of "designated troop contributors" and a description of how data concerning them were compiled.

2. See, e.g., Security Council Report, "Twenty Days in August: The Security Council Sets Massive New Challenges for UN Peacekeeping," Special Research Report no. 5, September 8, 2006, www.securitycouncilreport.org; Mark Turner, "Peacekeeping Blues," *Financial Times*, December 9, 2006, www.ft.com; and D. C. F. Daniel and Leigh C. Caraher, "Characteristics of Troop Contributors to Peace Operations and Implications for Global Security," *International Peacekeeping* 13, no. 3 (September 2006), 297.

3. All troop and defense budget numbers for this chapter are drawn from the yearly issues of the *Military Balance*, published by the International Institute for Strategic Studies in London.

4. The macro numbers are much lower than the national means and medians because some countries with extremely large ground forces contribute only small proportions of their troops, while other countries with small forces contribute relatively large percentages.

5. Much of the information provided in support of this proposition is presented in greater detail in Donald C. F. Daniel et al., *Coercive Inducement and the Containment of Crises* (Washington, D.C.: US Institute of Peace Press, 1999), chap 1. For a recent analysis of the trend toward robust peace operations, see also Ian Johnstone, "Dilemmas of Robust Peace Operations," in *Annual Review of Global Peace Operations 2006*, ed. Ian Johnstone (Boulder, CO: Lynne Reiner, 2006), chap 1.

6. The seven countries for which data were not available were Afghanistan, Cuba, Guyana, Iraq, Liberia, Timor-Leste, and Trinidad-Tobago.

7. Consistent with the counting rules described in chapter 2 of this volume, this percentage applies only to the twenty-four missions in 2006 where there was at least one participant who contributed at least one hundred troops.

8. The sixty-two comes from adding together the number of high-quantity states and the number of high-quality states, while also accounting for overlaps. It also excludes three high-quality states whose ground forces were so low (below 4000 troops) as to raise major doubts as to their abilities to become consistent designated contributors, much less significant contributors. On the issue of a low end for size of ground forces, see Daniel and Caraher, "Characteristics of Troop Contributors to Peace Operations," 303.

9. It was 45 percent in 2004 and increased to 53 percent by the end of 2007. U.S. Department of Defense data on "Military Occupational Specialties" are reproduced in www.globalsecurity.org/military/agency/mos.htm.

10. Excellent analyses are found in William Langewiesche, "Peace Is Hell," *Atlantic Monthly*, October 2001, 51–80; and in Lynn Davis et al., *Stretched Thin: Army Forces for Sustained Operations* (Santa Monica, CA: RAND Corporation Arroyo Center, 2007).

11. John J. Spinelli, "Peacetime Operations: Reducing Friction," in *QDR 2001 Strategy-Driven Choices for America's Security*, ed. Michelle Flournoy (Washington, D.C.: National Defense University Press, 2001), 272–74. The complexities of rotation cycles are well laid out in Adam Talaber, "Some Implications of Increasing U.S. Forces in Iraq," [U.S.] Congressional Budget Office Report, April 2007, http://fpc.state.gov/c4763.htm. This report indicates that the Army's plan for the post-Iraq era is an "arrangement that would leave one-quarter of the force deployed at any one time, one-half . . . available to respond to other contingencies, and one-quarter recovering from deployments" (6). This would mean a one-in-four rule. It should also be noted that in June 2006, one-third of the active U.S. ground forces personnel (as opposed to units) were deployed. The general consensus then (and now) among informed observers was that American ground forces were stretched to their limits. See Carl Connetta, "No Good Reason to Boost

Army, Marine Corps End Strength," Briefing Report #20 of the Project on Defense Alternatives, January 31, 2007, as found at www.comw.org/pda.

12. A listing of peace operations centers is found at the site maintained by the International Association of Peacekeeping Training Center, at www.iaptc.org.

13. International Institute for Strategic Studies, *Military Balance 2007* (London: Routledge-Taylor and Francis, 2007), 52. All future references to an annual volume will be cited as *MB* [year, page]. *MB* 2004–5, 272. *MB* 2007, 25 and 100. *MB* 2007, 52. *MB* 2006, 5; see also *MB* 2004–5, 161; *MB* 2005–6, 5, 45, and 152; *MB* 2007, 332. *MB* 2004–5, 37–38. *MB* 2004–5, 288; *MB* 2005–6, 45. *MB* 2004–5, 37–38; see also *MB* 2007, 101. *MB* 2004–5, 37–38, 273; *MB* 2006, 49. *MB* 2005–6, 152; see also p. 154. *MB* 2006, 24 and 49.

14. *MB* 2006, 58. *MB* 2007, 95. *MB* 2005–6, 356. *MB* 2004–5, 37–38. Ibid. *MB* 2006, 49. *MB* 2004–5, 288. *MB* 2006, 47 and *MB* 2007, 187. *MB* 2004–5, 37–38. Ibid. *MB* 2007, 339. *MB* 2003–4, 321 and *MB* 2007, 258.

15. *MB* 2005–6, 45. *MB* 2003–4, 104. *MB* 2005–6, 251. Ibid., 252.

16. See inter alia *MB* 2004–5, 220, 272, 273, 288, 318, 319, 333; *MB* 2005–6, 45, 216, 264, 308, 355, 359, 408; *MB* 2006, 56 60, 347; *MB* 2007, 55, 98, 99, 257, 259.

17. This observation was made at an off-the-record meeting in 2001 in Washington, D.C., devoted to the topic of trends in peace operations. The meeting was organized by the U.S. National Intelligence Council and the United States Institute of Peace.

18. Four high-quality states were dropped as not being critical because of the very small size of their active forces. These were Ireland, New Zealand, Slovakia, and Switzerland.

Chapter Four

1. United Nations, *Report of the Panel on United Nations Peace Operations*, A/55/305 and S/2000/809 (transmitted to the UN on August 17, 2000), paragraphs 92–117.

2. Citation is from SHIRBRIG website, http//www.shirbrig.dk/html/facts.htm.

3. Leonard Hawley, "Enhancing Capacities of Others: Lessons Learned from East Timor," unpublished briefing notes, September 19, 2001.

4. Author's observation during a field visit to Afghanistan in August 2006.

5. Combined Forces Command Briefing, November 29, 2006, Kabul, Afganistan.

6. The author was the UNTSO Security Officer at the time and carried out the investigation.

7. The author was present at a number of heated UNOSOM II staff meetings on this subject.

8. The author was the military advisor to the U.S. Liaison Office to UNOSOM II in the summer of 1993.

9. General Charles Krulak, the commandant of the Marine Corps, coined this phrase to describe the complex urban operating environment. See his *Commanders Planning Guidance* (Washington, D.C.: Marine Corps Headquarters, 1996).

10. Thomas E. Ricks, *FIASCO: The American Military Adventure in Iraq* (New York: Penguin, 2006), 139–40.

11. Ibid.

12. The author was on the team in Mogadishu that evaluated that threat in July 1993.

13. Author's nonattribution interview with a French officer familiar with the UNIFIL situation on December 14, 2006.

14. Dan Ephron, "Hizbollah's Secret Weapon," *Newsweek*, September 11, 2006, 28.

15. The exception here is that in August 1993 in Somalia, General Aideed circulated the rumor that he had obtained Stinger anti-aircraft missiles from Afghanistan. The threat grounded

UN contract helicopters for several days due to skyrocketing insurance rates until the rumor was proved to be false.

16. John Mackinlay, "Opposing Insurgents, during and beyond Peace Operations," in *Peace Operations after 11 September 2001*, ed. Thierry Tardy (London: Frank Cass, 2004), 173–74.

17. Gary Anderson, "UNOSOM II: Not Failure, Not Success," in *Beyond Traditional Peacekeeping*, ed. D. C. F. Daniel and B. C. Hayes (London: Macmillan Press, 1995), chap. 14.

Chapter Five

1. Robert Oakley et al., eds., *Policing the New World Disorder* (Washington, D.C.: National Defense University Press, 1998). See also William Lewis, Edward Marks, and Robert Perito, *Enhancing International Civilian Police in Peace Operations*, USIP Special Report No. 85 (April 2002).

2. Mark Kroeker, "Contingent Owned Equipment (COE) Reimbursement," conference notes from briefing on "Overcoming Challenges to Stability Policing," given at the Centre of Excellence for Stability Police Units, Vicenza, Italy, December 7, 2005.

3. Author interviews, Ministries of Foreign Affairs and Defense, Buenos Aires, July 2004.

4. For a detailed look at the modern use of constabulary forces in peacekeeping operations, see Robert M. Perito, *Where Is the Lone Ranger When We Need Him? America's Search for a Postconflict Stability Force* (Washington, D.C.: USIP Press, 2004).

5. Author interviews, Buenos Aires, July 2004.

6. Author interviews with advocates from Refugees International, who, on a mission to Haiti in early 2005, noted the willingness of Chilean special police to confront gangs and attempt to disarm them while also intervening to stop Haitian-on-Haitian violence. Other national contingents were noted as refusing to leave their compounds.

7. Author interview with Chilean Embassy official, Washington, D.C., November 2006.

8. Author interviews, Centre of Excellence for Stability Police Units, Vicenza, Italy, February 2005; author interviews, Italy, March 2007.

9. Author interviews, National Gendarmerie Training School, Bucharest; Romanian Special Police Unit, Kosovo, January and February 2005.

10. Author interviews, National Gendarmerie Training School, Bucharest.

11. Most national gendarmerie forces fall are under the leadership of the Ministry of Interior when they are at home, and some, when deployed abroad, come under the auspices of the Ministry of Defense. In certain instances, national governments have refused to allow their gendarmerie forces to come under a foreign military chain of command when deployed abroad, fearing they will be used in place of the military. Unfortunately, this often defeats the purpose of deploying gendarmes at all, as their abilities to act in an intermediate force environment is critical in postconflict settings.

12. Officials and former force commanders in Singapore and Indonesia repeatedly praised the professionalism of the Thai armed forces.

13. Author interviews, Bangkok, September 2004.

14. Author interviews, Ministries of Defense and Foreign Affairs, Singapore, October 2004.

15. Ibid., and author interviews, Ministry of Foreign Affairs, Brasilia, July 2004.

16. The United States Department of Defense Security Cooperation Agency, News Release: "Brazil to Acquire S-70B Helicopters and Engines," September 27, 2006.

17. Author interviews, Chilean Ministry of Defense and Joint Forces Headquarters, Santiago, July 2004.

18. Author interviews, Tokyo, October 2004.

19. Author interviews, Ministries of Defense and Foreign Affairs, Singapore, October 2004.

20. NATO Topics: Strategic Airlift Interim Solution (SALIS), www.nato.int/issues/strategic -lift-air/index.html.

21. Author interviews, South African National Defense Forces (SANDF) Headquarters, Pretoria, South Africa.

22. Author interviews with representatives from the main private security contractors who have provided demining and UXO support for operations in peacekeeping and stability operations in Ethiopia, Bosnia, Kosovo, Croatia (UNTAES), Afghanistan, and Iraq. Companies have asked to remain anonymous. Interviews conducted in Washington, D.C., on July 16 and 18 and September 22, 2006. (While it is recognized that the private security industry has filled a critical role in the provision of specialized requirements in peacekeeping operations from the Sierra Leone mission in 1998 to the current missions in Kosovo and Afghanistan, this chapter seeks to explore those contributions made by national and regional actors only, as the role of the private industry in this regard is extensive and cannot be addressed within the confines of this chapter.)

23. Author interviews, Washington, D.C., May 2005 and September 2006.

24. Author interviews with the Bosnian, Croatian, and Serbian ministries of defense and interior, January and February 2005. Additional interviews conducted with the diplomatic representations of each country to the United States in October 2006.

25. Author interview, Washington, D.C., October 12, 2006.

Chapter Six

1. Address by Salim Ahmed Salim, then secretary-general of the OAU, at the Second Meeting of the Chiefs of Defense Staff of Member States of the OAU Central Organ, Harare, October 25, 1997.

2. The OAU authorized missions in Chad (2), Rwanda (3), Burundi (1), Comoros (3), DRC (1), and Eritrea/Ethiopia (1).

3. ANAD is the French acronym for the now defunct Francophone West African security arrangement, the *Accord de Non Aggression et D'Assistance en Matiere de Defense*, which was signed in June 1977 by Burkina Faso, Mali, Mauritania, Niger, Senegal, Côte d'Ivoire, and Togo.

4. In August 1998, Zimbabwe, Angola, and Namibia intervened militarily in the DRC conflict. The intervention was endorsed at a meeting of SADC defense ministers in Harare on August 18, 1998, and President Mugabe subsequently claimed that SADC had come to a unanimous decision to help President Laurent Kabila. On September 22, 1998, a 600-strong South African (SA) military task force entered Lesotho, ostensibly to assist the Lesotho government in restoring law and order following election-related unrest. Although South Africa stressed that this was a combined military task force, consisting of Botswana Defense Force and SA elements, only two hundred BDF troops arrived in Maseru—and after most of the fighting was over. The SA government insisted that the intervention was requested by Lesotho in accordance with SADC agreements and was thus undertaken under the auspices of SADC.

5. The mission, authorized in December 2001, became operational in January 2002 and comprised peacekeepers from four CEN-SAD countries serving in Bangui.

6. The Institute for Security Studies provides a detailed profile of these and other African regional rganizations. See www.issafrica.org/index.php?link_id=3893&link_type=12&tmpl_id=2.

7. Mark Malan, *Developing the ECOWAS Civilian Peace Support Operations Structure*, Kofi Annan International Peacekeeping Training Center, March 2006, www.kaiptc.org/_upload/ general/ecowas.pdf.

8. Africa Center for Strategic Studies, *ECOMIL after Action Review Final Report*, August 2004.

9. As a consequence of these shortcomings, the ECOWAS Secretariat requested and received authorization by the Mediation and Security Council in December 2003 to establish a Mission Planning and Management Cell.

10. Arusha Agreement for Peace and Reconciliation for Burundi, Protocol V, Article 8, August 28, 2000.

11. Festus Aboagye, "The African Mission in Burundi: Lessons Learned from the First African Union Peacekeeping Operation," *Conflict Trends* 2 (2004).

12. Ibid.

13. Lansana Gberie, *The Darfur Crisis: A Test Case for Humanitarian Intervention* (Accra, Ghana: Kofi Annan International Peacekeeping Training Center, 2004).

14. These are the words of an expert seminar participant. Catherine Guicherd, *The AU in Sudan: Lessons for the African Standby Force,* IPA meeting report, 2006, www.ipacademy.org/asset/file/166/AU_IN_SUDAN-Eng2.pdf.

15. Ibid.

16. There have been allegations of U.S. support of Ethiopian intervention, and of U.S. combat operations from a base in Kenya against ICU forces driven south by the Ethiopians. There were also rumors that two thousand Eritrean soldiers were aiding the ICU.

17. UN Security Council, Resolution 1725, S/RES/1725, 2006.

18. UN Security Council, Resolution 1744, S/RES/1744, 2007.

19. UN Security Council, *Report of the Secretary-General on the Situation in Somalia,* S/2007/115, 2007.

20. See, for example, Margaret Vogt, ed., *The Liberian Crisis and ECOMOG: A Bold Attempt at Regional Peacekeeping* (Lagos: Gabumo, 1992); W. Ofuatey-Kodjo, "Regional Organizations and the Resolution of Internal Conflict: The ECOWAS Intervention in Liberia," *International Peacekeeping* 1, no. 3 (1997).

21. See, for example, Max Sesay, "Civil War and Collective Intervention in Liberia: A Strange Case of Peacekeeping in West Africa," *Review of African Political Economy,* no. 67 (1996).

22. See, for example, Mark Malan, "The OAU and Sub-Regional Organisations: A Closer Look at the 'Peace Pyramid,'" *ISS Papers,* no. 36 (1999).

23. Eboe Hutchful, "Peacekeeping under Conditions of Resource Stringency: The Ghana Army in Liberia" (paper presented at a SAIIA/ISS conference with the theme "From Peacekeeping to Complex Emergencies? Peace Support Missions in Africa," Johannesburg, March 25, 1999).

24. U.S. Department of State, *Summary of the African Crisis Response Initiative,* July 10, 2001, http://allafrica.com/stories/200107100090.html.

25. Eric G. Berman, *French, UK and US Policies to Support Peacekeeping in Africa: Current Status and Future Prospects,* a report for the Norwegian Institute for International Affairs, 2002, par. 57.

26. Elizabeth Turpen et al., *Following the Money: The Bush Administration FY03 Budget Request and Current Funding for Selected Defense, State, and Energy Department Programs* (Washington D.C.: The Henry L. Stimson Center, 2002).

27. Nina Serafino, "The Global Peace Operations Initiative: Background and Issues for Congress," *CRS Report for Congress,* 2006, 2.

28. Partnership for Effective Peacekeeping, "The Global Peace Operations Initiative," www.effectivepeacekeeping.org/pep-pubs/.

29. Serafino, "The Global Peace Operations Initiative."

30. Eric G. Berman, *French, UK and US Policies to Support Peacekeeping in Africa,* par. 69.

31. Benedicte Franke, "Enabling a Continent to Help Itself: U.S. Military Capacity Building and Africa's Emerging Security Architecture," *Strategic Insights* 6, no. 1 (2007): 9.

32. Independent Task Force, "More than Humanitarianism: A Strategic U.S. Approach Toward Africa," *Council on Foreign Relations Task Force Report No. 56* (January 2006): 81

33. Alexander Ramsbotham, Alhaji Bah, and Fanny Calder, *The Implementation of the Joint Africa/G8 Plan to Enhance African Capabilities to Undertake Peace Support Operations: Survey of Current G8 and African Activities and Potential Areas for Further Collaboration* (London: Chatham House, 2005), 10.

34. During the center's first phase (1995–1999) only twelve short courses were presented to a total of 520 participants. After November 2000, the RPTC ran only four short courses, with 135 students in total.

35. Spokesperson of the French Foreign Ministry, March 26, 2007, www.ambafra-pk.org/article.php3?id_article=1057.

36. National War College Nigeria, www.nwc.gov.ng/ACSRT/Departments.htm.

37. Main activities are presented in detail on the KAIPTC website, www.kaiptc.org/home/.

38. KAIPTC, Commandant's Annual Report, December 2004.

39. Ibid.

40. William Nhara, "Conflict Management and Peace Operations: The Role of the Organization of African Unity and Subregional Organizations," ISS Monograph Series, no. 21 (1998): 39.

41. African Union, Protocol Relating to the Establishment of the Peace and Security Council of the African Union, adopted by the First Ordinary Session of the Assembly of the African Union, Durban, July 9, 2002. Hereafter referred to as the "PSC Protocol."

42. Policy Framework for the establishment of the ASF, Exp/ASF-MSC/2 (1), adopted by the Third Session of African Chiefs of Defense Staff, May 15–16, 2003, and noted by the Heads of State and Government at the Maputo Summit in July 2003.

43. Implementation Report by Africa Personal Representatives to Leaders on the G8 Africa Action Plan, Evian, June 1, 2003. The full report, including the Annex: Joint Africa/G8 Plan to Enhance African Capabilities to Undertake Peace Support Operations, is at www.g7.utoronto.ca/summit/2003evian/index.html#chair.

44. The idea of a 6th ASF brigade, which may well have provided the AU with a quick reaction force, met with strong objections by South Africa at the Third ACDS meeting, May 2003, and was removed in the revised policy framework document.

45. African Union, Report of the First Meeting of the African Ministers of Defense on the African Standby Force and the Common African Defense and Security Policy, January 20–21, 2004, Addis Ababa, Ethiopia. MIN/Def.&Sec.1(II)Rpt.

46. The EU-sponsored Africa Peace Facility is a mechanism that allocated an initial amount of €250 million to the AU for the purpose of financing peacekeeping in Africa. It is based on three principles, the first of which is *ownership*, implying that it provides "support to the African Union and the sub-regional organizations in taking care of African conflicts and stimulating the search for an African continental solution." This is intended to reinforce the political authority of the AU as well as its technical potential. The €250 million comes from the European Development Fund (EDF) under the Cotonou Agreement. Of this, €126.4 million comes from each African country's contribution of 1.5 percent from its allocated envelope. The remaining €123.6 million is transferred from unallocated resources (reserves) of the Ninth EDF. The €250 million can be used to finance costs incurred by African countries deploying their peacekeeping forces but may not be used to cover expenditures on hardcore military equipment and weaponry.

47. A draft MOU between the AU and the RECs has reached its fifth version.

48. African Union, *Roadmap for the Operationalization of the African Standby Force*, Report of the Experts' Meeting on the Relationship between the AU and the Regional Mechanisms for Conflict Prevention, Management and Resolution, Addis Ababa, March 22–23, 2005, EXP/AU-RECs/ASF/4(I), par. 10.

49. According to the PSC Protocol, Art. 10 (4): "In the exercise of his/her functions and powers, the Chairperson of the Commission shall be assisted by the Commissioner in charge of Peace and Security, who shall be responsible for the affairs of the Peace and Security Council. The Chairperson of the Commission shall rely on human and material resources available at the Commission, for servicing and providing support to the Peace and Security Council. In this regard, a Peace and Security Council Secretariat shall be established within the Directorate dealing with conflict prevention, management and resolution."

50. PSC Protocol, Art. 13 (6) and (7).

51. *Securing Peace and Stability for Africa: The EU-funded African Peace Facility* (Brussels: European Commission, 2004).

52. James Dobbins, *A Comparative Evaluation of United Nations Peacekeeping*, Testimony presented before the House Committee on Foreign Affairs' Subcommittee on International Organizations, Human Rights, and Oversight, June 13, 2007.

53. Business Executives for National Security, *Peacekeeping Perils and Prospects: "The Big Ten" Lessons Learned from Recent Operations in Somalia, Rwanda, Haiti and Bosnia*, www.bens.org/library/publications/archive.html.

Chapter Seven

1. Michael O'Hanlon and Peter W. Singer, "The Humanitarian Transformation: Expanding Global Intervention Capacity," *Survival* 46, no. 1 (2004): 77–100.

2. Compare NATO, *The Alliance's New Strategic Concept. Agreed by the Heads of State and Government, North Atlantic Council, Rome 7-8 November* (Brussels: NATO, 1991); NATO, *The Alliance's Strategic Concept. Approved by the Heads of State and Government, North Atlantic Council, Washington DC, 23–24 April* (Brussels: NATO, 1999); NATO, *Final Communiqué, Ministerial Meeting of the North Atlantic Council, Reykjavik, 14 May* (Brussels: NATO, 2002).

3. European Union, *Declaration of the European Council and Presidency Report on Strengthening the European Common Policy on Security and Defence, Cologne, 3–4 June* (Brussels: European Union, 1999).

4. The Constitutional Treaty, which was agreed upon by EU member governments but put on hold after being rejected in Dutch and French referenda, would have significantly revised the Petersberg tasks.

5. All quotes are from European Union, *Presidency Conclusions, Nice European Council, 7–9 December 2000, Annex III to Annex VI* (Brussels: European Union, 2000).

6. See European Union, *Presidency Report on ESDP, Brussels, 12 December 2003, 15678/05* (Brussels: European Union, 2003), 16; EU Military Staff, *Impetus: Bulletin of the EU Military Staff, Spring/Summer 2006* (Brussels: EU Military Staff, 2006), 3 and 20.

7. See, for example, "NATO and the EU: Time for a New Chapter," Keynote speech by NATO Secretary-General Jaap de Hoop Scheffer, January 29, 2007 (Brussels: NATO, 2007).

8. Aside from the operations mentioned here, the EU has launched a variety of civilian crisis management missions. Information on all operations, both civilian and military, is available at www.consilium.europa.eu/showPage.asp?id=268&lang=en&mode=g.

9. European Union, *A Secure Europe in a Better World: European Security Strategy* (Brussels: European Union, 2003), 12.

10. This does not imply that fatalities will lead to withdrawal, as the example of ISAF in Afghanistan shows. By October 2006 European contingents had sustained the following 109 fatalities without persistent public calls for withdrawal: United Kingdom (41); Spain (19); Germany (18); France (9); Italy (9); the Netherlands (4); Romania (4); Denmark (3); Sweden (2).

11. For a recent example of an intracoalition division that jeopardized deployments, see the Dutch decision to increase their commitment to ISAF. See Mark Joyce, "Nato's Future Credibility Is Now in Dutch Hands," *Financial Times*, January 19, 2006, 17.

12. For an in-depth discussion of the concept of strategic culture and its application to several cases in Europe, see Bastian Giegerich, *European Security and Strategic Culture: National Responses to the EU's Security and Defence Policy* (Baden Baden: Nomos, 2006).

13. IISS, *The Military Balance 2006* (London: Routledge, 2006), 56–60.

14. European Defense Agency, *National Breakdowns of European Defence Expenditure* (Brussels: European Defense Agency, 2007), www.eda.europa.eu.

15. See Michael Alexander and Timothy Garden, "The Arithmetic of Defense Policy," *International Affairs* 77, no. 3 (2001): 509–29; Michael Clarke and Paul Cornish, "The European Defence Project and the Prague Summit," *International Affairs* 78, no. 4 (2002): 777–88.

16. European Union, *Headline Goal 2010, Approved by the General Affairs and External Relations Council on 17 May 2004* (Brussels: European Union, 2004).

17. European Union, *Military Capabilities Commitment Conference, 22 November* (Brussels: European Union, 2004).

18. Since the November 2006 declaration of full operational capability, significant shortfalls have emerged. The NRF concept is thus under review and can be expected to be revised during 2008.

19. Jeffrey P. Bialos and Stuart L. Koehl, *The NATO Response Force—Facilitating Coalition Warfare through Technology Transfer and Information Sharing* (Washington, D.C.: National Defense University, 2005).

20. See Jean-Yves Haine and Bastian Giegerich, "In Congo, a Cosmetic EU Operation," *International Herald Tribune*, June 13, 2006, 8.

Chapter Eight

1. The CIS was founded in December 1991. Today it includes Armenia, Azerbaijan, Belarus, Georgia, Kazakhstan, Kyrgyzstan, Moldova, Russia, Tajikistan, Ukraine, and Uzbekistan. Turkmenistan withdrew its membership and became an associate member in August 2005. For more information on the CIS, see www.cis.minsk.by; and Alyson J. K. Bailes, Vladimir Baranovsky, and Pál Dunay, "Regional Security Cooperation in the Former Soviet Area," in *SIPRI Yearbook 2007: Armaments, Disarmament and International Security* (Oxford: Oxford University Press, 2007), 165–92.

2. The Treaty on Collective Security was concluded on May 15, 1992, in Tashkent by heads of six CIS states: Armenia, Kazakhstan, Kyrgyzstan, Russia, Tajikistan, and Uzbekistan. For the text of the treaty see http://dkb.gov.ru/start/ (in Russian). In September 1993 Azerbaijan signed the treaty, as did Belarus and Georgia three months later. (Belarus had been interested in signing from the very beginning of the initiative but had to find legal ways to circumvent the political neutrality proclaimed in the country's new constitution.) The treaty came into force for all nine participants in April 1994 for five years without automatic prolongation. In 1999, Azerbaijan, Georgia, and Uzbekistan did not extend their membership to the treaty for various political reasons. Armenia, Belarus, Kazakhstan, Kyrgyzstan, Russia, and Tajikistan signed the Charter of the Collective Security Organization on October 7, 2002, at Chisinau, Moldova, formally

establishing the CSTO as a regional organization. In 2006 Uzbekistan returned to the treaty, discouraged by experimentation for several years with the Western vector of military cooperation, and became a full member of the CSTO.

The SCO was established by a declaration issued in Shanghai on June 15, 2001, by six states: China, Kazakhstan, Kyrgyzstan, Russia, Tajikistan, and Uzbekistan. India, Iran, Mongolia, and Pakistan have since become observer states. The text of the Declaration on the Establishment of Shanghai Cooperation Organization, June 15, 2001, is available at www.sectsco.org.

An informal alignment of Azerbaijan, Georgia, and Ukraine existed from late 1996, with Moldova moving closer to it. An unofficial "group of four" emerged in May 1997 in the course of discussions on redefinition of the flank zone of the Treaty on Conventional Armed Forces in Europe. Zdzislaw Lachowski, "Conventional Arms Control," in *SIPRI Yearbook 1998: Armaments, Disarmament and International Security* (Oxford: Oxford University Press, 1998), 501–17. GUAM's formal structure was established in October 1997, when the presidents of the four states held a meeting during the summit of the Council of Europe. See the GUAM website, www.guam .org.ua. In 1999, Uzbekistan joined the group, making it the GUUAM, but it left in 2005. At the GUAM Summit in Kiev, May 22–23, 2006, the GUAM member states formally established the Organization for Democracy and Economic Development–GUAM as an international organization. English translations of the 2006 GUAM Charter and of the Declaration on Establishment of the Organization for Democracy and Economic Development—GUAM are accessible at www.mfa.gov.az/az/guam/. Institutionalization of GUAM has been hindered by the failure of the Moldovan and Ukrainian parliaments to ratify the charter. See Vladimir Socor, "Summit Takes Stock of GUAM's Projects, Institutional Development," *Eurasia Daily Monitor* 4, no. 20 (June 20, 2007), www.jamestown.org/edm/article.php?article_id=2372242.

The Community of Democratic Choice was established in December 2005, when Kiev became a meeting place for leaders and top officials from Estonia, Georgia, Latvia, Lithuania, Macedonia, Moldova, Slovenia, Romania, and Ukraine (member states), and from Azerbaijan, Bulgaria, the Czech Republic, Hungary, Poland, the EU, the OSCE, and the United States (observers). See Jean-Christophe Peuch, "Ukraine: Regional Leaders Set up Community of Democratic Choice," Radio Free Europe/Radio Liberty, December 2, 2005, www.rferl.org/ featuresarticle/2005/12/045ad9d6-04ea-41ac-9c8e-6501191f1cd8.html.

For an assessment of the security functions of the CIS, CSTO, GUAM, and SCO, see Bailes, Baranovsky, and Dunay, "Regional Security Cooperation in the Former Soviet Area."

3. The North-Atlantic Cooperation Council was later renamed the Euro-Atlantic Cooperation Council (EACC).

4. The Collective Security Treaty entered into force in 1994. For the treaty, see http://dkb .gov.ru/start/ (in Russian).

5. Interview of N. Bordyuzha to RIA-Novosti Agency, October 8, 2004.

6. It would be incorrect to consider the dependency of CSTO Staff on Russian General Staff communication lines or satellite information network a weakness of the CSTO Staff, since this is a normal international practice: many NATO and EU central operational military command structures are dependent on U.S. satellite information and navigation, as well as on communication, reconnaissance, and other elements of military support.

7. Chapters VIII and VI of the UN Charter allow regional security organizations to undertake peacekeeping-type operations (operations in consent with the deliberately expressed political will of legitimate authorities of the states on whose territory conflict occurs). The CSTO Charter speaks of operations under UN, OSCE, or CIS mandates, though CSTO itself was recognized in 2004 by the UN as a regional security organization under Chapter VIII credentials.

8. Negotiated military and border arrangements were formalized in the Treaty on Deepening

Military Trust in Border Regions (April 2006) and the Treaty on Reductions of Military Forces in Border Regions (April 2007).

9. The SCO was formally founded as an organization on June 14, 2001.

10. The official wording of the organization's mission has no reference to relations with Moscow and is aimed to promote the Black Sea–Baltic Sea axis of interstate cooperation. Membership of the community is still not exactly clear. At the Vilnius conference of 2006, the two founding members, Macedonia and Slovenia, did not take part; instead, Poland was one of the hosts, and the prime minister of Sweden, G. Persson, expressed Sweden's intention to join the organization.

Chapter Nine

1. Paul Kennedy comments on the important role of Latin American nations as force contributors, describing them as being among "the traditional leading contributors to UN peacekeeping missions (the Scandinavians, Dutch, Latin American states, old British Commonwealth countries)." Paul Kennedy, *The Parliament of Man: The Past, Present, and Future of the United Nations* (New York: Random House, 2006), 258. In addition, we should note here that the term *peace operations* applies to all forms of peacekeeping: traditional peacekeeping, also known as PKO; wider peacekeeping (sometimes called Chapter VI and a half operations); and peace enforcement operations. All peace operations imply a degree of consent between the disputing parties, but consent diminishes as the operation becomes more one of enforcement (under Chapter VII of the UN Charter). Moreover, all require impartiality from the peace forces. However, this is not the same as neutrality, which makes no judgment regarding the legitimacy of the parties, while peace operations do not preclude such a judgment as long as the rules of the operation are applied equally to all sides.

2. At the Congress of Panama (also known as the Amphictyonic Congress), held in Panama, June 22–July 15, 1826, the former Spanish colonies of Latin American came together to establish closer links and define a common position toward Spain. The Treaty of Union, League, and Perpetual Confederation, drawn up at the Congress and including commitments to mutual defense and peaceful settlement of disputes, never came into effect.

3. The Columbia Encyclopedia, 6th ed. (New York: Columbia University Press, 2001–5), s.vv. "Organization of American States," "Pan-American Union."

4. Colonel Jorge Rosales, draft paper for workshop on Haiti PKO, presented at the Center for Hemispheric Defense Studies, Washington D.C., 2004; cited in John T. Fishel and Andres Saenz, "Lessons of Peacekeeping and Capacity Building: What We Have Learned from the Case of Haiti," *Security and Defense Studies Review* 5, no. 1 (Spring 2005); available at www.ndu.edu/chds/journal/indexarcspring05.htm.

5. Paul Kennedy, *The Parliament of Man*, 258.

6. This account of the IAPF is drawn from the work of Lawrence A. Yates, *PowerPack: U.S. Intervention in the Dominican Republic, 1965–1966*, Leavenworth Papers, no. 15 (Fort Leavenworth, KS: Combat Studies Institute, U.S. Army Command and General Staff College, July 1988); and "Intervention in the Dominican Republic 1965–1966," in John T. Fishel, ed., *The Savage Wars of Peace: Toward a New Paradigm of Peace Operations* (Boulder: Westview, 1998), 135–54.

7. Harold E. Bullock, "Peace by Committee: Command and Control Issues in Multinational Peace Enforcement Operations" (thesis, School of Advanced Airpower Studies, Maxwell Air Force Base, Alabama: Air Force Press, February 1995), accessible at http://aupress.maxwell.af.mil/saas_Theses/SAASS_Out/Bullock/bullock.pdf.

8. The RSS was formally established by the Treaty Establishing the Regional Security System, signed at St. Georges, Grenada, March 5, 1996.

9. This account of the establishment of the Multinational Force and Observers (MFO) is based on information provided in the Multinational Force and Observers website, www.mfo.org (accessed July 7, 2007). The full texts of the Treaty of Peace between the Arab Republic of Egypt and the State of Israel, signed at Washington, D.C., March 26, 1979, and of the Protocol establishing the MFO, signed on August 3, 1981, can be accessed at www.mfo.org/1/54/base.asp.

10. Panama withdrew with the abolition of its army after the U.S. 1989 invasion (Operation Just Cause). In fact, the last unit of the Panama Defense Force to be disbanded was the MFO unit, which returned under a new government and furled its flag with full honors.

11. This account of MOMEP is based on Stephen C. Fee, "Peacekeeping on the Ecuador-Peru Border," in Fishel, *The Savage Wars of Peace*, 57–70.

12. Author's observation during a visit to the Uruguayan Army school, November 2005.

13. Personal communication with Robert Pike of the U.S. Army South, CAA Liaison Office.

14. Joint exercises involve two or more military services, while combined exercises involve two or more nations. Thus, a joint and combined exercise involves at least two different military services (e.g., army and air force) and at least two nations (e.g., the United States and Honduras).

15. A CPX trains a military staff to deal with a series of problems. It is usually conducted without troops on the ground. A field training exercise (FTX) trains troops on the ground as well as the staff.

16. Rosales, draft paper for workshop on Haiti PKO, 141.

17. Ibid.

18. Personal communication from Robert Pike. The CAA is made up of the armies of: Antigua and Barbuda, Argentina, Bolivia, Brazil, Canada, Chile, Colombia, Dominican Republic, Ecuador, El Salvador, Guatemala, Honduras, Mexico, Nicaragua, Paraguay, Peru, Trinidad and Tobago, the United States, Uruguay, and Venezuela. Observer states are Bahamas, Barbados, Belize, Costa Rica, Guyana, Jamaica, Panama, St. Kitts and Nevis, and St. Lucia. Observer organizations are the InterAmerican Defense Board and CFAC.

19. Personal communication from Robert Pike.

20. This section is based on Walter E. Kretchik, "Getting There from Here: Multinational Force and Haiti's Quest for Democracy," in John T. Fishel and Andres Saenz, "Lessons of Peacekeeping and Capacity Building,", 9–13.

21. Ibid., 10.

22. "Agreement of Governors Island," signed by President Jean-Bertrand Aristide and Lt-Gen. Raoul Cédras, July 3, 1993, at Governors Island, New York; in Center for Law and Military Operations, Law and Military Operations in Haiti 1994–1995: Lessons Learned for Judge Advocates, Charlottesville, VA: Center for Law and Military Operations, The Judge Advocate General's School, U.S. Army, December 11, 1995, 174–76, accessible at www.globalsecurity.org/military/library/report/1995/OL_Haiti_Lessons_19951211.pdf.

23. A joint civilian OAS-UN mission, MICIVIH predates UNMIH.

24. Walter E. Kretchik, "Getting There from Here"; and UN Department of Public Information, *The United Nations Mission in Haiti: Background*, September 1996, www.un.org/Depts/DPKO/Missions/unmih_b.htm.

25. UN Security Council, Resolution 940, July 31, 1994.

26. An advance UNMIH team had been in Haiti since September 23, 1994.

27. Joseph Napoli, "The U.S. Role in Establishing the Multinational Interim Force and the UN Stabilization Mission in Haiti (MINUSTAH)," *Security and Defense Studies Review* 5, no. 1 (Spring 2005): 38.

28. Ibid.

29. Enzo Di Nocera Garcia and Ricardo Benavente Cresta, "Construyendo Capacidades para América Latina y el Caribe: Las Operaciones de Mantenimiento de Paz y el caso Haití," *Security and Defense Studies Review* 5, no. 1 (Spring 2005): 62–89. Several Chilean liaison officers to the U.S. Army Command and General Staff College at Fort Leavenworth, KS, made this point to me over the course of five and a half years.

30. UN Department of Public Information, "UN Mission's Contributions by Country," May 31, 2007, www.un.org/Depts/dpko/dpko/contributors/2007/mayo7_5.pdf.

31. Ibid.

32. UN Department of Public Information, "UN Mission's Contributions by Country," August 31, 2006, www.un.org/Depts/dpko/dpko/contributors/2006/augusto6_5.pdf.

33. Aldunate was accused by the "human rights" community of complicity in the violations of the Pinochet regime, but the democratic government of Chile has firmly maintained his innocence. Aldunate was the Chilean liaison officer to the U.S. Army Command and General Staff College at Fort Leavenworth, Kansas, while I was teaching there, and I count Aldunate among my friends.

34. This section derives from Fishel and Saenz, "Lessons of Peacekeeping and Capacity Building," 196–207.

35. This section draws on Hans Morgenthau's writings on prestige.

36. Cited in Luciana Micha, "Una visión integrada de la participación Argentina en MINUSTAH (An Integral View of Argentina's Participation in MINUSTAH)," *Security and Defense Studies Review* 5, no. 1 (Spring 2005). Translation from John T. Fishel and Andrés Saenz, "Lessons of Peacekeeping and Capacity Building."

37. Fishel and Saenz, "Lessons of Peacekeeping and Capacity Building," 197.

38. Luciana Micha, "Una visión integrada de la participación Argentina en MINUSTAH (An Integral View of Argentina's Participation in MINUSTAH)," 115.

39. Fishel and Saenz, "Lessons of Peacekeeping and Capacity Building," 198–99.

40. Ibid.

41. Ibid., 199–201.

Chapter Ten

1. See "Declaration of ASEAN Concord II (Bali Concord II)," signed on October 7, 2003, in Bali, Indonesia, by all ten ASEAN members, www.aseansec.org/15159.htm.

2. For more on these discussions, see the Asian Regional Forum website, www.aseanregionalforum.org.

3. See *United Nations Report of the Panel on United Peace Operations* (New York: United Nations, August 21, 2000), www.un.org/peace/reports/peace_operations/docs/a_55_305.pdf.

4. ASEAN comprises Brunei Darussalam, Cambodia, Indonesia, Lao PDR, Malaysia, Myanmar, the Philippines, Singapore, Thailand, and Vietnam.

5. For more about the history of ASEAN and background about the political and security environment that defined the regional dynamics, see, among others, J. A. C. Mackie, *Konfrontasi: The Indonesian-Malaysian Dispute 1963–1966* (Kuala Lumpur: Oxford, 1974); Arfinn Jogensen-Dahl, *Regional Organisation and Order in Southeast Asia* (New York: St. Martin's Press, 1982); and Michael Antolik, *ASEAN and the Diplomacy of Accommodation* (Armonk, NY: M. E. Sharpe, 1990).

6. Michel Leifer, *ASEAN and the Security of Southeast Asia* (London: Routledge, 1989), 19.

7. "The ASEAN Declaration (Bangkok Declaration)," signed August 8, 1967, at Bangkok, Thailand, by the five founding members of ASEAN, www.aseansec.org/1629.htm. "Zone of Peace, Freedom and Neutrality Declaration," signed November 27, 1971, at Kuala Lumpur,

Malaysia, by the five founding members of ASEAN, www.aseansec.org/1647.htm. "Treaty of Amity and Cooperation in Southeast Asia," signed February 24, 1976, at Denpasar, Indonesia, by the five founding members of ASEAN, www.aseansec.org/1654.htm.

8. Antolik, *ASEAN and the Diplomacy of Accommodation*, 8.

9. Tobias Nischalke, "Does ASEAN Measure Up? Post-Cold War Diplomacy and the Idea of Regional Community," *The Pacific Review* 15, no. 1 (2002): 93. See also Mely Caballero-Anthony, "Mechanisms of Dispute Settlement: The ASEAN Experience," *Contemporary Southeast Asia* 20, no. 1 (1998): 59.

10. Ibid.

11. The current participants in the ARF are Australia, Bangladesh, Brunei Darussalam, Cambodia, Canada, China, the European Union, India, Indonesia, Japan, the Democratic People's Republic of Korea, the Republic of Korea, Lao PDR, Malaysia, Myanmar, Mongolia, New Zealand, Pakistan, Papua New Guinea, the Philippines, the Russian Federation, Singapore, Thailand, Timor-Leste, the United States, and Vietnam. See www.aseanregionalforum.org.

12. See, for example, Tan See Seng et al., *A New Agenda for the ASEAN Regional Forum* (Singapore: Institute of Defense and Strategic Studies, 2002); and Alastair Iain Johnston, "The Myth of the ASEAN Way? Explaining the Evolution of the ASEAN Regional Forum," in *Imperfect Unions: Security Institution over Time and Space*, ed. Helga Haftendorn, Robert A. Keohane, and Celeste A. Wallander (Oxford: Oxford University Press, 1999), 287–324.

13. David Dewitt, "Common, Comprehensive and Cooperative Security," *Pacific Review* 7, no.1 (1994): 285.

14. For more on this topic, see Mely Caballero-Anthony, *Asian Attitudes and Approaches to Peace Operations*, UNISCI Papers, 29 (Madrid: Complutense University, 2003).

15. See, for example, Jurgen Ruland, "ASEAN and the Asian Crisis: Theoretical Implications and Practical Consequences for Southeast Asian Regionalism," *Pacific Review* 13, no. 3 (2000): 421–51; Jeannie Henderson, *Reassessing ASEAN*, Adelphi Paper 323 (London: Oxford University Press for IISS, 1999); John Garofano, "Flexibility or Irrelevance: Ways Forward for the ARF," *Contemporary Southeast Asia* 21, no. 1 (April 1999).

16. For a more comprehensive discussion, see Mely Caballero-Anthony, *Regional Security beyond the ASEAN Way* (Singapore: Institute of Southeast Asian Studies, 2005).

17. See Michael Barnett, "Partners in Peace? The UN, Regional Organizations and Peacekeeping," *Review of International Studies* 21, no. 4 (October 1995).

18. Since the 1990s forty-one peacekeeping operations had been initiated, compared to eighteen from the period 1948–1989. See UNDPKO, *United Nations Peacekeeping 1948–2005*, www .un.org/Depts/dpko/dpko/timeline/.

19. Boutros Boutros-Ghali, *An Agenda for Peace: Preventive Diplomacy, Peacemaking and Peace-keeping*, Report of the Secretary-General pursuant to the statement adopted by the Summit Meeting of the Security Council on 31 January 1992, June 17, 1992, UN Document no. A/47/-77-S/24111, www.un.org/Docs/SG/agpeace.html.

20. Lakhdar Brahimi, *Report of the Panel on United Nations Peace Operations*, August 21, 2000, UN Document no. A/55/305 - S/2000/809, www.un.org/peace/reports/peace_operations/.

21. Kofi Annan, *Prevention of Armed Conflicts*, Report of the Secretary-General, June 7, 2001, UN Document no. A/55/985 – S/2001/574, www.reliefweb.int/library/documents/2001/ un-con flprev-07jun.htm.

22. International Commission on Intervention and Sovereignty, *Responsibility to Protect: Report of the International Commission on Intervention and State Sovereignty* (Ottawa: International Development Research Centre, December 2001), www.iciss.ca/report-en.asp.

23. Ibid., 13n31.

24. Kofi Annan, *In Larger Freedom: Towards Development, Security and Human Rights for All*, Report of the Secretary-General, March 21, 2005, UN Document no. A/59/2005, www.un.org/largerfreedom/.

25. Juanito P. Jarasa, "The ASEAN Troika on Cambodia: A Philippine Perspective," in *The Next Stage: Preventive Diplomacy and Security Cooperation in the Asia-Pacific Region*, ed. Desmond Ball and Amitav Acharya (Canberra: Australian National University, 1999).

26. Ibid., 212.

27. See Sorpong Peou, *Intervention and Change in Cambodia: Towards Democracy?* (Singapore: Institute of Southeast Asian Studies, 2000), 386–90.

28. Jarasa, "The ASEAN Troika," 213.

29. President Joseph Ejercito Estrada, Republic of the Philippines, "Chairman's Press Statement on ASEAN 3rd Informal Summit," Manila, Philippines, November 28, 1999, www.aseansec.org/5300.htm.

30. ASEAN, "The ASEAN Troika: Terms of Reference adopted at the 33rd ASEAN Ministerial Meeting," Bangkok, July 24–25, 2000, www.aseansec.org/3637.htm.

31. Kofi Annan, People of East Timor reject proposed special autonomy, express wish to begin transition to Independence, Secretary-General informs Security Council, Press release SG/SM/7119 - SC/6722, September 3, 1999, www.un.org/peace/etimor99/result_frame.htm.

32. For a more detailed account of the crisis, see Ian Martin, *Self-Determination in East Timor*, International Peace Academy Occasional Paper Series (Boulder, CO: Lynne Reinner, 2001); and Leonard Sebastian and Anthony Smith, "The East Timor Crisis: A Test Case for Humanitarian Intervention," in *Southeast Asian Affairs 2000* (Singapore: Institute of Southeast Asian Studies, 2000), 64–83.

33. The ASEAN countries that eventually participated in the INTERFET were the Philippines, Singapore, Malaysia, and Thailand. Australian Department of Defense, Countries involved, Website on Interfet, http://pandora.nla.gov.au/parchive/2000/S2000-Nov-7/easttimor.defence.gov.au/index.html.

34. Malaysia, the Philippines, Singapore, and Thailand contributed personnel to UNTAET. UN Department of Public Information, East Timor—UNTAET: facts and figures, 2002, www.un.org/peace/etimor/UntaetF.htm.

35. Rodolfo C. Severino, ASEAN Secretary-General, "Sovereignty, Intervention and the ASEAN Way," Address at the ASEAN Scholar's Roundtable, Singapore, July 3, 2000, www.aseansec.org/3221.htm.

36. Alan Dupont, "ASEAN's Response to the East Timor Crisis," *Australian Journal of International Affairs* 54, no.2 (2000), 163–64.

37. Ibid.

38. Surin Pitsuwan, "Regional Efforts in Peace Operations," Comments delivered at the Wilson Park Conference, Wilson Park, Essex, July 2, 2002.

39. For more details, see Aceh Monitoring Mission website, www.aceh-mm.org/.

40. For more on this topic, see Pang Zhongying, "China's Changing Attitude to UN Peacekeeping," in *UN Peace Operations and Asian Security*, ed. Mely Caballero-Anthony and Amitav Acharya (London: Routledge, 2005), 73–87.

41. Bonny Ling, "China's Peacekeeping Diplomacy," International Relations and Institutions, *China Rights Forum*, no.1, 2007.

42. Speech by China's Assistant Foreign Minister Cui Tiankai at the Opening Ceremony of China-Norway Peacekeeping Workshop, March 26, 2007, www.fmprc.gov.cn/eng/zxxx/t306951.htm.

43. UN Department of Public Information, UN mission's summary detailed by country, and monthly summary of contributions (military observers, police and troops), May 31, 2007, www .un.org/Depts/dpko/dpko/contributors/.

44. For more on this topic, see Pang Zhongying, "China's Changing Attitude to UN Peace-keeping," 73–87.

45. See Katsumi Ishizuka, "Japan's Policy towards UN Peacekeeping Operations," in Caballero-Anthony and Acharya, *UN Peace Operations and Asian Security*, 56–72.

46. "Law concerning Cooperation for United Nations Peacekeeping Operations and Other Operations," adopted June 15, 1992. Revised in 1998 and 2001. See Japanese Cabinet Office, International Peace Cooperation Headquarters, Japan's record in international peace cooperation activities, www.pko.go.jp/PKO_E/cooperation/progress_e.html.

47. Japanese Ministry of Foreign Affairs, "Record of Japan's International Peace Cooperation Activities Based on the International Peace Cooperation Law," 2005, www.mofa.go.jp/policy/un/ pko/pamph2005-2.pdf. For up-to-date information on Japanese contributions to peace operations, see Japanese Cabinet Office, International Peace Cooperation Headquarters, "Japan's Participation in UN Peacekeeping Operations," www.pko.go.jp/PKO_E/cooperation/results_e.html.

48. Japanese Ministry of Foreign Affairs, Record of Japan's International Peace Cooperation Activities.

49. Yasushi Akashi, "Japan Should Expand Peacekeeping Role," *Yomiuri Shimbun*, July 31, 2000, reprinted in Global Policy Forum, www.globalpolicy.org/security/peacekpg/general/ japan.htm.

50. Ibid.

51. "Indonesia Proposing ASEAN Security Community Concept," *Jakarta Post*, June 16, 2003, www.thejakartapost.com.

52. See *The ASEAN Security Community*, www.aseansec.org.

53. See *Vientiane Action Programme*, www.aseansec.org./VAP-10thASEANSummit.pdf.

54. "Indonesia Proposes Southeast Asian Peacekeeping Force," February 21, 2004, www.ase ansec.org/afp/20p.htm.

55. See "Asean's Peace," *The Straits Times* (Singapore), March 8, 2004.

56. See "Executive Summary on the Third Meeting of the CSCAP Study Group on Regional Peacekeeping and Peace-building," New Delhi, India, December 8–9, 2006.

57. For a recent study, see Sam Bateman, Catherine Zara Raymond, and Joshua Ho, *Safety and Security in the Malacca and Singapore Straits: An Agenda for Action* (Singapore: Institute of Defense and Strategic Studies Policy Paper, Nanyang Technological University, May 2006).

58. So far, twelve countries have signed the ReCAAP Agreement, namely, Brunei Darussalam, the Kingdom of Cambodia, the Republic of India, Japan, Republic of Korea, the Laos Peoples' Democratic Republic, the Union of Myanmar, the Republic of the Philippines, the Republic of Singapore, the Democratic Socialist Republic of Sri Lanka, the Kingdom of Thailand, and the Socialist Republic of Vietnam. Of these twelve, eleven have ratified the agreement, which came into full force on September 4, 2006. For more on ReCAAP, see www.recaap.org/html/.

59. "ASEAN Agreement on Disaster Management and Emergency Response," Vientiane, July 26, 2005, www.aseansec.org/17587.htm.

60. The Twelfth Meeting of the ASEAN Regional Forum (ARF), Vientiane, July 29, 2005.

61. "Asia to Strengthen Civilian-Military Disaster Cooperation," Agence France-Presse, July 28, 2006. See also Sharon Wiharta et al., *The Effectiveness of Foreign Military Assets in Natural Disaster Response* (Stockholm: Stockholm International Peace Research Institute, 2008).

62. See *Kuala Lumpur Declaration on the Establishment of the ASEAN Charter*, December 12, 2005, www.aseansec.org.

Chapter Eleven

1. Jean-Marie Guéhenno, "Third World Conflicts: A Plan to Strengthen UN Peacekeeping," *International Herald Tribune*, April 19, 2004, www.iht.com/articles/2004/04/19/edguehenno _ed2_.php.

2. UN Department of Public Information, "United Nations Peacekeeping an Indispensable Weapon in International Community's Arsenal, Secretary-General Says in Anniversary Message for First Mission," Press release SG/SM/10714, November 3, 2006, www.un.org/News/Press/ docs/2006/sgsm10714.doc.htm.

3. Brig. Gen. Indarjit Rikhye commanded the Mission of the Representative of the Secretary-General in the Dominican Republic (DOMREP); he served for over a decade in the UN Department of Peacekeeping Operations and helped set up the United States Institute of Peace, a congressionally funded think tank in Washington, D.C. Dewan Premchand had the signal honor to command three UN Forces on two continents over a span of three decades, in each case with success and distinction. Lt. Gen. Nambiar was the force commander and the head of the United Nations Protection Force (UNPROFOR) in the former Yugoslavia during its first turbulent year.

4. Philip Mason, *A Matter of Honour: An Account of the Indian Army, Its Officers and Men* (London: Jonathan Cape, 1974).

5. Defense Talk Forum, www.defencetalk.com (accessed February 7, 2006).

6. See "Bush Names Pakistan Major Ally," *BBC News*, http://news.bbc.co.uk/2/hi/south _asia/3814013.stm. Non-NATO ally is a designation given by the U.S. government to exceptionally close allies who have close strategic working relationships with American forces but are not members of NATO.

7. For a comprehensive, balanced, and well-researched history of the Indian and Pakistani armies, see Stephen Cohen, *The Pakistan Army,* 2nd ed. (New York: Oxford University Press, 1998); and Stephen Cohen, *The Indian Army: Its Contributions to the Development of a Nation,* 2nd ed. (New York: Oxford University Press, 2001).

8. United Services Institution of India, Centre for United Nations Peacekeeing, "Indian Army Peacekeeping Doctrine," New Delhi, 2007, www.usiofindia.org/Indian%20Army%20 Peacekeeping%20Doctrine%20.pdf.

9. UN Department of Peacekeeping Operations, "United Nations Peacekeeping (2) Fatalities by Nationality and Mission up to 31 May, 2007," www.un.org/Depts/dpko/fatalities/StatsBy NationalityMission%202.pdf.

10. Ramesh Thakur and Dipankar Banerjee, "India: Democratic, Poor, Internationalist," in *Democratic Accountability and the Use of Force in International Law,* ed. Charlotte Ku and Harold K. Jacobson (Cambridge: Cambridge University Press, 2002) 176–206.

11. Ibid., 176.

12. See "Constitution of India" (New Delhi: Universal Law Publishing Co., 2000), http:// lawmin.nic.in/coi.htm.

13. Thakur and Banerjee, "India: Democratic, Poor, Internationalist." Even at the time of the 1962 war with China, India had an infantry brigade and attached troops in Congo, and they remained there till completing the task in 1963.

14. Statement by Mr. Kamalesh Sharma, March 26,1999, to the UN Special Committee on Peacekeeping Operations, www.un.int/inida/ind117.htm.

15. International Commission on Intervention and State Sovereignty, *The Responsibility to Protect: Report of the International Commission on Intervention and State Sovereignty* (Ottawa: International Development Research Centre, 2001); also available at www.idrc.ca/openebooks/960-7/.

16. Thakur and Banerjee, India: Democratic, Poor, Internationalist," 204.

17. UN News Service, "First Woman Appointed UN Civilian Police Adviser," *UN News Centre*, January 10, 2003, www.un.org/apps/news/story.asp?NewsID=5847&Cr=civilian&Cr1=police.

18. See UN Department of Peacekeeping Operations, "Military Division—Key Personnel," www.un.org/Depts/dpko/milad/md/key_pers.htm.

19. P. R. Chari, *The IPKF Experience in Sri Lanka*, ACDIS Occasional Paper, Program in Arms Control, Disarmament, and International Security, University of Illinois at Urbana-Champaign, February 1994, www.acdis.uiuc.edu/Research/OPs/Chari/Chari_IPKF.pdf.

20. Ralph Buultjens, "The Ethics of Excess and Indian Intervention in South Asia," *Ethics & International Affairs* 3 (1989): 73–100.

21. "Pakistan's Contribution to UN Peacekeeping Operations," an Inter Services Public Relations (Pakistan) Publication, January 2007.

22. UN Department of Public Information, "UN Missions Summary: Detailed by Country," May 31, 2007, www.un.org/Depts/dpko/dpko/contributors/2007/may07_3.pdf.

23. UN Department of Peacekeeping Operations, "Military Division—Key Personnel," n.10.

24. "UNOSOM II Takes 'Decisive Action' to Restore Peace; Killing of 24 Peacekeepers is Biggest Single UN Loss Ever - United Nations Operations in Somalia-United Nations developments," *UN Chronicle*, September 1993.

25. "Pakistan's Contribution to UN Peacekeeping Operations," an Inter Services Public Relations (ISPR) Publication, 2002.

26. Kabilan Krishnasamy, "UN Peacekeepers as 'Reliable' Forces: Pakistan's Somalia Experience," *Islamabad Policy Research Institute Journal* 11, no. 1 (2002): 94–105.

27. Global Policy Forum, "Troop and Other Personnel Contributions to Peacekeeping Operations: 1996," www.globalpolicy.org/security/peacekpg/data/pkotrp3.htm.

28. Kabilan Krishnasamy, "Bangladesh and UN Peacekeeping: The Participation of a 'Small' State," *Commonwealth and Comparative Politics* 41, no. 1 (March 2003): 24–47.

29. Nepalese Ministry of Foreign Affairs, "Nepal's Role in the UN Peacekeeping Operations," 2006, www.mofa.gov.np/nepalun/statement7.php.

30. Ibid.

31. Based on Sri Lankan Ministry of Defense, Public Security and Law and Order, Sri Lanka's Participation in the United Nations Peace-keeping Operations, 2006, www.defence.llk/new.asp?fname=20061207_02 (accessed July 2, 2007).

32. Data from the SIPRI Multilateral Peace Operations database, www.sipri.org/contents/conflict/database-Intro/ (accessed July 2, 2007).

33. Sri Lankan Ministry of Defense, Public Security and Law and Order.

34. UN Department of Public Information, "UN Missions Summary: Detailed by Country," n.23.

35. Information about the Bangladesh Institute of Peace Support Operation Training comes from the institute's official brochure.

36. Information about the Centre for UN Peace Keeping is taken from the USI-CUNPK website. See "Training for Peace," Official brochure of USI-CUNPK, 2005, http://cunpk.org/.

37. Karniol, Robert, "Pakistan Eyes Peacekeeping Training Centre," *Japan Defence Weekly* 42, no. 24, 15 (June 2005): 24.

38. Sri Lankan Ministry of Defense, Public Security and Law and Order.

Chapter Twelve

1. The current Arab League member states are Algeria, Bahrain, Comoros, Djibouti, Egypt, Iraq, Jordan, Kuwait, Lebanon, Libya, Mauritania, Morocco, Oman, "State of Palestine," Qatar, Saudi Arabia, Somalia, Sudan, Syria, Tunisia, United Arab Emirates, and Yemen.

2. "Charter of the League of Arab States," signed at Cairo, March 22, 1945, by Egypt, Iraq,

Jordan, Lebanon, Saudi Arabia, and Syria. The text of the charter is available in Arabic and English at www.arableagueonline.org.

3. Robert W. Macdonald, *The League of Arab States: A Study in the Dynamics of Regional Organization* (Princeton, NJ: Princeton University Press, 1965), 43.

4. Hussein A. Hassouna, *The League of Arab States and Regional Disputes: A Study of Middle Eastern Conflicts* (Dobbs Ferry, NY: Oceana, 1975), 16.

5. Macdonald, *The League of Arab States*, 42.

6. "Joint Defense And Economic Cooperation Treaty between the States of the Arab League, Signed at Cairo," April 13, 1950. English translation available at www.arableagueonline.org/las/english/details_en.jsp?art_id=736&level_id=272.

7. Joseph A. Kechichian, *Security Efforts in the Arab World: A Brief Examination of Four Regional Organizations* (Santa Monica, CA: Rand, 1994), 10.

8. Reuters, "Arab Parliament Meets in Cairo," *alJazeera.net*, December 29, 2005, http://english.aljazeera.net/NR/exeres/9C0B6509-D352-41C6-9800-6B398D62671D.htm.

9. Ibid.

10. This account of the 1961 crisis in Kuwait is based on Hassouna, *The League of Arab States and Regional Disputes*, 100.

11. This account is based on Istvan Pogany, *The Arab League and Peacekeeping in the Lebanon* (New York: St. Martin's Press, 1987).

12. John Graham Merrills, *International Dispute Settlement*, 3rd ed. (Cambridge: Cambridge University Press, 1998), 272.

13. The Taif Agreement, signed by the Lebanese Parliament on October 22, 1989, at Taif, Saudi Arabia, was designed to end the civil war in Lebanon. For the full text of the agreement, see www.monde-diplomatique.fr/cahier/proche-orient/region-liban-taef-en.

14. Middle East Institute, *Encyclopedia of the Modern Middle East* (New York: Macmillan, 1996), 1083–84.

15. J. E. Peterson, "The GCC and Regional Security," in *The Gulf Cooperation Council: Moderation and Stability in an Interdependent World*, ed. John A. Sandwick (Boulder, CO: Westview, 1987), 173.

16. John Christie, "History and Development of the Gulf Cooperation Council: A Brief Overview," in Sandwick, *The Gulf Cooperation Council*, 18.

17. Michael Barnett and F. Gregory Gause, "Caravans in Opposite Directions: Society, State, and the Development of a Community in the Gulf Cooperation Council," in *Security Communities*, ed. Emanuel Adler and Micheal Barnett (Cambridge: Cambridge University Press, 1998), 172.

18. Kechichian, *Security Efforts in the Arab World*, 13.

19. International Court of Justice, "Maritime Delimitation and Territorial Questions between Qatar and Bahrain (Qatar v. Bahrain)," Press release no. 2001/9, March 6, 2001, The Hague, www.icj-cij.org/presscom/index.php?pr=234&pt=1&p1=6&p2=1.

20. James T. Quinlivan, "Coup-proofing: Its Practice and Consequence in the Middle East," *International Security* 24, no. 2 (Fall 1999), 131–65.

21. Military force sizes given in this section come from International Institute for Strategic Studies, *The Military Balance 2007* (Abingdon: Routledge, 2007). Figures are approximate and include only ground forces on active service.

22. Contributions to UN peace operations given in this section come from UN Department of Public Information, UN mission's summary detailed by country, May 31, 2007, www.un.org/Depts/dpko/dpko/contributors/2007/may07_3.pdf.

23. Despite this, Yemen currently contributes fifty-three troops and military observers to

nine UN peace operations in the Greater Middle East, including UNMIS and the United Nations Mission for the Referendum in Western Sahara (MINURSO).

24. Azzedine Layachi, "Morocco: Will Tradition Protect the Monarchy?" in *The Middle East in 2015: The Impact of Regional Trends on U.S. Strategic Planning*, ed. Judith S. Yaphe (Washington, D.C.: National Defense University Press, 2002), 54.

25. Associated Press, "Arab League Nations Offer Peacekeeping Troops for Darfur," *Washington Post*, October 9, 2006, A18.

Conclusion

1. The total of 130 here, two more than the 128 total for the overall number of operations, is explained by Heldt in note 8 in chapter 1 of this volume.

Contributors

GARY ANDERSON retired as a colonel from the Marine Corps in August 2000. While on active duty he served as commander at every level, from platoon to surveillance and reconnaissance group, including command of Camp Hansen on Okinawa. While on active duty he served in several operations; chief among them was Operation Continue Hope in Somalia in 1993, where he served as military liaison officer to the U.S. Liaison Office in Mogadishu. His nonoperating force assignments have included Marine Officer Instructor at Vanderbilt University, speechwriter and deputy director of the HQMC Special Projects Directorate, UN observer in Lebanon and Israel, faculty member at the Marine Corps Command and Staff College, and director of war gaming at Quantico.

MAJOR GENERAL DIPANKAR BANERJEE (ret.) is the founding director of the Institute of Peace and Conflict Studies in New Delhi, India. Previously, General Banerjee served as the deputy director of the Institute for Defense Studies and Analyses, where he was also a senior fellow, and the director of the Regional Center for Strategic Studies in Colombo, Sri Lanka. He has also held visiting fellowships at the United States Institute of Peace and the Henry L. Stimson Center, Washington, D.C. He has been a consultant to the United Nations on the Conventional Arms Register and was an international advisor to the International Committee of the Red Cross from 2000 to 2004. He has edited *Comprehensive and Co-operative Security in South Asia* (1998), *Confidence Building Measures in South Asia* (1999), *CBMs in South Asia–Potential and Possibilities* (2000), and *South Asia at Gunpoint: Small Arms and Light Weapons Proliferation* (2000).

MELY CABALLERO-ANTHONY is an associate professor at the S. Rajaratnam School of International Studies (RSIS) in Singapore. She is coordinator of the Non-Traditional Security Program (NTS) and secretary-general of the Consortium of Non-Traditional Security Studies in Asia (NTS-Asia). She is interested in regionalism and regional security in the Asian Pacific, multilateral security cooperation, and human security. She worked as lead researcher and manager for the Project on Health and Human Security in East Asia and was a researcher at the Human Security Project (Harvard University). Her publications include *Understanding Non-Traditional Security in Asia: Dilemmas in Securitization* (2006) and *Studying Non-Traditional Security in Asia: Trends and Issues* (2006). She is a member of the Council for Security and Cooperation in the Asia-Pacific (CSCAP), of the CSCAP Working Group on Peace Operations, and of the ASEAN Institute of Strategic and International

Studies (ASEAN-ISIS); she is also an associate fellow at the Institute of Development and Strategic Studies (ISDS).

DONALD C. F. DANIEL is a member of the core faculty in the Security Studies Program at Georgetown University. He recently served as a special advisor to the chairman of the National Intelligence Council. Prior to assuming that post in January 2001, he was Milton E. Miles Professor of International Relations at the U.S. Naval War College. He has also been a research associate at the International Institute for Strategic Studies in London, a visiting fellow at the Brookings Institution in Washington, D.C., and a fellow at the UN Institute for Disarmament Research in Geneva. His book *Coercive Inducement and the Containment of Crises* (coauthored with B. C. Hayes and Chantal de Jonge Oudraat) was a runner-up for the Grawemeyer Award for Ideas on Improving World Order. His expertise includes international affairs, peacekeeping, the UN, U.S. security policy, global trends, strategy, and U.S. military affairs. Dr. Daniel received his Ph.D. in international relations from Georgetown University.

JOHN T. FISHEL, a specialist in Latin American affairs, is a member of the faculty of the School of International and Area Studies of the University of Oklahoma. He was professor of national security policy and research director at the Center for Hemispheric Defense Studies of the National Defense University until 2006. He was formerly adjunct professor at the School of International Service of American University and served as president of the Midwest Association for Latin American Studies (MALAS) and as president of the North Central Council of Latin Americanists (NCCLA). While on active duty in the U.S. Army, he held several positions, including chief of research and assessments of the Small Wars Operations Research Directorate (SWORD) and deputy chief of the U.S. Forces Liaison Group. He has authored and coauthored numerous publications, including *Uncomfortable Wars Revisited* (2006), *Civil Military Operations in the New World* (1997), and *Invasion, Intervention, "Intervasion"* (1997).

BASTIAN GIEGERICH is a research associate at the International Institute for Strategic Studies (IISS), focusing on EU security and defense policy and on strategic culture. Before joining IISS in 2005, he was a research associate at the National Defense University in Washington, D.C., and a project manager at the Aspen Institute, Berlin, and he taught at the Department of International Relations at the London School of Economics, where he obtained his PhD. Recent publications include *European Security and Strategic Culture* (2006).

BIRGER HELDT is an associate professor of peace and conflict research and a research adviser at the Folke Bernadotte Academy (FBA). He leads the FBA's international working group on peacekeeping. He has published extensively on peacekeeping; his most recent book is *Peacekeeping Operations: Global Patterns of Success, 1948–2004* (second edition, 2006).

KATRIN HEUEL is a research analyst at the International Institute for Strategic Studies. In May 2007, she completed her master of arts in security studies from the School of Foreign Service at Georgetown University, where she also worked as a research assistant on peacekeeping. Before coming to Georgetown Ms. Heuel worked at the Aspen Institute, Berlin, as a senior program manager for three years. Prior to joining the Aspen Institute Ms. Heuel worked as a freelance journalist. Her articles have appeared in various publications, including the *Washington Times* and the *General-Anzeiger* in Bonn, Germany. She also holds a master's degree in political science from Hamburg University.

MARK A. LOUCAS is a research associate at the Fund for Peace. He is an analyst for the 2007 *Failed State Index* and works with the Peace and Stability Operations Program and the Foreign Policy Program. He has been coleader of the Regional Response to War Program since September 2007.

MARK MALAN is peacebuilding program officer at Refugees International and serves as the executive coordinator for the Partnership for Effective Peacekeeping. Before he joined Refugees International in 2007, he headed the Conflict Prevention, Management and Resolution Department of the Kofi Anan International Peacekeeping Training Center in Ghana (2004–07) and the Peace Missions Program at the Institute for Security Studies (1996–2003). Until 1996, he lectured in political science at the Faculty of Military Science, University of Stellenbosch. Malan has published extensively on issues relating to regional security and peacekeeping in Africa.

BENJAMIN MARGO is a research assistant at the Center for Peace and Security Studies at Georgetown University. He received his master of arts in security studies from the School of Foreign Service at Georgetown University, where he also worked as a research assistant on peacekeeping. He received an A.B. from Harvard College.

ALEXANDER I. NIKITIN, director of the Center for Political and International Studies (CPIS) and of the Center for Euro-Atlantic Security of the Moscow State Institute of International Relations (MGIMO), is vice-chairman of the Russian Pugwash Committee of Scientists for Disarmament and International Security and a member of the Advisory Board of the Center of Political Studies. He has also been a researcher at the Institute for the U.S. and Canadian Studies, research fellow at the NATO Defense College and at IFRi Institute, and a member of the USSR permanent mission to the UN. He has authored and coauthored several publications, including *Eurasia: New Peace Agenda* (2005), *Peace Support Operations, Parliaments and Legislation* (2004), and *Peace-Keeping and Peace-Enforcement Operations: Theory and Practice* (2000).

PAUL R. PILLAR, visiting professor and member of the core faculty of the Security Studies Program at Georgetown University, retired in 2005 as national intelligence officer for the Near East and South Asia. Formerly he was executive assistant to the CIA's deputy director for intelligence and executive assistant to Director of Central Intelligence William Webster. He also was deputy chair of the DCI Counterterrorist Center and was a member of the National Intelligence Council. In addition Dr. Pillar worked as federal executive fellow at the Brookings Institution. His publications include "Intelligence, Policy, and the War in Iraq" (*Foreign Affairs*, 2006); *Terrorism and U.S. Foreign Policy* (2001); and *Negotiating Peace* (1983).

PATRICIA TAFT, who has published editorials and journal articles on international law, humanitarian intervention, regional cooperation, and civil society empowerment, is a senior associate in the Peace and Stability Operations and Foreign Policy programs at the Fund for Peace (FfP). She currently leads the Threat Convergence Project and works for the Fund's annual *Failed States Index*. While working for FfP she has co-led field missions to Africa, the Americas, Asia, and Europe. Prior to her employment at the FfP she worked for the United States Institute of Peace and was a senior associate with the Public International Law and Policy Group, where she still serves on the Special Advisory Council. In addition, she serves on the board of directors of the Peace Operations Institute and teaches at American University's School of International Service.

SHARON WIHARTA is researcher in the Armed Conflicts and Conflict Management Project at the Stockholm International Peace Research Institute (SIPRI). She is SIPRI's principal researcher on peacekeeping and peacebuilding issues, focusing particularly on efforts to promote justice and to establish the rule of law in postconflict situations. In 2005–06, she co-led a study on local ownership and the rule of law during the peacebuilding process, which involved field missions to Afghanistan, Liberia, and Sierra Leone. She is also a member of the international Challenges of Peace Operations: Into the 21st Century Project. She is the author of several publications on peacekeeping, peacebuilding, postconflict justice, and humanitarian issues; and most recently she coauthored *Transition to a Just Order—Establishing Local Ownership after Conflict* (2007) and *The Effectiveness of Foreign Military Assets in Natural Disaster Response* (2008).

Index